DAVE RUST

David D. Rust

DAVE RUST | *A Life in the Canyons*

FREDERICK H. SWANSON

Foreword by
MICHAEL F. ANDERSON

THE UNIVERSITY OF UTAH PRESS
Salt Lake City

The Defiance House Man colophon is a registered trademark of the
University of Utah Press. It is based upon a four-foot-tall, Ancient
Puebloan pictograph (late PIII) near Glen Canyon, Utah.

12 11 10 09 08   1 2 3 4 5

LIBRARY OF CONGRESS CATALOGING-IN-PUBLICATION DATA

Swanson, Frederick H. (Frederick Harold), 1952-
  Dave Rust : a life in the canyons / by Frederick H. Swanson ; foreword by Michael F.
Anderson.
    p. cm.
  Includes bibliographical references and index.
  ISBN 978-0-87480-944-2 (cloth : alk. paper) 1. Rust, David D. 1874-1963. 2. Outfitters
(Outdoor recreation)—United States--Biography. 3. Mountaineering guides (Persons)—
United States—Biography. I.Title.
  GV191.52.R87S93 2008
  796.522092—dc22
  [B]   2007025512

Frontispiece photograph courtesy of Blanche Rasmussen

Printed by Sheridan Books, Inc., Ann Arbor, Michigan

For David Schleicher

Contents

Foreword by Michael F. Anderson | *ix*

Prologue | *xiii*

Acknowledgments | *xxi*

Maps | *xxiv*

1. Free Range | 1
2. A Valuable Course of Training | 17
3. Building Trail | 30
4. Bridging the Canyon | 44
5. Rougher and Wilder As You Go | 61
6. The Jumping Off Place of the World | 77
7. Roads to the Wilderness | 93
8. The Cowboy and the Lawyer | 110
9. The School of the Desert | 127
10. Wide Horizons | 144
11. Into the Escalante | 159
12. Return to Glen Canyon | 175
13. Adventures from Rim to River | 189
14. Unusual Campout Excursions | 203
15. The Search for the Ancients | 220
16. Monuments in Sandstone | 237
17. Wilderness Park | 250
18. Last Journeys | 264
19. The World Open to View | 279

Epilogue | 292

Notes | 299

Bibliography | 325

Index | 337

Illustrations follow page 164

Foreword

WRITING HISTORY is remarkably selective. For thousands of years men recorded only great men and great epochs. Only in the last century have men and women expanded historical horizons to include great women and lesser men, long looks at mundane human existence, accounts of varied ethnicities, and people from all walks of life. But even today, most biographers devote whole books to the few persons popular culture considers "great," while the rest of past humanity lingers in obscurity, awaiting their own personal scribe.

Grand Canyon historiography is little different. There are a number of good books that survey the pioneer history of the Grand Canyon region and highlight some of its movers and shakers, both early rugged individualists and subsequent federal administrators. Ralph Cameron is one of the former, a man who used hard work, a liberal interpretation of the law, favorable partnerships, and his own political influence to control some 17,000 acres of prime canyon real estate. Pete Berry is another, who settled for hard work alone to build the Bright Angel and Grandview trails and the Grandview Hotel while working copper mines at Horseshoe Mesa. John Hance, Louis Boucher ("the Hermit"), James Thurber, Bill and Ada Bass, and Martin Buggeln are others who spent much of their adult lives at Grand Canyon, influenced its early development, and are today remembered as canyon-era snapshots only because someone chose to write about their time here in broader tomes. There are few comprehensive biographies of canyon denizens, with the notable exception of Tom Myers and Elias Butler's recent book, *Grand Obsession*, the life of inveterate canyon hiker Harvey Butchart.

Colorado River history is another genre that illuminates some of the men and women who dared to run Grand Canyon's rapids before Glen Canyon Dam. Until recently, however, one would think that their lives began and ended when they floated down from Lees Ferry and emerged some weeks later at the Grand Wash Cliffs (with one exception, several biographies of John Wesley Powell). These truncated tales are told in an excellent river-running summary by C. Gregory Crampton, and in the published river journals of John Wesley Powell, George Flavell, the Kolb brothers, and a few others. Brad Dimock has escaped the mold in recent years with wonderful lifelong biographies of Glenn and Bessie Hyde, Buzz Holmstrom, and Bert Loper. Richard Westwood has done the same with *Woman of the River*, a biography of early commercial river runner Georgie White, and *Rough-Water Man*, a biographical account of Elwyn Blake's role in the early Colorado River surveys.

And then there is the north rim of Grand Canyon and the shadowy territory to the immediate north known as the Arizona Strip. Writers since the 1960s have taken tentative steps toward revealing the pioneer history of the national park's northern edge in some comprehensive manner. No one, to my knowledge, has zeroed in on an overall history of the entire region, but authors have probed the past of Pipe Spring National Monument, for example, and settlement of the Mount Trumbull area. Helen Fairley, in one chapter of *Man, Models, and Management* (an excellent but obscure multi-disciplinary examination of the region), outlines the history of cattle ranching on both sides of the Kaibab Plateau. Jerry D. Spangler, writing for the Grand Canyon Trust, has recently cast a perceptive glance at regional history and prehistory in *Vermillion Dreamers, Sagebrush Schemers*, but it is clear to Spangler himself that much of the story is incomplete, and there are no lifelong biographies of the men or women who settled this remote region in the late nineteenth and early twentieth centuries.

This is where Fred Swanson's biography fits into the historiography of the Grand Canyon region. When I researched *Living at the Edge: Explorers, Exploiters and Settlers of the Grand Canyon Region* in the 1990s, I had little luck uncovering published sources on North Rim and Arizona Strip history. I began to look in the local archives and made several trips up to the few libraries and newspaper offices on the Strip, and while there, managed to interview a few of the old-timers. My modest sleuthing unveiled a ghostly figure named David Rust and his efforts to build the first tourist trail from the north rim down to the Colorado River, following the banks of Bright Angel Creek. He seemed to appear suddenly in 1906, only to disappear the following year, with few clues as to where he came from or where he ended up. No canyon place name honored his presence, but I did sense from his 1906–1907 journal, which I had managed to acquire, that this was another of those important canyon pioneers that the historical community knew little about simply because no one had chosen to write about him.

After my book was published in 1998, and I had come to work for the National Park Service as a park historian in 2001, I was contacted by Fred Swanson, a Salt Lake City writer with an interest in the pioneer history of Grand Canyon.

I told him what I knew of the North Rim and Arizona Strip, and he sent me several excerpts from the journals of George C. Fraser, a wealthy easterner who took long wilderness trips to northern Arizona and southern Utah in the first third of the twentieth century in the company of a regional guide named David Rust. All of a sudden, Rust was less the chimera I had stumbled upon a few years earlier and more a long-term regional actor. I was intrigued, and over the years encouraged Fred to send me more about Rust and the region north of Grand Canyon. Eventually he sent me this wonderful manuscript about a man who struggled with poverty in his youth on the Strip and throughout southern Utah, who made it through university in spaced installments, who scratched a living like many canyon pioneers with many types of jobs, became a self-taught expert on regional natural history, and lived a very long life that was enriched by his love for Grand Canyon. In this book, David Rust emerges as an important figure, not only in early canyon tourism but as one of the first, if not the first, person to offer guided boat trips down the Colorado River—a fact heretofore not widely known.

I loved reading Fred's manuscript, not only because the story is so well written and the subject so dear to my heart, but because it again illustrates the value of biography, the confluence of one man, one woman, or one family with a region's overall history. Nothing introduces the human element better, and if one is already familiar with a region's history, reading about a life within that geographic, political, or economic context makes the story so much richer and far more, well, human. I welcome Fred into the community of recent biographers that includes Brad Dimock, Richard Westwood, Tom Myers, Elias Butler, and the few others who find value in a single life. David Rust, at long last, has found his personal scribe.

Michael F. Anderson, Ph.D.
Grand Canyon, Arizona

PROLOGUE | *Lookout Ridge*

You must love my country. Powell loved it,
Dutton loved it; I love it, and so must you.

DAVE RUST
as told to Harrison R. Merrill (1929)[1]

OF ALL THE MOUNTAIN PEAKS and cliff edges he had stood upon in his years of exploring the Colorado Plateau Province, Dave Rust considered Navajo Mountain quite possibly the finest of all. This massive summit rose four thousand feet above the desert floor along the Utah-Arizona border, giving a stunning perspective over the surrounding canyons and mesas. The mountaintop itself was cloaked with scrubby pines that blocked the view, but jutting out from its northwest flank was a buttress Rust called "Lookout Ridge"— and it was here that he brought some of his favorite clients to take in the expansive scene. Rust was a connoisseur of the far view, and during the thirty-three years that he worked as a backcountry guide, no trail was too long to reach another vantage point.

One chilly April afternoon in 1919, Rust led a New York newspaper publisher named Donald Scott over the frost-broken rubble at the crest of Navajo Mountain, heading for Lookout Ridge and the view they had ridden two hundred miles to reach.[2] But the weather was not cooperating: a sea of clouds encircled the mountain, leaving them as cut off from their surroundings as a ship in fog. The two men settled down to wait. To come this far only to have the world around them hidden from view would be a major disappointment.

It had taken them four days to reach the mountain on horseback, starting at Dave's home in Kanab, Utah, far to the west across an isolated territory where pack string and wagon were still the preferred modes of travel. Few white explorers came this far; automobiles had only begun to probe these primitive tracks. The native Paiutes and Navajos rarely climbed the mountain, except when they found it necessary to conduct a rain ceremony at one of its key spiritual sites.

Resting on the exposed ridge that evening, the temperature plummeting in the thin air at an elevation of over ten thousand feet, Rust and Scott watched for breaks in the enveloping blanket of clouds. Toward sunset their luck turned. The mists, now glowing pink, gradually gave way to reveal an intricate system of sandstone canyons at the northern foot of the mountain. Incised drainages twisted their way down to the San Juan and Colorado rivers, forming a seemingly impenetrable maze. Rust pointed out the span of Rainbow Bridge off to the northwest, from their height an insignificant feature lost in the interlocked canyons. Beyond it they discerned the course of the Colorado River as it flowed through Glen Canyon—familiar territory to Rust, who as a young man in the 1890s had prospected the river's sandbars. Now he was laying plans to return to the river with other clients, this time to search for scenery instead of gold.

Past Glen Canyon more landmarks emerged from the clouds. Sixty miles to the north, the three summits of the Henry Mountains rose out of the desert, flanked by the craggy satellite peaks of the Little Rockies. Like Navajo Mountain, the Henrys had formed from the welling up of huge volumes of molten rock, forming giant blisters in the earth's crust. The crests of the Waterpocket Fold and Fiftymile Mountain splayed away from Navajo Mountain like spokes on a giant wheel, revealing ancient warps and uplifts in the sedimentary strata. The Aquarius Plateau dominated the skyline to the northwest—Rust had ridden clear across it four years before and had stood at the brink of its lava cliffs, looking across to where they now stood. To the east the tawny desert lay in shadow, with the strange pinnacles of Monument Valley rising far in the distance.

Here was a geology textbook on display, showing how millions of years of erosion had carved a complex drainage network out of the thick Mesozoic layers. Though he was not a scientist, Rust had read the growing body of work on the Colorado Plateau, and on summits like this he always took the time to explain to his companions how these astonishing landforms had come to be.

The men returned in semidarkness to their camp on an aspen-covered bench not far below the summit, where War God Spring gave its clear flow. Leaving the mountain the next day, they returned to the trading post at Kaibito, where they met John Wetherill of Kayenta. The famed explorer had led the first expedition to Rainbow Bridge, Utah, just ten years earlier. Scott traveled with Wetherill eastward across the Navajo Reservation, while Rust, after buying a couple of Navajo rugs at the trading post, headed back to Kanab. When he reached home he discovered that his wife, Ruth, had given birth to their seventh child. He presented a rug to the doctor as payment. It was not the first time that he had been out in the backcountry on such an occasion.

A year later Donald Scott wrote to Rust, recalling their mountain sunset as "one of the most uplifting and glorious panoramas I shall ever see." This whole section of the Southwest was a revelation for him: "I cannot tell you what a great comfort my trip through these wide open spaces was, where everything seems fresh from creation and you can almost see the handmark of the Lord upon it."[3] Rust would have been pleased that his friend had been able to enjoy their dramatic mountaintop vista. He felt that his job involved much more than finding the trail and cooking the meals. It was his privilege to pass along a thorough appreciation of the Plateau Province of Utah and Arizona.[4] There was no better place to achieve that understanding than from the summit of Navajo Mountain, and—though Rust was too modest to claim this—there was no one better suited to the job.

David Dexter Rust (1874–1963) grew up in America's forgotten outback—the deserts and plateaus of central and southern Utah. Unlike the explorers and literary men and women who visited the region and extolled its wonders to the outside world, Rust knew it from the inside. At the age of nine he was tending sheep with his older brothers in the high meadows of the Fishlake Plateau; when he was thirteen he was placed in charge of the family's herds ranging through the blue-shale hills along the Dirty Devil River. Overcoming an impoverished upbringing and primitive schooling, he latched onto books like a lifeline. Education opened the gate to the wider world—"my American birthright," he called it. He spent four years, off and on, studying at Brigham Young Academy in Provo and another year at Stanford. But he never lost his love for the desert and for primitive ways of travel. He told an interviewer, "I've gone through two colleges without receiving a degree except perhaps an M.D. I am a mule driver."[5]

He was a good deal more accomplished than the average muleskinner. He published a small-town newspaper for a few years, served a term in the Utah legislature (always a maverick, he ran as a Kane County Democrat), and was active in the "Good Roads" movement of the early 1900s. He was an advocate of dryland farming and for a time grew crops in the desert under the Vermilion Cliffs. Rust worked in the region's schools as a teacher, principal, and district superintendent, beginning at the age of nineteen as the sole schoolteacher in the desert hamlet of Hanksville. A stint as a Colorado River gold miner introduced him to Glen Canyon—a stretch of river that would figure prominently in his later career. In 1923 he began the first regular river-guiding service in the Plateau Province, leading curious explorers down Glen to view its serene sandstone walls and abundant historical features.

In 1906 he hired on as foreman of an ambitious project to build the first tourist trail down Bright Angel Creek in the Grand Canyon. At the mouth of the creek, he and his men installed a cable-tram crossing over the Colorado River and erected a tent camp underneath the cliffs of black schist. Here he found his calling as a guide, taking visitors on extended pack trips across the Kaibab Plateau, making stops at the North Rim's fabulous overlooks. Soon he branched out to explore the little-charted landscape beyond the Canyon, where the Colorado, Virgin, and San Juan rivers and their tributaries had shaped the Earth's surface into forms that defied imagination and beckoned to the explorer.

Dave Rust, one of his clients said, could follow a blind trail across the slickrock better than anyone.[6] He knew how to thread his way through the desolate badlands surrounding the Henry Mountains and climb up to the summit of Mount Ellen, where his guests would take in the hundred-mile views out over the Utah desert. He loved to traverse the flower-decked meadows of the Aquarius Plateau—a "rendezvous for poets," he called it—to camp by the cliff at Bowns Point, overlooking the weird slickrock domes and shadowy fissures of the Escalante River drainage. He would lead trips into those canyons starting in 1920, long before the rest of the country—or even many of its natives—knew of the wonders hidden there.

In the first few decades of the twentieth century, many travelers were looking for some relics of the Old West—a crusty Grand Canyon prospector, a taciturn cowhand with a flair for roping, or perhaps a weathered outfitter full of extravagant yarns. What people like Donald Scott found when they stepped off the train and met Dave Rust was altogether different. He was a native son, to be sure, but he had an extraordinary thirst for knowledge, and a rare ability to impart his learning to others. He made sure that his clients saw the finest examples of the region's startlingly exposed geology. But he asked much of his guests, too: not only did they have to cope with harsh, unforgiving terrain, Rust insisted that they learn from the experience.

In the course of month-long trips covering hundreds of miles, he took time to explain the lay of the land as seen from high viewpoints, discuss the long human history of the area, and read from geologic and literary works around the campfire. In contrast to many purveyors of the tourist West, his approach to guiding was grounded in careful study and preparation. Adventure was not the main point of his trips; for Rust, the goal was to comprehend the landscape. He liked to quote Thoreau that "traveling is no mere pastime"; he believed that scenery was inextricably connected with geology and history. "I have failed if I fail to assist you to love my country," he told his friend and fellow teacher Harrison R. Merrill. "I count whatever money I may receive from any group of travelers as nothing, absolutely nothing, less than nothing, if they do not leave these breaks loving these gorges, these painted cliffs, and these dusty deserts."[7]

The alert explorer could reap great rewards in the American Southwest, and Rust was ahead of his time in preaching this gospel. He was the first guide to understand the potential of the entire Colorado Plateau as a source of physically and intellectually challenging experiences that went well beyond mere tourism. Refusing to restrict himself to a handful of well-worn trails in the national parks, he ranged throughout the canyon lands, trekking from mountain peaks to river gorges and back again, journeying by horseback, wagon, and boat through what was still poorly mapped territory. Other southwestern explorers and scientists, including his heroes John Wesley Powell and Clarence Dutton, were far better known. But if you were a traveler of some means and had a zest for adventure, Dave Rust could take you into canyons and mesas that had yet to appear in the pages of *National Geographic*.

His clients included scientists, business leaders, world travelers, and writers. Two would go on to careers in the U.S. Senate. Whatever their background, Rust showed them how to live for weeks at a time within the region's isolated canyons and plateaus. These were not package tours with stops at plush lodges and tricked-up trading posts. His guests enjoyed rough-and-ready hospitality from the sheepherders, prospectors, and cattle ranchers they met in the back-country. His "campout excursions," as he called them, involved long days in the saddle through all types of weather and terrain, often in the oppressive heat of the canyon bottoms, enduring dust, biting gnats and ants, and occasional hunger or thirst. Camp might be pitched out on a shadeless greasewood bench; water, when it was available, sometimes trickled along a salt-encrusted mudflat. Bed was usually a couple of blankets and a tarp laid out on a mattress of sand or pine boughs.

His guests felt pampered, though, when Dave would scrounge a leg of mutton from a sheepherder and accompany it with his trademark "doughgod" biscuits. And a night under the stars in that pollution-free era was something to behold.

These trips were a natural extension of Rust's teaching career, and he shared his knowledge with infectious enthusiasm. His book learning supplemented an ample native understanding of the land. The archaeologist J. O. Brew wrote in 1971 that "when, as a rank tenderfoot, I spent two months on the trail with him in 1931, he seemed to me to know everything about the geology, geography, flora, fauna, history, and folklore of the area. Forty years later, I still think he did."[8]

For a man of an intellectual bent, Rust possessed the physical toughness that came from a life in the wild. Tall, lean, and erect, his bearing suggested pride in a life of hard work. A friend described him at age forty as "about 6 feet in height, very slight, but muscular and wiry.... We learned from experience that he has endless endurance."[9] Fair-haired as a youth, he turned prematurely gray, and with his penetrating gaze and long, striking face he projected an air of competence. The resemblance to the Marlboro Man ended there, however. A lifelong reader of literature, science, and biography, he never let his mind idle. He could quote from Dutton or Shakespeare, and was an admirer of progressive leaders from Susan B. Anthony to Theodore Roosevelt. Often jovial, quick with a sly quip, he savored the company of his many distinguished guests.

He saw deeper meanings in the rocks, too. His early writings describe a spiritual wonder at the Grand Canyon's glories. He witnessed the awesome power of the Colorado River in all its seasons and sometimes felt the isolation of the Canyon's gloomy recesses. He fit these impressions into the framework of his Mormon faith, but anyone who has been deeply moved by this landscape will see a kindred spirit in his writings.

Standing atop Navajo Mountain in 1919, Rust could survey the Plateau Province's most inaccessible topography, some of it familiar, much of it still awaiting his exploration. The year was a milestone for Dave. His tourist-trail venture at the Grand Canyon was slipping from his grasp as a new federal agency, the National Park Service, replaced the more accommodating forest rangers he had dealt with. Autos were driving to the North Rim and into Zion Canyon, where commercial tent camps had opened to serve the tourists. But out beyond the gorges of the Colorado and San Juan rivers lay country that few city dwellers had seen. During the next two decades Rust would expand his guiding horizons to include almost all of this expanse.

Today, the parklands of the Colorado Plateau are seeing an unprecedented boom in tourist traffic, and both the land and the visitor's experience have, in places, suffered. More and more people who think of themselves as travelers rather than tourists are seeking a deeper, more intimate experience with the land. More and more entrepreneurs are catering to this interest through specialized travel programs. With countless sources of information to draw on, we no longer have to hire a guide and pack string to see the best parts of the canyon country.

What you got out of your travels, not how many places you visited, was Rust's chief concern. Though his beloved canyon lands have changed, his approach to seeing them remains instructive. He made something of his wanderings, and his clients had the good fortune to experience a rare encounter with one of the earth's most dazzling landscapes. Their impressions of the Southwest would always be bound up with memories of their friend, guide, and fellow adventurer, a man for whom travel became far more than a pleasant diversion.

Acknowledgments

SO OFTEN AN OLD PHOTOGRAPH opens a door to the past. Dave Rust was unknown to me until nine years ago, when I needed to find a photo of a young canyon explorer named Dodge Freeman to illustrate a booklet on southern Utah's red rock country. Freeman had taken a long and intriguing pack trip through that region with a fellow he identified only as Dave Rust. This led to the David D. Rust Collection in the Archives of the LDS Church in Salt Lake City, where, to my surprise, I found a black-and-white negative of the two of them standing in a dilapidated desert corral. I showed the photo to William W. Slaughter, an archivist in the Church's extensive historical collection, who looked at me and asked pointedly, "So are you going to write a book about Rust?" That was not my intention, but he persuaded me to have a look at Rust's writings. Bill's enthusiasm and patient assistance over the years, as well as the help of his colleagues, made this book possible. Thanks also to the Church Archives, the Church of Jesus Christ of Latter-day Saints, for making Rust's papers available to the public—a noteworthy service.

I also owe much to Blanche Rust Rasmussen, who in many fine conversations shared memories of her parents and gave me open use of her albums of Dave's photographs, writings, and clippings. The late Quentin Rust gave me the benefit of his long interest in his father's explorations. Joseph C. Rust and Harold Rust made available their considerable research into Dave's life and career. Nora Mickelson recalled Dave's stories of six decades ago with crisp precision. Ned Chaffin brought to life his days on the trail with Dave Rust. To all of you I owe heartfelt thanks.

Much useful material—maps, photographs, digitized newspapers, and manuscripts—was provided by the staffs of the special collections departments at the J. Willard Marriott Library, University of Utah; Harold B. Lee Library, Brigham Young University; Gerald R. Sherratt Library, Southern Utah University; Cline Library, Northern Arizona University; Huntington Library; Denver Public Library; Princeton University Library; Utah State Historical Society; and the Utah State Archives. Roy Webb of the Marriott Library shared his expertise in river history and contributed a thorough and useful review of the text, as did historian Laurance D. Linford—many thanks for your efforts.

A number of friends reviewed drafts of early chapters, for which I thank them, but their support and encouragement have been the greater contribution: David Schleicher, Jennifer Anderson, Melissa Helquist, Dave Bastian, Randy Eggert, Gavin Noyes, and Julie Zych.

Several of George C. Fraser's descendants—Dorothy Shore, Ian Fraser, and Leighton C. Coleman—generously made their family's photographs available. The late Sarah Fraser Robbins offered her recollections of a Glen Canyon voyage with her father, Dave Rust, and Bert Loper in 1930. Brad Dimock provided background on Frederick Dellenbaugh's 1929 visit to Utah. Michael Quinn of the National Park Service at Grand Canyon National Park helped with photo identification. Michael F. Anderson, also with the NPS at Grand Canyon, is undoubtedly the leading expert on North Rim history, and his help in identifying old roads and trails is much appreciated. His Foreword is a wonderful addition to this book.

Peter DeLafosse of the University of Utah Press shares a great appreciation for Colorado Plateau history, and his suggestions strengthened the book. Copyeditors ply an unsung craft, and Virginia Hoffman brought skill and thoroughness to her review of the manuscript.

For close to a decade I've retraced Dave Rust's trails through the canyon country with two steady companions. My wife, Bessann, who has had boundless faith in this project, has been my tripmate, sounding board, and best reviewer. Our daughter, Ellie, started out with us on the trail to Cape Final with an oversize teddy bear hanging precariously out of her rucksack, but a few years later she was scrambling around the rocks by the Colorado, helping me locate Rust's tram anchorage. From river to rim, we three have enjoyed some great Dave Rust sunsets—thanks for the journeys.

MAPS

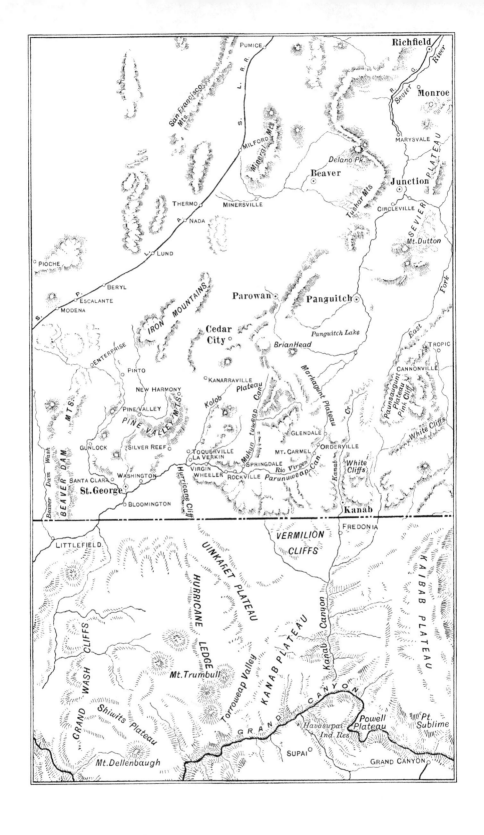

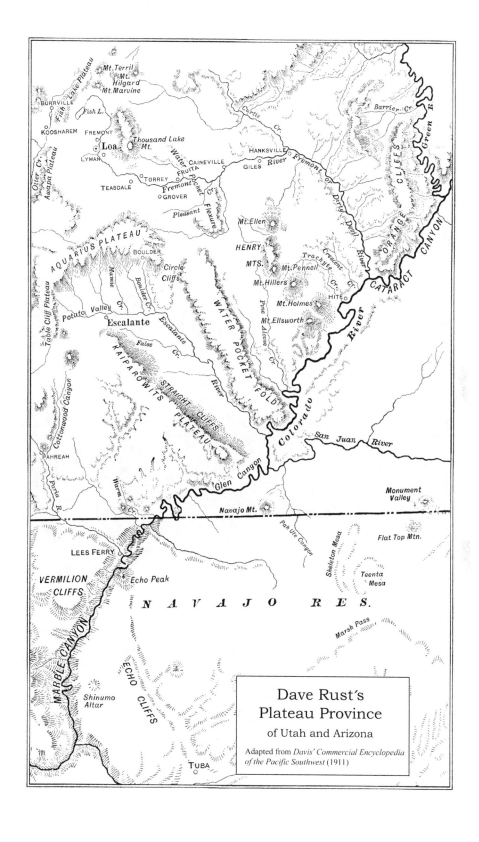

Dave Rust's
Plateau Province
of Utah and Arizona

Adapted from *Davis' Commercial Encyclopedia
of the Pacific Southwest* (1911)

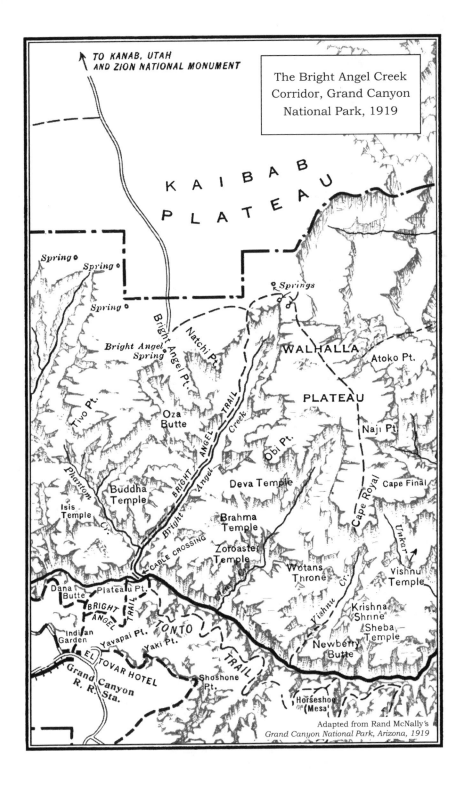

TO KANAB, UTAH
AND ZION NATIONAL MONUMENT

The Bright Angel Creek
Corridor, Grand Canyon
National Park, 1919

KAIBAB PLATEAU

Spring
Spring
Spring
Springs

Bright Angel Pt.
Bright Angel
Spring
Natchi Pt.

WALHALLA
Atoko Pt.

PLATEAU

Tivo Pt.
Oza Butte
Naji Pt.

Obi Pt.

Cape Royal
Cape Final

Phantom Cr.
Buddha Temple
Deva Temple

Isis Temple
Brahma Temple

Unkar

BRIGHT ANGEL TRAIL

Zoroaster Temple
Wotans Throne
Vishnu Temple

CABLE CROSSING

Dana Butte
Plateau Pt.
BRIGHT ANGEL
TONTO
Krishna Shrine
Sheba Temple

Indian Garden
Yavapai Pt.
Yaki Pt.
TRAIL
Newberry Butte

EL TOVAR HOTEL
Grand Canyon R. R. Sta.
Shoshone Pt.

Horseshoe Mesa

Adapted from Rand McNally's
Grand Canyon National Park, Arizona, 1919

DAVE RUST

1 | *Free Range*

My coming out of the wilderness is a marvel to me.

DAVE RUST
Interview, 1937

OF THE THOUSANDS OF PILGRIMS who have come to love the landscapes of the Colorado Plateau, many can recall an incident that struck them with particular force—an encounter with the wild that helped to define their sense of the place. For Donald Scott, the amazing sunset atop Navajo Mountain in 1919 was one such moment; many of Dave Rust's other clients had their own. A Vermont industrialist named Ralph Flanders wrote of a summer day on the Aquarius Plateau when he watched thousands of sheep being driven up from the desert to the verdant mountain pastures, a scene he found almost biblical in its beauty. Henry Dodge Freeman, a young Chicago man with an affinity for the Southwest, recalled coming across a pair of snowy egrets elegantly posing in a fern-lined grotto near the Escalante River—a brief but memorable vignette from the dozens of weeks he had ridden with Rust. Out on the trail, far from the routines and pressures of city life, stirring moments such as these had a way of standing out and becoming emblematic of a great trip.

The outdoor life also had its less uplifting intervals; Rust understood that fine memories could be fashioned from discomfort and challenge as well as from scenes of grandeur, and he did not try to cushion his clients from the vagaries of the trail. "I think with wonder of our cold nights & hot stones for cold feet," wrote Jane Fraser, who with her husband George C. Fraser brought their family west from New Jersey in 1921 to ride with Rust over the high Paunsaugunt, Markagunt, and Kaibab plateaus. In those days the mountains and deserts of Utah were not so well stocked with comfortable tourist cabins, and camping beneath the stars might require some extra warmth under the blankets. Another client recalled the horseback and river trips he had taken with Rust through the Glen Canyon country: "I'll never forget my first night out there, down in Rainbow Canyon near the Arch. Nor shall I forget our nights on the River, especially that one when heat pressed down like a blanket and a sudden sand storm drove us under blankets. I took a picture that night by moonlight with the moon glittering on the River. Remember?"[1]

Such were the conditions Rust had known from his boyhood, growing up in the remote settlements of central Utah where summers were short and conveniences nonexistent. Young men were often away from the safety of home and were expected to take care of themselves. Rust's first experiences in the woods came a few years after his father moved his family and their twelve hundred sheep to take up a homestead in Grass Valley, located in south-central Utah about twenty miles southeast of the town of Richfield. In this high, cold valley, a pleasant clear stream called Otter Creek meandered under the shadow of the Fishlake Plateau. Here, through the months of summer, Dave's older brothers looked after the family flock. Dave joined them when he was nine years old.

By day, it was gorgeous country—there was the lovely long jewel of Fish Lake, sitting deep and pretty in its glacial trench below the bulk of the Hightop, one of several summits that climbed over eleven thousand feet into the sky. The mountain's open meadows, fringed with aspens and dark spruce forests, were pleasant places to watch the sheep. Come nightfall, however, these woods could breed elemental fears, as Dave discovered during an outing with a friend up into the hills. He recounted the adventure in a high-school essay, one of the few events from these years that he set to paper.[2]

His friend, identified only as "Andrew," carried a rifle, intending to shoot a deer. Dave was well equipped with a revolver and a double-barreled shotgun. With the latter he obtained a grouse for dinner, which they plucked and roasted over an evening campfire by a small lake. It was too late in the day to ride down the mountain for home, so they settled in by the fire and pulled their blankets around them. "The moon shone in splendor above us," Rust wrote, "making the shadow of the trees look black and lonely." They had seen the tracks of a large bear earlier in the day, so they were already somewhat on edge. In his flowing longhand, Rust described the dread that came on them:

> About mid-night we were awakened by an awful scream which reminded me of a hungry panther in pursuit of its prey. Our horses snorted and tried to get loose but nothing could be seen but a canopy of darkness for the moon had left us in the dark.
>
> Again and again we heard that dreadful yell as we stood there almost scared to death. At length I managed to start a fire and the remainder of the night was spent with our toes in the ashes and our fingers on the triggers of our guns. It seemed a long time until morning and when the sun came to

chase away the fear of the night, we felt like acknowledging the wisdom of the Creator when he said, "let there be light."

This was a more direct encounter with the terrors of the wild than most tourists would ever experience. It was certainly not Rust's last; he knew the hold this country could have on one's mind—whether it was gloriously uplifting or a serious challenge to one's existence.

David Dexter Rust was born on March 10, 1874, to George Smith and Eliza Brown Rust, who were among the Mormon homesteaders seeking to get established in the valley south of Utah Lake, some fifty miles south of Salt Lake City. George Rust had arrived in the Salt Lake Valley with the first wave of Mormon emigrants, but his quest for land, grass, and mineral wealth would propel him beyond the edges of the Utah settlements. At the time of Dave's birth, the Rusts made their home on Spring Creek, several miles west of the town of Payson. The Rusts stayed at this home only until Dave was four, leaving him with few memories of his birthplace. In his unpublished memoirs he recalled that he "rambled in the brush along the creek, with white hair and red dress." More than once his older sister, Julia, rescued him after he waded into the creek. Even then he displayed an instinct for survival by holding onto the grass-lined bank until she spotted him. Flowing water would continue to attract Rust throughout his life, even as he maintained a healthy respect for its dangers.[3]

Payson at that time was a growing community of more than a thousand people. The town and its surrounding fields were set in the wide, flat bed of ancient Lake Bonneville, described by a member of John C. Fremont's 1856 exploring expedition as "beautifully verdant."[4] When George and Eliza Rust arrived in 1857, the settlers were still defending themselves against dispossessed Ute Indians, and Eliza later told her children of anxious moments when destitute natives would come to their door looking for food.

The Latter-day Saints have always been considered a distinctive group in the history of the western United States, surviving religious persecution and making a dramatic exodus to the Great Basin of Utah under the leadership of Brigham Young. Despite the unique institutions that separated them from and sometimes antagonized their fellow citizens, the Saints were full participants in the westward expansion. The story of individual Mormon pioneers such as the Rusts reads much like those of the Methodist emigrants to the Oregon Territory or the Scandinavian farmers in the Dakotas: they searched for arable land; battled drought and insects; made alternating attempts to drive out or coexist with the Indian population; and struggled to establish new communities a thousand miles from supply sources. The Rusts brought as much energy to their quest as any other pioneer family; what marked them was the classic tension between George Rust's wanderlust and Eliza's determination to forge a secure home for her children. Their conflicting drives would determine how Dave's childhood would play out and, it is safe to say, set a direction for much of his adult life.

In his later years Dave spent part of his free time recording his family history, which has always been an activity of some importance among the Latter-day Saints. His notes, though sketchy (it would remain for his niece, Ethel Jensen, to compile a more complete story), show the family's close ties to their church—and also document a degree of rootlessness in his father's life from childhood onward. George Smith Rust was born in 1834 in Lowell, Vermont, a small town at the foot of the Green Mountains in the northern part of the state. His father, William Walker Rust, left the family when George was four years old and in his travels westward was baptized into the Mormon faith. George's mother, Mary Rand Rust, died of typhus in 1839, followed soon thereafter by George's infant sister. George and his brother were sent to an orphanage. The family's accounts differ, but it seems that in 1841 William Walker Rust brought the boys to Nauvoo, Illinois, the new center for the Mormon Church, where he remarried. George continued to live apart from his father, learning various occupations and attending school when he could.[5] These were the formative days of the LDS religion, when their founder and prophet, Joseph Smith, was actively recruiting members. George Rust recalled that the prophet himself baptized him in the waters of the Mississippi in 1843.

William Walker Rust joined the Mormon Battalion of the U.S. Army in 1846, accompanying the detachment as far as Santa Fe but mustering out after being kicked by a mule. He arrived in the Salt Lake Valley in the late summer of 1847 with one of the first Mormon emigrant parties. George joined the emigration in the company of a family named Haight, arriving in the Salt Lake Valley in September 1847, a few weeks after his father.

In 1854 father and son both were called to serve on an LDS mission in St. Louis, Missouri, under Erastus Snow. While stationed at Mormon Grove,

Kansas, in 1855 following his stay in St. Louis, George met, baptized, and married Eliza Brown, then seventeen years old. A Pennsylvanian by birth, Eliza had traveled west with her mother, Catherine Slauson Brown, also an LDS convert, to this jumping-off point for the Mormon emigration.

Following their marriage George and Eliza Rust headed west to Salt Lake City, where George worked at ranching jobs for a time. Their first child, George Brown Rust, was born in 1856 while they were living in Spanish Fork in the Utah Lake valley. The next year they moved to Payson, where five of their seven children were born. George Rust took a second wife, Sabra Beckstead, while at Payson and had one child with her. At first the Rusts made their home in a bare sheepherder's cabin that offered meager comfort; their subsequent dwellings improved their state only marginally. George divided his time between caring for his cattle and sheep and attempting to run a dry-goods store in town. These were relatively settled years, but a chance discovery would soon put other prospects in his mind.

Around 1864 LDS Church authorities, who controlled much of the territory of Utah, granted George Rust and a partner the right to graze their livestock throughout the Tintic Valley west of Payson. The story has persisted through the years that one day in 1869, while Rust was out on the range, his horse's hoofs turned up a chunk of unusual-looking rock. He took the specimen to an assayer and was told that it consisted of high-grade silver ore.[6] One account states that Rust showed the rock to others in town and that a group of men left the next day to stake a claim. Rust may or may not have accompanied them; he is said to have traded his interest in the find for a wagon and team, believing little would come of it. The seven men who proceeded to locate the Sun Beam claim on Rust's site put it into production the following year, inaugurating one of Utah's richest mineral districts. Rust located his own claims at Tintic soon thereafter, but none developed into a profitable mine. Thus tantalized, Rust continued over the years to search for gold and silver in Utah and Nevada, but without much success. His ambition, like that of so many other fortune seekers of the time, would define the better part of his adult life and have strong repercussions for his family.

For the first years of Dave's life, George Rust managed to set aside his fascination with the Tintic mines and pursue whatever income he could find in the Payson area. He eventually found the region too thickly developed for his taste, and by some family accounts he was unable to successfully earn a living from his farm and store. In 1878 he relocated the family more than a hundred miles to the south, taking up a homestead near the new town of Burrville in Grass Valley. It would not be his last move in search of better pasture.

The journey southward took a week, with Dave's older brothers herding the sheep as they progressed through the towns and fields of central Utah, heading for wilder country. Grass Valley had been opened to homesteading only four years earlier, following a peace treaty that had been negotiated with the Ute Indians. Ethel Jensen described the homestead as being "as inviting as a desert oasis. Subsurface springs had made of the plot a veritable marsh. A sizeable stream flowed through the grassy plot. It was fed by little rivulets, crystal clear, with a hint of ice in their coolness."[7] The surrounding hills offered pasture; the new community, a fresh start.

Dave first went to school here starting at about the age of seven. The one-room stone schoolhouse had, he recalled, a door at one end, a big fireplace at the other, and not much else. The pupils sat on slabs of wood, there being no chairs, tables, or desks. His teacher, a seventy-three-year-old pioneer named Lewis Barney, was hard of hearing; the small community could not afford to hire a younger teacher from outside. Eliza had already taught Dave to read and write using a reader she had saved from her childhood; she would guide his education for another fifteen years. In their three remaining years in Grass Valley, Dave would spend only about twenty weeks in a classroom, yet he showed such an interest in learning that his older brothers gave him the nickname "Doc." He described himself as a "ravenous" reader who was strongly driven to learn. He would gravitate toward books for the rest of his life, seeking the vantage they gave him of the world beyond his horizon.

The long winters at Burrville hampered the Rusts' attempts at growing grain or garden crops, and to complicate things George Rust had failed to obtain water rights to go with the property. Again he found himself wishing for open land and a new beginning. As it was for many Westerners, the chance to make a real showing always seemed to lie over the mountains. But by the 1880s most of the arable, relatively temperate valleys in Utah were occupied. There remained the much less hospitable land at the fringes of settlement—either in the highest, frost-ridden mountain valleys or in the desert to the south and east.

Two of the Rusts' children, George B. and Orion, had wintered the family's stock at the base of the Henry Mountains, many miles to the east of Grass Valley, where the snows did not pile up as deep. They had visited the recently occupied homesteads along the lower Fremont River—then called the Dirty Devil[8]—and had noticed good grass in the valley. George Rust decided to take his chances there. In 1884 he traded his Grass Valley homestead for one of Mosiah Behunin's claims located along the Dirty Devil, close to the young village of Caineville, which Behunin and other pioneers from Grass Valley had settled in the early 1880s. There, under the blue shale slopes and high cliffs bounding the shallow stream, they would begin anew.

The journey to Caineville took them over the dry, sage-dotted Awapa Plateau, descending into an inviting valley where the Fremont River wandered gracefully down from the highlands east of Fish Lake, and eastward into a bewildering jumble of red cliffs and bare, shining sandstone domes. This was the Waterpocket Fold, one of the rocky barriers that the early cattlemen called "reefs"—for it presented a serious obstacle to travel. The only wagon road through the Fold, opened only a few years before, followed a narrow, boulder-strewn cleft called Capitol Wash, named for the monumental white sandstone domes surmounting the cliffs.[9] One kept an eye to the sky while going through this gorge, lest a flash flood turn the route into a deadly trap.

The prospect they met on the far side of this canyon must have been daunting. The outwash slopes from the Fold led down to a series of painted clay hills as barren as the surface of the moon. Beyond them rose sheer rims that delineated treeless mesas. Between the two principal mesas the Dirty Devil River meandered through a cottonwood bottom, in those days still a pleasant stream, flowing several feet deep between gentle banks that permitted irrigation water to be drawn off.[10] Nearby, the cabins of a half-dozen families spread out along the river, in contrast to the usual tightly clustered Mormon villages. They called the place Caineville in honor of John T. Caine, Utah's territorial delegate to Congress. The town's setting was hardly lush, but it offered timber and firewood for a homestead. The climate was warmer at this lower elevation, with the advantage of winter range close by in the surrounding desert. Still, this place promised only unrelenting hard work. It would have taken a hopeful man and woman, perhaps aided by a sense of promised destiny, to see any chance of creating bounty here.

The Rusts moved into Behunin's one-room cabin and made do with its clay roof and clay floor. Clay chinked the gaps between the crooked cottonwood logs.

"Primitive place to grow up" was Dave's succinct recollection of his teenage years in this setting. "No school, no post office, few books.... Plenty of ledges to climb, a river to swim in." The settlers held dances in a farmer's cabin; Dave recalled that some of the girls danced barefoot for want of shoes.

George Rust soon returned to the mines of Tintic with the hope of bettering his family's chances. At first, Eliza could count on help from Dave's older brothers, George B., Will, and Orion, but within a few years they were settling families of their own. Dave's oldest sister, Laura, married while the family was living at Burrville, although she and her husband followed the Rust family to Caineville. Dave's other sister, Julia, helped Eliza with the household and at times taught school in their home in the years before the village built a one-room schoolhouse.

In time more of the hard work fell to Dave, since his youngest brother, Roy, was only five years old at the time of their move. There were always the livestock to look after, a large and crucial garden to tend, and wood to haul. They grew wheat as a staple crop and for cash, Dave learning to thresh it by hand, using a flail to break open the seed heads and tossing them in the ever-present wind to separate the chaff. He would then grind it in their hand-cranked mill, pure tedium for an adolescent boy. The family also grew sorghum for molasses—another crop they could sell or trade in the local subsistence economy.

The residents of Caineville never achieved even the small degree of prosperity that came to Mormon villages in more favorable locations. The town remained little more than a collection of cabins strung out along the river, although the settlers eventually erected a small building for use as a school and church meeting-house. By 1890 the Rusts built a larger house with a real roof. Dave was assigned the task of planting and watering dozens of apricot seedlings, which, he observed proudly, grew into the best orchard in Caineville. Only a few hardy kinds of fruit could survive the parching winds that roared down from the plateaus and the bitter cold that settled into the valley in winter. As Dave wrote many years later, the "long, lean winter ate up the good months," leaving only a "short summer with the flaming sword of frost at each entrance."[11]

Remoteness blanketed the land, coloring the settlers' days. Distance and weather limited how often they could replenish their slim stocks of cloth, medicine, ironware, and other necessities. Self-reliance went without saying, and anyone with a special skill was admired. George Rust's particular gift was for danc-ing; when he paid a visit to town, he was in demand as a "dancing master" who could instruct and lead these important social occasions.

Some of the first settlers in the lower Fremont–Dirty Devil river valley were specifically interested in the region's distance from rails and roads; after passage of the Edmunds Act in 1882, the area's considerable unmapped topography gave Mormon polygamists seeking to avoid federal marshals a chance at their free-dom. This does not appear to have influenced George Rust's decision to move to Caineville, since his plural wife, Sabra, had divorced him in 1872. Dave's oldest brother, George B. Rust, had taken a second wife, and like many men of the pe-riod he moved frequently between his family's homes to stay hidden.

Despite the hard work of maintaining a homestead, Eliza insisted on conti-nuing her children's education, schooling them at home that first winter—Dave recalled how Eliza would wash his face in the morning with cold well water to wake him for study. In the coming years she took Dave and Roy back through Capitol Wash and over the mountains to board in Richfield and attend school. The family's finances permitted this for only three winters, when Dave was twelve, fourteen, and eighteen years old. His first school year was spent at the Rich-field public school, with subsequent years at the Sevier Stake Academy, an LDS Church-owned school that had been established in 1887. These academies were set up throughout the Mormon lands as an alternative to public schools, which church leaders believed were growing too lax in matters of moral and religious instruction. Tuition was required of the students, and local church members supported the schools through their tithes.[12] The Richfield academy enrolled as many as 186 students in its eight grades; Dave would have found it a considerable contrast to the tiny schoolhouses he had attended in Burrville and Caineville. In the winters between school years he read whatever books were available, but there were few places to get them and little money for extra purchases. As much as he wanted to pursue the world of adventure, biography, and ideas, scant time was allowed a young man in the Utah outback for such diversions. If childhood want leaves a lasting yearning in the adult, Dave's was clearly for books and the possibilities they represented.

When he was not in school and could be excused from household chores, Dave took his turn tending the family's livestock. Out in the nearly barren hills surrounding Caineville, he formed his first impressions of the wild terrain of the Colorado Plateau. Years later, when he was sketching ideas for a Western novel set in this same region, he would draw on his memories of those long vigils, describing the "gaunt cliffs starving and choking" that surrounded the river, the "crude materials for the making of a landscape."[13]

Most of the time the family ranged its cattle and sheep north of the Dirty Devil, in a limitless maze of cliffs and rimrocks that sloped up to the foot of Thousand Lake Mountain. What little water made its way down from the high country soon withered into the sandy washes and clay pans of the South Desert, Middle Desert, and the Hartnet, the latter named for a man who pioneered a primitive wagon road through this forbidding country.

The drainages here followed no discernable plan, wandering among nameless pinnacles and mile-long outcrops, eventually joining the arsenic-tinged flow of Salt Wash. Landmarks appeared and disappeared with each turn in the trail; there was little with which to orient oneself. Clarence Dutton, in his 1880 work titled *Geology of the High Plateaus of Utah*, described this place as "the extreme of desolation, the blankest solitude, a superlative desert." Eighty years later, the novelist and historian Wallace Stegner would call it "a lovely and terrible wilderness, such a wilderness as Christ and the prophets went out into; harshly and beautifully colored, broken and worn until its bones are exposed."[14] These were remarkably poetic descriptions, but neither Dutton nor Stegner had to live in this country—they could look forward to returning to comfortable homes in well-watered places following their explorations. Rust knew no such amenities during his years at Caineville. Only the mountain forests of the high plateaus to the west relieved the emptiness.

At first Dave accompanied his father, his brothers, or a hired sheepherder on their forays into the region. George Rust, like any homesteader, expected his children to handle whatever conditions they might encounter miles from home. As long as Dave had someone older nearby there was probably not too much to fear, but as he came of age he was once again given new responsibilities. He learned to manage his own affairs in this unforgiving country. While in the Middle Desert on one occasion, his father assigned him the task of leading a heavily laden mule back to Caineville. Partway through the trip the load shifted; lacking the strength to right it, he was forced to retrace his way back through the confusing terrain to camp.[15]

Rust wrote very little about these trials; they were not all that unusual for young people of his generation. A solitary sojourn in the winter of 1887, though, became one of the mileposts he noted in his autobiographical sketches. That Christmas it fell to him to watch the family's flock by himself. He was thirteen. The Hartnet desert, at an elevation of over five thousand feet, was often subfreezing in winter; with no other human within a dozen miles, the nights especially would have seemed endless. He never welcomed enforced solitude; a stint in the wilds by oneself was something to endure, not relish. Like other young people raised in the out-of-the-way Mormon towns of southern Utah, he learned early the value of community; during his guiding career he would take pleasure in the company of his guests while roaming this same landscape.

The following spring Dave again made his camp in the Hartnet among a few sheltering trees. He had recently turned fourteen, and he was not yet aware that some government scientists and explorers regarded his surroundings with awe and wonder. He was alone, again, and as he related years later to Ethel Jensen, he didn't much care for it.[16] The sheep ranged between the cliffs, searching for the sparse grass in the valley floor. All he had to do was keep the herd moving, which his dog mostly took care of, and watch for coyotes.

Lacking anything to read, he determined to set himself a project. Taking out his knife, he selected a likely cottonwood branch and began shaving off strips of the soft wood. Within a few days he had carved the body and neck of a crude fiddle. He fashioned strings using sinew from a dead ewe's back. Tail hairs from his horse, stretched across a supple branch, made a serviceable bow. The sound it made was pleasing enough and he had plenty of time to practice.

Dave packed up his fiddle when it came time to head down the draw to his family's home in Caineville. There he proudly showed his creation to his mother and played a couple of tunes for her. Eliza sent a letter to George Rust, who was off again in the gold camps of Tintic, strongly suggesting that he come up with the money to buy Dave a real fiddle. Her husband managed to comply, and a few months later Dave had a usable instrument in his hands. He would find many chances to use it at dances in the Hanksville assembly hall and in other towns, as well as playing for his clients on the backcountry journeys he would lead throughout southern Utah. But he kept the old cottonwood fiddle as a reminder of his days in the loneliest of deserts, where a little initiative could make a long sojourn more pleasant.

The demands of a desert life fostered strong capabilities in the children that grew up on the Dirty Devil. Not the least of these was the awareness of danger and the ability to determine when one could run a risk. Still, like any youth, Dave stretched the line at times. In the late spring of 1891, when he was seventeen years old, he and a companion (whom he identified only as "Joe") hired on to drive a herd of horses from the Gunnison Valley in central Utah to Blake City, as the Utah town of Green River was known then. Rust wrote about the incident four years later in a college essay titled "Crossing Green River." It shows a young man who had learned self-reliance but who could still find himself out on a limb.

From Gunnison, the two young men drove the herd south to Salina and east over a divide between the Wasatch and Sevier plateaus, which separated the cultivated Sevier River valley from the desert to the east. After the long, dusty trek across the San Rafael desert, the cottonwood-lined banks of the Green would have looked plenty inviting. Rust and his friend expected to cross the horses fairly easily, but the river was running high. A ferry that might have aided them was stuck on a sandbar on the opposite bank. Cottonwood snags, torn loose from the banks by the flood, drifted by. They found a possible crossing a mile upstream from a railroad trestle bridge. "Here we went," Rust wrote, "and proceeded to drive the frightened animals into the black foaming stream. After about an hour's work we persuaded them to take [to] the water, but instead of going across, they followed the bank for about a quarter of a mile and then returned on the same side from which they were driven." After a few more tries, the boys managed to get all but two of the horses across. These were "large yellow studs belonging to the owners of the herd. They fought us like monsters when we would try to make them take the water."

Dave and his friend finally got the balky animals across. Now only their bags remained. They walked back down to the bridge and waited until a train passed, hoping that indicated a lull. They made two trips across without incident. Rust returned and fetched his saddle and rifle, making it halfway back across before hearing a shrill blast from an oncoming locomotive. Encumbered by his load, he realized he could not make it across. "My gun and saddle were on my back thus making me all the more feeble. These I cast at my feet and grasping one of the huge iron pillars I swung out and there on that shaking bridge I shivered like a bird on a swaying willow. I was almost like a phantom, the black monster snorting and puffing at every moment and now and again giving off his boiling breath."

The scene was classic silent-movie material, but it would have left a powerful impression on a young man. Rust did not record any further daredevil stunts during his adolescence. His brushes with danger—in such places as the Colorado River in the Grand Canyon—would come unbidden, and he would develop considerable skill with which to respond.

That summer he traveled to Mancos, Colorado, where his brothers George and Orion had leased a farm and needed help with the haying. After returning to Caineville that fall to help Eliza with the homestead, he was able to complete his high school classes in Richfield during the 1892-1893 school year. Composition was a favorite subject, and he wrote poetry and short essays in the heartfelt style of the time. His graduation portrait shows him dressed in starched collar and coat, bearing a slight smile that seems to belie pride in his accomplishment.

In the winter of 1893 Dave was asked to teach school in Hanksville, a slightly larger community located twenty miles farther down the river from Caineville. This was a considerable honor for a young man of nineteen with only three years of secondary education, but that was sufficient for the local school directors, and Dave gave his students the best he could offer. The job came with little pay, but the experience showed him an alternative to farming and herding that better suited his interests. He told an interviewer years later how he "pitied" the four first-graders in the school, "for I didn't know how or what to teach them. Somehow before the year was over they had mysteriously learned to read."[17] The older children seem to have given him more trouble: a family story has it that a group of perennial eighth graders took it upon themselves to run off new teachers and boasted that they would make things tough for Dave as well. On his first day, Dave set his briefcase on the desk, opened it, took out a revolver, and laid it carefully on the desk. Then he addressed the class, telling the would-be ruffians, "Now boys, I am here to teach, not to be taught." The boys all graduated that year.[18]

He spent the summer of 1894 herding a local rancher's cattle in the Henry Mountains, but with a higher goal in mind: "I turned cowboy with the determination to go to school when I had earned enough money," he recalled, telling Eliza that he wanted to attend Brigham Young Academy in the fall. This Provo school, the forerunner of today's Brigham Young University, was considered a "normal" school, specializing in the education of future teachers. A degree or at least some coursework there would enhance Dave's prospects; however, it is likely that the lure of classes taught by trained professors was sufficient inducement.

In the fall of 1894, Dave wrote in his memoirs, he had "a span of wild horses, a wagon, and very little money" with which to pursue his dream. Eliza also had little cash, but she offered to accompany Dave, Roy, and his half-brother Sidney to Provo, where she would find them a place to live and do what work she could. Dave appreciated her devotion, recalling that "when you have your mother you can do anything you want—if she's with you." To help pay expenses, Eliza ran an improvised boarding house in three rooms she had rented. Roy and Sidney attended the free public school while Dave took classes.[19]

Dave again herded cattle in the Henry Mountains during the summer of 1895 to save up money for his second year in Provo. He majored in English and pedagogy, obtaining an underpinning to his scattered education that would help him throughout his teaching career. It was an exciting time for a young man reared in the backcountry, and he made the most of it, editing the school newspaper, taking part in dramatic performances, and singing in the college choir. His finances did not permit him to continue for a third year. It would be another three years before he could return.

Dave returned to his home country in the fall of 1896 to take a position as the principal of the Loa public school, located west of Caineville in the high upper valley of the Fremont River. His education was paying off, and the work may have been a welcome contrast to his summers as a cowboy. Public, taxpayer-supported schools generally paid better in those years than the Church-owned stake academies such as the one he had attended in Richfield. For the next twelve years, however, he never stayed more than a year at any one school. "I was always glad to get a job some place else," he said, "and the board of education was glad to see me get it."[20] In reality, his employers were probably delighted to employ someone with his enthusiasm and dedication. While he may have lacked some of the finer points of pedagogy, he possessed a deep love of learning—always a key asset for a teacher.

Opportunities in Caineville were severely limited, and Dave never returned home for long. All of the villages along the Dirty Devil experienced trouble in the 1880s and 1890s. Typhoid fever was a recurring nightmare; the villagers drew their drinking water from a common well and the shallow groundwater next to the river was often contaminated. Adding to these miseries, a diphtheria epidemic hit the valley in the winter of 1893–1894, taking the lives of seven children. Eliza Rust, who made a study of herbal remedies, attended many of the sick during these crises.[21]

While the villagers could withstand periodic drought and disease, they could not hold back the floods that afflicted the Dirty Devil valley. Overgrazing of the surrounding drainages probably exacerbated the natural flood events common to any desert landscape. In September 1897 heavy rainfall sent runoff down countless small tributaries in the surrounding sandstone-and-shale desert, rapidly swelling the river beyond its shallow banks and inundating communities from Caineville to Hanksville. In the 1930s the geologist Charles B. Hunt talked with Rust and other old-timers about the extent of the flood for his geological monograph on the region, the *Geology and Geography of the Henry Mountains*. Dave told him how the flood washed out the settlers' dams and buried their farmland; even more critically, the river cut deep into its bed, lowering the water table and leaving irrigation headworks high and dry.[22] Many families, including the Rusts, tried to hang on, but additional floods every few years worsened the problem. Another major deluge swept through the valley in 1909, ending for all practical purposes any chance at agriculture. Most of the families moved out and the population of the valley plummeted.

Eliza hung on to the Rust homestead until 1910, her sons helping with the home and garden when they were in the area. It was George Rust who decided to sell, relocating Eliza to Manti, Utah, where he had found work as a guard at the LDS temple. He received very little for their property—a few hundred dollars by one account; Ethel Jensen wrote that he received no more than a sorrel horse. The elder Rusts remained in Manti for the rest of their lives, occupied with the offices of the LDS Church known as "temple work," which consisted of such services as proxy baptisms for the dead and the sealing of wives to husbands in eternal marriage.

Dave maintained close ties with Eliza for several more years following his school job in Loa, even while he broadened his travels. His father was a more distant figure, the children faulting him for his long absences and for sinking so much of the family's finances into his mining ventures. Surprisingly, though, Dave soon heard the same call himself, and in the fall of 1897 he decided to join the hundreds of men who were searching the sandbars of the Colorado River for placer gold. He had been getting a good education, it was true, but the great river that plowed through the slickrock on the other side of the Henry Mountains held its own allure. Some of his father's boomer heart lived in Dave as well, and the notion that men might be uncovering wealth so close to home was too much for him to ignore.

Rust would find something of great value in Glen Canyon, only it would not be gold. Instead, he would take part in what Wallace Stegner called the "life-curve" of many Westerners. His course was to be, in Stegner's words, "shaped by the bigness, sparseness, space, clarity, and hopefulness of the West."[23] He had experienced all of these salient qualities of the open ranges and deserts of Utah. While working in Glen Canyon, he would begin to understand what this immense landscape might hold for his future—and how these magnificent canyons could become meaningful to many other people as well.

2 | A Valuable Course of Training

> If by some magic I could carry you away to that strange
> laboratory of nature, and take you for a few hours' ride
> down that turbulent old river, the wonders you would
> see, the raptures you would feel, the truths that would
> be flashed upon you, would exceed in character-forming
> power all that could be given in hundreds of expositions.
>
> DAVE RUST
> "Boating on the Colorado" (1901)

FOR YEARS FOLLOWING Maj. John Wesley Powell's pioneering voyages down the Colorado in 1869 and 1871, Glen Canyon remained as it always had been, little more than a barrier to cattlemen and emigrants. Powell mentioned the canyon only briefly in his publications, which focused on the more dangerous stretches of river above and below Glen. Clarence Dutton and G. K. Gilbert treated the canyon peripherally in their works on the geology of the region. Such studies, moreover, held little interest for most Americans. It took Cass Hite's discovery in 1883 of small quantities of gold in the Colorado River's sandbars to set off real interest in Glen Canyon: news of mineral finds, however sparse or far away, got talked about. While there was no stampede to the canyon, hundreds of men rode down the long desert trail from Hanksville or across the plateau from Blanding over the next few years to see if they could make the river sands pay.

Placer gold—which simply means gold found in waterborne deposits instead of hard-rock veins—may consist of gleaming nuggets like those James Marshall found at Sutter's Mill in 1848, but it is usually much finer and requires painstaking separation from its substrate. The Colorado River's gold was so fine—"flour" was the name given it—that it took as many as two thousand tiny flakes to make a single cent's worth.[1] Miners who panned promising sandbars on the Colorado often found a little color, but more elaborate methods were needed to separate the flakes from the sand. Pearl Baker, in her book *Trail on the Water*, described the apparatus that the prospector Bert Loper used. This was a sluice box lined with carpet and covered with quarter-inch screen, into which the gold particles burrowed while gravel and stones passed over. After days of shoveling sand into the box and pouring buckets of river water through it, Loper would remove the carpet and rinse it in a tub. The residues accumulated over a season were further sluiced and then amalgamated with mercury. This toxic mess was boiled off to leave the remaining gold. Loper used a retort to conserve the expensive mercury, but other miners probably exposed themselves to a hazardous pall.[2]

The best sandbars were not those along the river but farther up on the banks, where floods at prehistoric river levels left deposits that were now high and dry. The miners either had to haul water up to the banks for sluicing or carry the sand down to river level. Either way it was daunting work. Yet by 1889 the hamlet of Hite, located near the head of the canyon, boasted a post office serving around a hundred miners scattered between the mouth of the Dirty Devil and the bars located a few dozen miles downstream.[3]

No one seemed to be getting rich from the Colorado, but by 1888 Dave's older brother Will decided to try his luck. He left his name inscribed on a cliff near Halls Crossing alongside those of dozens of other miners. Will returned in 1896 during a second wave of interest in Glen Canyon spurred by gold discoveries in the San Juan River, a tributary to the Colorado. On this venture Will joined a fellow prospector named Ed Meskin to hunt for a likely sandbar. Meskin bought out an existing claim near the Crossing of the Fathers and Will worked with him for part of that year.[4]

News of the workings on the Colorado must have reached George S. Rust at Tintic, though he was not sufficiently tempted to leave the diggings he hoped would bring him riches. By 1897, though, Dave had heard enough to persuade him to try. He may have been encouraged by the rise in gold prices that followed the election of William McKinley, who campaigned in favor of a monetary gold standard.[5] Possibly he was influenced by the news of steamships arriving in San Francisco and Portland that summer bearing $1.5 million in Klondike gold. While the Alaska discovery may have stoked Dave and Will's enthusiasm, they decided to search for their glory hole closer to home. That fall, rather than resume teaching at the Loa school, Dave set about gathering supplies for a jaunt down to the Colorado. Had he headed to the Yukon he would have met with about the same degree of success, but with a far more expensive and arduous route getting there.

When he wasn't mining, Will Rust was living with his family in Hanksville, just down the river from Dave's home in Caineville. There he built a sixteen-foot wooden boat and, with his brother Orion's help, hauled it down to the Colorado at the mouth of Crescent Creek, also called North Wash.[6] A few miles down-stream on the west bank lay Hite, a rude collection of log shacks befitting a typi-cal gold-rusher's center. The two men floated more than a hundred miles down-stream to Wildhorse Bar, located far below the mouths of the Escalante and San Juan rivers. Dave was to meet them with a pack string he was taking overland. He did not record which route he took from Caineville, but the shortest way was to head south along the edge of the Waterpocket Fold. After forty miles' riding he could turn west and follow Charles Hall's wagon road through Muley Twist Canyon, a sandstone slot that climbed through the Fold in a series of tight bends. From there the route involved a long trek southward to reach the river. He likely followed the route of the 1879–1880 Hole-in-the-Rock party, a group of Mormon colonists who had sought a route across the canyons to the San Juan River. This party was nearly thrown back at the brink of Glen Canyon, and succeeded in get-ting their wagons down the cliffs only by extraordinary effort. Dave's route would have veered off to the southwest around the base of the Kaiparowits Plateau.

At Wildhorse Bar the three brothers pitched their shovels into sands that yielded only a few dollars on a good day. Orion headed home after a couple of weeks; Dave and Will labored on. The amounts they saw from their "wash-ups" were neither so discouraging as to induce them to quit nor so great as to make the effort worthwhile. Many canyon miners were turning up gold, but the high cost of bringing food and supplies so far down the river ate up most of their returns. A miner at Klondike Bar bragged to the entrepreneur Robert Stanton that he took out $1,500 in seven months—but still came out on the losing end.[7] Rust's friend Lou Chaffin told the historian Gregory Crampton that he mined $16,000 from Moqui Bar using a commercial amalgamator. Chaffin worked into the early 1900s after many of the early miners had given up. Although he did not mention his expenses, he was one of the few truly successful miners in Glen Canyon. Rust told Lou's son, Ned Chaffin, that "your father took more gold out of Glen Can-yon than all the other miners put together."[8]

As the fall progressed, Will and Dave could see the sun's course sink lower in the sky, rising above the rims a few minutes later each morning. Ice began to form at the river's edge. Isolation made work on the bars that much harder. For men used to company, living on the river for three months would have seemed pretty lonesome; unlike some miners, neither of them had much incentive to escape society. Other prospectors would occasionally float by and stop to share news or a meal. When Christmas came that year, Dave and Will rode fifty miles west to the settlement at Pahreah, where they enjoyed a pleasant holiday dance under the Paria River's red cliffs. On January 12, 1898, back at work at Wildhorse Bar, the brothers were paid a visit by a crew of prospectors who were locating claims all along the river. Heading the crew was Robert Brewster Stanton, one of the Colorado River's larger-than-life characters. He was preparing the ground for a grand scheme to build a fleet of dredges that he hoped would extract millions of dollars' worth of gold from the river bars.

In 1900, workers for Stanton's Hoskaninni Mining Company laboriously disassembled their first dredge at its Ohio manufacturing plant and shipped it to Green River, Utah. From there they hauled it overland to the Colorado, following a rough road they had built south of the Henry Mountains. The dredge proved a spectacular failure, with two months' operation netting just sixty-seven dollars' worth of gold. Their crude processing method could not separate the impossibly fine gold flakes from the sand and silt of the river. The dredge was abandoned and remained for years as a curious monument visited by river runners.[9]

That January another group of prospectors pulled a boat in to Will and Dave's camp, ready to quit the river and find a route out to the north. The men were uncertain of the terrain that lay beyond Glen Canyon's cliffs, but Dave was willing to lead them. He gathered up his gear, said goodbye to Will, and headed up the barren drainage of Last Chance Creek to the foot of the Kaiparowits Plateau. The prospectors were headed for the town of Escalante, but Dave did not record whether he led them west via the Paria River, or east along the Hole-in-the-Rock trail. It was Dave's first experience guiding a party of horsemen. Though he was not terribly familiar with the country, he knew enough landmarks to make the journey successfully.

Dave resumed work at Wildhorse Bar with Will, but they met with little success. They decided to float on down to Diamond Bar, where Ed Meskin and another prospector named Nathaniel Galloway were working. The Rusts traded one of their horses for Meskin's interest in the claim, and stayed on with Galloway. Nathaniel "Than" Galloway was a prospector, trapper, farmer, and part-time vagabond from Vernal, Utah, who achieved his own place in the history of the Colorado River. Dave and Will had met him earlier at their Wildhorse Bar camp while he was towing a boat upstream. He is often credited with introducing the stern-first method of running rivers, whereby the oarsman faces downstream and pulls against the current to position the boat for running a rapid. His method, with refinements, has become standard among modern-day river runners. He showed Dave some of his techniques of river maneuvering, practicing in Glen's relatively easy rapids. Once Dave asked him how he figured out which channel to take when running a complex rapid. "Go through and figure out afterwards," was his answer.[10]

When high water came in the spring and flooded their sandbar, Dave headed upriver to Halls Crossing. This required rowing against the current and taking advantage of shoreline eddies as much as possible, as well as using the winds that often blew up canyon. As a last resort he would get out and tow the boat from the bank. Will floated downstream to Lees Ferry with Galloway. Will's journey overland back to Hanksville presented its own difficulties. His saddle horses ran off at one point and he wandered back through the cliffs toward the Escalante River, nearly starved, until he reached the camp of some cowboys who fed him and pointed out the way home.[11]

In the summer of 1898 Dave and Will signed up for wage work with the Good Hope Mining Company, one of several outfits that gathered together the foot-loose miners and brought in enough capital to purchase some heavy machinery. The Good Hope was run by Ben Hite, brother of Cass Hite, and had in its employ as many as a hundred men at one time.[12] Their location at Good Hope Bar, just fifteen miles downstream from Hite, required less time and effort to resupply than the claims farther downstream. The operation featured a forty-foot-high water wheel that powered some simple pumps with which to hose the river gravels. Dave made a dollar and a half a day tending the sluice box, but like many of the young men working there that summer, he was not willing to work for wages for long, and lasted only the summer before heading home.

While at Good Hope Bar he got in more time on the river, maneuvering the wooden freight boats that the miners used to haul gear up and down the river. The company owned a twenty-foot boat, which, lacking a motor, had to be rowed back upstream to Hite for supplies. He later described this work as "... steady, hard pulling, determination in every stroke, and strokes in quick succession."[13] On a good day he and his companion could cover twenty miles upriver.

Glen Canyon did not put Dave much ahead, but it was a stimulating and independent time. Unlike Will, he had no family obligations other than to help

Eliza where he could. Looking back on the adventure, he saw the unlikelihood of it all, as suggested in some lines he wrote:

> Oh, farmers drop your grubbing hoes
> Your shovels and your picks
> Don't linger any longer
> To work your water ditch.
> But leave your wife and family
> All out in the cold,
> And shove for Dandy Crossing
> To hunt the shining gold.[14]

His verse reads like a parody of Brigham Young's frequent exhortations to the Saints not to leave their farms for the lure of the goldfields. Perhaps this was intended. Dave knew well what his father's obsession at Tintic had cost his family, but his own interlude on the Colorado was little more than a youthful adventure, harming no one and costing only sweat and aching muscles. Dave was one of many young men who tried their luck and, as Gregory Crampton wryly observed, "obtained for their pains an exhilarating life in the open air." Perhaps Dave was aware of the sparse record of success among Colorado River miners, where, as he later wrote, you were "as likely to find gold in sand-rock as hair on a rattle-snake." Nonetheless, he saw other values in being out on the river. A member of Powell's surveying team observed in 1872 that "the discovery of gold on this river has caused many a man to go back 'broke,' as it is termed, and perhaps not much pleased with the Colorado, but let the man who admires nature visit this place and he will be well paid for his trouble." If Rust did not arrive in Glen with this view, he soon adopted it. Years later, when he recounted to interviewers his growing fascination with the landforms of the Colorado Plateau, he fixed the beginnings of this interest to his days along the river in Glen Canyon.[15]

Dave rode home at the end of the summer of 1898, visiting Eliza in Caineville and then continuing up the Fremont River valley and on north to the town of Emery, located at the eastern base of the Wasatch Plateau. He had arranged to teach the fourth and fifth grades at the Emery elementary school that winter. Conveniently, his sister Laura and her husband had moved to Emery that summer—they may have been the inducement to take the job—and Dave lodged with them for the school year. He made a favorable impression on the county school superintendent, who commended him as "a hard working and earnest teacher."[16] His services as a fiddler also were in demand for social occasions that season, and Ethel Jensen's history records that he made several fiddles that year. Presumably he had a better source of materials than his horse's tail and a cottonwood branch.

Teaching school provided a more assured income during the winters, but he had not forgotten the excitement of prospecting. In the summer of 1899 he set out for the Henry Mountains with Will Rust and Nathaniel Galloway to try the hardrock side of mining. The steep eastern slope of Mount Ellen had seen its own gold rush beginning in 1889 when Jack Sumner (of Powell's 1869 Colorado River expedition) and a companion located a paying vein in a place they called Bromide Basin. At the peak of the boom, the mountainside town of Eagle City boasted a hundred workers, but the rush was over by the time the Rusts and Galloway got there.

Dave may have made a little money from his pick-and-axe work, for that fall he resumed his studies at Brigham Young Academy. He completed his third year at a time when his first classmates were graduating from their own six-year program. As much as he valued education, he could not afford to continue. Nor was a return to Glen Canyon in the works. While he was attending school at Provo, Robert Stanton's Hoskaninni mining venture was going under, and so Dave missed an opportunity to take part in that massive operation. It was just as well; his brother Roy spent a summer working for Stanton and, like much of the crew, failed to collect his wages.

He decided instead to leave Utah in the summer of 1900 to search for work. He and a college buddy rode the rail cars west of Salt Lake to work at an assortment of laborer jobs, first on a railroad in Nevada, then at a logging camp in the High Sierra. They made it as far as San Francisco before their money ran out. There he enjoyed his first view of the ocean, which he described as the highlight of his trip. In a letter to Eliza he urged her not to worry about him, saying "if you could see this beautiful country, this great City, the Pacific beach with its great mad waves, the steamers, the transports, the war ships, you would not tremble except with admiration."[17] As impressive as these sights were, he was not tempted to stay. Before heading home, he and his friend spent a few weeks putting up hay at a family friend's ranch near Lovelock, California, in the Sierra foothills.

That fall he took a job as the principal of the Deseret Stake Academy at Hinckley, a farming community in Utah's West Desert. His months there were one of the few times he kept a daily journal; he recorded his attempts to instill an interest in learning among his thirty-two pupils, who ranged from the first to the eighth grade. Maintaining order in the classroom proved onerous. "The dogged drudgery of discipline I can't endure," he wrote. "If all there was in being teacher was to teach, then the pleasure of the occupation would be manifest."[18] He had his upper classes read *Robinson Crusoe*, *Gulliver's Travels*, *Uncle Tom's Cabin*, and James Fenimore Cooper's *The Pathfinder*; for many of his students, this would be their last exposure to literature. Today's teachers would recognize his lament that some of the parents did not require their children to do their homework and remonstrated against his disciplinary efforts.

The social life of the community, as everywhere in Utah, revolved around church meetings and dances. Rust observed that "much time is given to dancing which if spent in reading good books would revolutionize the literary status of the country." Nevertheless, he noted that he was "raised to dance" and was "always ready to take a whirl." Several of his women teachers proved to be pleasant companions, and there were laughter-filled wagon rides under cold, starlit skies and tête-à-têtes on front porches. No serious romances seemed to have developed, however.

Rust returned to Brigham Young Academy in the fall of 1901 for his fourth year of classes. As part of his studies in English composition, he wrote an article about his experiences on the Colorado River, submitting it to the Mormon youth magazine *Improvement Era*. "Boating on the Colorado" was the first of seven pieces he would publish in this magazine, which were his only writings for a wider audience. In it he described the hard work of pulling freight boats up the river and the dangers of negotiating its rapids. There were compensations, though. "A trip on the river is a most valuable course of training," he wrote. "Although no formal studies in morality are given, still the sermons that may be read in the great temples of stone, are redolent of moral influence. The dangers of life on the river tend to sharpen the mind and give to even the mediocre a resolute will and a conquering determination." His finding moral lessons in stone—he knew his Shakespeare—may sound a little Victorian to modern minds, but he clearly took pride in his labors on the river. It was not a bad way for a young man to test himself.

During this year Dave was also introduced to the psychological theories of John Dewey, one of the founders of American progressive education. Dewey published "My Pedagogic Creed" in 1897, establishing him as an innovative thinker, and he was invited to give a series of lectures at Brigham Young during the 1901 summer session. That fall Dave assumed the editorship of the student newspaper and arranged to reprint all ten of the lectures, prefacing the series as "something fresh from the mind of one of our greatest men."[19] He took some criticism for filling half of each issue with these lengthy expositions, but he felt that Dewey bore important advice for teachers-to-be. While Dewey's theories and his vast body of writing yielded many interpretations, Rust was drawn to his notion that an educator represented the values of the larger community, which, in Dewey's words, permitted the child "to emerge from his original narrowness of action and feeling, and to conceive of himself from the standpoint of the welfare of the group to which he belongs."[20] Such views meshed perfectly with the Mormon emphasis on participating in the life of the community. That their children would come to adopt the community's values went without saying.

While progressivism in education has come to be taken for permissiveness and overemphasis on the individual, Dewey still held to the idea that children must develop strong capabilities and exercise good judgment. "To prepare him [the student] for the future life means to give him command of himself," he wrote. "It means so to train him that he will have the full and ready use of all his capacities; that his eye and ear and hand may be tools ready to command, that his judgment may be capable of grasping the conditions under which it has to work, and the executive forces be trained to act economically and efficiently."[21] These words could serve as Rust's personal motto, and he would paraphrase them in his 1911 essay "The Worth of a Boy."

Rust did not complete the coursework necessary to graduate that year, and he somewhat regretfully saw more of his former classmates finish their program. It must have been difficult for him to get so close to the coveted degree in education, which would have assured him good jobs in his field. But he had come a long way from his one-room schoolhouses, amassing some fair experience in the classroom and good recommendations as well. In the fall of 1902 he signed on as the principal of the public school in Fredonia, Arizona, a tiny community just south of the Utah line. It paid $125 a month—a good deal more than the private Deseret Academy or any other rural district in southern Utah. He turned down an offer of a principal's position in Provo because it paid forty dollars less.

The northern Arizona desert was new territory for Rust. To get the Fredonia job he took an examination in Flagstaff, crossing the Colorado River at Lees Ferry and traveling through the Painted Desert into Indian country.[22] The land here was as wild as the Dirty Devil mesas. But Fredonia, and the larger community of Kanab back over the line in Utah, were Mormon towns with a strong social network. A college friend named Royal Woolley came from Kanab, and he arranged to introduce Dave to his family. Royal's father, Edwin D. Woolley Jr., was a prominent Kane County rancher, businessman, and civic leader. The son of a wealthy Salt Lake City pioneer, Woolley arrived in southern Utah in 1866 as part of the so-called "Dixie Mission," the great expansion of Mormon settlers into southwestern Utah. His second wife, Florence, was the daughter of the Apostle Erastus Snow, the leader of the Mormon settlers in Dixie. "Uncle Dee," as he was known, had previously operated an LDS Church-owned ranch at Pipe Spring, Arizona, and another in the high country north of Kanab. He finally settled in Kanab, where he served for many years as president of the LDS Church "stake" in Kane County.

The Woolleys lived in one of Kanab's finer homes and frequently hosted visitors, as there was no hotel in town. Dee Woolley's daughter Mary Elizabeth, who wrote a brief family history in 1934, recalled that "our home was always open to friends and strangers alike.... we were the only ones who boasted a 'spare-room,' which was usually occupied."[23] Thus the family welcomed Dave during the autumn LDS stake conference held in Kanab. There he met Royal's sister Ruth, the daughter of Dee Woolley and his first wife, Emma Bentley. She found Dave to be an intelligent fellow with wide-ranging interests—a bit higher-toned than the cowboys she had been dating.

Ruth Woolley had a male friend who was completing an LDS Church mission and she was seeing another local man as well. Undeterred by this, Dave asked her to the Christmas dance. The two of them caused something of a stir at this occasion, Ruth recalled, since her missionary friend (and presumed intended) had just returned home. Dave stayed as a guest of the Woolleys through the holiday season and he and Ruth went to more parties and dances. She related how "after the dance on New Year's night, we stood by the fireplace in front of a good pitch pine fire. I was a green country girl and I didn't comprehend what Dave was telling me of his plans for the future."

Dave eventually let his intentions be known, for they were engaged in March and made plans to be married at the LDS Temple in Manti, Utah, in May 1903, after the school year was out. The two-hundred-mile ride to Manti took the better part of a week in a borrowed white-topped buggy, spending nights at the homes of acquaintances along the way. The temple at St. George would have been a shorter journey, but Dave's father worked at the Manti temple, and he, Eliza, and another Caineville family welcomed them. After the wedding Dave and Ruth continued on to Salt Lake City to visit two of Ruth's sisters. While there, they attended a speech given by President Theodore Roosevelt at the Salt Lake Tabernacle. He spoke on the need for conserving the forests and rangelands of the West, and on the importance of the small farmer and stockgrower in developing the state's resources.[24] Roosevelt's progressive ideals appealed to Dave, who would go on to serve the role of yeoman farmer and rancher for some years.

Dave attended the summer session at Brigham Young Academy and hoped to return to Fredonia that fall. When the school hired a different principal, he decided on a more ambitious agenda, applying to study at Stanford University. Dave had been impressed with San Francisco during his brief visit in the summer of 1900, but more important, the Leland Stanford Junior University was emerging as the most prestigious school in the West. Its president, David Starr Jordan, attracted some of the leading intellectuals and authors of the day to his faculty. A program of study there would take Rust well beyond the teacher's curriculum at Brigham Young. Curiously, Rust was able to attend Stanford under the auspices of the LDS Church, having received a call to an "educational mission" there.[25] It is likely that Dee Woolley, as an influential stake president, arranged for this honor. Such missions were somewhat unusual in the Mormon Church, and typically went to young men and women who showed a particular intellectual or artistic talent that could be developed to the benefit of the church. The mission would fulfill Dave's duty in this regard and he would never serve the more usual role as a proselytizer for his church. There does not appear to have been any stipend attached to his mission, however.

Dave and Ruth arrived in Palo Alto in mid-August, traveling with a group of Salt Lake Civil War veterans who were attending a G.A.R. convention in San Francisco. They boarded with a local family for a couple of months, then set up housekeeping with another student couple in a rented home in College Park, a mile from campus. Dave tried out one of the new "wheels"—a bicycle—to get to classes, and in the evenings he would walk with Ruth to the library to study. He majored in English literature and rhetoric; he kept a few of the essays and poems he wrote there, which display the serious, flowery style of the time.

The cosmopolitan life in the Bay area was a far cry from what Kanab or even Provo could offer. They attended plays at the university and visited the Pacific shore when they could. It was a huge change for Ruth, especially, who had never been outside of Utah. She arrived shortly after learning that she was expecting their first child—a time when a prospective mother might want to be close to her family. She wrote frequent letters to her sisters that betrayed no particular homesickness. Funds were tight, though, and she took in ironing to help pay the bills. She also sold some of the livestock she owned back in Utah. Dave, appreciative of her support, promised to pay her back when he returned to teaching in Fredonia.[26]

Their first child, a boy, arrived that April. Ruth's sister Rae, a nurse, came to stay with them and help care for the baby. The Rusts named him David Jordan, honoring Stanford's president as well as the biblical David, "the great poet of Israel," in his father's words. Life was full of changes—new surroundings, a baby, interesting studies. Ruth's letters home spoke of Dave's enthusiasm for his work and his delight in his son. While she may have missed the rest of her family, she accepted their move as an adventure, one that would help place a good foundation for their life together.

The summer after the regular school year at Stanford, Dave took classes from several distinguished visiting professors, including John Dewey, who was teaching a guest course in "Psychology and Education." Equally notable was a course in physiography and geology from Harvard's William Morris Davis, the founder of the field of geomorphology. Davis had established his reputation by elucidating the "cycle of erosion," in which landforms were repeatedly uplifted and worn away according to a predictable pattern, leaving a so-called mature landscape or peneplain.[27]

Davis was probably an ideal lecturer for Rust, who had grown up among the most spectacularly eroded landscape in the hemisphere. Davis had studied the Grand Canyon and surrounding region during visits in 1900 and 1902. He believed that the Plateau Province had been sculpted by the long, slow action of streams, not by cataclysmic earth movements. By Davis's time, geologists had largely accepted the concept of "uniformitarianism," in which physical processes acted at a steady rate over the millennia. While his model of wholesale landscape wasting and the development of a peneplain has been updated in the age of plate tectonics, Davis's theories gained wide acceptance in an era when scientific discoveries were beginning to filter into the common understanding.

At a minimum, Rust would have learned from Davis a new language for understanding the physical geography of his home country. Equally likely, he would have absorbed Davis's enthusiasm for his subject—the professor was known for his emphasis on education and placed a high value on geographic literacy among nonspecialists. Listening to Davis's lectures would have helped Dave realize that whatever attraction he felt for his home ground had a strong intellectual justification as well. The Colorado Plateau was more than merely scenic; it was the bones of the earth exposed, and he was in an enviable position to understand and exploit that knowledge.

This stimulating summer ended Dave's work at Stanford, since there was no money to continue his studies. In the fall of 1904 he took a job as principal of the Cassia Stake Academy, an LDS-run school south of Burley, Idaho. Their second child, Emma, was born during this stay. But they longed to get back home, and when the school at Fredonia asked him to return for the 1905–1906 school year, they moved once again. This was a blessing for Ruth, who could again be close to her family; Fredonia lay seven miles south of Kanab and her sisters and mother visited them often while they were there.

Dave's years of wandering were not quite over, but henceforth his travels would take on a new focus and direction. He knew that his father-in-law had plans for promoting tourism on the north side of the Grand Canyon; Dee Woolley had asked Dave to spend the summer of 1905 working on a trail he was building down from the North Rim. Dave thought he might get involved in this project. At Stanford he had gained a new understanding of the magnificent workings of nature in the Colorado Plateau. Within a year he would find a way to tie his career to this intriguing landscape.

3 | *Building Trail*

The river trip on horseback down the Woolley Trail in Bright
Angel Creek… is a royal journey through an ever deepening and
narrowing gorge of majestic towers and walls, terminating at a
River Tent Camp usually maintained at the Cable crossing by
those faithful prophets who have seen the north rim come into
its own, D. E. Woolley, and D. D. Rust, of Kanab, builders of
the trail.

J. Cecil Alter
"Utah Recovers the Grand Canyon of Arizona" (1920)

Dave and Ruth Rust's move to Fredonia in the fall
of 1905 placed them in one of the more remote spots in the American West, a
slice of desert territory called the Arizona Strip. Mormon polygamists had settled
Fredonia in 1885 as a refuge from federal raids, originally calling it Hardscrabble.
The name fit the locale, but Erastus Snow, an LDS Church leader in southern
Utah, suggested "Fredonia" to emphasize the freedom that Mormon women (in
Spanish, *la dona*) would have there.[1]

There was not much to say for the town's setting other than its location in
Coconino County, far from any sheriff with jurisdiction. The Arizona Strip had
its beauties, but on this vast Permian terrace that stretched for a hundred miles
beneath the Vermilion Cliffs, water sources were scarce and the wind whipped
unimpeded across the land. The early-day stockmen, cowboys, and homesteaders
of the region learned to live with its stinting rainfall and searing heat. You could
always look to the south, though, where a broad, gently arched curve of a mountain reached clear across the southern horizon. The locals called it "Buckskin
Mountain" for the deer herds that thrived there, and its parks and forests offered
pleasant summertime pastures for the settlers' herds. Residents of Kanab and Fredonia enjoyed picnics up on the mountain, despite the long day's ride needed to
reach its cool forests.

Major Powell named this sprawling highland the Kaibab Plateau, after Paiute
words that he translated as *Kai-vav-wi*, or "mountain lying down."[2] Exploring the
plateau in 1872–1873 from their base camp south of Kanab, Powell and his men
found it a disorienting, practically featureless terrain. It was anything but flat;
its uplands were dissected by innumerable ravines and small canyons that made

travel a challenge. Only a few high points surmounted its endless pine forest. The plateau gave no hint—either by drainage or by slope—of the great chasm that formed its southern boundary. One of the scientists in the Powell Survey's employ, an army captain named Clarence E. Dutton, wrote that "whenever we reach the Grand Cañon in the Kaibab it bursts upon the vision in a moment. Seldom is any warning given that we are near the brink.... [T]he forest reaches to the sharp edge of the cliff and the pine trees shed their cones into the fathomless depths below."[3]

Dutton's remarks were part of an engaging geological overview he wrote of the Grand Canyon and the cliffs and terraces to the north of the Arizona Strip, titled *Tertiary History of the Grand Cañon District*. The book featured as many observations of the region's scenic and aesthetic qualities as of geologic faults and unconformities. In time, Dutton's report would come to define the Grand Canyon as a world-class wonder in the minds of the intellectuals and travelers of the day.[4] Rust would adopt the book, and Dutton's congenial way of explaining geology, as his personal guide to the canyons.

Several local cowboys helped guide and provision Powell's exploring parties, and they must have brought back impressions of the Grand Canyon. But the North Rim and its views were generally of little interest to cattlemen, other than as a natural fence line. The notable exception was Dee Woolley, who as a young man had worked as a cowboy on the Kaibab. Local legend says that when Woolley first saw the Grand Canyon from the North Rim in 1880, he was so amazed that he nearly fell off his horse. (More likely, his horse spooked upon reaching the sudden drop-off, but the tale fit his expansive character.) He recovered, the story goes, and "bowed his head in reverence to the wonderful works of the Creator."[5] His cowboy companions, it is reported, only laughed. But Woolley had an enterprising mind. He understood at once that what he was viewing ranked among the world's great geological spectacles. He would spend the better part of the next four decades trying to get other travelers to make the trip and would become the most active tourism promoter on the north side of the canyon.

In 1892 Woolley accompanied a party organized by John W. Young (a son of Brigham Young) that brought Buffalo Bill Cody and various English noblemen to the Kaibab with the intention of creating a hunting camp. The long, dusty ride from Flagstaff via the Painted Desert and Lees Ferry did little to stimulate interest among the Englishmen, and nothing came of the scheme. Woolley hosted a party of geology students from the University of Utah under Prof. James E. Talmadge at the Grand Canyon in the early 1900s, and in the summer of 1902 he brought the entire Kanab high school student body to spend three weeks at the North Rim.[6] But the journey discouraged most travelers.

Woolley heard from his friends in northern Arizona how tourist traffic to the South Rim was growing year by year. Former South Rim prospectors such as Bill Bass, Ralph Cameron, and John Hance turned to guiding "dudes" down the steep trails they had hacked out of the cliffs and slopes below the rim.[7] By 1901 the Atchison, Topeka & Santa Fe Railway completed a rail line from Williams, Arizona, to the South Rim, giving a boost to tourist traffic at the hotels and camps located there. Then the Santa Fe opened the elegantly rustic El Tovar hotel in 1905 and put the Grand Canyon on America's tourist map. From then on, the general public's view of the canyon would be firmly linked to the South Rim.

President Theodore Roosevelt set aside some of the forest lands atop the Kaibab as a game preserve in 1906, and he designated part of the Grand Canyon and Marble Canyon as a national monument in 1908. These actions brought additional public attention to the north side of the canyon, but tourist development continued to be concentrated at the South Rim, the only place where private landholdings overlooked the chasm. The monument itself, as well as the rest of the Kaibab Plateau, was in the hands of the Agriculture Department's Forest Service, which at that time had little interest in tourism.

Access to the North Rim country remained difficult. Rail stops in Utah came no closer than two hundred miles from the canyon, and the few wagon roads that led up onto the Kaibab were of poor standard. Woolley believed he could tap into the South Rim's tourist traffic with a cross-canyon trail, as well as improve the roads on the Kaibab and farther north so that travelers could continue on into Utah. This would mean more business for guides and outfitters based on the Arizona Strip, and it would route lucrative business through his hometown of Kanab.

At that time the only constructed trail across the Grand Canyon was William W. Bass's route that led down to the Colorado River from his South Rim tourist camp, twenty miles west of the emerging tourist center at the Santa Fe's terminus. Bass had installed a cable crossing on the Colorado upstream from the mouth of Shinumo Creek and kept a rudimentary tourist camp near the river.

From there his trail led up Muav Canyon to the North Rim, some twenty-five miles west of Bright Angel Point. Bass took the occasional hunting or tourist party across his trail, but the steep, rugged route—particularly the rocky ascent up the north side—discouraged most visitors from making the trip.

Woolley had in mind a different route that would start from the North Rim, east of Bright Angel Point, and follow the long gorge of Bright Angel Creek to the river. A trail here would offer advantages over Bass's route: by extending it across the Colorado and up to Indian Gardens, it would meet Ralph Cameron's toll trail coming down from the South Rim. The way would then be clear for tourists to cross the canyon in relative comfort. Sportsmen would be attracted to the Kaibab's deer herds, which were at that time open to hunting, and to the prospect of going after the elusive mountain lions that preyed on the deer.

To this end, in 1903 Woolley and four of his business friends organized the Grand Canyon Transportation Company to build a tourist trail across the canyon. His partners were Thomas Chamberlain, a Kanab businessman; Jim Emmett, a noted northern Arizona cattleman who had operated Lees Ferry for a time; E. S. Clark, an attorney from Flagstaff; and a third Kanab man, Timothy C. Hoyt. The initial capital stock was ten thousand dollars, divided equally among the five directors.[8]

The men voted to begin work on the trail that summer. They filed a "certificate of location" to what they called the "Grand Canyon Toll Road" with Coconino County on June 15, 1903, and attached a plat sketch of the route. It showed the road or trail beginning from "Woolley's Station," an undefined point that may have been in or near Harvey Meadow, north of Bright Angel Point. (The actual road, once it was built, started at a pasture Dee Woolley used in Fuller Canyon, where the company eventually built a small outfitting cabin.) The route reached the rim above a side canyon of upper Bright Angel Creek, and from there descended into Bright Angel Canyon and went on to the river. Two Flagstaff prospectors, Porter Guffy and Wash Henry, had filed an earlier claim to the portion of this trail along Bright Angel Creek, but their claim does not seem to have interfered with Woolley's venture.[9]

The project ran in fits and starts for several years. Woolley had already spent some time scouting for a route off of the rim east from Bright Angel Point. Sometime around 1902 or 1903, Woolley, Emmett, and Hoyt located a deer trail that might afford a descent. "We followed it," Woolley recalled, "until we came to an immense slide of loose stuff (shale) on Marble Ledge. We thought it feasible to make a trail through it—it being the only possible place along a 100 mile ridge."[10]

The men might have been aware of a U.S. Geological Survey party under Francois E. Matthes that had used this same game trail, or one very close to it, in the fall of 1902. Their route could hardly be called a trail. "So steep was it in certain places," Matthes recalled in a 1927 article, "that the animals fairly slid down on their haunches. So narrow between the rocks was it at one point, that the larger packs could not pass through and had to be unloaded."[11] Dee Woolley probably followed the same route in the summer of 1903, but he did not indicate in his memoirs that he knew Matthes or had discussed the route with him.

Tim Hoyt and a small crew of hired men began work on the trail in the summer of 1903, starting from a minor promontory on the rim that they named "Hoyt's Point."[12] They managed to hack out some rock and vegetation, but it would have been a stretch to call their route a tourist trail. In late June Hoyt sent an optimistic note to Dave Rust, who had been his classmate at Brigham Young Academy. He anticipated an easy job of it:

> When are you coming down this way? And are you going to Flag [Flagstaff] this summer. If so, why not get someone else to come down with you, a photographer, a correspondent, a sketcher, etc. and then I would pilot you over Buckskin, across our new trail, and up the hill on the other side. We're anxious to catch a few suckers for advertising purposes, and would scoot them over toll-free if they were the proper stuff.... There is not a dangerous place on the entire trail and horses can be taken to the river and across.[13]

Hoyt may have been correct about being able to get horses down to the Colorado River, but a tremendous amount of work remained to smooth the path enough that tourists might actually enjoy the journey. From the edge of the canyon three miles northeast of Bright Angel Point, the route zigzagged down a steep ridge, dropping three thousand feet in a straight-line distance of just over two miles. From there the "trail" followed the creek bottom, crossing the stream repeatedly as the cliffs rose higher. Three miles above the confluence with the Colorado, the canyon narrowed into a defile known as "The Box," a long, sometimes gloomy gorge that forced riders repeatedly into the stream. Three-quarters of a mile from the river, the cliffs opened again to reveal a habitable bench along Bright Angel Creek.

At the mouth of the creek, one had to row across the Colorado, assuming someone had left a boat handy. Pack stock could negotiate the river only at low water levels. Then came a stiff climb up the drainage of Pipe Creek to the first outpost of civilization at Indian Gardens, an old mining camp that had recently been reopened for tourist use. Here Ralph Cameron's toll trail, the precursor of today's Bright Angel Trail, led up to the South Rim.[14]

The cross-canyon route was not exactly a boulevard, and the prospect of fording the river was itself daunting. The keystone to Woolley's plan was to rig a cable crossing of the Colorado above the mouth of Bright Angel Creek. Outfitted with a metal tram cage, this cable would take passengers and stock across in comparative ease and safety. When the river was in flood, as it often was, a tram would be the only way to cross the river. Why not simply build a footbridge? Woolley and his partners probably reasoned that a tram could generate tolls and thus pay for itself, whereas traffic across a bridge would be harder to regulate. A tram may have appeared easier to build, too, although events would prove otherwise.

The third leg of the plan was to be a tourist camp near the mouth of Bright Angel Creek. The benches along the creek offered one of the more hospitable environments in the depths of the Grand Canyon, at least during the spring and fall. The clear, pleasant waters of the creek would make the site usable in summer, when inner-canyon temperatures soared. Once tourists were hauled across the river to the north bank, they could stay in camp a few days or be outfitted for hunting trips up to the Kaibab Plateau.

The company filed for a right-of-way with the Forest Service in 1904, apparently to consolidate their claim filed the year before with Coconino County, and had their trail professionally surveyed that March. That fall, the Forest Service's field personnel inspected the route and recommended to the General Land Office that the right-of-way be granted.[15] Following some back-and-forth paperwork, including communication with the office of the Chief of the Forest Service, the agency on May 29, 1905, approved the Grand Canyon Transportation Company's trail application. It stipulated, though, that the company build a "free public road or trail, but not a toll road." This left the company able to charge only for use of its tram crossing. The agency further required that "no stone, timber or earth be removed in excess of amount actually needed for constructing this road, and that in procuring construction material and building the road, neither the scenic beauty of the canyon shall be in any degree marred, nor the forest reserve injured."[16]

The Forest Service need not have worried about the company significantly marring the forest; the trail was little more than a footpath. That did not stop Woolley from promoting it. In 1905 he and Jim Emmett traveled to Salt Lake City to talk up their plan. They induced a number of Utah's political leaders to have a look at the Kaibab's development possibilities. Utah senator George Sutherland and governor A. L. Thomas trekked to the North Rim that summer under Woolley's guidance, while Reed Smoot, Utah's other senator, and Congressman Joseph Howell visited in September.[17] Tim Hoyt helped with guiding duties on the latter trip, which included a deer hunt on the Walhalla, or "Greenland" Plateau. Woolley enlisted Sutherland's help in obtaining the Forest Service's approval for their trail.

Aside from permits and publicity, the trail itself still needed considerable work. Continual erosion on the steep slopes threatened to erase the pathway, and in general it required construction to a higher standard. The project would benefit from an energetic boost, and Woolley decided that his son-in-law could provide it. That spring, while Dave and Ruth were finishing their school year in Idaho, Woolley wrote to ask whether Dave might be available to work as a cook that summer for the trail workers. He mentioned the Sutherland-Thomas party, and Rust thought it would be fun to entertain such a crowd. "I have been very much amused & taken up with the thought of cooking for Governors & senators next summer," he wrote to Eliza. "They might think truly of [the] strenuous life if they ate my cooking."[18]

But Dave did not hire on with Woolley that summer, and in the fall he returned to Fredonia as the school's principal. The following April the superintendent of schools for Coconino County asked him to return that fall, saying "the school there needs a man with your push and energy."[19] By the summer of 1906, though, Dave was ready to try working in the field. On June 25 he hired on as manager and construction foreman for the Grand Canyon Transportation Company. Woolley raised $1,500 toward Rust's salary of $50 a month—the same as the other hired men. Rust was also to receive one-twelfth of the company's stock, to be paid for from half of his salary.[20] It was not a lot for Ruth and the family to live on in Dave's absence. Woolley may have assisted the family in other ways, and in any event he continued his mentorship that had begun with Dave and Ruth's move to Stanford.

Rust's eagerness to take on the project is all the more noteworthy in that he was giving up a relatively well-paying position—$125 a month for eight months—as the principal at Fredonia. Few jobs in the region offered this much. But perhaps he felt that by working for his father-in-law he would be getting in on the ground floor of an ultimately successful enterprise, with prospects for even more money. There may well have been an element of excitement to the position, too—being in charge of an endeavor that could open up the region to greater development.

Rust began work immediately. He would spend the better part of two years getting the trail built and installing the cable crossing on the Colorado River. More work would follow to set up the tent camp at Bright Angel Creek and begin guiding visitors over the trail and along the Kaibab.

Throughout the West, in precipitous canyons and on high mountain talus slopes, one can still see evidence of the incredible energy that early-day prospectors and entrepreneurs poured into developing their dreams. Today only a trace of the Rust tram is visible: some eyebolts and a few scraps of cable sunk in a rock buttress on the north bank of the river, fifty feet upstream from the present-day Kaibab suspension bridge above the mouth of Bright Angel Creek. The tram was to have been the main transportation link between the South and North rims, allowing Woolley and his fellow tourism developers, including Rust, to share in the bounty brought to the South Rim by the Santa Fe Railway.

Rust only occasionally kept a journal during his life, but he must have been excited about what he was doing in the canyon, for he kept a substantial record of his years there.[21] It is filled with his joys at occasional successes and his pain at numerous setbacks, and shows his determination to fulfill the vision he inherited from his father-in-law. In it he said little about his role as leader of the crew, but his work as a school principal gave him some experience with supervising others. Probably his style was to lead with a pickaxe in hand; the journal indicates that he labored as hard as any of his men.

Rust set out from Kanab on June 27, 1906, with Dee Woolley and five hired men; a sixth man was already in the canyon. Laden with tools and gear, they took three days to climb over the Kaibab and reach the rim at the head of their trail.

Woolley accompanied them down the trail they had built thus far, pointing out what remained to be done and leaving the party to its work. The crew would take until mid-August to complete the trail to the river.

Day after day the men swung their pickaxes and chipped out a graded trail snaking down the steep sidehills from the rim to Bright Angel Creek. It was heavy effort, and initially it had to be done under the full force of the sun on the canyon's south-facing slopes. Keeping everyone in good health proved to be a recurring problem. Rust's journal mentions one hazard they ran into early on:

> JULY 11. The trail is completed from Emmett Creek to the Spring—a good grade, and taken as a whole a splendid trail. Dalton is poisoned, either with poison oak or ivy, we can't say. I have a touch of the same thing. We were in the brush during a rain storm, and were thoroughly wet. As soon as we reached camp I took a bath & changed clothes. Dalton still has on the same clothes.
>
> JULY 12. Dalton is better. I am worse. We are contemplating starting home.—P.M.—Have decided we have the *itch*, some kind, 7 day perhaps—instead of poison. We took hot bath and composition tea, used plenty of soap and changed all clothes.

The men worked through the punishing heat of midsummer, pushing the trail far down from its 8,500-foot elevation at the rim to the canyon of Bright Angel Creek where, at less than 4,800 feet in elevation, the sun felt considerably warmer. At first they worked out of a temporary camp they called "Take a Rest," located on a dry ridgetop 1,100 feet below the rim. Farther down there was a pleasant spring issuing from a side canyon, and still lower down, Bright Angel Creek offered ample water. This was augmented by the flow of "Emmett Creek"—their name for Roaring Springs Creek, a spectacular short stream that issued from a cave in a limestone cliff. After sidehilling above the east bank of the creek for a mile, they descended to the welcome coolness of the creek bottom. From there work proceeded swiftly. They planned to eventually get the trail located higher up and out of the water, but with few exceptions it remained intertwined with the creek for as long as they used it.

By August 17 the crew had carved a suitable trail through the narrow "box" of Bright Angel Canyon to the Colorado River. "The [last] few rods are finished this morning," Rust wrote. "The boys take a plunge in the River and we go to the upper part of the Box for dinner and to Rock Cache before evening. The Trail is finished!"

Their moment of exultation was well deserved, but harder work lay ahead as they set to bringing down the heavy main cable and stretching it across the river. Dee Woolley had already made arrangements for the ironmongery needed to build the tram car. Through Bowman & Co., a Kanab dry-goods store Woolley owned, he ordered a large steel cage to be made that would hang from five hundred feet of heavy cable, to be shipped from Salt Lake City's venerable Zion's Cooperative Mercantile Institution. Its specifications were as follows: "Now we want a steel cage as light as can be made to have it strong enough to carry a horse and rider or eight or ten persons.... The dimensions wanted are, six feet by ten feet (6x10) and six feet six inches high. You can readily see what this is for. It's to carry passengers across the great gorge of the Colorado river."[22]

Woolley hired the Trent Engineering & Machinery Co. of Salt Lake City to design the cable supports, the most critical part of the tram. The Colorado River at Bright Angel Creek was more than four hundred feet wide—a huge distance to span without the use of cranes or other heavy equipment. The firm suggested that the cage be made narrower—"four or five feet at most"—to insure better balance, and that it hang from two cables—"to insure the steadiness of the cage, and thereby make it as attractive as possible to tourists, even the most nervous ones."[23] Woolley opted to stick with one main cable, from which the cage would be suspended by two sets of double wheels. Smaller cables would serve as haul lines. The cage had an airy design, but it did have a plank floor to minimize vertigo and permit livestock to be carried.

The disassembled tram and the wire cables had been stored up on the plateau for more than a year while the men worked on the trail. The crew brought the first of the smaller cables down to the river during breaks while working on the trail, and now, with that job completed, they went back for the heavy main cable. Rust spent a day helping the men rewind the seven-hundred-pound spool into eight rolls, distributing them between four horses, one coil on each side of a pack frame. Tethered head-to-tail with a man leading and following, the horses negotiated the tricky route down to the river. It was, Rust recalled, "some feat to get [the] procession along the one-foot trail around the curves and down hill."[24] Then he climbed back out and rode back over the Kaibab for home and a month's vacation. He was in Kanab for the birth of his and Ruth's third child, Richard, on September 19.

Rust returned to the Grand Canyon on September 24 to finish carrying the disassembled tram cage and timber supports to the river. Two weeks were needed to ferry the materials down the long trail, with a break midway to let the horses rest. They encountered several tourist parties using their trail, including one led by Ralph Cameron, the owner of the Bright Angel toll trail on the other side of the river.

Proper support and installation of the tramway was essential. If too much sag was left in the main cable, the loaded tram car could not be pulled up to the opposite shore; if it were stretched too tight, the stress placed on the cable's supports would be extreme. In the best of circumstances, the abutments on each bank would have to withstand a force of many tons. The engineering firm specified a counterweight system at each end of the main cable, consisting of a large wheel leading the cable down to a twelve-foot-tall wooden box filled with ten thousand pounds of rock.[25] These weights would travel up and down to compensate for the load on the cable. Rust, however, decided the abutments on each side of the river could support a static cable anchorage. He arranged for heavy timbers for the cable towers to be cut at a sawmill near Big Springs, at the northern edge of the Kaibab Plateau, and hauled to the trailhead. Lacking any real construction experience, Dave relied on instinct, not to mention trial and error, to construct the critical supports and anchorages.[26] Even so, the engineering problems almost overwhelmed the crew. During their attempts to rig the tram, Rust and his men would witness memorable displays of the physics involved.

By October 8 they were ready to string cable. First they towed the smaller wires across the river with a rope, using a portable steel boat they had brought down the trail and assembled at the river. These wires were then used to pull the heavy main cable across. Rust's journal entries during this period were terse, suggesting that he and his men were fully occupied:

OCT 8. Brown, Pratt, Cram and I go to River & carry small steel boat from lower ferry to our crossing before dinner. In the afternoon we swing two wires.

OCT 9. Set up the winch and forge and swing the small cable but lose her just before she reaches anchorage. The wire broke. Adams and Kitchen are still above finishing the packing.

OCT 10. At noon we have the little cable anchored O.K. The boys came from above with last packs. Adams returns to Rock Camp. We set the winch & continued to make slot for anchor shaft. The rock shatters so we cannot get a good place. Some one from the other side is working on the trail below us. He has been there since we came in and has a new boat.

OCT 11. Begin to prepare rock for wooden butments. Go above and find a splendid drift. Bring down a big raft of it. Anchor seat has caved in so begin again. Aim to start over. Adams is on Top after 200 feet of cable.

OCT 12. Make wooden buttments & finish the anchorages. A large hunting party comes down trail below.

OCT 13. Abandon the anchorage on this side & go above and bring large timbers for purpose. The anchorage is arranged & large cable put over. The tourists cross their stock & prove to be Armour and Harvey with three other men. In stretching the large cable the wire broke and all had to be done over. The poor wire has now cost us about $40.

OCT 14. Harvey examines tramway & pronounces it O.K. We fasten end of cable across the River and begin stretching. The rope fastened to this end breaks and the cable goes into the River. We finally succeed in attaching a rope and drawing her out. At noon she is in place again but not stretched or fastened at this end.

Adams goes above for scow lumber to put floor in cage. Some of the boys find some excellent ruins just above anchorage on this side.

OCT 15. Fix pulleys for small cable to run in, & prepare winch etc. for same.

OCT 16. Prepare cage for swinging.

OCT 17. Swing cage and made first trip over. No one rode. The pulleys etc. are out of true, there is something wrong with the little draw cable, & in general the whole concern needs doing over, new buttments must be made before she will be a success.

Despite their difficulties with the tram, the work brought moments of camaraderie—Dave kept a snapshot that shows three of the crew shoulder to shoulder, grinning, Rust wearing his military-style hard hat. Most of the workers were from the Kanab area and probably got along well. About once a week Dave would hike up to Indian Gardens or to the South Rim (a 4,400-foot climb) to get mail, have a meal, and visit with the acquaintances he was making among the men who worked on the south side of the canyon.

Life at camp, too, could be pleasant. Bright Angel Creek brought a steady flow of crystalline water in contrast to the muddy Colorado's flow. Near its mouth the canyon opened up enough to relieve the feeling of hemmed-in oppression so common in the inner gorge. When deep snows hung onto the North Rim in the spring, wildflowers were blooming on sunny ledges by camp. With Rust's plantings and garden, the place promised to become a haven for cross-canyon journeyers. In a small way, he and his crew were replicating the improvements that Utah's pioneers had made in the towns and villages of the Colorado Plateau.

Their tent camp shared one problem common to all homesteaders:

DEC 13. Have broken all records on catching mice. Night before last, caught 23. Last night, 14 mice and 1 rat. The rat and one of the mice either committed suicide or accidentally fell. They were in the water bucket. Four of the others were caught in my water trap and the rest in the patent traps. I set two traps for the first time in the new quarters night before last. I am wondering if I can catch a million by May 1.

In early December of 1906, a photographer named Ellsworth Kolb rode into Rust's camp on Bright Angel Creek. He and his companion, Howard Noble, were returning from a late-season hunting trip on the Kaibab, where they had encountered snow and cold. Dave invited them to have supper and spend the night. The next morning Dave helped Kolb and Noble swim their horses and pack stock across the river (the tram was not yet in operation) and went with them along the river's south bank as far as the mouth of Pipe Creek. Along the way he studied the next section of trail they would have to build in order to connect to Cameron's Bright Angel trail farther up at Indian Gardens. Noble rode on up, but Kolb came back to camp and the two men sat up after dinner comparing their experiences in the canyon. Ellsworth offered to take some photographs around the camp for publicity purposes, and Rust, for his part, offered to hike with him up the river so he could photograph scenes in the inner gorge. The next day, Rust ferried Ellsworth back across the river, "since he was a new hand with the oars."

The two men had much to talk about and Dave was undoubtedly happy to find a friend who shared his love of the canyon. Ellsworth Kolb had arrived at the South Rim in 1901; his brother Emery joined him the following year. In 1904 they opened a cliffside photography studio where they specialized in taking photographs of tourists departing on mules for Indian Gardens. Soon they branched out to become accomplished photographers of the entire Grand Canyon. Rust soon met Emery and his wife Blanche, with whom he and his family would enjoy a lifelong friendship (Ellsworth left the Grand Canyon in 1916). The Kolbs' photography studio remains one of Grand Canyon National Park's historic attractions.

In the years he spent working on the tram, Dave would frequently visit the Kolbs, enjoying a family atmosphere that was missing from the river camp. In return, he would invite them over to his side of the canyon for hunting trips on the Kaibab. These and other Grand Canyon pioneers forged their own community, an antidote to the isolation of this far-off remnant of the southwestern frontier. For Dave, separated for months at a time from his family, these interludes made his strenuous years in the canyon more tolerable.

Rust's December visit with Ellsworth Kolb stretched the season about as far as it would go. Winter was settling into the canyon; they noticed ice forming along the edge of the river. "No place for oranges," Dave observed. On December 17 he accompanied Ellsworth up to Indian Gardens and went on to the South Rim to get the mail and socialize a bit. Then it was time to head back for the Kaibab and home.

4 | Bridging the Canyon

> Why this deep hole in the ground should inspire more won-
> der and awe than the loftiest snow mountain or the grand-
> est waterfall I will not attempt to explain, but it does. One
> cannot leave off gazing and wondering.... Morning, noon,
> and evening the same unchanging precipices show their
> unchangeable colors, cliffs looking across at cliffs as they have
> done for millions of years and will do for millions more.
>
> JAMES BRYCE
> *Memories of Travel* (1923)

RUST RODE THE LONG TRAIL out of the Grand Can-
yon five days before Christmas, 1906, heading home for Kanab. A foot of snow
at the North Rim signaled a tough haul across the Kaibab, since the trail climbed
another four hundred feet to reach the summit of the plateau.[1] But the prospect
of time with his family offered ample incentive. After slogging across the top,
Dave began the long descent into Naile Canyon, the usual route down to the
desert towns. (The canyon was named for John Nagle, a German immigrant who
had Anglicized his name to Nail or Naile.[2]) By the time he reached Big Springs,
Rust was out of winter's worst conditions. The thirty miles of wagon road to Fredonia and Kanab were relatively easy going.

The holiday season in Kanab was a time to celebrate the year's accomplishments and look to the future. The close-knit community offered a warm respite
from the strenuous challenges of the trail and tram. Dave and Ruth would have
enjoyed spending evenings at the Woolley's beautiful Victorian home, and perhaps they found time for a family sleigh ride as they had during their first Christmas in Kanab three years before.

Worse conditions lay ahead, however, when Dave and two of his men started
back for the canyon on January 3, 1907. Traveling by way of the House Rock Valley instead of their customary route via Big Springs, they encountered deep snow
and fierce winds that forced them to return home. Rust spent the next two weeks
on a trip north to Salt Lake City, stopping in Manti and Provo to visit his parents
and other relatives. While he was in the city he dropped in at the office of Trent
Engineering to discuss the problems they were having with the tram. The firm
recommended that the tram cage be loaded with rocks and drawn across a num-

ber of times to break in the cables and pulleys.[3] Rust took the advice to heart, but he would meet with disaster in its application.

With the Kaibab snowbound, Dave made his way back to the South Rim via a long railroad journey from Salt Lake to Los Angeles and back east to Flagstaff. On January 27 he returned to the river camp at Bright Angel Creek to find it "secure and very lonely." He surveyed a location for their permanent tent camp along the creek, then made out an application for use of the site to send to the Forest Service.[4] A trek back up to the South Rim to post the letter gave him a chance to have dinner with Ellsworth Kolb at the El Tovar. "I don't like to be alone much better than Adam," he wrote in his journal.

The rest of the crew resumed work in February 1907. Much of the men's effort was spent in blasting out a "high-water" trail in the section of cliff west of the north tram tower. Drilling holes in the dense schist by the river was no picnic. "We have a time to get drills sharpened. No blacksmith & the meanest kind of rock," Rust reported to Dee Woolley. "Two men have been about one week on one pillar along the high water trail & still it is scarcely half done."[5]

They also set about making improvements to their tent camp, which would one day accommodate tourists crossing the river on their tram. What became known as Rust's Camp was located underneath the cliffs on the east side of Bright Angel Creek, a quarter-mile northwest of the mouth of Bright Angel Creek. They built a bridge across the creek and plowed the stony soil for a garden. A ditch brought in water from the creek. This camp was a crude predecessor to the much more elegant Phantom Ranch, constructed a half-mile farther up the canyon in the 1920s.

In March Rust cut hundreds of fresh branches from cottonwood trees in upper Phantom Creek, a tributary of Bright Angel Creek, planting them near the tent camp. The survivors of these trees, along with additional seedlings he obtained from Indian Gardens in 1909, are among those giving welcome shade to today's tourists and hikers who pause along the creek.

The sheer effort of blasting out the high-water trail and then getting heavy cables strung across the river took a toll on all hands. Rust repeatedly suffered flare-ups of a painful lung condition he diagnosed as pneumonia, but which may have been pleurisy aggravated by the strenuous work. He missed his family and made trips back over the Kaibab when he could, again braving the plateau in winter conditions. Sometime in the spring of 1907 he and Israel Chamberlain, a Kanab friend and employee of the Transportation Company, managed to take a buggy from near the rim as far as Pleasant Valley, south of present-day Jacob Lake, where snowdrifts stopped them. They continued on horseback after hoisting a side of venison they were bringing out. It was still thoroughly frozen when they returned several weeks later.[6] These were men who had heard firsthand of the hardships of the Mormon pioneers, and they had experienced danger themselves often enough. Their work on the trail probably did not seem that extraordinary to them. Still, their efforts wore them down:

> MARCH 5 [1907]. Last night it rained and nearly all day it rains. The boys get in a few hours work. I lie in bed practically the whole day. I have been getting worse since the 1st and now I must rest and heal up. Sort of general break down due from strain or cold or both or something else. I cannot sleep and eating doesn't agree with me. So I just lie and twist and sort of "nightmare" it.

In late March they finally were able to hang the cable car and attach a haul line to it. Dave took a hacksaw to the cage to trim some of its excess weight and reduce the sag on the main cable. The men piled five tons of rock to secure the "deadman" anchor on the north side. A trial run with the tram car proved successful, although it took them twenty-five minutes to haul it across the river and back.

Their hopes for early success were soon dashed. The main cable spanned nearly five hundred feet and was under tremendous strain.[7] The clamp that secured it to the anchorage on the south side was not up to the task:

> APRIL 1. An ill omen, a sad day for us, a heart breaker. We had salty coffee for breakfast, but that isn't the trouble. Just as we have finished the platform landing on this side and readjusted the little cable, we load the cage with about 2000# of stone and start her across. All goes lovely and jubilant until the car is nearly half way over, then buzz! whang! ka-splash. She sinks out of sight—the river eats it up like the monster she has proved herself. In the morning my joy was at its height, to think we had succeeded in making things go. Now, as she all goes into the river, a pall comes over me, stunning, like some friend were stricken dead. I am incapable of action for several minutes. Then we row across to discover the weak place. The clamps have

slipped off the other end of the big cable. We take blocks over and attach to loose end which is right at the edge of the water. We pull on the slack and go to camp sad, sad!

It took a week of enormous effort to free the cage from the river, which was now in flood. All they had to pull on the submerged cable was a chain block, a simple pulley device. They were able to get the tram cage partly above water, but no farther, and while reefing on the pulley chain Rust reinjured his chest. The high water made conditions dangerous; a boat tied to shore broke loose in the current and disappeared. "Everything seems to be going down the canyon," Rust wrote. "Thank God no human lives have gone that way & pray none shall."

APRIL 3. My lungs are painful. We try to attach line to cage but I cannot stand to row. We come to camp and Ted starts to Gardens for supplies. Alex fences garden. It rains and thunders as it has been doing since the 1st. I have been wet a time or two which I should not have been.

APRIL 4. Spend the day in making fast a line to the cage and to winch. A very hard day, but we succeed. Ted is afraid to work on the river so, tho I am unfit—should be in bed, I go with Alex and we make attempt after attempt before we get the attachment made. We make a pull and the cage moves toward the shore. We are glad.

APRIL 5. Continue to pull. It is slow work with a chain block to attempt to draw the cage 200 feet. We have to cross with the block and ease up the propel rope on other side then return & draw the cage till that slack is taken up.

Tonight we bring wood block to this side and expect to draw big cable some in the morning.

APRIL 6. Tug and tug and tug but she comes slow. We get power enough to draw big cable but anchorage to block gives way. The cage in going down, tipped over, thus tangling the ropes.

APRIL 7. We make block anchorage solid and draw big cable. Ted goes to Gardens and Alex and I intend to try to detach farther end of propel rope from cage, since the cage is out of the water pretty well by drawing big cable. Wind makes boating dangerous so we rest and do odd things about camp. Just at sundown the wind calms and we test the intention with the result that we cannot get at propel rope.

I am very tired and anxious. If word goes out about our misfortune we shall be greatly damaged. Each tomorrow I am determined to get her out. She has been there five days and it is not a pleasant responsibility.

APRIL 8. Success today. Cage drawn to shore, big cable raised, and propel rope partly out. It is broken, near the middle. Tomorrow I will go to meet President Woolley at Flag. The tram will remain undone till I return. We have tested the thing pretty severely and learned much about it. Now I'll be able to put things up about right.

At 4 p.m. on April 9, after a day spent repairing the retrieved cage, Rust left for the South Rim and a rest in Flagstaff. He noted in his journal that he "barely made it to the top."

Their difficulties were not over. On the night of April 15, with the crew back at camp, the river rose fifteen feet and swept away the steel boat they were using to ferry across the river. Work on the south-side anchorage was halted until the river dropped. They would have to keep close watch on their remaining canvas boat. For three days, while the flood raged past them, they reinforced the anchorage on the north side of the river and attempted to stretch the main cable tighter.

After the water dropped enough to enable them to cross the river, they tried to get a haul cable across to the other side by tying one end to a log and launching it into the river. This experiment failed in the strong current, and the ensuing work to retrieve the cable gave Rust "such a fright that my lungs are bad again."

According to Dave's later recollection, they then built a makeshift suspension footbridge across the river to aid their work.[8] His 1907 diary makes no mention of this bridge, which would have predated the 1921 Park Service footbridge that replaced the Rust tram. Probably it was a crude affair designed for the workmen and not for tourists. One wonders whether it would not have been easier to build a decent bridge and station someone at one end to collect tolls.

Returning to work on April 18, the crew managed to get the haul line across the river and attached to the tram cage. After spending a week making adjustments, they discovered to their horror that the main cable was worn and was starting to unravel. They would have to go out and get a new one. On April 30, 1907, Rust wearily rode the fifteen miles up to the North Rim and crossed the Kaibab for home. For the next month he would occupy himself with odd jobs around Kanab until the new cable arrived.

A brief vacation from these travails came later in June when a friend of Dee Woolley's, Charles J. "Buffalo" Jones, asked Rust to help out with one of his lion-roping expeditions. Jones was an adventurer in the classic Western mold, known for his exploits in roping wild animals in various exotic locales. Over the years Jones had made a project of importing bison from Canada and stocking them on suitable ranges in the United States. In 1905 he met with Woolley and Jim Emmett to examine the range on the Kaibab and the House Rock Desert for an unusual breeding project. From Jones's imports they experimented with creating a bison-cow hybrid they called *catalo*.[9] Now Jones was showing his roping tricks to a San Francisco writer named Grant Wallace, who was on a three-week stay in the Kaibab. Jones tracked and treed a large mountain lion they called the "Greenland King," named for the lush peninsula now known as the Walhalla Plateau. Wallace was given the honor of shooting the animal. "Nothing but his last track remains to prove this story," Rust wrote, "for the great and brave beast refused to render up his body even in death. He fell—2,000 ft. towards the mouth of the Little Colo. river." It was one of Rust's first experiences guiding a party of "dudes," and was a taste of things to come.

Rust joined another of Jones's lion-roping hunts later that year, and packed the live, trussed-up animal down his trail and up to the South Rim. Ellsworth Kolb featured a photograph of the lion in his 1914 book *Through the Grand Canyon*. The lion was taken to Las Vegas, where it escaped and ran down the main street.[10]

Rust also joined a Woolley family outing to the Kaibab and Grand Canyon that July. Jim Emmett and some other family friends joined them. While inspecting the tram's winch set into the cliffs at the cable's north abutment, Woolley fell and slid dangerously close to the drop-off. Emmett jumped to the rescue and caught him before he went over a cliff. Woolley badly sprained his ankle; Rust noted that he had a long, painful ride back up the trail.[11]

Finally, on July 20, they were able to get the replacement cable to the river and resume work. Rust's brief journal entries at this point indicate a state closer to exhaustion than jubilation. After taking a break in Kanab during August and the first half of September, the crew returned to complete their work. Finally, on September 21, they took "Rose Evans and Lida Belveal, two young ladies from El Tovar and Los Angeles" across and back—their first passengers. They did not charge them for the ride. One can imagine the crew's expectant looks as Dave escorted their passengers onto the fearsomely exposed tram cage that dangled by the black cliff above the south bank of the river. Once the ladies were seated and instructed as to the procedure, he signaled to his man at the opposite shore to start cranking the winch. Gravity assisted at first as the cage took advantage of the sag in the main cable. Then came the hard work of winching the laden tram car over the final two hundred feet, working against the sag. With a creak and clang as the cage came to rest on a rock jutting above the north bank, the ladies stepped off, the smell of axle grease on sun-heated metal mingling with the hot breeze coming up the canyon. A precarious series of steps led off the rock to the trail heading over to Bright Angel Creek. Perhaps they enjoyed a cool drink of creek water under the brush arbor at Rust's Camp before they were escorted back to retrace their journey.

After this mammoth investment of sweat, skinned hands, and close calls with injury, one could excuse the men for hoping that they would be rewarded with a rush of tourists. Unfortunately, a trickle was all that ensued. Further work on the trail, they hoped, would bring more traffic. Their chief aim was to complete a link on the south side of the river up to Indian Gardens, where it would connect with Ralph Cameron's trail coming down from the hotels on the South Rim. But the company would have to continue without Rust's help, at least for a while. By the fall of 1907, funds were low and the company could no longer pay him a salary. Dee Woolley, casting around for some way to finish the project, suggested that Cameron provide some workers to build the last trail link down the "granite" from the Tonto Bench to the tram. He even suggested to E. S. Clark, the company's agent in Flagstaff, that the whole tram operation be turned over to Cameron. "If Mr. Cameron doesn't want to take hold of it," he told Clark, "see what the railroad wants to do." Cameron replied that he was willing to link trails, but he offered no funds and his workers were busy maintaining his own trail. He was already one of the more colorful tourist operators at the South Rim, and acquiring the Woolley-Rust operation would have expanded his business's scope, but he was embroiled in conflicts with the Forest Service and the Santa Fe Railway over his Grand Canyon properties and probably had little incentive to take on a cross-canyon trail.[12]

The project was stalled at least through the winter. Rust still had his teaching career to fall back on, and he obtained a position as the principal of the high school at Orderville, Utah, located in the green swales of Long Valley in the upper East Fork of the Virgin River. He may well have been ready for a break.

The Mormon village of Orderville was noted for having been organized under strict communitarian principles derived from the United Order of Enoch, Brigham Young's attempt in the 1870s to direct the growing capitalistic economy of Utah along more cooperative, locally oriented lines. Kanab and other towns in Kane County had formed short-lived chapters of the United Order, but only in its namesake town did citizens make the system work, at least for a time. By 1890 this experiment in social engineering had broken down throughout Utah, including in Orderville, and was officially abandoned.[13]

Rust and his family spent a pleasant winter in a home close by the schoolhouse. Although Dave kept no journal that fall, Ruth recalled taking outings in the countryside and watching their three young children play in the muddy yard. Jordan was three years old, Emma was two, and the family had just celebrated Richard's first birthday. A favorite activity was attending the school basketball games that Dave organized. Ruth was inclined to cheer for her home team, Kanab, but Dave held no favorites and promoted his code of sportsmanship and fair play.[14]

The day after school was out in late April 1908, a terrible incident occurred that colored the Rusts' memories of that year. One of his best students, an eighth grader named Mary Stevens, was brutally killed by another student, Alvin Heaton Jr., in a sensational case that shocked and appalled people throughout southern Utah. Heaton had gotten the girl pregnant, and he murdered her to try to avoid scandal. The crime was traced to him and he confessed, but he served only a few years of a life sentence before being pardoned.[15]

What made the crime especially awful for Dave and Ruth was that they had seen Miss Stevens sitting on a rock reading a book as they were returning from a trip to Panguitch.[16] The girl was expecting to meet her lover and hear his proposal of marriage. Instead, Heaton shot her three times and hid her body in some rocks. The boy belonged to one of the wealthier families in Orderville, while Stevens came from poverty, and family disapproval (real or anticipated) may have further confused his thinking. Dave's grandson, Joseph C. Rust, after looking into some of the undercurrents that affected this unusual village, concluded that life in Orderville operated under a rigid social structure despite its communitarian background. He believes that the tragic incident reinforced his grandfather's strong distaste for social hierarchies.[17]

Dave and Ruth had traveled to Panguitch that April so that he could take the Civil Service exam preparatory to finding work with the Forest Service in its Kaibab Division. Part of the test involved packing a mule, which Dave passed with a perfect score. There was also a written exam containing such questions as: "State how you would construct a 14 by 18-foot log cabin. Give the amount of material necessary and approximate cost of construction."[18] He did well enough overall that he received a job offer to work on the forest south of the Grand Canyon (as yet, the agency had few personnel on the Kaibab itself). Since he was unwilling to relocate his family out of Utah, Dave passed up the opportunity. Further work on the Grand Canyon project, though, was still uncertain.

The summer of 1908 began with a month-long hunting trip to the Markagunt Plateau with his old friend Nathaniel Galloway. One of the few surviving grizzly bears in the region was attacking livestock in the Panguitch Lake area, and Galloway was known as an expert trapper. It is not recorded whether they got the bear, but tramping around the woods with his old friend, living once again like a footloose bachelor, was reward enough. Afterward, Dave returned to the Grand Canyon project. That spring, Dee Woolley had managed to obtain a five-thousand-dollar investment in his company from Jesse Knight, a Utah mining magnate who had made his first strike in the silver mines of Tintic. On one of his frequent trips to Salt Lake City, Woolley happened to see Knight get on his train at Provo. He introduced himself and before the train had arrived, he had Knight's check in hand.[19]

The cash influx was enough to get Dave back to work. He headed out for the Grand Canyon with four new men on the crew, including two, Scott Dunham and Rees B. Griffiths, who would continue to work with Rust and guide clients for the Transportation Company for years to come. The enterprise was still not self-supporting, and Dee Woolley contributed additional funds to keep the men at work. Jim Emmett chipped in a little money, too, and Tom Chamberlain contributed a hundred pounds of dried Jersey Blue apples.[20]

Rust received a pay increase to seventy-five dollars per month, with an additional allotment for his expenses. He was to be responsible for making a new trail on the south side and setting up "at least 1 good camp that will accommodate 12 tourists."[21] This referred to the tent camp along Bright Angel Creek that Dave had surveyed earlier. He was also to purchase saddles and tack so that he and the company's guides could outfit tourist parties on more extended trips.

The company's most notable party that year included Utah senator George Sutherland, who arrived in late August to hunt cougars on the Kaibab. "Lion" hunting was still the main attraction of the North Rim country; later that year an unknown author named Zane Grey would visit the Kaibab for the same purpose, meeting Dave along the way.

Through the fall of 1908 Rust and his crew fixed up various parts of their operation, regraded sections of eroded trail above Bright Angel Creek, and blasted out a rock face on the north side of the river to improve their high-water trail. They erected six white canvas tents alongside the creek, stocking them with cots and mattresses so their guests could enjoy relative comfort. A cook tent completed the camp, with most of their meals prepared outside under a brush arbor.[22] To help stock the larder they brought with them a small herd of sheep which they let loose somewhere in the upper part of the canyon, returning as needed to butcher a ewe for meat.

They also continued to work on the connection with the Bright Angel Trail at Indian Gardens. The existing trail followed the Tonto Platform from Indian Gardens to Pipe Creek, descending that steep side canyon to the river, more than a mile below the mouth of Bright Angel Creek. Dave had scouted a connecting route along the river's south bank from the tramway to the mouth of Pipe Creek, but he decided it would require excessive blasting through the cliffs rising above the river. They had had enough experience with this on the north bank. Instead, Rust envisioned improving an old prospector's route—he referred to it as the "Wash Henry" trail—that led directly up the steep canyon side to the south of their tram. Rust and his crew reworked this route up to the Tonto Platform at a place they called the Tipoff. Here they followed the relatively gentle benchland westward, aiming to connect with Cameron's trail in the upper Pipe Creek drainage.

Although the tram now operated smoothly, they experienced misfortune with their animals. Late that fall, two of their horses died from a mysterious cause. Rust suspected some poisonous weed they might have been eating. "I feel that I am Job's relative," he wrote, "—all my horses dying off." His troubles did not end there. He had another attack of what he termed pneumonia—"exposure & overstrain on boulders the cause. I am in hopes of bluffing it off." Griffiths, too, was sick and could not work for a few days. Then, nature intervened again:

DECEMBER 20 [1908]. The night of the 17th the river rose nearly 15 feet. Took away our new boat, & threw the old cable into the river. We have been trying to pull her out but she is in the quick-sand. We will save 1/2 of her anyway. Another dead horse—that boat getting away. When will this kind of fortune cease?

At Christmas the crew took a break from their difficulties by visiting their friends, including the Kolb brothers, at the South Rim:

All went to Rim for an Xmas. Walked. Rees & I had the *best* lunch at Gardens a decent man could wish for. Other 2 caught us before we reached top. I gave dinner at Bright Angel Hotel. Went to a funny party at Barn & returned feeling *paid* the next day. Brought a little phonograph Ed [Ellsworth Kolb] gave me for Xmas present.

Rust and his crew returned to camp to find yet another of their horses dead. He concluded his 1908 journal by noting (and underlining) that "*the year has not been a howling success.* Moderate—rather. Hope the next year will be no worse." His inveterate optimism, coupled with sheer persistent effort, carried him through the trials of the canyon. All involved with the Grand Canyon Transportation Company hoped that 1909 would see their trail come into its own.

Their first milestone in the new year was the completion of the trail along the Tonto Platform to Indian Gardens:

JAN. 10, 1909 (SUNDAY). The Connection trail completed on the 8th inst. A red-letter date. The Plateau took 30 days' work. And it's a good path. We ate a complimentary dinner with Mr. Montgomery near Indian Gardens the 8th. And the same afternoon brought the motor to the brink from Gardens where C.C. had brought it. A few moves now & we'll be in the king. Our cots etc. are on Rim & we'll soon shape up for first party.

Rust had ordered a small gasoline engine to install at the tram in order to relieve some of the effort of hauling the cage across. The 2.5-horsepower "Little Giant" engine, sold by Montgomery Ward, weighed 500 pounds and would have required disassembly to haul it from the South Rim to the river. It needed constant tinkering in order to operate in the canyon environment:

FEBRUARY 3. We had been 10 days installing, & trying to get to work, our Little Giant. I went on [across?] River for an engineer. He promised to come down the 28th. He did not come or write so I said to Rees, "We'll fix the engine ourselves." For 5 days we have been experimenting first with one part and then another. Today we fixed the pump, the last thing it seemed to us to get out of fix. But we have mastered it.

The canyon was not a place for specialists. Each of the men took turns as mechanic, wrangler, cook, general laborer, and, as needed, doctor. The remainder of Rust's entry for February 3 reveals something of their diverse operation:

66 trees were brot from Gardens Sunday by Israel. They are set out, a new canal made, some garden seeds put in, some oats planted, high water trail raised, winch fitted to engine so we can make round trip in 6 minutes, all tents put up & cots fixed up for tourists, old cable coiled & put away in cave, about 10 pack loads of stuff brot from Gardens, and today we are making a wall around one side of camp plot. We are not Chinese but we make a good deal of wall.

Now we are sure ready, and I'm going to get someone to come down. Tomorrow I go to rim to "wrangle dudes." —And I hope by next Sunday to have something different to say.

The weather has been too cold for campout parties until now. It is coming Spring.

The cold weather continued, discouraging travel on their trail for several more weeks. "We are all taking things pretty easy just now," Rust noted, "sleeping good long hours, eating considerable, reading much in magazines, and trying to endure this monotony." He climbed up to the South Rim several times to talk up his trail; the manager at El Tovar, Charles Brant, said he would try to help. On February 22 a man and his wife came down to the river and wanted to cross. Rust proudly headlined his journal entry that day "*Our First Dollar*.... I feel something like Lincoln felt over his first $1.00. And he earned that by crossing someone." Over the next month a few more parties would use their tram, but as yet the company did not charge a fixed toll. Rust simply accepted what people chose to pay, which rarely amounted to more than a couple of dollars.

With the coming of warmer weather their garden showed promise, with "radishes, peas, lettuce, oats up nicely." They supplemented their diet with mutton, and obtained fish from the Colorado with what Rust would later describe as "illegal bait"—sticks of dynamite left over from their rock work, which they carefully lit and hurled into the river. The resulting explosion would bring dozens of humpback chubs and other fish to the surface, stunned and easily harvested.

Several parties of notables came down the trail from Indian Gardens that spring. Rust was especially impressed by a chance meeting with two of America's most prominent naturalists, John Muir and John Burroughs, who visited the canyon together in early March and walked down the Bright Angel Trail. Rust, hiking up to get the mail, recognized them at once and introduced himself. "It didn't take me long to get acquainted with them," he told an interviewer in the 1930s.[23] "They were real people. We would sit down about every hundred yards, chatting and observing. When they found out I was camping at the river bottom, they were immediately interested in me." Rust later wrote of the encounter in his unpublished essay "Genuine Travelers": "That hour with them is cherished now as one of my fondest recollections. They had passed the 'allotted age of man,' their white beards glistened in the sunshine, yet their eyes snapped with the vigor of their young spirits as they discoursed like prophets concerning the world of Nature about them." Muir had visited the canyon several times before; in 1902 he wrote an essay for *The Century* magazine that helped bring this wonder to Americans' attention.[24]

On March 15 Lord James Bryce, the British ambassador to the United States, descended the canyon for a brief tour, part of a circuit he was making of America's parklands. Rust met him at the river, though Bryce was traveling with his own guide. He later described Bryce as approachable and friendly. Bryce included a glowing description of the Grand Canyon in his book *Memories of Travel*, published posthumously in 1923.

It seemed that business on the trail would take a turn for the better. On March 20 a Dr. Morrill and his wife crossed the river and stayed overnight at their tent camp—their first paying guests at the camp. Even the recurring health problems Dave faced could be taken in stride:

APR. 4. (SUNDAY). I'm in the hospital again with my old friend Pneumonia. Israel [Chamberlain] is head nurse & physician in charge. Case getting on beautifully. He wont let me do a tap. He has gone to Burro springs now for prescriptions. Nice to be sick in such a great place where 100 people are not trying to dose you.

The prospects for an early start to the tourist season, however, were washed out with the spring thaw. As snow in the upper reaches of Bright Angel Canyon began to melt, the creek began to rise, augmented by percolation coming down through the layers from the Kaibab Plateau. By April 15 the rushing current made the narrow "Box" section impassable to man or horse, and it remained so for weeks. Several parties were interested in getting across to the North Rim to make an early lion hunt, but it was no go. From the Kolbs' studio high up at the South Rim, where he had gone to meet a potential tourist party, Rust watched the creek with a telescope. On May 10 he could see it was running "high & black with mud." A few days of cold weather reduced the runoff, so Rust returned to camp and scouted up into the Box. The creek was "barely passable—belly deep to the horses in nearly every crossing." He decided it was safe, however, and sent word for the party to come down. But the tourists dispatched a South Rim guide with a note explaining that one of them was ill and the trip would have to be postponed—another disappointment.

Tourist traffic across their tram also was scarce. Rust wrote to his parents on April 30, saying that they were seeing "a small party about once a week." Although he had been away from home seven months, he expressed no particular loneliness: "All goes well with us.... Ruth & children have had their own way all right this winter—sick some of the time of course but got thru any way."[25] Their fourth child, Milton, had been born the previous August, while Dave was in the canyon. Dave had hauled out in mid-May to spend a couple of weeks in Kanab with his family.

By June the Colorado was running high against the rock wall they had built on the north bank, although with the tram in place, parties could still cross. Rust, now working on his own, tended camp and garden. In his journal he had taken to calling the place "home." He had given the better part of three years to his dream.

JUNE 8 [1909]. The River is "way up"—higher than 2 years ago. Wall entirely inundated. B. A. [Bright Angel Creek] is still carrying about twice usual amount.

And I'm here *alone*. Some may think I have a great quality—stay with. But I "figger" that it is just as important to be a dropper as a stayer.

The canyon doesn't thrill me now as it used to. Seems like I've always been here. I *love* it yet, & revel in its pictures—in fact find new ones every day. Good deal like the change after a few years in husband & wife. More deep affection but not so much electro-magnetism.

There were diversions. In mid-June he rode up to the Kaibab with Ellsworth Kolb, visiting Point Sublime and a lookout he called "Thompson's Point," which gave "one of the finest views of the Canyon." Dave was learning the lay of the Kaibab, a seemingly level plateau which in fact required considerable skill to navigate. Without obvious high points or major valleys, one could easily lose track of one's position in its vast forest. By following stockmen's trails, though, and keeping their bearings through the tall pines, Dave and Ellsworth were able to make their way west along the plateau. Side jaunts to the rim were the main goal. At these points they witnessed some of the greatest viewpoints the canyon had to offer; he would return to them often in the coming years.

Dave also found time to take family members and friends up to the Kaibab for a break from the desert heat. Emery and Blanche Kolb and their daughter Edith joined the Rusts for an extended vacation through most of August, including a camping sojourn on the Kaibab and a stay in Kanab. Ruth Rust recalled that the Kolbs "loved camping out in the forest, cooking their food in a bake oven over a camp fire and sleeping under the stars on spruce boughs."[26]

Dave's focus remained in the Canyon, though. While he was working on the trail and tramway he found time, perhaps during those days when he was alone, to look up at the cliffs and buttes and speculate on how they fit into a larger order. In "The Bright Angel," a short piece he wrote for *Improvement Era* in 1908, he played on the name that Major Powell had given the narrow gorge that held his tourist trail. Powell had supposedly named the creek to balance the name "Dirty Devil," which his men had applied to the silty tributary they had found at the head of Glen Canyon. Rust felt that both names were appropriate, representing as they did the angels of darkness and light. In Bright Angel Canyon it was not hard to discern higher meanings: "There is every suggestion of the Master. In the shadows of the depths of solitude seem to appear Golgotha, Gethsemane and Calvary; high up in the sunlight is the mighty truth that has swept the deck of the world. There are lurking moods of evil, and bright pictures of everlasting hope;

there is the remorse of Peter, and the halo of the light of the Pentecost." Rust was not just indulging in fancy. The dark inner walls of this canyon could indeed appear ominous, and he had spent plenty of time in all seasons laboring within its confines. Climbing up out of the canyon into the welcome sunlight, especially in winter, must have seemed a great release. "It is fit ground for pilgrimages," he felt, "and whoever passes through must be filled with awe and reverence." He would return to this theme of pilgrimage in some of his later writings; he understood the powerful hold the landscapes of the Plateau Province could have on those who spent time there.

With Bright Angel Creek running at a safe level by the early summer of 1909, traffic across the Grand Canyon gradually picked up. Rust was kept busy shuttling visitors up to the Kaibab and back down to his river camp. On June 17, returning from the North Rim with Ellsworth Kolb, he decided to accompany his friend on the climb back to the South Rim and a night in a hotel bed. There he found a telegram waiting for him requesting his help in taking a party of seven men across the canyon:

> I had to hustle to North Rim for horses where Ed & I had placed them a week before. Made trip all right to meet appointment June 22 5 P.M. Crossed the 7 & their beds etc. and also unexpectedly, Frank Onstott & 3 dogs & bed, saddle etc. Had my hands full. Took Gaddin's bunch to B. A. cabin[27] 23 & brot G— back to meet companions 24th. Came from B. A. cabin to river in 5 hrs. Best record yet.

When the Transportation Company had a man stationed at the tram, all this traffic could be accommodated, but Scott Dunham and Rees Griffiths had been let go for a time to reduce the payroll. Rust was left to ride back and forth between the rims, meeting tourists and hunting parties and crossing them on the tram. Inevitably this led to confusion when a party would reach the river to find the tram unattended. If a group arrived from the south, one of them would have to cross hand-over-hand on the cable, using a painter's chair, to reach the winch on the north bank. And the tram itself looked rather dubious to many visitors. Rust's friend J. Cecil Alter set down his impressions of the crossing when he visited Rust during the latter years of its operation, accompanied by the famous mountain lion hunter James T. Owens:

> Jim Owen and I got in observing with some misgiving that it was fifty-five feet to the sand-laden water.... We directed the operator to "Let her go" about as reluctantly as a convict might signal to the hangman; and as the wheels behind the cliff rock anchor began to rattle, the whole canyon side and the water's edge moved slowly away from us. We glided breathlessly outward on the sag in the cable to the middle of the stream, where the cage halted, but swinging like a bell to and fro. Jim and I were the unwilling bell-clappers and we clung to the girders of the cage until our hands hurt. When I looked down through the open end of the swinging cage toward the swirling water and observed the drunken river careening wildly, my whole insides, legs, bones all tried to climb into my chest.... It didn't quiet me a whit to visualize Dave's previous escapade of drawing himself across the cable seated in a trapeze because the cage was on the far side of the canyon.[28]

When confronted with this uncertain apparatus, some visitors chose not to cross on their own, and either waited for Rust to show up or simply returned to the South Rim. The undermanned operation thus may have lost considerable traffic.

The tram was working, however, and the river camp was ready to host overnight stays. The summer of 1909 was the first full season of business for the company. Dee Woolley's dream was in operation, and Dave was making it work. Neither Rust nor Woolley recorded use figures for their Bright Angel Canyon trail, but it is unlikely that it averaged more than a few parties per week. Such sparse traffic would hardly have supported a tollkeeper, let alone returned profits on the company's investment. Most tourists arriving at the South Rim were not inclined to set off for the far side of the canyon, despite Rust's assurances that the North Rim was even more spectacular, and the Transportation Company lacked the funds to advertise their new route. In the years ahead Woolley, Rust, and others involved in North Rim tourism would look northward for business. If few people were willing to cross the canyon, surely the means could be found to bring people in from the Utah side. In fact, until Arizona was granted statehood in 1912, many residents of southern Utah considered the country lying north of the Colorado River to belong more properly to their state.[29] It would be up to Utahns, they felt, to boost the Kaibab Plateau and the North Rim to the prominence it deserved.

5 | *Rougher and Wilder As You Go*

There has been a call to the city. There is now a call to
the wilderness. The temples, spires, turrets, monuments, domes, —
all the forms of architecture of the mountains—
are more inspiring than the works of man. Solitude is as
necessary as society. The awful depths, the pinnacles of glory,
and the gloomy shadows of the canyon, give the keenest
impressions, and would be fitting for a sacred excursion.

DAVE RUST
"From Salt Lake to the Grand Canyon" (1910)

AS THE SUMMER WARMTH began to clear the snow off
of the Kaibab Plateau in June 1909, Rust once again left his river camp and made
the long climb up to the North Rim. Traveling with Frank Onstott, a ranching
partner of Dee Woolley, Rust hitched up his wagon at Jim Owens's ranger cabin
near Bright Angel Point and started out for Big Park (also called De Motte or
V. T. Park) at the crest of the plateau. Their route followed a draw called Robbers Roost Canyon, which climbed gradually northward through a grand forest
of ponderosa pine. The ride would have been glorious, with pinegrass sprouting
under the trees, new buds on the aspen, wildflowers in bloom, and everywhere
the rich smell of the warm earth as it emerged from the snowbanks. While the
Grand Canyon may have been everyone's ultimate destination, Dave had a special
fondness for the forests and meadows of the Kaibab, particularly in summertime
when they offered up their cool and bracing pine-scented breezes.

Partway up Robbers Roost Canyon, the men were startled by a loud sput-
tering noise punctuating the calm. Dave's horses spooked at the sight of two
automobiles making their way down the canyon. After getting his animals under
control, Rust peered ahead at the approaching vehicles. In the passenger seat of
the lead vehicle was the unmistakable figure of his father-in-law, Dee Woolley,
wielding an axe and sporting his customary grin. Driving the car was Woolley's
nephew, E. G. "Gordon" Woolley Jr. of Salt Lake City. A second vehicle carried
friends and family members from Salt Lake and Kanab. They were headed for
Bright Angel Point, completing a marathon 425-mile run from Salt Lake City.
Theirs were the first vehicles to have journeyed that far.

Rust took photographs of the party and heard them tell of their adventure. Gordon Woolley was driving a Thomas Flyer, a five-thousand-pound, sixty-horsepower workhorse, the model that had won an exciting race in 1908 from New York across North America and Siberia to Paris. The other was a Locomobile, an elegant, expensive vehicle with its own racing heritage, belonging to David Affleck, Gordon Woolley's brother-in-law. The cars had made the distance across Utah without serious breakdown. Dee Woolley had arranged to spot caches of gasoline and oil every thirty miles, and they carried a full complement of tools to work over the rocky wagon roads. By the end of their 850-mile journey, they had worn out nine tires priced at eighty dollars each.[1]

Dee Woolley had hit on the idea of an auto expedition to the Grand Canyon in 1908, during a visit to Salt Lake City for the fall conference of the LDS Church. Gordon Woolley had recently purchased the Thomas car and offered to take his uncle for a ride. It was Uncle Dee's first experience with the new vehicles, and he was entranced, realizing that here lay the answer to his dream of getting large numbers of people to visit his scenic lands in southern Utah and northern Arizona. He determined on the spot to persuade his nephew to undertake the journey the following summer.

Uncle Dee had a hard sale to make. Few automobiles had been as far as the Dixie country, and none had as yet braved the rutted wagon roads that led to the North Rim. Gordon Woolley understood what such a journey would entail and was reluctant to subject his expensive new machine to such punishment. Uncle Dee pressed his case enthusiastically, promising to get the townspeople along the route to work on the bad spots in the road, and to personally see about caching the needed gasoline. In May, Gordon tried to back out. In a plaintive letter to his uncle, he wrote that "since the news has spread, of our proposed trip, my friends have come to me by the dozens to try to persuade me against such a fool hardy undertaking. They tell me it is utterly impossible to get an automobile over those roads." He told Uncle Dee that "I have decided to give up the trip. I am sorry to disappoint you."[2]

Dee Woolley, however, was not one to be dissuaded once he had latched onto an idea. He wrote back to his nephew with further plans, leaving no room for argument: "We have fixed up all the places in the road down Johnson's Canyon and you can come spinning right along.... I shall send a team out a few days ahead to take sufficient [gasoline] for your needs to Bright Angel Point and along the way.... Will be looking for you about the 15th or 16th, until then Goodbye, Uncle

Dee."[3] Faced with this irresistible force, Gordon resigned himself to the venture. He enlisted Affleck, a mechanic, to pilot the other car, and various other family members joined in.

The motorists found the roads south of Provo to be fully as bad as they feared. High centers and deep ruts required careful driving, but uncovered irrigation ditches caused the most trouble. There was no question of taking on the sand hills past Mount Carmel, so they were forced to take the longer wagon road down Johnson Canyon. This route, too, had sandy stretches in which the narrow wheels were useless. The crew spread straw on the roadway and covered it with tarpaulins so the vehicles could proceed, repositioning the tarps every dozen yards or so. The scene would have been comical but for the endless repetition as the two cars inched ahead toward the mouth of the canyon.

After they emerged at the base of the Vermilion Cliffs, ten miles east of Kanab, Dee Woolley met the party for the triumphant drive into Kanab. Most of the town turned out to see Uncle Dee astride the engine of the Thomas car, waving his hat and whooping war cries. Their visit was a sensation for the isolated community. But many thought they were foolish to attempt the North Rim, and a few shouted their derision. This, of course, only redoubled Dee Woolley's determination.

Upon leaving Kanab, the motorists followed the wagon road that had been used for years by Woolley, Rust, and others in the Grand Canyon Transportation Company. This route came south through Fredonia, then headed southeast to the mining camp at Ryan, at the foot of the Kaibab Plateau. From there the route went past Big Springs and up Naile Canyon to the crest of the plateau at Big Park. A downhill run through Robbers Roost Canyon led to Jim Owens's ranger cabin, located in a small meadow a few miles from Bright Angel Point. Rust accompanied them the last few miles to the overlook. Afterwards the motorists made a side trip east through the Walhalla Plateau. Over the course of the trip the cars averaged six miles per gallon, and "drank oil," according to accounts. The road they had taken from Kanab would remain the primary route to Bright Angel Point until 1913, when the Forest Service constructed a new road via Jacob Lake farther east on the plateau.[4]

Rust celebrated the Woolleys' expedition in an article for *Improvement Era* that appeared the following year. Mechanized travel would revolutionize tourism, he predicted. The crowds in Kanab might scoff, but even greater accomplishments lay ahead for those who wished to see the nation's wonders:

To satisfy this longing, two motorcars were steered down through the counties, rougher and wilder as you go, towards the Buckskin Mountains, that might as well be a thousand miles away.... The way they chased along through woods, across ravines, down the slopes to the very drop of the canyon wall, —it would have seemed a proper sequence if they had kept right on, amid air, till, like a bird, they withered from view, or landed safely on the opposite brink.

And this will be done. The most distinguished tour of the next decade will be across the canyon in an airship, a mile above the Colorado. Yet all around are men who squint their eyes and say, "You'll never do it."[5]

Following this excitement, Rust returned alone to his river camp. In his journal he referred to his "loco-plane"—the tram—which was his own technology for getting across the river. "Pioneers have always builded better than they knew," he concluded his article on the daring motorists. He probably counted himself among those whose risk-taking would lead to greater things. The tram was but a first step.

With the way clear for autos to reach the North Rim, at least in theory, Woolley and Rust became two of the most active boosters for better roads in the region. Until these improvements came, though, Dave remained in the business of guiding visitors to the North Rim by horse and pack mule. As much as he anticipated the easing of distances in his region, he remained wedded to primitive means of transport. In his article on the Woolley motor expedition, he observed that "it is not expected, nor wished, that the Grand Canyon will ever become as familiar to people of Salt Lake City as is Garfield Beach or Lagoon. The God of the wilderness will see to that." But the tension between the two forms of travel would grow, in his mind as well as in others.

There were plenty of Americans and world travelers who were interested in discovering the far corners of the West, whether by auto or horseback. Outdoor travel and camping were on the rise nationwide. "Appreciation of the wilderness by the early years of the century was more than a mood," wrote historian Earl Pomeroy, "it was becoming a movement."[6] The Grand Canyon stood high among the symbols of wild, spectacular country. President Roosevelt and John Muir were among its famous exponents; other writers, such as George Wharton James, published detailed accounts to guide hikers and riders over the South Rim's Hermit, Bass, and Boucher trails. Sportsmen, too, found adventure in some sections of the Plateau Province. With the establishment of the Grand Canyon Game Preserve in 1906, the Kaibab Plateau became well known as a place to hunt cougars—one of the last Wild West experiences available in the country.

Most sportsmen visiting the Kaibab sought the services of James T. "Uncle Jim" Owens, a colorful Texan who had been appointed warden of the preserve in 1907. Owens's chief duty was to rid the Kaibab of predators, "lions" among them, which he pursued and treed with his trained hounds.[7] Dave was a good shot with a rifle and had experience tracking game, so he occasionally joined up with Owens to guide a hunting party. This sport remained a sideline, however, and his later writings suggested that he found treeing and shooting lions to be a little unsportsmanlike, at least in comparison with hunting other predators such as grizzlies.

Sometimes Rust's guests arrived from other countries, drawn by the promise of hunting that was no longer possible in their own land. Rust and Owens once guided a Norwegian diplomat (Dave never recorded his name) on the Kaibab for four months. "He had never gone out except with three servants and a special woman cook, but he went out there with me and Uncle Jim Owens," Rust recalled in 1937. "We did everything for him. He was much bigger than I and every so often he'd stop and say: 'You must take good care of me.' We'd tell him he should be looking after us." The experience proved salutary. At the end of his wilderness sojourn, the diplomat told Dave that he and Owens had made a man out of him.[8]

In the spring of 1907 an obscure writer from New York City named Zane Grey arrived in Flagstaff to take part in what he hoped would be a genuine Old West adventure. Earlier that year Grey had attended a lecture by Buffalo Jones on his exploits roping wild animals, including the mountain lions of the Kaibab Plateau. Grey was enthralled by Jones's personification of the Wild West and paid a visit to his hotel room following the lecture. Jones invited Grey to have a look at his catalo breeding operation and hunt mountain lions as well.[9]

The literary industry that stoked the popular image of the West was already well established by then, with such titles as Owen Wister's *The Virginian* (1902) leading the field, but there was plenty of room for an adroit newcomer to make his mark. By 1906, when Grey first visited the South Rim, he had completed three minor novels set on the Ohio frontier. He had recently quit his dentistry practice for the life of a writer and needed to find a convincing way to capture the public's attention. Characters such as Buffalo Jones might provide the color and adventure he sought.

Grey met Jones at the El Tovar hotel on March 27, 1907. Rust, who had guided with Jones, hiked up to the South Rim and was introduced to the author two days later.[10] The initial plan was to have Rust take Grey across the canyon to the Kaibab, but with snow lying heavy on the plateau and Bright Angel Creek still running high, this approach was abandoned. Grey took the train to the West Coast, returning to Flagstaff two weeks later to meet Jones, Jim Emmett, and Dee Woolley for a longer trek to the Kaibab through the Painted Desert and Lees Ferry. Dave bunked up with Grey at a crowded Flagstaff hotel the evening before the group set off for the Kaibab. The author carried a pistol that he placed under his pillow that night, which amused Dave. He told Grey, "We're damn near civilized out here." It was, he related years later, "a precaution altogether un-necessary at that late period in frontier history."[11] Dave left Flagstaff for his river camp to await the party as they returned from the Kaibab. However, after Jones, Grey, and Emmett had spent several weeks wandering along the plateau in search of mountain lions, two of Jones's men escorted Grey down Muav Canyon to Wil-liam Bass's Colorado River cable crossing—the only other tram crossing in the Grand Canyon. Dave thus missed the opportunity to guide the young author.

Grey's experience that year with Buffalo Jones gave him material for his first book set in the West, *The Last of the Plainsmen*, which was published in 1908. This mostly nonfiction work (Grey included several chapters colorfully recount-ing Jones's exploits in the Far North) did not sell particularly well, although Grey's descriptions of the Painted Desert, Lees Ferry, and the Kaibab Plateau car-ried a more authentic flavor than most of his fiction.

Grey returned to the Grand Canyon in April 1908, making a long pack trip with Buffalo Jones and Jim Owens across the Kaibab to the Powell Plateau. Be-sides hunting lions, they detoured down into the Thunder River area below the rim. This rarely seen wonder of the desert entranced Grey and gave him a setting for one of his favorite literary devices: the hidden oasis in a rock-walled strong-hold where his hero and heroine could hide out. Interestingly, Grey wrote to his wife that Rust had told him about the Thunder River area, presumably at their 1907 meeting in Flagstaff, and that Dave claimed to have been the first white man to visit the locality.[12] Dave made no mention of meeting the author in his brief journal for 1908, although he recalled much later that Grey was "decidedly green in saddling a mustang though a fancy shot with a rifle. Several lions yielded to his marksmanship within a month." This appears to be secondhand information, however.[13]

Rust was away once again when the author came through Kanab at Dee Woolley's invitation to interview local people about their culture and history. Grey used his impressions of the Mormons in his first successful novel, *The Heritage of the Desert*, published in 1910. The story is set in the Lees Ferry country, with the Vermilion Cliffs taking shape as an ever-present backdrop Grey called the "Red Wall." Grey wrote to Rust after the book's publication that he had based the character of Dave Naab on Rust.[14] As the son of the stern Mormon cattleman August Naab, Dave Naab saw plenty of frontier action and was depicted as being handy with a mustang or rowing a boat on the turbulent Colorado. Jack Hare, the Easterner who came west to recover from tuberculosis and find adventure, stood well for Grey himself. While nowhere did Rust ever mention traveling with Zane Grey, the author seems to have talked and corresponded enough with Rust to have formed a fairly accurate impression of him. Dave Naab, for example, was the only one among his clan who smoked—a minor vice that Rust occasionally enjoyed. Rust invited Grey to join him and Nathaniel Galloway on their grizzly-hunting expedition to the Markagunt Plateau in the summer of 1908, but Grey expressed an aversion to trapping. Rust found this interesting for someone who enjoyed treeing lions with hounds.[15]

Grey hoped that Rust would be pleased with his depiction of the Mormons in *Heritage of the Desert*, in comparison to the negative stereotypes generally found in stories of the day. August Naab, for example, is presented as a strong, fair-minded man, slow to anger, who resorts to force only to protect his family and his hard-won homestead against rustlers and outlaws. For this character Grey borrowed from Jim Emmett, who operated a ranch and ran the ferry at the head of Marble Canyon. Following the publication of *Heritage*, Grey told Rust, "I shall not write anything about the Mormons that would hurt anybody's feelings. I simply want to tell of the wonder and beauty of their desert struggle as I see it. So you can safely take me anywhere."[16]

Rust corresponded with Grey during the winter of 1910–1911 in preparation for a journey the author wanted to make across the Navajo Reservation. Grey told him, "I'd rather have you [as guide] than any one I know." Their plan nearly foundered over costs; Dave held out for ten dollars a day as guide, while Grey insisted he could pay no more than five, plus food and other expenses. In the end, Rust agreed to his price and made arrangements to meet Grey at Flagstaff in mid-April. But shortly before their trip, Rust learned that the Colorado River was in flood and that the ferry boat at Lees Ferry had sunk on March 9. He wired Grey that he could not cross the river to meet him. Grey, disappointed, hired a Flagstaff man, Al Doyle, to be his guide. Upon reaching Lees Ferry, Grey noted that people were fording teams across the river, and he sent Rust an irritated note. Rust had no subsequent encounters with Grey, for the author again contracted with Doyle when he returned to the Navajo country and Rainbow Bridge in 1913. Rust told historian Otis R. "Dock" Marston in 1960 that after their night at the Flagstaff hotel in 1908, he never saw Grey again.[17]

Despite his promise to Rust, Grey's portrayal of Mormons was far less positive in his next novel, the phenomenally successful *Riders of the Purple Sage*, published in 1912. Here the patriarch Tull is depicted as intolerant and domineering, and the heroine, Jane Withersteen, must ally herself with gunslinging Gentiles to preserve her ranch and her freedom. The other Mormon women in the story are depicted as tireless workers who suffered under the men's control. It was a curious turnabout for Grey.

With his Colorado River tram completed, Rust looked increasingly to guiding as a summer occupation. Instead of tending to guests at Rust's Camp, he ranged farther afield with the adventurous tourists who were beginning to arrive from across the country. Rust's grandson, Joseph C. Rust, who compiled Dave's Grand Canyon journals, observed that guiding offered better prospects than sitting by a trail and hoping people would come by. A client engaged for a few weeks or a month was a steady source of income, and could be shown around a much wider region than the Bright Angel corridor.[18] Too, guiding was a more active occupation than running a camp or a toll trail, and Dave rarely liked to stay put for long.

Business started gradually, with a few of the men and women who used his trail wanting to arrange hunting trips on the Kaibab or make visits to nearby scenic destinations. In early July of 1909 he joined Buffalo Jones and Jim Owens in guiding a party of Bostonians on a mountain lion hunt. Leading the group was a prominent businessman and manufacturer named Charles Sumner Bird. A supporter of President Theodore Roosevelt and later a Progressive Party candidate for governor of Massachusetts, Bird was typical of the well-heeled outdoorsmen who saw their adventures as a worthy complement to the civilized life. Bird was impressed when Jones roped a two-hundred-pound lion during their trip, and he later related the adventure to a gathering of the Camp Fire Club of America in New York City. Bird described how Jones climbed up after the treed cougar, "halted it a moment with a steady gaze," and slipped a noose over its head.[19]

Rust's association with such well-known outdoorsmen helped to bring him future clients. After working in and out of the Canyon that summer and fall, and visiting his family in August, he arranged for what appears to be his first campout party of his own. His client was George A. Agassiz, son of the famous Harvard botanist Louis Agassiz. He and Rust made a difficult November traverse of the Markagunt Plateau and the broken country overlooking the North Fork of the Virgin River, ending at Cedar City. They encountered snow and cold that weakened and later killed one of Rust's horses. Agassiz commemorated the trip by sending Rust an aneroid barometer along with detailed instructions for its use. Rust made no mention of using it in the field; one dealt with the Colorado Plateau's storms as they came.

While working at the Colorado River's edge, Rust thought about the great river adventures undertaken by men like John Wesley Powell and those who followed him. (One of the books he kept at camp was Frederick Dellenbaugh's *A Canyon Voyage*, an account of his 1871 voyage with Powell.) While he occasionally took the Transportation Company's canvas boat upstream a few miles from Bright Angel Creek, most of his river experience had taken place in Glen Canyon more than a decade ago. While Glen contained no truly dangerous rapids, Rust did hear other miners' tales of near mishaps. Several occurred in the small rapid at the mouth of the Paria River at Lees Ferry. Once, as he related in his 1901 article "Boating on the Colorado," two "inexperienced gentlemen" took the ferryman's boat out on the river and were rapidly swept downstream. "They screamed for help, but no help was near. Then they settled down to pull for life, and barely escaped the terrible rocks over which no boat could be saved from wreck." In later years this rapid would be given the unimposing name of "Paria Riffle," but to a young man in a big canyon, it appeared dangerous enough.

In the same article Rust expressed his admiration for Nathaniel Galloway's 1897 voyage with William Richmond down the Green and Colorado rivers to

Needles, California. Their trip covered more distance on the Colorado than either of Powell's voyages, and established Galloway as the Colorado's most accomplished boatman. It was only the fifth documented run of the Grand Canyon.

Galloway returned to the river in the fall of 1909 as a hired boatman for Ohio industrialist Julius Stone, who was making what has been called the first pleasure voyage down the Colorado.[20] Stone had invested in Robert Stanton's unsuccessful mining venture in Glen Canyon at the turn of the century, but despite his financial losses he retained a love for the canyons of the Colorado. The expedition was two years in planning, and Galloway had issued Rust a standing invitation to come along. In December 1907 he wrote to his friend in his untutored longhand, "So I Want You to Begin to Round Up your Shoulders Some, For A Trip Thru the Canyons With Mr. Stone. Next Season. For as Sure as I Have Any Say about it you Are Going to Be invited to Join the Co." Galloway repeated the invitation a few months later, saying that "Mr. Stone Has Given Me permission to invite you to join this Co on the trip thru the Canyons & if you Choose to Except He Will prepare a Boat Special For you. I hope you May See Your Way Clear Later on So you Can Join the party. I Am Sure you Would appreciate it in years to come."[21] The expedition was delayed a year, but the invitation stood.

Rust declined to join them, telling Galloway that he feared he would have a recurrence of the pneumonia that had plagued him while working on the tram. He was aware that the Green and Colorado rivers held rapids far harder than any he had rowed in Glen Canyon. Foregoing the trip remained a disappointment. Years later, he told river historian Otis R. "Dock" Marston that he had wanted to accompany Galloway and Stone. Rust's journal for January 1, 1941, contains the wistful note that "in spirit I was with them." Dave was guiding George Agassiz through the Zion country when Stone, Galloway, and their party pulled in at Bright Angel Creek on November 2; Galloway was disappointed not to see his old friend.[22]

Despite passing up the opportunity to accompany Stone and Galloway, Rust remained fascinated by the Colorado. He admired (and perhaps envied) the men who took on its challenging rapids. In the spring of 1909 he and Emery Kolb undertook a strenuous excursion upriver from the tram, rowing against the heavy current and taking advantage of shoreline eddies where they could, making it to the foot of what they believed was Sockdolager Rapid. Rust wrote in his journal, "There are 2 ordinary rapids & 3 big whoppers that we went over to get to the Sockdolager. We didn't go up over it but took several interesting pictures from a point several hundred feet overhead by the rapid. The wind blew hard up canyon as we were coming home & made things tough. Reached camp after dark." When the Kolbs made a run through the canyon in 1911, they determined that Sockdolager was actually farther upstream.

The Kolbs were novice boatmen, so Dave imparted what experience he had in river maneuvers, including Galloway's method of running rapids by facing downriver. Ellsworth and Emery were confident learners and soon made plans for a major Green-Colorado river expedition. The Kolbs intended to make this a business venture, taking motion pictures of the voyage to be featured on a lecture tour. Their trip from Green River, Wyoming, to the Gulf of California eclipsed anything Rust would do on the river, and their filming of daring runs through the Colorado's rapids established them in the public's mind as adventurers of the first order.

The Kolbs invited Dave to join their 1911 expedition when they reached Lees Ferry. Rust wired back that this was not possible, but he offered to greet them as they emerged from Glen Canyon. He rode down to the ferry and waited there several days, but left before the Kolbs showed up. Rust told Dock Marston in 1948 that he would have accepted the Kolbs' invitation had he been considered an equal member of the party, but he would not go as their assistant. "I was as independent as they were," he wrote. He explained further that he was afraid of contracting pneumonia and becoming a burden to the Kolbs—the same reason he had given Nathaniel Galloway. It seems unlikely that these reasons were the whole of it, though. The Grand Canyon's rapids held fears for Rust, as shown in a strange incident that occurred after Dave left Lees Ferry. On his way home he stopped for the night at the rim of Marble Canyon above Soap Creek rapid, where he could look down on the stretch of river that had drowned railroad promoter Frank M. Brown in 1889. Though Brown's inadequate boat had only been caught in an eddy below the actual rapid, and his drowning was largely due to his not wearing a life preserver, the rapid looked intimidating enough. That night Rust awoke after dreaming about a disaster befalling his friends in the rapid. He was sufficiently disturbed that he sent a note back to Lees Ferry for the Kolbs, recounting his dream and suggesting that they portage the rapid. His friends, however, were not to be deterred. Ellsworth wrote in his book *Down the Colorado* that "Rust should have known us better."[23]

Dave had been worried about his friends even before they set off, urging them to take along an experienced boatman such as Galloway. He even took the step of writing to Galloway and suggesting that he contact the Kolbs. Galloway did just that, but Ellsworth told his brother that he wanted to row his own boat.[24] The Kolbs undertook the voyage on their own; whatever success they would meet with would be theirs alone.

Rust's premonition about Soap Creek rapid, though, was very nearly on the mark. After the Kolbs reached Bright Angel Creek and climbed out to the South Rim to a warm welcome from their families, Ellsworth wrote a long letter to Rust relating their adventure up to that point.[25] Mostly he described his harrowing experience in Soap Creek rapid. "Say, what was that impressive dream?" he wondered. He recounted how Emery got good pictures of him running the first boat through, "even if I did touch a rock and get dumped out but I'm sure I was back in so quick that even the moving picture camera did not catch me at it."

Ellsworth then went back to bring the second boat through while Emery waited at the foot of the rapid. This time he had more trouble. "I blame the darkness for missing my channel," he told Rust, "but sometimes the current is just a little stronger than you are when you make the high dive and any how I got some where else and you can guess the rest. Emery says the boat shot its entire length out of the next wave and fell upside down. All I know is that I was trying to touch bottom by holding on to the end of the oar with my right hand. I did not touch."

Ellsworth, struggling beneath the waves, grabbed a line that they had tied to the oars to keep from losing them. "I did not give a sigh of relief as I needed the air but I gently pulled myself up until I could catch the gunwale of the boat. My head was under the cockpit and we were traveling as fast as the Grand Canyon Limited. I got my head on the outside just as we climbed one of those big combers and it curled over and gave me a biff on the side of the head.... After that I held pretty close to the boat."

By this time he had floated down to where Emery waited in the first boat. In the growing dark Emery was not sure of his brother's position. Ellsworth called out and Emery, seeing him at last, grabbed his life preserver. Together they drifted down, Ellsworth's boat still upended in the current. As they headed into the next, smaller rapid—the one that had taken Frank Brown's life—Ellsworth shouted out to Emery that "all he had to do was keep cool and pull us all away from the bank—and he did it." The men beached their boats below the rapid and spent the night there, happy to be through with it.

After reading Kolb's letter, Rust must have felt just a little vindicated for his warning, and perhaps relieved that he had not opted to join his friends on their

Grand Canyon voyage. He preferred to keep outright danger at arm's length. Though he was certainly enticed by the prospect of a great river voyage, he was simply too cautious to tempt fate. These were still the early days of Grand Canyon river running: the Colorado had claimed three victims in Marble Canyon from the Brown-Stanton party and other men had lost their lives attempting to cross in boats at Bright Angel Creek.[26] Men were still using inadequate wooden or canvas boats and dubious life preservers, if they wore them at all, and although Galloway's technique was becoming generally accepted, no one had successfully run all of the Grand Canyon's rapids. Since Rust was at best a poor swimmer (one of his daughters recalled that he could not swim at all), his caution was probably wise.

Over the years Rust would become friends with some of the Colorado River's best-known river rats, including Galloway, the Kolbs, Bert Loper, Harry Aleson, and Dock Marston. But he would never make the voyage through the Grand Canyon, even as boats and safety techniques improved. Still, he felt the insistent tug of the river's untamed current. Soon after the Kolb's voyage, he would begin planning a Colorado River dream of his own—a return to Glen Canyon, this time as a river guide, not as a prospector.

The summer season of 1910 brought a significant change in Rust's work in the Grand Canyon and on the Kaibab. Dave spent most of the guiding season away from the river, leaving Scott Dunham to attend to the tram and camp. With the trail completed, he was free to range as widely as his guests wanted. A woman from Worcester, Massachusetts, Mrs. Helen White Sargent, wanted to see the scenic highlights of the North Rim and Zion country, and she had considerable time to roam. From June 10 to August 1, Rust piloted her and two companions (he recorded their names only as Flanders and Miller) on an extensive tour of the best the region had to offer.[27] Starting from Jim Owens's ranger cabin, they took the wagon road heading east to fine viewpoints of the Grand Canyon from the Walhalla Plateau, then backtracked and rode westward to Point Sublime and Powell Plateau. The crew enjoyed an unusual treat at Muav Saddle (where Powell Plateau connected to the main Kaibab) when William Bass rode up from his little garden at the mouth of Shinumo Creek with some fresh melons. After savoring spectacular views into the canyon, they took a wagon east off the Kaibab to visit Jones and Woolley's catalo ranch and peer down into Marble Canyon. Rust then took the party back to his home in Kanab for a rest and reprovisioning. This was no small need, for other than procuring mutton or a side of beef from the ranchers or herders they met, there were no other sources of food in the area.

From Kanab, Rust led his guests west across the arid plains of the Arizona Strip to Pipe Spring. As the only source of clear water for dozens of miles, this old Mormon outpost was a welcome stop. (To commemorate its importance to settlers, Pipe Spring would be designated a national monument in 1923.) Rounding the western edge of the Vermilion Cliffs, they dropped off of the Hurricane escarpment into the Virgin River valley. Here, after a stop at Thomas Judd's wine cellar in LaVerkin, they continued up the valley. Grand temples and parapets rose overhead as they drew up into the great canyon of the upper Virgin River.

This stunning gorge with its enormous sandstone walls was still little known outside of southwestern Utah. John Wesley Powell rode up the canyon in 1872 following his traverse of Parunuweap Canyon on the East Fork of the Virgin River; he named the larger valley Mukuntuweap, after a Paiute word that has been variously translated as "straight canyon," "land of the springs," and even "land of Mukun," after a supposed Paiute chief. Powell contributed the first published descriptions of the two canyons in his 1875 *Report on the Exploration of the Colorado River*. Clarence Dutton of the Powell Survey gave a brief mention of Zion Canyon in his geological monograph, the *Tertiary History of the Grand Cañon District*, published in 1882, but his focus was more on the immense temples of sandstone as seen from near the present-day town of Rockville. Dutton predicted that this view would one day become one of the most admired in the world, but such renown would be some thirty years or more away. Frederick Dellenbaugh visited the canyon in 1903. He published an article in *Scribner's Magazine* the following year, titled "A New Valley of Wonders," praising Zion's "incredible cliffs, buttes, pinnacles, gloriously painted, astonishingly sculptured."[28]

What is just as astonishing is that a writer at the start of the twentieth century could be describing as a new discovery a canyon as deep and magnificent as Yosemite. Mormon cattlemen had known about the canyon for decades, of course, and a few outsiders had investigated it out of curiosity. Several Mormon settlers built cabins and ranch buildings among Zion's soaring cliffs, but the canyon remained effectively cut off from the traveling public. In 1909, acting on a report of a government surveyor, President Taft designated a small national monument with the name Mukuntuweap. At 15,840 acres, the monument took in only a narrow corridor along the canyon's most spectacular walls.[29] But until Zion National Park was designated in 1919, the valley remained in obscurity. The name "Zion" at that time was often used to denote the whole of the Mormon enterprise in Utah, and was not generally applied to the canyon of the Virgin River until it was given national park status. Locals used the term "Little Zion."

Rust could offer Mrs. Sargent's party a breathtaking experience as he led them up the crude, rutted, and often horribly muddy road along the Virgin River east from the little communities of Hurricane or Toquerville, drawing nearer to the magnificent towers that guarded the entrance to the valley. At Springdale, then only a small cluster of homes, the canyon turned north. After passing through a difficult stretch where the canyon walls closed in on the river, they entered a different world, a delightful valley of cottonwood groves under the shadow of huge red cliffs. Still higher up, brilliant white towers, some capped with red, oversaw the scene. It was a more intimate and less forbidding experience than the Grand Canyon's immense vistas.

The national monument covered only part of the canyon, and without any rangers or other federal government presence, its effect was mostly to prevent further homesteading. Ranchers from the Kanarra Valley to the west were building cabins in high meadows on the plateau west of the canyon, and a local man named Flanigan had strung a cable from a promontory on the canyon's east rim clear to the bottom of the canyon, on which he lowered lumber from a sawmill located back from the cliffs. This cable became a local attraction, and daring people would brave the 2,500-foot ride up to the rim, clinging to a seat while they were hoisted up the dizzying cliffs. On his 1910 trip with the Sargent party, Rust saw the cable as a useful way to reach the rim of the canyon. First he unloaded his mules and sent the packs up the cable. Then it was his guests' turn. Mrs. Sargent was game to ride the contraption. The sawmill operator at the top of the cable attached a small load of lumber to be lowered while she sat in a wooden seat at the bottom. The weight of the descending load was sufficient to hoist her skyward, under the hopeful control of a brakeman. She reported a splendid view from the top. After the others made it up, Rust joined them, having enlisted a fellow to bring the animals up the steep stock trail to the east rim.

Following this adventure, Rust took the group up to the high Pink Cliffs that rose like a parapet above the fissured upper canyons of Little Zion. Behind this rampart lay the Markagunt Plateau, an expansive upland that offered charming meadows set among spruce, fir, and aspen. Leaving this pleasant high country, they descended gradually to Panguitch Lake and its namesake town. The return to the Grand Canyon was accomplished over easier trails through Long Valley and the Mormon villages of Orderville, Mount Carmel, and Kanab. It would have been a stunning adventure for any traveler, but still more awaited them: after Dave saw them off, Mrs. Sargent and her friends journeyed to the Navajo Reservation, where they made a trip to Rainbow Bridge with John Wetherill.

During these prewar years, with automobile travel still a novelty, wealthy individuals such as Helen Sargent could still undertake extended journeys into the Southwest that were simply not available to the average city dweller. Such travels kept an aspect of gentility to them, even though their devotees camped on bare ground and rode through rainstorms and baking sun. Here was a lingering remnant of the Victorian age, which sought as its stage the last few relatively untouched landscapes of the world. For Rust, the Kaibab and the Markagunt uplands were not all that different from home. For Mrs. Sargent and her fellow explorers, this was about as unusual a life as one could find. This encounter between world traveler and trail-wise native had stimulating possibilities—which Dave would put to advantage in the years to come.

Although Rust could not have known it at the time, this seven weeks' journey became the template for his most successful trips. He would revisit much of the same country over the next decade, reaching far from the main attractions of the North Rim and Zion Canyon to include such seldom-visited places as the Shivwits Plateau and the Pine Valley Mountains. In later years he would extend his backcountry tours throughout the Colorado Plateau, spending weeks at a time away from towns, using a wagon where feasible to make time between attractions and venturing farther on horseback to get into the most inaccessible country. The Sargent trip, though he gave it only brief mention in his journal, proved to be a turning point in his guiding career. He noted that the "expense was too much for charges made," but he would work on those details in the future. While the North Rim would remain his focus for a time, he was no longer tied to Rust's Camp and the Grand Canyon. With a characteristic restlessness, he would seek new vistas throughout the Plateau Province. Indeed, the hunt for new vantage points would become his chief preoccupation as he led adventurous companions to one promontory after another. His vision was expanding to include tens of thousands of square miles of stunningly exposed bedrock.

6 | The Jumping Off Place of the World

Our family slogan is, "Strict economy and unceasing industry." We test each want seven times to make it a necessity, before making a purchase. When we don't need the horses, they are sent out to graze away from expensive hay. When the weather drops to zero, we crowd into half the house to save fuel. We avoid gambling, except when we plant corn on an arid farm and wish for rain to win a crop.

DAVE RUST
"Stretching the Dollar"

BY THE FALL OF 1909 Rust had been working on the Grand Canyon trail and tram for more than three years, with time out only for trips home and for teaching in Orderville during the winter of 1907–1908. He could reflect with some pride on his accomplishments: a new cross-canyon trail that was beginning to attract visitors; a tent camp in the Inner Gorge; a sturdy tram to ferry tourists across the great river. He had guided several notable travelers on extended outings across the Kaibab Plateau and into the sandstone gorge of Little Zion. For a man who had grown up in the shale hills of the Dirty Devil, it was a considerable privilege to sit around the campfire with such people as George Agassiz, Grant Wallace, Helen White Sargent, and Charles Bird.

There was also satisfaction in dealing with the challenges and dangers of rigging the tram, then savoring the day's work with one's companions back in camp. Although the labor was taxing and he suffered recurrent chest injuries, he pitched in with the rest of the men with pickaxe or rock hammer. Those who knew Dave described him as outgoing and sociable; he loved a joke and was comfortable in any company. His quick mind could figure an engineering problem or lay out an irrigation ditch. There were plenty of such puzzles to grapple with on the tram project. Like most outdoorsmen, he was experienced with pack animals and more than once had to steady a balky horse on a tight spot in the trail. One friend noted that he had "a fine, gentleman's vocabulary which any pack animal is apt to mistake for swearing."[1]

While he found it rewarding to be working amid one of the world's great natural wonders, he was still not able to make a sufficient living in the Canyon. The Transportation Company did not have the resources to build the lodges, cabins, or campgrounds that would attract the average tourist. Nor could it pay him as much as a schoolteacher's salary, at least until trail traffic picked up. Guiding visitors to the Kaibab Plateau and Zion Canyon, though highly satisfying, brought in limited income. While he noted at the end of the 1909 season that "things look fair for a 5 to 10 thousand dollar run next summer," the expense of supplying their guests with provisions and saddle horses ate up much of the profit.[2] Their pack stock continued to suffer losses in the harsh canyon environment. At the start of the 1910 season, Dave and Scott Dunham discovered to their shock that five of the ten horses they had left in Bright Angel Canyon were dead. Rust speculated that it was from the same poisoning that had affected their herd over the last few years. They could ill afford the loss, but maintaining their operation so far from their homes meant that such setbacks would inevitably occur.

As breadwinner for a growing family, Rust needed to look for every available source of income. Villages such as Kanab, however, had no large, established businesses where a man could expect to earn a steady salary. It was commonplace for enterprising men of the time to have their hands in many ventures, for an income never was assured in any line of work. Rather than return to teaching, he tried a new tack. On the last day of 1909 he and his friend Israel Chamberlain, a co-employee of the Transportation Company, each filed a homestead claim east of Kanab under the Enlarged Homestead Act of 1909. This law, sponsored by Utah Senator Reed Smoot, allowed settlers in several western states to file for 320-acre homesteads—twice the former amount—as long as they put one-fourth of the land under cultivation and lived there for five years. Rust purchased an adjacent parcel to bring his homestead up to 500 acres and set about plowing it to raise winter wheat and summer corn. He never lived on the property, although this requirement was probably not watched very closely.

The first two decades of the twentieth century saw unusually beneficent precipitation on the Colorado Plateau and throughout the semi-arid West. As reports of bumper harvests circulated back east (and were touted by railroad and land agents), thousands of settlers moved into previously uncultivated lands where they hoped to turn virgin soil into a cash bounty. The plains of eastern Montana saw a major boom as the railroads advertised plentiful crops practically for the taking. During this period the land around Kanab and the Arizona Strip, while far drier on average than the northern plains, saw sufficient winter snowfall and summer rain to permit so-called "dry farming." The town of Springdale, for example, located just south of Zion Canyon, recorded twenty inches of precipitation in the years 1906, 1907, and 1909—well above the long-term mean.[3] This gave the soil enough reserve moisture to mature a winter wheat crop without supplemental irrigation, something normally required for agriculture in this desert region.

Rust did not expect to make a killing from this venture, and his annual harvests amounted to only a hundred bushels or so.[4] Relatively little outlay was involved, however, and he supplemented his income by grazing livestock on his land. Dry farming enjoyed a boom in southern Utah during the 1910s. Its greatest advocate was John A. Widtsoe, president of the Agricultural College of Utah at Logan. Widtsoe wrote an encouraging letter to Rust sixteen months after he had started his farm, saying that "there is no doubt in my mind as to the ultimate success of dryfarming over a very large area of Kane County, provided the right methods be adopted and practiced.... It is not necessarily easy farming, but it is profitable farming. It requires a high degree of intelligence, as well as persistence in the practice of proper methods."[5] Perhaps such requirements drew Rust to the work, and contrasted enough with the toil of his former jobs pitching hay or threshing wheat. He even presided over a group of local farmers called the Vermilion Arid Farming Association. Dave persuaded Nathaniel Galloway, his buddy from mining days in Glen Canyon, to invest in a nearby plot, but farming did not appeal to Galloway for long, and he soon withdrew from the venture.

This was not Dave's first attempt to secure a homestead. In 1906 Congress had passed the so-called Forest Homestead Act, which allowed would-be settlers to file for title to any arable land within the national forests. Rust did so for a 160-acre tract within the Grand Canyon Forest Reserve, and although he did not mention its location in his journal, it may have been at the mouth of Bright Angel Creek, one of the few perennial streams in the region. Here, he told Dee Woolley, he planned to "make a ditch, raise garden and farm products as well as trees. I shall want to fence a little, make a rock house or so."[6] The Forest Service had to review the application and determine whether the land was in fact arable, and it seems to have either delayed or denied Rust's bid. Had he succeeded in privatizing a quarter-section of land at the bottom of the Grand Canyon, there today might be a very different scene greeting the tourist along the river's bank. As it was, Dave would have to be content with a smaller garden serving his tent camp.

Dave's brother Will and his wife Sarah took up a homestead near Short Creek, Arizona, in 1911. This community lay to the west of Kanab in the equally inhospitable desert of the Arizona Strip. They raised goats and exotic sheep, and were able to "prove up" on the property within a few years.[7] The two brothers remained close, and Dave often arranged to stop by with his clients when he was heading around the Vermilion Cliffs toward Zion Canyon. Dave acquired a second homestead near Pipe Spring some time later, eventually building a cabin on the property and renting it to a friend who worked the land. Will and Sarah moved to Pipe Spring in 1915 and for several years ran a tourist stop at the old ranch building by the spring. Travelers were few in those days, when the roads through the Arizona Strip had hardly progressed beyond wagon tracks.

In August 1910 Dave and Ruth welcomed the fifth member of their family, a girl they named Laura. Dave was once again working up on the Kaibab when the baby arrived. Ruth managed the Rusts' busy household during her husband's long absences. Following their return from Orderville, they had rented a house in Kanab that had only three rooms and no indoor plumbing, but few Kanab families knew anything different. Dave and Ruth found their harvests ample, as long as they kept to the economical, self-sufficient way of life they had known from childhood. Dave would take time in the spring to plow their large garden plot next to their house and tend to the homestead east of town. Then he would head for the Grand Canyon to earn whatever cash income he could. Come autumn they would harvest and put up half a ton of grain, a ton of potatoes, and, Ruth recalled, "at least 500 quarts of fresh fruit and gallons of preserves."[8] Whatever they couldn't store they sold to neighbors or to the occasional tourist. To augment this harvest they kept a milk cow, pigs, and chickens. The children were still too young to be of much help, but Ruth counted on assistance from her relatives in town. The Rusts lived a frugal life, closer to the ways of the previous century than the modern era, but it suited Dave's inclination to economize. Ruth went along with this program, her children recalled, but her workdays were long.

In the fall of 1911 another business opportunity arose, once again the result of Dee Woolley's initiative. Charles H. Townsend, the owner and editor of Kanab's local newspaper, the *Kane County News*, was interested in selling. Townsend was one of a number of Kanab newspapermen over the years with an independent viewpoint, and he had angered enough local people with his anti-Mormon statements that he was unable to attract sufficient advertising to support his paper. Dee Woolley joined with his friend William W. Seegmiller to buy the *News*.[9] Rust, with his wide-ranging interests and his talent for writing, was a natural choice for editor. He found the work congenial, if not especially remunerative; it was a good position for a man with connections to the community and who had something to say on occasion. Few copies of the paper have survived, but those that did display his personal style: he ran the usual columns boosting local progress or reporting on the comings and goings in nearby towns, but he also wrote accounts of his friends' activities in the outback. There might be news of a Kaibab lion hunt with Uncle Jim Owens; mention of Nathaniel Galloway's efforts to trap a huge grizzly that was raiding sheep on the Aquarius Plateau; or items on the projected new auto road to the North Rim.

Rust gained a reputation for fairness and good humor in print. His friend J. Cecil Alter, a weather bureau official from Salt Lake City who later wrote a history of Utah journalism, noted that he stressed "education, religion and the home" and avoided too much controversy.[10] Dave was willing to use the paper to promote his progressive views. The people of Kanab gave him such an opportunity when, in 1912, they elected a town board consisting of five women. This was said to be the first instance in the country of a town governed entirely by women. Ruth's sister, Mary Woolley Howard, was elected president of the board, a position corresponding to mayor. She explained how their election came about in a letter to Arthur Woolley, a family relation, the following summer: "There had been no primary held previous to the morning of election day. That morning a little bunch of the locust-tree orators were discussing the prohibition question in their usual place.... The ditch-bank politicians wrote out a ticket composed entirely of ladies, as a joke, and they presented it to father [Dee Woolley] on his morning trip down-town, and to which he said, 'We'll elect them!'"[11]

In contrast to the chauvinistic manner of their election, the women set about their duties seriously, passing ordinances aimed at ridding the town of rubbish and stray dogs, and, controversially, requiring cattlemen to keep their livestock from wandering the streets. They undertook to enforce the local "dry" law, but had difficulty finding a town marshal willing to tackle the duty. After several men proved reluctant to corral the town's moonshiners, Howard told Arthur Woolley that "we are seriously considering the appointment of a lady to that office."

When the women's term was over, Rust congratulated them in a laudatory article, saying that they "closed an administration that from the standpoints of integrity, ability, and enforcement of ordinances has never been equalled in Kanab before." They had served "in the face of some very bitter ridicule" and were "in no mean sense of the term 'suffragettes.'"[12]

Townsend, the paper's former editor, took exception to the new voice in town. He saw himself as the defender of the "little guy" and in 1912 founded a rival paper, the *Kane County Independent*. In it he ran editorials accusing Dee Woolley of conniving to get public funds appropriated to build a road to the Grand Canyon to his own benefit. "There is in the minds of the promoters not a thought of preserving any national play-ground—only a hanker for more tourists," Townsend wrote. The criticism was hardly fair and had little effect on Woolley's high standing in the community, where he was respected as a man who could get things done. The main result of Townsend's efforts was to divide the advertising revenue available to the two papers. Townsend's *Independent* lasted only few years. Rust continued to edit the *Kane County News* until the summer of 1914, when he turned the reins over to Jack Borlase. Borlase and his successor, Will Dobson, were inclined toward muckraking and enjoyed exposing the affairs of the moneyed interests in Salt Lake City. In all, Kanab got quite the reputation for daring journalism.[13]

None of these ventures, interesting though they were, brought in much cash income. With five children to support, Dave decided in the fall of 1912 to return to his former profession, running for the position of superintendent of schools for Kane County on the Republican platform. He won handily, 549 votes to 3. He served one term as superintendent, holding the position concurrently with his newspaper editorship, before being defeated in 1914. He won re-election as superintendent in 1921 and served four more years.[14]

Kane County's schools in those days ran only through the eighth grade; students wishing to attend high school had to board in Panguitch in adjoining Garfield County. Kanab residents managed to scrape funds together for a high school in 1914, which operated from the second floor of a local office building. A proper school building was erected four years later. As superintendent, Dave oversaw the work of eighteen teachers scattered among the district's towns, and occasionally doubled as principal at the Kanab high school. He sought to hire enthusiastic, dedicated personnel—much as he had brought his own enthusiasm to Utah's small-town schools a decade or two earlier. Most of the district's teachers were local, but he also looked elsewhere for qualified people. The daughter of a college classmate, a young woman named Helen Candland, was one such promising teacher. In 1922 she applied for an opening at the Kanab high school, much to her father's dismay. She recalled her father telling Dave, "You can't do such a thing to this girl. The salary is poor—Kanab is the jumping-off place of the world." Dave asked his friend to let her give it a try, saying he would pay her a thousand-dollar bonus—in scenery. As he anticipated, Candland discovered a love for the red-rock desert and the North Rim country, though she stayed only one year.[15]

Rust continued to pursue his interest in civic betterment through Kanab's Commercial Club, a businessmen's organization found in most cities and towns of the era. Kanab's group had its beginnings in 1908, when Dave invited some of his friends to meet at his house in an informal society they called the Bull Pups Club.[16] Later, as the leaders of the community sought to advance their business interests, they formalized the group and made contact with civic leaders in surrounding counties and in Salt Lake City. Their chief concern was to improve the transportation infrastructure in rural Utah. Distance and isolation limited access to markets and kept Kanab and other small towns from joining in the nation's growing prosperity. There was also the unfulfilled promise of the Grand Canyon trail and tram, into which Rust had poured so much effort. His operation would see little business as long as it remained disconnected at its north end—dangling, as it were, at the edge of the Kaibab. Over the next few years, Rust and Woolley would focus much of their effort on this problem.

While tourists could reach the South Rim by rail, those crossing on Rust's trail to the North Rim needed a better way to connect with rail lines in Utah. The Union Pacific's Salt Lake Route came no closer than Lund in Utah's Great Basin, two hundred miles from the North Rim; the Denver & Rio Grande's branch line to Marysvale was just as distant. Better roads to the Kaibab were important, of course, but were not the only option. Scheduled rail service was far more reliable than the autos of the day, and local boosters fervently hoped that their towns might be blessed with new track. When Dee Woolley rode into Kanab on the hood of his nephew's automobile in 1909, he told the excited citizens that a railroad would one day climb the slopes of the Kaibab and disgorge tourists at Bright Angel Point. This was his ultimate goal: to see tourism at the North Rim achieve the same prominence as the Santa Fe's operations at the South Rim.

Talk of new rail lines was nothing new around Utah; newspapers were even then predicting an imminent southward extension from either Lund or Marysvale. The *Washington County News* touted the superior views of the Grand Canyon from the North Rim and speculated that the new railroad would bring more than 50,000 tourists there each year—exceeding the Santa Fe's traffic to the South Rim. Soon, people said, there would be an elegant rimside hotel on a par with the El Tovar. There was even discussion that the line would cross the Colorado River at Lees Ferry and continue on to Santa Fe.[17] The excitement built like a summer thunderhead over the Kaibab, promising a rich economic boon for the communities along the line. Railroads had brought progress throughout the westward expansion of the country, and the Grand Canyon was merely one of the last prospects awaiting development.

Tourist traffic alone, though, could not support a new rail line to the Kaibab. Mineral and timber wealth, and to some extent agriculture, made branch lines profitable. The plateau had only a few small, unproductive mines, but timber it had in abundance, and the U.S. Forest Service, which controlled both the Grand Canyon National Monument and the Grand Canyon Game Preserve, was interested in placing the rest of its timber holdings on the Kaibab under modern forest management. The stately pine forests that blanketed the plateau were one of the wonders of the world: thick-boled ponderosa pine predominated, many of them hundreds of years old and displaying the distinctive yellow-orange, jigsaw-puzzle bark that gave them their common name of "yellow pine." Centuries of slow-burning grass fires, set by Indians to promote new grass and thus increase game, had created a wonderful park-like setting throughout much of this forest. (Townspeople in Kanab recalled seeing smoke from Paiute fires up on the plateau even into the early 1900s.) The great trees grew dozens of feet apart with little brush between them.[18] Heavy cattle grazing beginning in the late 1800s also cleared out undergrowth.

While the Kaibab's pines might amaze eastern visitors, the Forest Service, under its founding chief Gifford Pinchot and later under Henry S. Graves, was determined to put them to good use. In 1907 the chief inspector for the agency, R. E. Benedict, visited the Kaibab in Dee Woolley's company, where they discussed matters regarding the Grand Canyon Game Preserve and Woolley's catalo breeding scheme. The subject of the plateau's timber potential also came up, and Benedict, according to Woolley, tossed out some staggering sums—the agency could offer for sale fifteen million board feet per year for a hundred and fifty years, a total of more than two billion board feet.[19] This was an almost incomprehensible volume for a region accustomed to lumber scarcities, where men still operated tiny sawmills in such unlikely spots as the east rim of Zion Canyon and on Canaan Mountain, using cables and winches to lower the prized boards to the valley floors.

In 1909 the agency sent a crew of timber cruisers to the Kaibab to verify the extent of the resource. Woolley understood that the timbering program was intended for outside markets, and would serve as an inducement for eastern capitalists to build a railroad to the Kaibab and commence industrial logging operations. This was precisely the development he hoped for, as a rail line would bring tremendous ancillary benefits in tourism, trade, and commerce for southern Utah and the Arizona Strip. Thus his hopeful prediction from the hood of his brother-in-law's automobile to the citizens of Kanab.

The foresters must have seen plenty to like on the Kaibab, for they soon drew up plans to harvest the timber. Tim Hoyt, now working as the assistant district forester in the agency's regional office in Ogden, also put his oar in the water for the benefit of his Kanab friends, urging Pinchot to proceed with the logging program. (Hoyt had left the Grand Canyon Transportation Company for the Forest Service in 1906, and Rust had bought out his stock in the company.) Hoyt informed Woolley in September that Pinchot had approved the sale of one hundred million board feet of timber to a company affiliated with the Union Pacific's Salt Lake Route. Hoyt excitedly noted that the railroad men "have practically said they would build the road if the Forest Service would sell them that amount of timber for a starter."[20] Such sweetheart deals were still common even in those years of Progressivism, and in fact represented an improvement over the outright giveaways of the public domain to the railroads of the previous century.

During the summer of 1910 a distinguished forestry group came to see what their timber cruisers had found. They included Chief Forester Graves, who had just replaced Pinchot, Congressman Herbert Parsons of New York, and Tim Hoyt. The Transportation Company handled arrangements for the party, their most impressive to date. Rust drew the guiding assignment while Scott Dunham and Rees Griffiths took care of the tram and the tent camp at the river.

The trip may have been a formality, since the agency's field personnel had already done their calculations, but it must have satisfied Graves of the Kaibab's potential, for later that year he authorized an even larger sale of ponderosa pine timber from the forest—a local newspaper put the sum at five hundred million board feet.[21] This prospective sale remained the subject of intense speculation in southern Utah for several years. The Union Pacific apparently lost interest, though, leaving room for a new beneficiary to seize the opportunity. On December 5, 1910, the Utah & Grand Canyon Railroad Co. incorporated for the purpose of building a rail line from Lund to St. George, along with a second line from Marysvale to Panguitch.[22] An extension southward into Arizona and the Kaibab Plateau was also planned. The principal investor, Frank A. Dudley of Niagara Falls, was connected to a New York engineering firm that was to undertake the actual construction of the line and purchase the timber for liquidation.

The capital outlay proved to be too much for these investors. Absent a federal land grant such as had aided the great transcontinental railroads, the distances to the Kaibab made the line appear unprofitable. Tim Hoyt continued to push his agency to make favorable terms for the public timber. In 1912 he told Rust that "when the big Kaibab timber sale and railroad talk was on I went to the very limit of my power to get the Forester and the Secretary to concede every thing it seemed necessary to get the capitalists to take hold of the matter. The result was that the terms were finally accepted by those with whom we were negotiating and the project was only delayed or possibly throttled by the difficulties in arranging traffic with other railroads concerned."[23] This may have been a reference to the Union Pacific or the Denver & Rio Grande, which controlled the tracks leaving Utah.

But the notion of a rail line to the North Rim persisted. By 1914 the Forest Service had upped its timbering plans again, offering to sell a billion board feet of timber from the Kaibab over a twenty-five-year period in order to finance the rail venture. Chief Forester Graves noted that as well as accessing timber stands, the railroad would bring development to "much unpreserved public land, which is now comparatively idle." With private financing not forthcoming, a congressman from Washington State, J. W. Bryan, introduced legislation in 1914 for the federal government to build the line. The bill went nowhere. In 1921, Utah congressman James Mays introduced yet another bill, but by then few in government were interested in the business of running railroads.[24]

Southern Utah's dream of a new railroad went unfulfilled. Had the line reached the North Rim, it would have meant a major change for the Grand Canyon Transportation Company's venture, bringing in tourists in numbers unimaginable for a horse-and-wagon operation. Improvements on this scale would likely have supplanted their little operation in the backcountry, but neither Rust nor Woolley ever indicated that they would mind. These men and their friends had grown up under the limitations of the frontier, chafing at the arduous journeys needed to conduct almost any business. Roads and rail lines would be Kane

County's and the Arizona Strip's salvation; the Grand Canyon and the Kaibab were the draw to make the improvements possible.

With no railroad in the offing, Woolley and Rust realized that the success of their Grand Canyon venture—and the economic future of their community as well—depended on improving the wagon roads to the Kaibab. At the time, motoring anywhere south of Marysvale or Cedar City was hazardous; to get as far as Kanab (let alone the North Rim) took real determination. Even traveling with horse and wagon had its hazards. One friend of theirs, Wesley E. King of the Salt Lake Commercial Club, found this out when he ventured south in the summer of 1911. Disembarking at the Rio Grande station in Marysvale, King and his wife hired a team and buggy to travel to Kanab and around the Little Zion country. The roads were bad enough through the high country of Long Valley south of Panguitch, but once they turned southeast at Mount Carmel to cross the sand dunes beneath the White Cliffs, they lost their way entirely. In this "Sahara," King wrote in the *Salt Lake Tribune*, "a lone sheep herder saved us, on the second morning out, and we floundered into Kanab over twenty-four hours late, just as Uncle 'D' Woolley was starting a posse of Indian scouts after us." King chided county officials for not posting adequate signs along the route. "A railroad or a line of commercial airships would help some," King suggested. "The one seems as early a possibility as the other."[25]

Rust joined the Kings at Kanab and piloted them westward across the Arizona Strip. King's description of the Vermilion Cliffs resembled Clarence Dutton's in his *Tertiary History*: "[W]e felt perfectly safe with our guide ahead and the magnificent cliffs to the right. It seemed as though we were passing in review at their feet while the sunshine and shadows on their towering sides kept us in a state of constant wonderment and awe."[26] Indeed, King mentioned both Dutton's and Dellenbaugh's writings, which were the standard references to the scenic features of the region.

Even this familiar route presented difficulties. On the third day out from Kanab, after the group had spent the night at an abandoned ranch, Rust's pack horses lit out for home. He overtook them ten miles back down the road and rejoined the Kings at noon. "Meanwhile," Wesley King reported, "our driving team had given us a further fright by breaking out of their pasture and straying into the recesses of the canyon at the rear of our habitat." Horses could negotiate bad roads better than automobiles, but at least the machines stayed where you pastured them.

Following Dutton's route, the party took the cutoff through the cliffs at Short Creek to descend into the valley of the Virgin. Rust then took the Kings on a long day's ride up into Little Zion. His guests enjoyed the scenery, but they felt a little like those tourists who made it to the bottom of the Grand Canyon and back: "[A]fter ten hours on a mountain pony," King wrote, "[we were] filled with tenderness and awe, but the tenderness and the awe were not in the same place."

After visiting Zion, Rust left the Kings and returned home. Wesley King's impression was that the communities of southern Utah held much promise for industry, but until better roads were built, little would come of the townspeople's hopes for more commerce.

In those years neither the state nor federal governments had worked out a formula for financing road construction. The Utah legislature's appropriations largely went toward roads between the state's urban centers; communities such as Kanab were left out. Seeking to redress this imbalance, Woolley and Rust, accompanied by other prominent men from Kanab and Richfield, traveled to Salt Lake City in the summer of 1913 to try to persuade the Utah State Road Commission to free up some money. Woolley told the commissioners that "for $10,000 I can build a road from the Utah state line to the [Grand] canyon, so that automobiles can travel over it at the rate of 20 to 25 miles an hour."[27] Within Utah, though, the state would have to help. He and Rust, along with other regional boosters, envisioned a "Grand Canyon Auto Road" from Salt Lake City to the North Rim that would compete both with the Santa Fe's line to the South Rim and with traffic northward from Salt Lake to Yellowstone National Park.

Woolley also brought up the subject of the immense timber resources of the Kaibab, and repeated his optimistic belief that a railroad might soon be built onto the plateau. The commissioners were enthusiastic about the plan and promised to support it, but without naming any sums. They did endorse the idea of employing convicts from the state penitentiary to work on road improvements—an idea that Rust would follow up on later. It would be several years, however, before state or federal funds were forthcoming, and in the meantime local and county officials essentially had to pass the hat to fund any improvements. Not until 1916 would the Feds chip in; in that year Utah senator Reed Smoot obtained $15,000 to build a road into Mukuntuweap National Monument.[28]

Along with the North Rim, the canyon of Little Zion was drawing the interest of tourism promoters in southern Utah. Its huge, colorful walls and intimate streamside groves, they felt, could make it the equal of the Grand Canyon as a touring destination. Utah governor William Spry visited Zion in the fall of 1913, accompanied by officials of the Salt Lake Route and the Wylie Way tourist-camp company of Yellowstone. Crowds of residents of the small towns along the Virgin River came along and celebrated with a picnic at the base of Cable Mountain. The governor declared the canyon to be the most beautiful sight he had seen, and he endorsed the idea of a rail line to bring commerce and tourists to the region.[29]

The North Rim and the Kaibab Plateau were also on the itinerary for the governor's trip. After taking in the views from Bright Angel Point and the Walhalla Plateau, Spry repeated his declarations that this was unmatched scenery. But he also expressed interest in future timbering on the Kaibab once a rail line was built. Nothing had yet come of the Forest Service's logging plans.

One of the businessmen accompanying the governor, H. H. Hays of the Wylie Way company, took a more realistic view of the prospects. His outfit had long benefited from the superior rail and stagecoach connections to Yellowstone, and in an article in the *Salt Lake Tribune* following the governor's trip, he pointed out that a good transportation infrastructure was sorely lacking in southern Utah. "We cannot tell the world about these places because they are inaccessible," he noted. "As long as it takes less time to go from Salt Lake City to New York than from Salt Lake City to the scenic wonders of southern Utah, it is idle to repeat and amplify what Powell, Dutton and other explorers have said about the marvelous country which lies to the south of Salt Lake City."[30] He had not been impressed with the road to Little Zion, calling it "the most treacherous highway in southern Utah." Local people, in their sober moments, would have had to agree.

The federal government's presence in southern Utah was still limited, but Forest Service officials felt they had a role in serving local communities' needs. Besides supplying timber for local sawmills and grass for ranchers' herds—activities separate from the prospective Kaibab timber sale—they could also play a part in developing tourism. In 1913 the Kaibab foresters undertook to build a road across the plateau from the forest boundary to Bright Angel Point. This road was an extension of the Grand Canyon Auto Road that was being pushed toward the

Kaibab Plateau by local residents under encouragement from Rust and Woolley. The road headed east-southeast from Fredonia for sixteen miles, turning south just beyond the forest boundary and climbing LeFevre Ridge to Jacob Lake.[31] From there it made its way south through the forests near the crest of the Kaibab, traversing the plateau's beautiful parks and meadows on the way to Bright Angel Point. It was the predecessor of the modern highways 89 and 67 and an alternative to the Big Springs–Naile Canyon route that Rust had used for years.

Dee Woolley was confident that the new road would develop into an important tourist highway, and to publicize it he contacted a former professional bicycle racer from Salt Lake City named Bill Rishel, who had begun mapping out auto-touring routes around Utah for the *Salt Lake Tribune*. These so-called "Pathfinder" expeditions were intended to boost the idea of vacationing by automobile, and during them Rishel kept detailed road logs of his routes, a necessary service for adventurous auto tourists. Rishel set off for the North Rim in the fall of 1913, independently of Governor Spry's trip, with an entourage of twenty-one motorists in eight vehicles.[32] As in 1909, it was necessary to ship gasoline ahead to Kanab and the Kaibab. They traveled the Panguitch–Johnson Canyon route that Gordon Woolley had used in 1909, finding it in similarly atrocious shape. In Kanab they were given a rousing greeting, and Rishel gave Mayor Mary Howard a ride around town. Dee Woolley and Forest Supervisor James Pelton accompanied the group over the new road to the Kaibab, where they camped at the Grand Canyon Transportation Company's new outfitting cabin in Fuller Canyon. The party trekked to Bright Angel Point on foot, perhaps wishing to avoid the beating that the last few miles of "road" must have given Gordon Woolley's and David Affleck's vehicles in 1909.

The notion of an auto highway to the Grand Canyon took hold among civic leaders in southern Utah and a rivalry arose between various counties over where the route would run. Kanab residents wanted to improve the Long Valley route south of Panguitch, continuing through the sand dunes north of Kanab, a shorter alternative to Johnson Canyon. Advocates in the Dixie country of southwestern Utah wanted the route, which they were calling the "Grand Canyon Highway," to go through the new community of Hurricane on the Virgin River and head out over the Arizona Strip past Pipe Spring. Rust had conflicting loyalties on the matter. He naturally wanted to see Kanab benefit from a more direct routing from the north, connecting his hometown with Panguitch and Richfield. In the end, though, he agreed with Washington County officials that the western route was superior; it could be kept open all year long and would provide closer access to Little Zion Canyon, a worthy co-attraction with the Grand Canyon.[33] In the ensuing years he would promote both routes as offering a scenic loop through the region's attractions.

With agreement reached among southern Utah leaders as to the routing of the new highway, there remained only the need to raise money to make the route a reality. Dee Woolley had been shaking the tree for some years to little avail. In 1909, shortly after his trip to the North Rim with Gordon Woolley, he wrote to E. S. Clark, his Flagstaff contact with the Transportation Company, suggesting that Clark badger Coconino County officials for funds to fix up the route in Arizona. "If I could get from six to eight hundred dollars to apply on the road," he offered, "I'll guarantee to make a road so that an automobile can go the seventy five miles [from Kanab to Bright Angel] in four hours including a stop for lunch." Woolley pointed out that on his nephew's trip he improved the road as they went, jumping out of the car at frequent intervals to clear the way of rocks and stumps. "So it seems to me that so trifling a sum to accomplish so much should be easily raised," he told Clark.[34] He also took up the matter with Ralph Cameron and anyone else who would listen, but these notables had their own projects to support.

It would come down to those most directly benefited by the road to raise the needed funds. In January 1915 Rust hosted a delegation from the Toquerville Commercial Club to drum up support in Kanab. A public meeting was called and the "Kanab Silver Band" was engaged to play, offering up a tune they called "The Rutless, Chuckless, Cussless Road." Speeches were given touting the good things that would come from the new road, and a committee of seven was chosen to canvass the town and nearby communities. Rust worked Kanab with two associates, collecting a thousand dollars from the public-spirited (and pointedly buttonholed) citizens. Dee Woolley chipped in two hundred dollars and Rust fifty toward the total.[35]

Rust, Woolley, and their associates formed an *ad hoc* committee to boost the "Utah–Grand Canyon Highway," enlisting members from Kane and Iron counties in Utah, and Coconino and Mohave counties in Arizona. Their letterhead trumpeted "Hurrah! Grand Canyon to Yellowstone 1915," expressing their hope of tapping into the growing traffic to America's flagship park. The committee successfully lobbied Utah state officials for the use of convict labor gangs from the state prison; these were pulled off of road projects in the northern part of the state and sent south to work during the winter.[36] Collections went up in other towns along the route. Iron County citizens pitched in a quantity of oats to feed the scraper teams operated by the convict laborers.

By the end of 1914 the Grand Canyon Highway had become a recognizable route from Cedar City to Hurricane, and tourist parties were beginning to venture farther on toward the North Rim. But the endless expanse of the Arizona Strip still dwarfed the road builders' efforts. Wind and sand, the constant factors on the Strip for thousands of years, could erase in a few days what the road crews took weeks to improve. Progress would come to the region at a slower pace than Kane County's boosters hoped for.

Rust was not one to record his innermost thoughts, but he was one of the hopeful ones. His position as a community leader must have brought him a good deal of satisfaction, and as the editor of the local paper, he served as a prominent spokesman for progressive ideas. He was not getting rich, but this never seemed to be at the top of his agenda. The country was opening up, and he was taking part in its development. There was talk of a new national park in the Grand Canyon—something that promised a future for his trail and tram. It was a time of rich possibilities for anyone involved in the economy of the region.

7 | Roads to the Wilderness

From frequent magazine stories, and even from recent geological documents, you might infer that the Canyon had only one side. Publicity comes so easy when the observations can be made from the cushions of Harvey hotels and Pullman-palace cars. Thus, by a lack of such accommodations as the average tourist demands, the mysteries of the north side have been kept sealed up. But now the way is opened, and beginning with the summer of 1915, the ordinary person of means and strength can follow the glorious trails of Powell, Dutton, and Moran and the rest of those remarkable explorers who have written so enchantingly.

DAVE RUST
Notes from a prospective tour brochure[1]

THE PAVED ROAD THAT LEADS through the Walhalla Plateau east of Bright Angel Point is surely one of the most beautiful drives in any of our national parks. After curving through twenty miles of aspen glades, ponderosa stands, and verdant ravines that gave the plateau its early name of "Greenland," the road ends a bit disappointingly at a huge, graveled parking lot, devoid of any shade. But a short trail leads from the car park to Cape Royal, one of the finest viewpoints in the Southwest. Hundreds of tourists stand at its guardrails on a summer afternoon, appreciating the close-up view of Vishnu Temple or scanning the Colorado River, a dizzying five thousand feet below, for passing raft parties.

Shortly after branching off of the park entrance highway that continues to Bright Angel Point, the Cape Royal road passes through a series of lovely meadows in a long draw called Fuller Canyon. Not long ago there stood a magnificent lone aspen tree in one of these meadows, an inviting register for passersby to carve their names. It is now dead and half fallen to the ground, but it once shaded visitors to the field headquarters of the Grand Canyon Transportation Company. In 1911 Dave Rust and Dee Woolley obtained a permit from the Forest Service to build a fifteen-by-sixteen-foot log cabin at the southeastern edge of this meadow. In it they stored saddles and tack for their outfitting business and accommodated overnight guests on cots during cold weather. A corral next to the cabin held the day's riding horses and pack mules, brought in from pasture in the surrounding meadow and woods. Here Dave and his fellow guides saddled up parties riding out to the North Rim and the start of their cross-canyon trail.[2]

Back behind the cabin, underneath branches of sweet-scented yellow pine, a tiny spring (now dry) oozed out into a stone catchment, providing just enough water for their operation. (In earlier years Dee Woolley sometimes pastured his "catalo" hybrids in this meadow, and the seep was called Catalo Spring.) The site had no views of the Grand Canyon, but the spring was the closest source of water other than at Uncle Jim Owens's ranger cabin on the road to Bright Angel Point. From the Woolley cabin, as it was known, it was a pleasant afternoon's ride to that overlook; visitors with a few extra days to spend could ride out to other viewpoints along the North Rim, including Cape Royal or Skidoo Point (now Point Imperial) at the eastern end of the plateau, or they could head west on cattlemen's trails to wonderful overlooks at Point Sublime or the Powell Plateau. Various guides, including Rust, worked out of the cabin under the auspices of the Transportation Company. Theirs was a highly informal operation, a far cry from the well-appointed sportsmen's lodges such as were found in the East, but it brought a small taste of civilization to the hundreds of square miles of the Kaibab's forest.

Visitors to the Woolley cabin ranged from world-savvy adventurers and hunters who wanted to add a Grand Canyon notch to their accomplishments, to curious Utahns willing to brave the roads and see if the famous canyon truly lived up to its billing. More and more automobiles were making the trip, harbingers of the sweeping changes that would overtake the more primitive modes of travel. But in its first five years, the cabin and trail still seemed like a far outpost, and many travelers wanted a guide to open up the country for them. By 1913 Rust's civic commitments were keeping him increasingly tied to Kanab, but he found time to accompany some friends to his favorite scenic spots, the Kaibab high among them. In early August of that year he arranged to meet J. Cecil Alter, a Weather Bureau official from Salt Lake City, his wife, and a third companion in Kanab for an excursion to the North Rim.

The Alters were on a horse-and-buggy tour from Salt Lake City to the Grand Canyon and Zion, a trip described in two articles he wrote for the *Salt Lake Tribune*.[3] They had driven south from Marysvale through Panguitch, but instead of descending into Long Valley, they turned east through Alton and proceeded to Kanab via Johnson Canyon—the same route that Dee Woolley had chosen for his nephew's auto expedition in 1909. The road was still in poor shape. Approaching the ranching community of Johnson, the Alters encountered a low stretch called Sink Valley, where, Alter wrote, "a few miles of clay makes the Circle[ville] valley look like a pavement by comparison." The Alters had to stop repeatedly to scrape mud off of the wheels so they could proceed. "It is truly the most picturesque mud hole on earth when at its best," he noted, "and there is no way around it."

Rust joined the Alters for the run to Bright Angel Point. After reaching Fredonia, they took the new Grand Canyon Auto Road, which by then had been extended south into the Kaibab. Forest Service crews were working on this route up on the mountain, and Alter assured his readers that the forest supervisor, James Pelton, would surely want to join any enterprising auto tourists willing to pioneer this route. It would be three more years, however, before the road was ready for regular motor traffic. Until then, Rust joked that the name meant that the new route "oughta be a road."

Once up on the Kaibab, the Alters enjoyed their slow progress along this attractive forest route, which was a worthy destination even without the lure of stupendous views at its southern end. The encompassing forest of spruce and fir was broken by meadows or "parks," as the settlers called them—among the most enchanting of the Kaibab's features. At their edges stood scattered stands of aspen, slender white trunks bearing a shimmering canopy. Some of the meadows were small, intimate openings of a few acres' extent, but along the crest of the plateau the road reached the grand corridors known to the pioneers of the region as Big Park and Little Park. Big Park also went by the name "V. T.," after the brand of an early cattle company that ran stock on the plateau. John Wesley Powell renamed this meadow in honor of his friend and colleague, Professor Harvey De Motte of Illinois Wesleyan University, with whom he surveyed portions of the Kaibab and North Rim country in 1872. Little Park, lying just to the south beyond a low divide that Dutton called the Sylvan Gate, became Little De Motte Park. Another meadow north of these parks was known as Pleasant Valley, and here Alter photographed their buggy traversing the scant tracks that constituted the Grand Canyon Auto Road. In August the late-summer asters would have been in bloom, the air fresh and cool in contrast to the desert they had left behind.

Dave regarded this stretch of the Kaibab as an ideal summertime destination, and in his 1911 essay "De Motte Park," he called attention to this overlooked Kaibab beauty spot. Were it not for the presence of the immense canyon to the south, this meadow would have been the premier destination on the Kaibab. Returning to the theme of outdoor pilgrimage that he had used in his 1908 essay "The Bright Angel," he presented the park as a worthy goal in itself:

As the "perfect days" of summer approach, they beckon us from the perspiring town to the shady groves and green banks and blossoms of wild flowers.... Schools have closed, social seasons run out, we must away to the silent places, the parks, the woods, the forests, to think it all over and slow down a little.

De Motte Park is a line of beauty in this magnificent American forest. It extends along the mountain for ten miles in curves as graceful as those of the human form.... Cowboys who have grown gray on the trails of the forest have a keen intuitive appreciation for it; they like to be there, yet they cannot sense the comparative sublimity of the place. They love it as if by instinct. So must any man who builds his campfire there, who sleeps under the pines and aspens, who sees the day break, and watches the sun chase away the dew of early morning.

In contrast to the labors of crossing the canyon of the Colorado, De Motte Park invited the traveler to picnic in the cool shade of a July afternoon. Rust called attention to this relatively unknown spot just two years after the discovery of Rainbow Bridge, a time when Americans favored monumental scenery that incited awe and wonder in the heart. De Motte Park offered a quieter aspect. Rust had spent many nights there, and he had seen it "dreary as an Alaskan lake in winter," as well as during its summer glories. Instead of viewing the place as just another stop on the trail to the North Rim, he had come to regard this park as a highlight of any trip. He passed along this appreciation to his guests, and one of his Boston clients, he recounted proudly, pronounced it "unquestionably the most beautiful park in the world." One imagines Rust standing by the campfire at dusk, explaining how the early geologists had theorized that the park was the course of an ancient river. Likely he would have read from the *Tertiary History*, wherein Dutton wrote, "The spirit of the scene is a calm, serene, and gentle one, touched with a tinge of solemnity and melancholy."

Leaving De Motte Park, the Alters and Rust were again in the forest, gradually descending the ridges and ravines that sloped down toward the North Rim, still hidden from view. Before reaching Bright Angel Point, they turned east up Fuller Canyon and made camp at the Woolley cabin. This would be their base for excursions along the rim.

Bright Angel Point was the chief attraction for the Salt Lake tourists. Alter photographed his companions clinging to the airy limestone outcrop that overlooked the fantastic abyss formed by two tributaries of Bright Angel Creek. Decades later, the Park Service would build a secure walkway to this same point, complete with guardrails and interpretive signs. From this vantage the full majesty of the Grand Canyon became obvious. The long trench of Bright Angel Creek, carved into an ancient fault line that split the canyon clean, pointed straight at the head of Ralph Cameron's Bright Angel trail on the opposite rim. (The trails on both sides of the canyon took advantage of the break in the cliffs created by this fault.) Remnants of an old erosion surface called the Tonto Platform flanked Bright Angel Canyon, and above these towered the massive buttes that Clarence Dutton had named for a mystical pantheon: Deva, Brahma, and Zoroaster temples. "It cannot be seen in a few minutes, nor a few hours," Alter wrote in 1920 of the view from this promontory. "Nothing less than a day, including an early morning and a late evening visit for contemplation from the extreme end of Bright Angel Point, will suffice, including such reconnoitering about The Transept and the Companion Alcove, which form the voids at the sides of Bright Angel Point."[4]

Dave took the Alters out to more viewpoints along the eastern edge of the Kaibab, and also to the head of his cross-canyon trail. They rode partway down Bright Angel Canyon, but did not go as far as the river. On their return trip the Alters dropped Rust off in Kanab and proceeded west through Pipe Spring and the Arizona Strip. Rather than circle around the Vermilion Cliffs via the new town of Hurricane, they took the steep road from Short Creek over the mountain, as Rust had done with the Sargent party in 1910. This road presented the traveler with a steep descent into the Virgin River valley. "Automobiles [coming the other way] might be taken up by block and tackle," Alter wrote, "one curve at a time, though a derrick would be better; but we cannot contemplate the pitiful plight of a lonely automobile safely landed at the top of this dugway and facing fifty-five miles of loose sand toward the Grand Canyon."[5]

Alter's second article for the *Salt Lake Tribune* likened the gigantic rock spires bordering the valley of the Mukuntuweap to dinosaurs' teeth, and contrasted the elegant names Dutton gave them (Western Temple, Smithsonian Butte) with the "plebian" local usage (the Steamboat, Bear Mountain).[6] They rode up the canyon as far as Cable Mountain, but the lumber hoist was not in operation, to Mrs. Alter's relief. Instead they paused to enjoy the showering stream at a nearby grotto now known as Weeping Rock.

Little Zion's isolation, Alter felt, was all that kept it from nationwide fame. "I realized why California's Yosemite, with an inferior performance, has gotten the confetti crowds, while Mukuntuweap is still all but lost in the native wilds; it is a mere matter of roads.... A twenty-mile gravel roof over the sand between Toquerville and Springdale is all it lacks."

This was still a day when most visitors to the North Rim and Zion Canyon needed a local connection—someone who knew the country and who could arrange logistics. Rust provided this essential service for the Alters in 1913, opening up an unseen world with his intimate knowledge of the Kaibab's beauty spots. The role suited him. He had already shown he could take charge of a work crew under the difficult conditions of the Grand Canyon. Guiding, however, demanded additional skills. Besides finding the trail, making camp, and cooking meals, he had to take into account each client's personality and expectations. Dave's wide range of social contacts—through teaching, newspapering, and (in later years) politics—undoubtedly served him well. While he fit in with his cowboy buddies out on the trail, Dave was also at ease with his highly educated and often wealthy clients. He could bridge the social gulf between the rough-hewn plainsman and the world traveler.

Rust's devotion to the cause of education cost him a chance at guiding the country's most famous advocate of the outdoor life. In mid-July of 1913, former President Theodore Roosevelt visited the Kaibab Plateau as part of an extended outing he was taking from the Grand Canyon through the Indian reservations of northern Arizona. His nephew, Nicholas Roosevelt, made arrangements with Rust for the Grand Canyon Transportation Company to guide the president's party while on the plateau. Rust was planning to attend a convention of the National Education Association in Salt Lake City during their visit, so he enlisted his brother Will's help. (Will and Sarah had moved to Kanab for the winter of 1912–1913 and lived for a time with Dave and Ruth.) Scott Dunham was to meet the party at the Colorado River tram and cross them to Rust's Camp; Will would be their cook while they hunted lions on the plateau for several weeks.[7]

While making preparations for the trip, Nicholas heard that the irrepressible Dee Woolley was talking up the president's visit to newspapermen. He telegrammed Rust in Salt Lake City, directing him to "shut up Wolley [*sic*]" and announce to the wire services that "it is not known when [Roosevelt] will cross the canyon or what his itinerary is he wishes it publically [*sic*] stated that he will do no hunting in Arizona."[8] Even in the wilds of the Kaibab, a famous person was not assured of privacy.

Nicholas, traveling separately, brought a string of his uncle's favorite horses up to the Kaibab from Lees Ferry, carrying with him "a great deal of importance and ostentation," according to Will Rust. Nicholas gave the guides detailed instructions for the provisioning of Colonel Roosevelt's party, and Dunham and Will Rust rode up to the Woolley cabin to put things in shape. Nicholas headed across the canyon to join his uncle. Unfortunately, the two guides miscalculated the date and failed to meet Roosevelt's party when they arrived at Rust's tram. Will blamed Uncle Jim Owens for wrongly informing him as to the calendar, but regardless of fault, Roosevelt found no one waiting for him on the south bank. The supervisor of the Bar Z Ranch, the principal cattle outfit on the Kaibab, happened to be on the other side of the river waiting for one of his men who was coming down from the South Rim, and he laboriously winched the tram cage across. Nicholas wrote in 1967 that "the cage went very slowly and irregularly, stopping for a minute at a time.... I couldn't imagine what was wrong.... For several minutes the car did not move at all." The ranch supervisor, an older fellow, was exhausted from cranking them across, and the Roosevelts were surprised to find that he was not the man whom they had arranged to meet.[9]

A thunderstorm that was building over the canyon let loose just as they were crossing the river; a reporter's dispatch to the *New York Times* observed that "lightning played about the cage." Despite the danger, TR was fascinated by the tram's winch system and once he was across he took charge and cranked the next party over.[10]

The Roosevelts spent the night at Rust's unoccupied camp on Bright Angel Creek. The two cattlemen assisted the party on the ride up to the North Rim, Roosevelt growing steadily more impatient at the Transportation Company's absence. Rust and Dunham, meanwhile, were preparing to descend from the North Rim, unaware that they were more than a day late. Pausing for lunch at the head of the trail, they were surprised to see the president's party making its way up the last switchbacks. Roosevelt was indignant and, according to Will, "would listen to no explanations.... [H]is anger would not be appeased." He had no further need for Rust's men, and he hired Jim Owens and some Bar Z men for their Kaibab lion hunt. Following these adventures, the Roosevelts headed east to the Navajo country with Jesse Cummings of Mesa, Arizona, as their guide.[11]

Even after the miscues with Roosevelt's party, Dave retained his admiration for the president and corresponded with Theodore Roosevelt Jr. occasionally over the years. In 1921 he and Ruth named their youngest child Quentin, after the president's son who was killed in the Great War. Dave admired not only TR's call to the "strenuous life," but his progressive politics, moral exhortations, and love of literature.

The Alters and the Roosevelts represented two poles of the travel spectrum in the pre-automobile years. While TR was certainly the most famous person to visit the Grand Canyon, his social and economic status was not terribly different from others who used Rust's and Owens's services. These wealthy individuals had the means to travel, but more important, their curiosity about the far-off places of the world, nurtured in supportive families and in the best schools of the country, induced them to make journeys of wide scope and modest challenge. Families such as the Alters, on the other hand, while decently educated and well-off by Utah standards, represented the more populist arm of tourism. They took natural pride in Utah's (and northern Arizona's) scenic wonders, but most of them were not interested in reliving the frontiersman's hardships. As the automobile came into wider use, the Alters and many other travelers would embrace it as a more convenient mode of travel. They were less concerned with the experience of roughing it than with seeing the marvels at the end of the road.

The more elite form of travel would continue to have its adherents, even as the wilderness shrank. Whether Roosevelt, Zane Grey, and their brethren (and the occasional woman) were merely partaking in a throwback atavism is at least debatable; both Roosevelt and Grey felt that tackling outdoor challenges was essential to manhood and even to good citizenship. One of Grey's biographers, Stephen May, draws a clear connection between the two adventurers, both of whom felt that their Western experiences made men out of them. May observed that TR regarded the West as "sanctified territory," and helped to make the cowboy a national symbol. Zane Grey followed in those same tracks, holding to "the idea that the sweat and exertion in attaining a goal must be equal to, or greater than, the prize itself."[12]

Both men had legions of readers, and their call to the rugged outdoor life stirred many. Some would make it to the Kaibab and, as word got around, request Dave's services as guide. His skill at primitive travel and his ability to relate to diverse clients might not bring him wealth, but they offered great satisfaction as he developed friendships with travelers from the wider world. The work was welcome, but that was only part of it. As prominent as he was in Kanab, he yearned for more of a connection to the outside world. At Brigham Young and at Stanford, he had tasted the cultural and intellectual heritage that was available to educated people. As he met other experienced journeyers, so would he be drawn outward. Kanab, like Caineville, had its limitations. There was more to see, more to understand, and his circle would continue to widen.

Rust's "God of the wilderness," however, proved unwilling to forestall many of the changes to the rugged country of his youth. The nascent tourism industry of the Southwest would devote its investments and advertisements to luring travelers who wanted an easier road to the backcountry. More and more touring parties sought North Rim views by car, taking advantage of the slowly improving roads. By the summer of 1914 the semiofficial route of the Grand Canyon Highway led south from Cedar City to Toquerville and had been signed in places, but beyond Toquerville, it was more dream than reality. This was discovered by a group organized by the Salt Lake Commercial Club that September.

The group included J. H. Manderfield, the assistant passenger representative of the Union Pacific's Salt Lake Route,[13] and one of the most energetic tourism promoters in the state. He was intent on getting some Grand Canyon business for his line, and he wanted to demonstrate how tourists could journey to Bright Angel Point without undue difficulty. Manderfield and his wife set out from Salt Lake with eight other motorists, taking a different route than the one Dee Woolley and his nephew had pioneered in 1909. While the roads may have been marginally better by then, their outfit suffered many more mishaps, as related years later by Frank Ensign, one of the participants.[14] At Toquerville, one of their party, driving a new Cadillac, mistakenly headed off on the rutted road leading to Zion Canyon and tore out the car's battery on a high center. Once the group had reassembled on the right road, they proceeded into the desert of the Arizona Strip. There they encountered troublesome dust and sand, causing their Pierce-Arrow car to grind to a halt every few miles with a clogged air cleaner. While traversing the Strip—one of the poorest sections of the road—the Cadillac suffered a broken steering knuckle and was abandoned. They replaced this vehicle in Kanab, but farther on, another car broke in two while crossing a sandy wash.

Further problems developed. One car had been mistakenly filled with wood alcohol in Kanab, which "dissolved the shellac off the cork float in the carburetor and stopped up the needle valve with the shellac. We lost a day on account of this mishap," according to Ensign. They made it to Bright Angel Point, but on the way home, driving in a sandstorm north of Kanab, one of the cars crashed into a rare oncoming vehicle. "The driver, Mr. Hughes, suffered two broken ribs in the collision," Ensign wrote, "and while rushing him to the doctor I ran into a twenty-foot desert arroyo and barely missed killing myself and passengers." The journey to the Grand Canyon was not one to take lightly. Clearly, before anyone could legitimately advertise the Grand Canyon Highway, much additional road work would be needed.

Manderfield was hardly deterred by his group's troubles, at least in public. Back home, he told the *Salt Lake Tribune* that this was "the greatest outing I have ever taken.... The roads were good in most places and always passable." He acknowledged that the section north of the Kaibab forest boundary needed work, but he saw much enthusiasm for the route among local residents.[15] Taking up the cause, the *Tribune* continued to sponsor its "pathfinder" expeditions throughout Utah as motor travel expanded in popularity. Dee Woolley accompanied one of these trips to the Grand Canyon in 1916, where he had another of his close encounters with the North Rim. One of the participants recounted how "they drove suddenly out of the trees near the rim and looked off into the vast space of the canyon. E. D. Woolley, sitting where he could not see the road ahead of them and getting the impression that they were headed straight for the edge, yelled 'Stop, stop, for God's sake stop.'"[16]

Though Dave was no longer one of the regular guides for the Grand Canyon Transportation Company, he maintained his connection to Woolley's outfit. Prospects looked good for a decent road to the Kaibab, and with it the hope of expanding tourist traffic to the North Rim. During the spring of 1915 Dave explored this possibility with J. H. Manderfield of the Salt Lake Route, who had brought up the idea of a joint venture as early as 1913. Manderfield envisioned a scheme something like that at Yellowstone National Park, where tent camps served tourists arriving by rail or stagecoach at the park's northern and western entrances. These were the kind of facilities that might attract real numbers of visitors—especially travelers who expected a measure of comfort and convenience. "We have one or two special parties in view that might make the trip," Manderfield wrote to Dee Woolley, "and I am sure if it is once started, it can be worked into a large proposition." He asked Woolley to come up with an itinerary, which Rust undertook to supply.[17]

The main problem was the two-hundred-mile gap that still remained between Bright Angel Point and the rail station at Lund in Utah's Great Basin. The road from Lund still presented many of the same obstacles that had confounded earlier parties. It started off south of Toquerville in decent shape, but beyond Hurricane it became steadily more miserable as it entered the sandy plains of the Arizona Strip. The section from Short Creek, Arizona, through the Pipe Spring area was the worst, where persistent sand traps waited to snare passing autos. Rust, who had acquired a second homestead property near Pipe Spring, put in some work on the road along with Dee Woolley in advance of the 1915 summer season. Together they located favorable road alignments, plowed sections with harrows, and smoothed out sandy stretches with split-log draggers. "It is pretty tough to have to donate work on Arizona roads and furnish our own board," Rust wrote to Manderfield, "but we ought to do that much at least to balance the unceasing efforts that you are handing out gratis."[18]

On the highway's southern end, the Forest Service had small crews working on its section up on the Kaibab, clearing trees, pulling stumps, and blasting out rocks. But much work remained. Convict gangs from Utah had worked on the section of road south to Hurricane during the winter of 1914–1915. Beyond Hurricane the prison laborers, to Dee Woolley's dismay, had only done "a little scratching with the grader...leaving the very worst part of the road untouched." Woolley told Manderfield that if he had been in charge, "you may be sure the dirt would fly." Rust had planned to lay down clay over the sandy parts, and tried to enlist some local farmers to help, but they could not leave their planting at the start of the season.[19]

Regardless of road conditions, Manderfield hoped to assemble a complete touring package that would be advertised through the Union Pacific's publicists. He arranged with a man in Cedar City to drive tourists from Lund to Bright Angel Point and back for forty dollars. Rust was to provide guide services at the end of the road, including an overnight stay at the Woolley cabin. He or one of his men would take visitors on the trail ride down Bright Angel Creek, spend another night at Rust's Camp at the Colorado River, and return to the rim, all for ten dollars plus the cost of meals. With hotel stays *en route* in Kanab and

Cedar City, the total package would come to seventy-five dollars per person for a six-day adventure. This was still a heavy outlay at a time when an average worker might only earn that much in a month.

To ensure the wayfarer's comfort, Manderfield felt that the enterprise should have dedicated automobiles in good repair to carry passengers on the motor leg of the journey. Perhaps recalling his 1914 journey, he advised Rust of what was needed: "You of course appreciate it is of the greatest importance that nothing be left undone to make the trip of the prospective tourist pleasant. On account of weather and dust conditions at times, there will be some objectionable features, but these can be cut down to a minimum." To that end, Manderfield had been talking with representatives of the Wylie Way company, then in operation at Yellowstone National Park, "to endeavor to get them to join in with you and form a strong company and put on two new heavy cars this year." He foresaw that they would need "competent and safe drivers" and "one or two repair stations enroute... also to see that these cars are put in first class shape before the opening of the season."[20]

Rust's correspondence with Manderfield indicates his excitement about the possibility of working directly with the railroad. This alliance could solve both the transportation and publicity needs that had kept his Grand Canyon trail and tram disconnected from the rest of the world. In response to Manderfield's request for an itinerary, he typed up some paragraphs describing the journey. Rust lacked the preferred style of the railroad's copywriters, but his words betray his thoughts regarding the significance of a trip to the Grand Canyon. "Many have made pilgrimages to the south side—the Coconino side, the Santa Fe side," he wrote, "in a search for the original. But they have gone back home either disappointed or satisfied with counterfeit. Few indeed are those who have actually visited the spot where Moran received his inspiration." Rust was referring to the painter Thomas Moran, who in 1873 accompanied Major Powell on a survey of the North Rim from the Toroweap to Marble Canyon, sketching as he went.[21]

"I do not wish to be understood as trying to underrate the features on the southern side," Rust went on. "They are well worth a trip around the world. But in comparison to the northern side, they are mediocre." Here he was writing like a good railroad publicist. But he could not resist putting in a plug for his preferred schedule for seeing the canyon: "A week for the round trip! That is all it takes. Of course, two weeks would be better and four weeks better still and two months not too long in which to get acquainted with the chief of all natural wonders."

Clearly he was not entirely assimilated to the modern, see-it-in-a-hurry style of travel. He was trying, though, to adapt to the new mode:

But here is what the busy man can do in a week: Leave the City of the Saints Sunday evening at midnight, after the day's worship is over, and be carried south on the soothing sleepers of the Salt Lake Line to wake up in the edge of the desert.

You will get off at Lund about 10 in the morning where you will change to an automobile and be taken to Cedar City before noon. From there to Hurricane is a downgrade joy ride of less than two hours and then you are in the "Dixie" fruitlands, on the Rio Virgen. You must rest there an hour or so and in the cool of evening go on to Kanab by early bedtime. A fair start the next morning puts you into the Kaibab before noon. You notice the heat of the 20 mile desert beyond Fredonia and early in the afternoon, less than 48 hours from Salt Lake, you reach the rim of the Canyon, get your first view and linger till sunset under the spell of an awful, everchanging panorama. Back to a safe distance from the brink, you will be comfortably cared for in an easy camp, and if you have ever written a diary, you will make some expression before retiring to your blankets to dream. The next two days, you would very likely choose to go to the river, one day down and one day back, on horseback, to spend a night at the bottom. A side trip to Desert View (Atoko Point) on Greenland (Walhalla Plateau) and back to Kanab completes the fifth day, and the sixth takes you to Lund in time for the evening train which puts you to bed and wakes you up early on the seventh day, Sunday, all refreshed and full of inspiration for your Sabbath contemplations.

While Rust may have been willing to accommodate the "busy man" who had only a week for the trip, this was really far too little time in his estimation. When he wrote these lines he had already taken several parties on much longer excursions from Zion Canyon to the North Rim, and he allotted five days or longer just to sample the viewpoints along the Kaibab. Rust probably understood that Manderfield's business experience exceeded his and that his friend knew what sort of operation would attract tourists. But the plan did not get off the ground that year. Rust had no background in setting up a coordinated travel venture, and Dee Woolley, who was nearly seventy years old, may not have been interested in starting another business. It was not clear that Rust even intended to do the guiding himself. That summer, Aldus "Blondie" Jensen, who had cowboyed on the Kaibab and rode with Uncle Jim Owens after mountain lions, started leading horseback trips out of the Woolley cabin, both for his lion hunts and for guests wanting to take Rust's trail down to the river.[22] Dave also had a man at the river, usually Rees Griffiths, to meet parties coming down from the South Rim and assist them at Rust's tent camp on Bright Angel Creek. Dave seemed not to want to be pinned down to one location, and he did have a family and business in Kanab to attend to. The result, however, was that he passed up a chance to develop what could have become a highly successful tourist business, one that would profit immensely from the coming fame of the two great parks, Zion and the Grand Canyon.

The Wylie Company proved better able to get in gear. Founded in Yellowstone National Park in 1893 by William Wallace Wylie of Bozeman, Montana (interestingly, he was a school superintendent like Rust), the eight "Wylie Way" camps in Yellowstone featured tent cabins with wooden floors, colorfully striped canvas walls, and bathroom and dining facilities close by.[23] By providing an alternative to the expense and formality of hotels, the Wylie camps were the first to open the parks to mass-market tourism.

Wylie sold his Yellowstone operation in 1905, but he saw opportunities at the North Rim and at Zion Canyon even before they became national parks. H. H. Hays of the Wylie Company again accompanied Utah governor William Spry on another of Manderfield's publicity trips to these locations in 1916. Three other Union Pacific officials came along, as well as a vice-president of the Raymond & Whitcomb tour company of Boston. The railroad men were suitably impressed; Gerritt Fort, the Union Pacific's passenger traffic manager from its Chicago office, told reporters that "it is no exaggeration to say that there is no grander scenery in the United States than in the Virgin river country."[24] The party continued on to the North Rim, experiencing the usual bad roads across the Arizona Strip. Rust met the party near Pipe Spring and helped locate a team of horses to pull their cars through a washout just beyond the spring.

Hays was evidently impressed with the country, for in the spring of 1917 the Wylie Company opened a tent camp in Zion Canyon. This camp, similar to the ones at Yellowstone, was set among the pines and cottonwoods along the Virgin River just south of the present-day Zion Lodge, and was reached by a newly improved (that is to say, graded dirt) road coming up the Virgin River from Rockville and Springdale. The company worked out an arrangement with Chauncey and Gronway Parry of Cedar City to shuttle tourists to the camps in sturdy, nine-passenger National autos, calling their combined venture the "National Park Transportation and Camping Company." The first group of twenty tourists from Salt Lake City arrived at Zion that summer. The cost for the entire trip, including transportation from the rail stop at Lund, five meals, and two nights' stay in a tent cabin, came to $26.50.[25] This was substantially less than what Manderfield envisioned for the longer journey to the North Rim and Rust's Camp on the Colorado.

The Union Pacific continued to seek greater awareness of Little Zion, as it was still called locally. The great canyon of the Virgin River was beginning to attract national interest. Frederick Dellenbaugh's 1904 article in *Scribner's Magazine* was followed in 1917 by a mention in Enos A. Mills's book *Your National Parks*, in which he described the Mukuntuweap National Monument as having "as spectacular a cañon, and as stupendous an array of vast rock forms, as is to be found anywhere in the world."[26] Still, the poor road leading up the valley of the Virgin River kept tourist visitation that year to only three hundred. One of those visitors, however, was Acting Park Service Director Horace Albright, who came at the railroad's urging. He was the first Park Service official to see the canyon. It had no custodian as yet, which Albright remedied on the spot by appointing Springdale resident Walter Ruesch to the position. At that time, the agency's entire budget for its twenty-one national monuments amounted to just $3,500, from which all maintenance costs and salaries were to be paid. Ruesch, like other monument custodians, earned a dollar a month. Typically, Albright's monument caretakers derived their income from guiding tourists, for which they were sometimes granted an exclusive concession.[27]

Albright loved the Mukuntuweap's cliff walls, hanging gardens, and shadowed gorges, and following his visit he took a personal interest in the monument. He was instrumental in obtaining an executive declaration from President Woodrow Wilson in 1918 that enlarged the monument substantially and changed its name to Zion.[28] The new name was retained the following year when Congress passed Utah senator Reed Smoot's legislation designating the canyon and surrounding rims as Utah's first national park. The Grand Canyon also achieved national park status in 1919, but without inclusion of much of the forested lands on the Kaibab Plateau, owing to Forest Service opposition (the park boundary was expanded northward in 1927).

The Park Service was interested in publicizing its holdings, but the main effort for at least a few years came from the railroads and their supporters. In 1919, the United States Railroad Administration, a federal bureau set up two years previously to administer the nation's rail lines during wartime, issued a sixteen-page booklet on Zion as part of its National Park Series. The text and photos extolled the beauty of this great sandstone canyon and promised visitors that they could make the trip in comfort.[29]

National recognition of Zion Canyon and the North Rim finally put southern Utah on the map as a tourist destination, and the Union Pacific now had a partner in the National Park Service. Its director, Stephen T. Mather, understood the need for a public constituency for his new agency, which had to compete for funds and recognition with other Progressive-era bureaus such as the Forest Service. Getting people into the parks was thus a priority. This was reflected in one of the original statements on management policy for the new parks, which took the form of a letter to Mather from Interior Secretary Franklin Lane. The letter, which one historian noted was probably drafted by Mather, made it clear that these were not to be wilderness preserves, at least in their entirety. It stated that "every opportunity should be afforded the public, wherever possible, to enjoy the national parks in the manner that best satisfies the individual taste. Automobiles and motorcycles will be permitted in all the national parks; in fact, the parks will be kept accessible by any means practicable."[30]

By ensuring that the parks would be open to automobiles, Mather was actually changing prior policy in some instances. Yellowstone, for example, was off-limits to the new machines, as Bill Rishel, the *Salt Lake Tribune*'s motor explorer, discovered on a trip in 1911. After a difficult 340-mile trip from Salt Lake City, he found two uniformed soldiers blocking the park's west entrance. Rishel blamed the established horse-and-wagon franchisees for the closure and spent several years working to lift the ban. Not until the end of the 1915 summer season was the park opened to cars, and for another year the motorists had to purchase an expensive permit.[31]

With the advent of modern tourist camps and tour companies, Zion Canyon and the North Rim emerged from the shadows of America's West, no longer hidden places that enterprising travelers had to discover on their own. Henceforth their wonders would be advertised and interpreted in tourist brochures printed courtesy of enthusiastic boosters within the Union Pacific and its subsidiaries. The Wylie camps set the pattern for tourism at Zion and the North Rim. In 1928 the Union Pacific would build a major park hotel at Bright Angel Point, offering a standard of comfort heretofore available only at the El Tovar. Auto-based tourism continued to increase, although slowly at first. The Grand Canyon Highway, and indeed the automobiles themselves, remained in such doubtful shape that tourists needed considerable fortitude and advance planning to undertake the trip. As late as 1922, one writer complained of the "stony, rough, dusty and wholly unimproved" road south from Cedar City, and the equally bad road that led south from Fredonia—where "we paused to fill our tank with fifty-cent gas" before heading on up to the Kaibab Plateau.[32]

Rust continued to guide in Zion Canyon for almost another decade, camping in the open under a special arrangement he had worked out with the Park Service. The North Rim and the Kaibab also remained a favorite destination. He made these trips with individual clients, not busloads of tourists, reflecting his preferred style—outfitting each party according to its particular needs, and tailoring the itinerary in line with his guests' experience and interests. This highly personalized approach, not mass-market camps, would be the basis for Rust's enterprise. He took clients down to his river camp less often, usually only as part of some longer venture.

It seems clear that Rust had little interest in becoming a tourist mogul in the fashion of W. W. Wylie or the Parry brothers. His interests were always centered on the landscape. Providing comfortable lodging and transport for large numbers of tourists would have kept him from ranging far across the Plateau Province. Dave's clients came west not to be pampered in hotels or even in tent camps, but to see the land—and he meant to show it to them. Simply shuttling tourists to one or two viewpoints, however grand, would not do. He knew that the Colorado Plateau offered much more, and that it would take real effort on the part of its visitors to even begin to sample its wonders. By focusing on what he did best, he would carve out a unique niche among the Southwest's tourism promoters.

From the top there stretches before you as far as the eye
can see a panorama of highly colored temples, towers,
numerous other rockforms that have been chiseled and
sculptured by nature from the rock plateaus that centuries
ago made up the wilderness. Cutting through these fantastic rock canyons is the mighty Colorado. —Oh, I can't
describe it. Nobody can. You have to see it, and thank good-
ness the eye of the camera isn't strong enough to snap it.

DAVE RUST
Interview, KSL Radio, 1930s

AMERICANS HAVE ALWAYS regarded the undeveloped
public domain as the ground on which they could build their dreams—whether a
homestead, a ranch, or for those with higher sights, commerce and industry. The
Kaibab and the North Rim country brought out the hopes of many in southern
Utah with its verdant pastures and its inexhaustible forests. Dee Woolley added
tourism to the North Rim's possibilities, and by the second decade of the new
century others were catching on. How best to exploit this scenic marvel, though,
was still up in the air. J. H. Manderfield of the Union Pacific hoped to get a tourist stage running to the rim, with comfortable touring cars dropping off travelers
at rimside camps, where Rust and his guides could entertain them with horse
rides out to scenic viewpoints. Dave, though, never fully embraced this vision.
For him, the Grand Canyon was still a place to see by pack string, at a leisurely
pace, with no more than a handful of guests at a time. His approach, common
during the previous century, sought intimacy with the land rather than speed.

In the summer of 1914 Rust met a gentleman from back east who, more than
any other of his clients, embodied this Victorian style of adventuring. In April of
that year, Manderfield received a letter on the stationery of a New York City law
firm asking for information about traveling to the North Rim, Zion Canyon, and
the surrounding region. Its author, an attorney named George Corning Fraser,
was interested in geology and appeared to know what he wanted to see. Manderfield sent Fraser a copy of J. Cecil Alter's newspaper account of his 1913 trip to the
Kaibab and forwarded Fraser's letter to H. J. Doolittle, his agent at Lund. Here
was an opportunity, he told Doolittle, to set up a tour with an apparently well-
connected easterner—one that might lead to more business.

Missing no chance, Manderfield also forwarded a copy of Fraser's letter to Alter in Salt Lake City, suggesting that he send more information to this New Yorker. Alter offered encouraging words about the scenery to be found in the Zion–Grand Canyon region, and suggested that Dave Rust would be the best guide for such a trip: "Mr. Rust could receive you at the Mouth of Little Zion, Springdale, and pilot you through both Mukuntuweaps, for he has been through them all. He could also take you into the Toroweaps, and Kanab Canyons [*sic*] where the thrills are never equalled. He also owns a cabin and a watering place adjacent to Bright Angel Springs, in addition to a herd of horses. I hope you make the trip! It will be worth many times what it costs, if you like roughing it."[1]

Rust arranged to meet Fraser and his seventeen-year-old son, George Jr., at Toquerville on July 5. Rust was to provide transportation to Little Zion Canyon (the Mukuntuweap's local name), thence out to the Uinkaret Plateau and the Toroweap, far to the southwest, and finally outfit an extended foray across the Kaibab Plateau. Fraser made arrangements with William W. Bass, who operated a tourist camp and guide service on the South Rim, to meet them four weeks later at Bass's Colorado River cable crossing.[2]

Years later, Fraser allowed that he was a bit concerned when Rust showed up in Toquerville with two horses to carry the three of them. But Dave had decided to hire a wagon and driver to haul most of their gear, with one of the Frasers riding on it as they made their way up into the imposing reaches of the Mukuntuweap. Like any guide, he had to assess his clients' capabilities as they proceeded up the road and camped in the upper part of Zion Canyon. The first test came in the narrows of the North Fork of the Virgin River, where the canyon closed down to a passage only a dozen or so yards wide, confined between sheer sandstone walls that rose hundreds of feet high. In 1914 this gorge had no special cachet; it was simply a barrier to further horse travel. Heavy rains had swollen the North Fork to a considerable depth and the three of them, having left their mounts behind, were at times wading in cold water up to their chests. Rust was impressed that both of the Frasers could handle this difficult hike without complaint. True, his clients were used to riding horses, but this was an entirely new experience for East Coast flatlanders.

Fraser wanted to see more than the well-described scenery within the Mukuntuweap and Grand Canyon national monuments. He had majored in geology at Princeton, where he had undoubtedly come across Dutton's *Tertiary History*; by 1914 he owned his own copy and packed it along on his trip as a reference. He decided that a worthy goal would be to retrace Dutton's paths and examine the scenes with his own eyes from the same vantage points. He was especially taken with Dutton's tantalizing descriptions of the Uinkaret Plateau and the Toroweap valley, which lay to the west of the Kaibab Plateau, and he was determined to get out there. It was an ambitious itinerary to undertake in the heat of midsummer.

Dutton told of the long distances and scarce water in that region, but he also promised much for the amateur geologist. There were recent lava flows bounding the sides of the Toroweap, faults displayed with great clarity, and the incomparable architecture of the western Grand Canyon itself. Even the long ride from Kanab could be lovely, Dutton wrote, proceeding through a desert that was "not without its charms, however repulsive in most respects," and with camps that revealed "the towering fronts of the Vermilion Cliffs, ablaze with red light from the setting sun. To the eastward they stretch into illimitable distance, growing paler but more refined in color until the last visible promontory seems to merge its purple into the azure of the evening sky."[3]

Reaching the Toroweap on July 17, Rust and the Frasers stood at the brink of the sheer cliff that looked directly down at the Colorado River. Dutton had described the "fiery cascades" of lava that "shot down into the abyss and pursued their way many miles along the bed of the river." Just as interesting were the magma dikes clearly displayed in the sides of the canyon. Dutton showed how these were intruded into the surrounding sedimentary strata before the Colorado dug the Grand Canyon: "It is manifestly impossible that a dike of basalt could rise hundreds or even two thousand feet through solid limestone, with one edge of it protruding laterally out of the face of a scarp wall.... We know that basalts play curious pranks sometimes, but they always keep within the limits of possibilities."[4]

Fraser was all for hiking to the river near Lava Falls, but Rust cautioned that they still had far to go in the two weeks they had allotted. By now he must have been getting some sense of his new client's remarkable appetite for discovery. For a man who worked in a well-appointed Wall Street office, Fraser was having little difficulty getting around on foot or on horseback. An even harder trail lay ahead, though, at the end of their trip—one that would tax Rust's physical and mental stamina as well as the Frasers'. But before they tackled the Grand Canyon, Rust took his guests to his hometown of Kanab for a rest and to restock provisions. Then they headed up onto the Kaibab for the culmination of their trip.

At the Woolley cabin in Fuller Canyon they stockpiled some of their food and traded their tired horses for fresh mounts. Rather than descend to the Colorado on Rust's trail, they chose to explore the entire reach of the Kaibab Plateau, riding first to the tip of the Walhalla Plateau at Cape Final and Cape Royal, then west to Point Sublime and the Powell Plateau. Fraser kept careful notes of his trip, detailing the impressive geologic exposures they could see from these and other vantages.[5] They spent hours at each viewpoint, comparing the scene at hand with the descriptions in the geologic reports Fraser had brought along. Dutton, in particular, laid out the Canyon's geology in understandable form, with W. H. Holmes's brilliantly drawn atlas sheets a perfect complement to the text.

Among the features of interest from Cape Royal was the spectacular Great Unconformity, Powell's name for the huge gap in the geologic record between Precambrian and Paleozoic strata. In places in the eastern Grand Canyon, tilted strata of the Grand Canyon Supergroup (a name not in use at the time of Fraser's and Rust's visit) had been cleanly planed off in a lengthy erosion cycle, with the overlying Cambrian Tapeats Sandstone capping them. Dutton noted that this unconformity cropped up elsewhere in the West, but at the Grand Canyon it was an obvious and remarkable feature.[6]

Nowhere in Fraser's experience was there such a clear delineation of geologic processes. He was captivated by the structure of the canyon. While Rust's previous clients had enjoyed the scenic delights of the North Rim, none had been as thoroughly versed in earth science. He was intrigued with this approach to sightseeing—studying the details of the landscape instead of merely admiring the view. In his later essay "Genuine Travelers," he recalled how they made their observations:

The Fraser method is to manage to reach the most comprehensive viewpoint in the afternoon when the lights and contrasting shadows are best (sometimes this is accomplished by fast riding as if we were in a cougar chase), dismount and leave the horses and mules with the wrangler, seek out a smooth spot (invariably the same spot where the early map-makers had set up their bench-marks), spread out the topographic and geographic maps, lay out the barometer and the compass, have at hand such reports and bulletins as might apply, and then with binoculars and camera proceed to capture the landscape panorama. As the "game" advances and the shadows deepen, crackers and coffee are brought from camp not far away—not a minute must be spared from the dramatic performance until darkness draws the curtain. The next morning, the observations continue from daybreak to nine or ten o'clock, lingering to read the relationships from foreground to horizon.

He was especially struck by Fraser's insistence that they make camp right at the edge of the canyon, "our feet sticking out over the rim," as Rust put it. At Point Sublime, one of the most fabulous of the North Rim viewpoints, they made their beds on a rocky perch at the very end of the little peninsula, enjoying a 270-degree panorama. (Holmes's triptych of this colossal view, included in the atlas accompanying the *Tertiary History*, is considered today to be one of the finest renderings ever made of the Grand Canyon.) On previous trips Rust had made sensible camps back in the trees like any outdoorsman would, but he agreed that these cliff-edge camps were "the only way to see the real thing. No other party has done it this way unless perhaps one or two of those early explorers such as Dutton or Powell."[7]

Fraser had made plans to meet William Bass at his Shinumo Creek camp at the bottom of the Grand Canyon around August 30, following his and Rust's exploration of the Powell Plateau. Bass sent instructions to Fraser before the trip, explaining how he and Rust must make two signal fires on Swamp Point the night before they planned to meet. Bass would answer from the South Rim with two fires of his own, then ride down the next day to meet them. He had a cable-car crossing at the river that would serve to get the Frasers across the river. This cumbersome method of communication proved to have its drawbacks. On August 28 Rust and the Frasers camped at the rim of the Merlin Abyss at the head of Shinumo Creek, still some miles from Swamp Point and the head of Bass's trail at Muav Saddle. They did not plan to reach the river for three more days. After building a campfire that evening back from the rim, they were perplexed to see two answering fires across the canyon near Bass Camp. Their prearranged signal had gone off ahead of schedule, leaving them wondering what to do. They chose to complete their exploration of Powell Plateau and take their chances upon reaching the river. As it turned out, Bass set out for the river on the twenty-ninth to find no one there. He pinned a note to his tram and returned to the South Rim. At dusk on the thirty-first, Rust and the Frasers arrived at the river after a tiring descent of Muav Canyon to find the crossing deserted. In his journal, Fraser recorded his deep worry over whether he and his son could get up to the South Rim on foot and on their own.[8]

It was not an idle concern. Rust had shorted their food ration for the trek westward across the Kaibab, believing that they could certainly scare up some game. If they did not come up with a few grouse for dinner, he was not above shooting a deer, even though they were in the federally protected Kaibab Game Preserve. This was probably standard procedure among the men who used the Kaibab frequently, where a deer would not be missed if it were butchered discreetly. But Fraser was averse to breaking the rules, and their larder shrank alarmingly. Nor did much small game come to hand. By the time they reached the river they were completely out of food—and the Frasers had a long climb out.

Rust bade the Frasers goodbye early on the morning of September 1, then headed up the difficult trail to Muav Saddle. He worried about his clients and had no way to ascertain how they were making out. In a letter to George Fraser after the trip, he told of his heavy mood on the trail up out of the canyon. He rummaged up a can of peas at Bass's campsite on Shinumo Creek, which gave him enough energy to make the climb, but he "ate the peas begrudgingly to think you could not share them."[9] He knew that his duty as guide was to see to the welfare of his clients, and it troubled him that he had left them in a precarious state, even if through no real fault of his own. "Everything was blue," he told Fraser, "not only the blue lime but every other formation in the canyon turned indigo. I was as glum as a doughsinker, pretty well worn from the previous day's tramp and gaunt as a Navajo, but the cause of my glumness was not the fatigue or lack of necessary nourishment." Rather, his mind was stuck on the thought that "perhaps I had not done right by you people, no amount of food or rest can remove such a feeling."

Fortunately, Bass headed down from the South Rim again on September 1, meeting the Frasers on their way up and providing them with horses. Rust need not have worried, for the Frasers were resourceful travelers and would have made it to the rim even without Bass's help. Still, he was glad to reach the North Rim and see his signal fires answered that evening. He shot a rabbit and a grouse for his own dinner and "retired very much relieved, with the assurance that you were all OK. Had my fires not been answered, I should have gone into the canyon the next day and hunted out the trouble."

Upon returning home, Fraser wrote to Rust to "acknowledge your concise and intelligible dispatch of the 1st instant, consisting of three bright fires on Swamp Point. I assure you they brought us a good deal of relief, because we were considerably worried about your making that long trip up Muav Canyon empty and alone."[10] Rust realized that he had just completed an extraordinary trip with an unusual and gifted fellow. He had learned not just the specifics of Grand Canyon geology but a whole new way of looking at the region. From then on, he would encourage his clients to take a more intellectual approach toward scenery, viewing the landscape as the result of powerful forces that left clear traces for anyone to see. Dutton, Powell, and their successors would become Rust's companions on the trail. "The fact is," he told Fraser, "that from the Little Zion to the Powell Plateau, we have followed the wake of those distinguished pathfinders, seeing as they saw."[11]

Fraser also held his new trail companion in high esteem. They continued to correspond following their trip, exchanging photographs and discussing the great things they had seen. Rust sent Fraser a copy of the Pearl of Great Price, a collection of Joseph Smith's writings. Fraser, a book collector who owned an original edition of the Book of Mormon, appreciated the gift, even if he did not agree with all of its theological points. That December, recalling their trek across the Kaibab, he sent Rust a Remington .30 rifle, saying "I hope it may prove like yourself, true and accurate, and serviceable when you are hungry."[12] Rust treasured the gift.

The two men barely finished reminiscing over their Grand Canyon trip when they began to lay plans for their next adventure. Rust had been thinking of trying to float through Glen Canyon as a new kind of tourist venture, and proposed the voyage to Fraser in early 1915. "Your suggestion about the river trip appeals to me very strongly," Fraser replied, "and I have worked it out with the aid of Powell's and Kolb's accounts of that portion of the voyages, extending from the lower end of Cataract Canyon to Lee's Ferry."[13] He included a typed itinerary for such a trip, to be followed by a visit to the "Moqui Villages—the snake dance, etc. and thence to Flagstaff, or the petrified forest, or through House Rock Valley to the Kaibab and across Rust's tramway to El Tovar." But in April Fraser returned to his idea of following Dutton's tracks, proposing that he and Rust tour the Utah High Plateaus that summer. This they undertook in July and early August, leaving Rust's Glen Canyon tour for later.

Their six-hundred-mile journey included mountain climbing on the Fishlake Plateau, a chilly camp below the summit of Thousand Lake Mountain, a climb of Mount Ellen in the Henry Mountains, a long ride across the Aquarius and Markagunt plateaus, a tortuous traverse of the upper forks of Zion Canyon, and a final climb to a sunrise view from Pine Valley Mountain in southwestern Utah.

Fraser accomplished much of this journey with a balky horse; before the trip, he requested of Rust, "[D]o not let the stock get too fresh. I do not want to add horse-breaking to my other accomplishments."[14] Rust considered this and supplied Fraser with a painfully slow mount that impeded their journey.

The two men also discussed some potential business prospects. In the fall of 1915 Fraser took an interest in buying the Crawford ranch in lower Zion Canyon, located outside of the small Mukuntuweap National Monument. He asked for Rust's assessment of crop yields in the area and even considered bankrolling some other land acquisitions nearby, Rust to act as his local agent and tenant farmer. Nothing came of the deal, and so Dave was spared from having the property bought out by the federal government when Zion National Park was created in 1919.

In the summer of 1916 Rust took the Frasers on a long trek from Flagstaff, across the Grand Canyon, and over the northern part of the Navajo Indian Reservation. Rainbow Bridge was among their destinations, a landmark that had only become known to the world seven years earlier as a result of the Cummings-Douglass expedition, led by John Wetherill and the Paiute Nasja Begay. Fraser's wife Jane and his daughter Myra had planned to come along, but in June Myra contracted measles and she and her mother decided to stay home. Fraser was disappointed, but he explained that "I prefer that she go through them at home, rather than in some Indian pueblo along the Santa Fe lines, or even on the salubrious Kaibab, though, in the latter contingency, I believe she would benefit from your resourceful care."[15]

Their Navajo trip put Rust in country he had not seen before, and the two men (again accompanied by George Fraser Jr.) were unable to trace a direct trail east from Rainbow Bridge. They wandered in and out of gigantic sandstone canyons and stumbled into Monument Valley, then an almost unknown destination. At one point, as they surveyed the terrain from the rim of another huge canyon, Fraser remarked in his journal that "we were lost, and glad of it, for if we had stayed on the trail, we never would have come this way."[16]

At the end of their trip in Bluff, Utah, the Frasers continued north by motorcar while Rust returned home across the reservation. The principal of the high school in Bluff, Dolph Andrus, heard the Frasers tell of the scenes they had encountered along the way: "They went so far as to say that in all their travels in foreign lands they had seen nothing to equal it." He wrangled an invitation to accompany Rust on the return trip. Dave wrote afterward that he and Andrus "rode straight south regardless of road into the arms of the Monumental Valley. Shook hands with the 'mittens' and filled our canvases to overflowing with monuments in every direction.... The Navajo Mountain shows his round head to the North-west and with the Square Rock in front we have certain landmarks to guide us on a trail we do not know." He observed that Monument Valley was "the great scenic ground of the region & should be reached by auto from Bluff & Kayenta." An-drus would accomplish this feat within the year, and his account of the journey would bring unexpected benefits for Dave.[17]

Following their Navajo trip, Rust and Fraser continued their friendly and remarkably intimate correspondence. Dave cherished their growing friendship, no doubt impressed that a man of Fraser's means and education regarded him as an equal. Fraser was particularly taken with Rust's competence as a pathfinder, in comparison with his own inexperience. "I reflect upon your accomplishments for four weeks," he wrote after their Navajo trip, "taking care of and bringing safely through all sorts of vicissitudes, six horses, one mule, and two dudes without the loss of even a stick out of the shaving soap box, or a nail out of the blacksmith out-fit, or a grain of Indian meal out of the flour sack." In a letter to J. H. Manderfield, Fraser remarked on Rust's "knowledge of the plains and of woodcraft, his unfailing good temper and resourcefulness.... Besides being a good scout, he is an educated and cultivated gentleman and is as agreeable a companion as one could find."[18]

Their backgrounds could not have been more different. Fraser had grown up in a privileged New York family, making trips as a youth to Europe and the Mid-dle East with his parents. His father was an amateur archaeologist and partici-pated in excavations in Egypt, during which George wandered the countryside. Where Rust had learned horsemanship out of necessity, Fraser had grown used to the saddle while riding across the Holy Land and visiting sites such as Lake Galilee and ancient Jericho. Even at this historic site, the young Fraser's attention was drawn to an exposed cliff, and his journal describes the geologic cross section he saw.[19] He would have plenty to interest him in the Colorado Plateau, where the entire landscape was open to view.

By 1917 Rust's guiding horizons had expanded well beyond the Grand Canyon, the Kaibab Plateau, and Zion Canyon. In George Fraser's company he had ex-plored the length of the Utah High Plateaus and the breadth of the Colorado Plateau. Fraser wrote to Rust in March of that year to outline their next trip together. He intended it to be as strenuous as their previous three outings. "I am perfectly certain," he wrote, "that no dude ranch or regular tourist route is going to satisfy me until I become a little more decrepit."[20] In fact, with his son doing wartime work in an iron foundry, Fraser felt that he and Rust "alone with three horses and the mule ought to make pretty good time."

There was plenty of new country to investigate. "How would you like to explore the Circle Cliff desert southeast of Escalante," he wrote, "look over the cliff at the southerly end of Fifty Mile Mountain, and cross the river at the Crossing of the Fathers, and go to the White Canyon Bridges, or instead make for St. George and see the Grand Canyon from the Grand Wash Cliffs and the base of the Shivwits?" These were ambitious plans, covering territory that most Americans had never heard of. Any of these destinations would have enticed Rust, and much of the country, notably the Escalante canyons, would have been new to him. But the martial fever growing across the nation caused Fraser to reconsider. On May 10, one month after America's entry into the European war, he told Rust, "I should state unequivocally and plainly that for me there is nothing doing in the way of travel this summer." There was simply too much uncertainty in the financial markets to allow a long absence from his office. Noting that after the war they might again resume their explorations, he offered a hopeful apology: "Please say you are disappointed at my reluctant decision, but satisfied it is right."[21]

By way of making amends, Fraser referred a new client to Rust. Le Roy Jeffers was an avid world traveler and lecturer, known for his mountaineering ascents in Europe and the western states. Fraser knew him through a mutual friend. He told Rust that Jeffers must be "some punkins" because of the letters he used after his name, denoting his rank as a member of the American Alpine Club and as a Fellow of the Royal Geographical Society of Great Britain. Fraser, upon meeting Jeffers, found him a bit on the egotistical side, and thereafter referred to him in his letters to Rust only as "the F. R. G. S."

That summer Jeffers came west to Utah and linked up with Rust for a tour of Zion, the North Rim, and Bryce Canyon. He made an unusual client. Besides his lofty rank, he was a strict vegetarian—Rust recalled that "his interpretation of the commandment not to kill included animals" and that he "turned his face away in resentment when I shot a grouse for dinner."[22] He was reluctant to ride horseback out of concern for the animal and, according to Rust, was unwilling to use a spur. Such views, needless to say, were not commonly appreciated in the Southwest.

After visiting Zion on the new road that had recently been opened to automobiles, Rust took Jeffers out via Hurricane and Pipe Spring to the Kaibab Plateau. There they virtually duplicated Rust's 1914 trip with George Fraser, stopping at Cape Royal, Cape Final, Naji Point and Atoko Point on the Walhalla Plateau, then heading west to Point Sublime and Dutton Point on the Powell Plateau.[23] Jeffers probably did not endear himself to Rust when, upon reaching Dutton Point, he took only a cursory look at the panorama that had enthralled Rust and Fraser three summers before. Dave's son Jordan, who was now old enough to help out as wrangler, recalled that Jeffers returned to the horses after ten minutes and said, "Well, I have seen it. Let us go." (Jordan adopted this phrase as a way of teasing his father on subsequent trips.)[24] Still, Jeffers must have been somewhat impressed with the view, for he described it in his 1923 book *The Call of the Mountains* as "one of the most comprehensive and satisfying panoramas of the canyon." He seems to have enjoyed his explorations of some of the lesser-known viewpoints along the North Rim as well, remarking (as a result of Rust's comments, most likely) that "only about a dozen travelers, including the U.S. Geological Survey, had stood upon them."[25]

After a stop in Kanab, Jeffers and Rust headed north to Panguitch by auto, getting out to push their vehicle through the sand hills north of town. Their goal was the view from the eastern edge of the Paunsaugunt Plateau, which Rust had yet to see close up. At Panguitch they consulted with the forest supervisor, J. W. Humphrey, about the condition of the road east from the Sevier Valley up onto the plateau. Humphrey assured them that cars could make it and encouraged them to try. In 1915 he had seen a great array of colorful fluted spires at the head of a small drainage above the town of Tropic—one named after a local cattleman named Ebenezer Bryce. Humphrey was already trying to raise interest in the area and had arranged for a Forest Service photographer to document it.[26]

Rust had just missed seeing Bryce Canyon in 1915 with George Fraser, and the scenic delights there were strangely unknown. Members of the Wheeler Survey, including the geologist G. K. Gilbert, had visited the locality in the 1870s and recorded the first descriptions and drawings of its brilliant pinnacles. Clarence Dutton, in his 1880 *High Plateaus* report, depicted the "mighty ruined colonnade" of the Pink Cliffs in the upper Paria River amphitheater, where "standing obelisks, prostrate columns, shattered capitals, panels, niches, buttresses, repetition of symmetrical forms, all bring vividly before the mind suggestions of the work of giant hands."[27] Dutton surveyed the Paria country from the southern end of the Paunsaugunt, a tremendous viewpoint to be sure, but not one that gave an intimate view of the smaller amphitheaters along the eastern edge of the plateau that have since become famous. Dutton's attention seemed to focus on the Table Cliff ramparts to the northeast, and it was there that Fraser and Rust sought their views in 1915.

Thomas Moran contributed a drawing of Bryce's spires, titled simply "Pink Cliffs—Eocene—Paunsagunt," to Dutton's *Tertiary History*, which was published in 1882; this illustration by the famous artist was based on a photograph by the Powell Survey artist W. H. Holmes. A government surveyor named T. C. Bailey was working in the area in 1876 and recorded the view into the Bryce amphitheater, where he saw "thousands of red, white, purple, and vermilion colored rocks, of all sizes, resembling sentinels on the walls of castles, monks and priests in their robes, attendants, cathedrals and congregations."[28]

These descriptions ought to have elicited some interest in the area, but poor roads and a general lack of publicity kept most visitors from reaching the views at Bryce. In 1916 the Union Pacific railroad, tipped off by the Forest Service, published an article on the wonders there in its magazine *Outdoor Life*. The *Salt Lake Tribune* would print an extensive article on Bryce in August 1918, titled "Utah's New Wonderland." Its author, Oliver J. Grimes, marveled at how this scenic gem had slipped past anyone's awareness. But no wonder: Grimes, too, had trouble finding the right road to the overlook. Stopping to ask a local cattleman how to get to it, he was told, "'Search me.... It's over to the south there somewhere.'"[29]

Jeffers described the scene in an article that appeared in *Scientific American* the following year. His "Temple of the Gods in Utah" was the first description of Bryce Canyon in the national press. He and Rust made their way through forest and meadows where no road signs marked the way; Dave's general recall of the plateau from his earlier trip sufficed. The views lived up to the forest supervisor's promise. Continuing Dutton's architectural metaphor, Jeffers called Bryce "a vast city of prehistoric ruins" whose coloring and sculpture looked like "the stage setting for a fairy opera." Dave led him down the steep, trailless slopes below the rim, where they explored the intricately cut walls. "One may wander for hours in this maze of canyons," Jeffers wrote, "studying the many colored walls and gazing upward at the narrow ribbon of blue sky.... [F]rom below the walls and towers have all the reality of castles, or elsewhere resemble the gigantic temples of India."

After surveying the main amphitheaters at Bryce, Rust and Jeffers headed south along the Paunsaugunt, where they inspected the flat-topped natural bridge located midway down the plateau. Dave would feature this little bridge on many subsequent trips. As Bryce Canyon grew in the nation's awareness, he was well positioned to guide clients there. In 1920 a local settler named Ruby Syrett built a small, rustic lodge on a parcel of former state-owned land close by the main viewpoint above Bryce Canyon.[30] Rust used the lodge as a jumping-off point for some of his longer pack trips.

Meanwhile, efforts were underway within the state of Utah to gain national recognition for Bryce. Building on the publicity from Jeffers's article, the Utah legislature in 1919 memorialized Congress to create a "Temple of the Gods National Monument."[31] Rust's friend J. Cecil Alter published an article that year in *Improvement Era*, also titled "The Temple of the Gods." This reached a more limited circulation, but the way was clear for tourists to begin enjoying Bryce. By 1923 the traffic was sufficient to induce the Utah Parks Company, a subsidiary of the Union Pacific Railroad, to buy the Syrett property and build a larger tourist camp. That year President Warren Harding signed a declaration establishing Bryce Canyon as a national monument under the administration of the Forest Service. Initially the monument covered only 2,320 acres—less than four square miles—leaving the remainder of the Paunsaugunt Plateau open to timbering and livestock use. Harding visited Bryce Canyon as well as Zion National Park that summer on the trip which later saw his illness and death.[32] Congress passed legislation the following year to create a "Utah National Park," providing for its transfer to the Park Service within the Department of the Interior. This was completed in 1928, when the park's name was changed back to Bryce Canyon.

Rust's 1917 excursion with Le Roy Jeffers opened up some interesting new territory for future trips, but little else in the way of guiding was happening while the war was on. He had plenty of other work. His farm property near Pipe Spring occupied much of his time over the next decade and became a sort of adjunct to the Rusts' home in Kanab. He kept as many as a hundred head of cattle there, and at times raised Angora goats.[33] Eventually he engaged a friend named Thomas Rauch, who had worked with him on the Grand Canyon tram, to live and work there as a caretaker.

Rust also continued to take an interest in dry farming on his acres east of Kanab. In 1917 he encouraged his fellow farmers to enter a contest sponsored by the LDS Church to see who could raise the most potatoes on a single acre of land. The contest was part of a national campaign to produce food for the war effort, and the Church offered a one-thousand-dollar prize to the winner—an enticing sum in those days. A man in Rust's LDS stake named Charles Pugh took the prize, growing 825 bushels on his well-watered farm located in the high country thirty miles north of Kanab.[34] Ironically, Rust would be credited with the prize owing to an erroneous report in *Improvement Era*. Rust dutifully corrected the mistake, noting that he was involved only to the extent of certifying Pugh's record to the church authorities.

In the fall of 1916 the Democratic Party of Kane County needed a man to run for the Utah state legislature, and few qualified candidates could be found in the predominantly Republican district. Rust was well known throughout the county, and the local party leaders persuaded him to switch parties and stand for election. As happens in committees, he was nominated before being asked. He accepted the call, he recalled later, in the spirit of fun as much as out of civic duty.[35] He attended a few political rallies with the rest of the party's ticket, letting others make most of the speeches, and spent no money on the race, since he did not expect to win. An unexpected Democratic landslide in Utah, led by wartime votes for Woodrow Wilson, allowed Rust to edge out his opponent, Joseph Swapp, by just five votes. Local officials had called the election in Swapp's favor before a box of ballots from an outlying town gave Rust the margin. It was "sheer luck," Rust wrote, "no management to it." George Fraser offered his congratulations, taking note of temperance efforts underway in Utah. "I suppose the result of your legislative efforts during the winter will be to make Milford as dry as the Kaibito Desert, and to drive those who would be cheerful in southwestern Utah to Caliente [Nevada]."[36]

The legislature convened the following January in Salt Lake City, with Rust serving on the appropriations, education, and public roads committees. His main goal was to secure additional state funding for road construction in southern Utah, and he proposed that roads be built to each county seat in the state. He also introduced legislation to complete the Grand Canyon Highway, envisioning it as a loop route from Salt Lake City through Cedar City, Hurricane, and the Arizona Strip to the North Rim, then returning via Kanab, Panguitch and Richfield. He told the *Washington County News* during the session that "The Yellowstone-Grand Canyon highway would do more to advertise the resources of the state than anything." His measure did not win approval, but he was able to secure the use of convict labor for road work during the winter season. He exercised his skeptical judgment on numerous appropriations when he felt they did not meet the test of the public good. "It was really great sport to decapitate some 'by request' pet measure," he recalled. He felt that the experience gave him an appreciation of the state's government. By coming "in close contact with the officials of the Commonwealth, I learned that they are not angels," he wrote afterward, "yet I learned, too, that they are deserving of confidence and respect and a fair hearing before conviction." Rust served a single term, losing re-election in 1918 by a considerable margin to William W. Seegmiller, who had long been active in local and state politics.[37]

In August 1917, with tourist travel to the region diminishing, Dave indulged a dream he had long held of showing the Grand Canyon to his parents. He wrote to George and Eliza, asking them if they would travel down from their home in Manti to see the great wonder that had occupied three years of his life. George Rust was eighty-three years old; Eliza was seventy-nine. Dave's niece Ethel Jensen joined her grandparents, and her account comprises the only written record of a Rust family outing.[38]

George, Eliza, and Ethel took the train south from Manti to Marysvale, where they boarded an old mail truck. Ethel noted that "the driver was a congenial old codger, badly in need of a bath and a shave." George was given a seat up front by the driver. Eliza and Ethel sat on boxes of goods, snugly wedged in between their luggage. Mail sacks served as a backrest.

Dave and Harold Bowman, a young Kanab friend, met the group in Panguitch, where they spent the night. The next day, after transferring to Bowman's battered Dodge, they headed for Kanab. The late-summer wet season was in progress, and with rain falling, the road grew steadily worse. When their vehicle got stuck near Long Valley Junction, Dave went to fetch help, returning with a farmer who claimed to be Butch Cassidy's brother. They made it only a few miles farther that afternoon, stopping to camp in the field of a friendly ranch owner.

Taking one's parents on a lengthy outing is always a chancy endeavor, especially if the accommodations are less than ideal. George Rust had spent many nights in the open and had little further use for discomfort. After overnighting in Kanab, they were joined by Ruth, Dave's brother Will and his family, and another family of Kanab neighbors for the trip to the Kaibab. Will was not feeling well, so they took a long stopover at Jacob Lake. Everyone enjoyed the cool air and scented pines of the plateau, and George was delighted to see one of the Kaibab's fabled tassle-eared squirrels.

Leaving Will and his family at Jacob Lake, they proceeded through De Motte Park and down Robbers Roost Canyon to the Woolley cabin. The day's storms cleared by evening and the chill mountain air settled into Fuller Canyon. Dave and his family made themselves at home in the cabin while the others sought the tents at the new Wylie camp a few miles away near Bright Angel Point. A cold night spent on a spartan canvas cot did little for George Rust's spirits. The next morning, upon reaching Bright Angel Point, he voiced many a diffident tourist's complaint: "'I can't see why in tarnation Dave had to drag us out here just to see this. I've lived around canyons most of my life, and I can't see this one is so different.'"

Even Eliza complained that she couldn't see the Colorado River as she had expected. Dave, though, had been around tourists before, and he was not going to let pass this opportunity to show his parents something of the canyon that meant so much to him. Ethel Jensen recalled Dave's bravura performance that morning:

"Come with me, Pa, I want to show you my canyon." He helped his father to his feet and steered him to a gorgeous lookout near Bright Angel Point. Eliza and Ethel tagged after them. They stood at the brink of his marvel of marvels.

"Be careful of your step," warned Dave. "It's a mile to the bottom.

"I suppose you want to know something about those Heathen Gods standing out there? Every last one of them, whether it be a spire, pyramid, or tower, has a name. Clarence Dutton named a host of them. Fresh from India and China, he came as a Government Surveyor to the Grand Canyon. He could see a marked resemblance between the Oriental Gods and Temples and the mimical forms that rose from the canyon depths.

"See that massive form a little to our left? Note the coloring; her reddish gray cap, stripes of greenish brown, even a subtle hint of yellow and purple, gorgeous, isn't she?"

"I think you are a bit color blind," interposed Eliza. "What do you mean, she?"

"Oh! This is Deva," explained Dave. "She is the wife of the Great Hindu God, Shiva. He stands over to the west about three miles. The story goes,

Deva got mad at Shiva and moved over here by Brahma, the big Hindu Boss, the evolver of the Universe. Now, isn't that just like a woman?" Dave's extravagant story had the desired effect. George S. smiled—almost.

"Just beyond Brahma, stands Zoroaster, founder of [that] ancient religion." Dave went on, pointing out buttes, temples, and spires as to color and identity. He had a way of breathing life into these huge masses of limestone; transforming the illusory into the real.

It was a proud moment for Dave as he showed his parents the landscape that was by now familiar to him. Ethel Jensen wrote of Dave's "fierce devotion" to the North Rim, expressed on this trip and in later conversations. "The North Rim is mine, clean, virgin, untrampled, just the way God left it," he asserted. The average tourist might enjoy the pampering service and luxurious amenities at the El Tovar, but to Dave, the genuine encounter with the canyon lay in riding rough trails and camping at its superb overlooks.

Dave did not seem too concerned about the competing camp outfit at the North Rim, at least by Ethel Jensen's recollection. He felt there was plenty of room for more tourists. What he could not have realized was how thoroughly the North Rim country would change within just a few years. The Wylie tent camp represented a fundamental shift in regional tourism, despite Dave's equanimity. Located close to the rim at the site of the present-day parking lot at Bright Angel Point, the camp was under the supervision of W. W. Wylie's daughter, Elizabeth McKee. She and her husband saw to the needs of as many as twenty-five guests, far more than Rust and his associates could handle at their tiny cabin in Fuller Canyon. The Wylies also offered trail rides and auto trips out to the Walhalla Plateau.[39] This operation was in a better position to take advantage of the growing numbers of tourists arriving by automobile on the newly completed road to Bright Angel Point. It is possible that Dave understood this, for he was already taking his parties farther and farther afield. The Grand Canyon Auto Road, as Dee Woolley and his son-in-law hoped, was indeed opening up the North Rim country. But while the world was discovering this scenic gem, Dave was already looking elsewhere.

9 | The School of the Desert

> Boys are the raw material. What can we do to make the most
> of their possibilities? Since there is no such thing as manhood-
> mills, that will take them in and turn them out men, it must be
> accomplished by painstaking development, chiefly under their
> own direction. Every boy has the choosing of what he shall be.
>
> DAVE RUST
> "The Worth of a Boy" (1911)

WITH THE WAR IN EUROPE consuming most Ameri-
cans' efforts, Rust found little in the way of guiding following his 1917 trip with
Le Roy Jeffers. He still wanted to stir up some business if he could, so early in 1918
he arranged to have a few lines put in a Salt Lake City travel newsletter called the
Good Roads Automobilist. It said simply that

> D. D. Rust, of Kanab, Utah, can be secured with his pack train or teams for
> trips to the Grand Canyon, Cliff Ruins, Rainbow Natural Bridge, etc.

This was about as much advertising as he engaged in. It might have seemed
odd for a horse packer to advertise in an automobile magazine, but there was not
so great a distinction between mechanized and horseback travel as there is today.
The machines traveled faster, but perhaps only for a few dozen miles before they
broke down or got stuck. And automobiles were extremely limited in where they
could go—from both lack of roads and the absence of service stations. Even basic
maps were scarce. Horse and mule were still the most reliable means to get into
the backcountry. Dave was willing to use vehicles on occasion, but he relied on
his packs and saddles for the real outback.

Many adventurers, though, were attracted to the mobility, excitement, and
challenge that the new machines promised—especially when they could take
them into new territory. Dolph Andrus of Bluff, Utah, who had ridden with Rust
on his return westward across the Navajo Reservation in 1916, set out the following May to repeat the trip by auto. His companion, a Salt Lake City dentist
named W. H. Hopkins, wrote a detailed road log of the route for the same issue
of the *Good Roads Automobilist* in which Rust placed his ad.[1] The roads were
poor, but Hopkins described them in optimistic terms, suggesting that the grand

pinnacles of Monument Valley and the remote trading posts on the reservation were available to be seen in relative comfort. Hopkins and Andrus were probably the first to traverse some of these wagon roads and desert tracks in a machine. That the Navajo country was not quite ready for large numbers of auto tourists was suggested by log entries such as at the arroyo of Laguna Creek, where Hopkins advised that "Wetherill at Kayenta, half a mile away, will provide team to tow you across and up the other side."

Road logs such as this were intended to encourage would-be adventurers to load gas cans and camping mattresses in their touring cars and set out for the hinterlands of the Southwest. The Hopkins article, however, happened to land in the hands of a young man from New York City who was ready for a different kind of adventure. Charles P. Berolzheimer was the son of a prominent German immigrant family that owned the Eagle Pencil Company. Charles's father, Philip Berolzheimer, had held the post of Chamberlain, or treasurer, of New York City and counted as his companions many of its Tammany Hall leaders. In 1908 Philip purchased a Georgia coastal island from an employee, turning it into an exclusive vacation retreat. His son Charles enjoyed visits to the island from an early age and developed an appreciation for the birds and animals that abounded there. Swimming in the ocean, pursuing sea turtles on the beach at night, and fishing in the island's backwaters all instilled in him a love of the outdoors.[2] It was only natural that he would dream of the infinitely greater adventures that were still possible in the western states.

The young Berolzheimer acquired the Hopkins article as part of his research for a trip he was planning with his longtime friend, Arnold Koehler Jr., also of New York City. When Charles was about to graduate from high school, his parents told him that as a gift he could have a vacation anywhere he wanted to go. Perhaps they were assuming he would go to Europe, as many children from wealthy families did in the tradition of the Grand Tour. Charles, however, was drawn west, and with Arnold planned an itinerary that included Yellowstone, Zion Canyon, Mesa Verde in southwestern Colorado, and Natural Bridges National Monument in southeastern Utah.

The boys wrote to the newly created National Park Service for information. None other than Acting Director Horace Albright wrote back, telling them that his agency had no personnel on the ground between Zion and Mesa Verde; indeed, he had no information at all on the territory of southern Utah that they planned to traverse.[3] Yellowstone, of course, was well established as a tourist designation, but the national monuments in the Colorado Plateau were barely mapped, let alone patrolled by uniformed rangers.

Albright did pass along a copy of the *Good Roads Automobilist* containing Hopkins's "Monumental Valley" road log. The boys were entranced. If the Navajo country was so wild that only one automobile had been across it, surely this was where one could find the Old West. They noticed the listings of guide services in the region, among them the same John Wetherill that stood ready to pull out stuck motors at Kayenta, Zeke Johnson of Blanding, and Dave Rust. The boys wrote to Rust, asking if he could guide them across the Navajo Reservation in the week they had allotted. Rust politely responded that if they wanted to make such a trip across the desert, they had better allow three full weeks for the horseback portion alone.[4] The country was even bigger than they imagined.

Though it meant reshuffling their itinerary, Charles and Arnold jumped at the chance to see what Albright described as "one of the wonderlands of America, and... one of the few remaining places that still possess many of the institutions of the wild West." They dropped Yellowstone from their plans and wrote back to Rust, confirming their desire to make the exciting journey across the Navajo deserts.

They were probably lucky to choose Rust as their guide. Berolzheimer and Koehler were undoubtedly the youngest men to attempt this trip as tourists, and they had no experience of the desert. The midsummer heat in this region could be extreme, and they would need someone who knew how to keep excitement from slipping over into danger. John Wetherill and Zeke Johnson, the only other men regularly operating in the area, were highly competent guides and were more familiar with southeastern Utah and the Navajo Reservation, but Rust had long experience working with young people. He enjoyed mentoring growing youths and took his duties seriously. In his work as a school principal, and later as a school superintendent, he had closer contact with students than would a typical modern administrator. He retained his strong interest, developed through years of classroom teaching and coaching sports, in what was then called "youth culture." This referred not to fashions of dress and attitude but to the carefully structured guidance of young people toward the ideals of the day.

Early twentieth-century America had only recently emerged from the strictures of Victorian society, in which young people were seen as small-scale models of adults and were subject to rather rigid training as to knowledge, religion, morals, and vocation. New ideas were afloat in intellectual circles as part of the Progressive reforms, but while its adherents favored suffrage for women and emancipation from slave-labor working conditions, the proper upbringing of young people was still very much on the table. Rust was no exception, and he put down some of his thinking in a lightly humorous essay for *Improvement Era*, which won a twenty-dollar prize offered by the magazine in 1911. Titled "The Worth of a Boy," Rust's essay stressed the need to provide young people with the proper social and cultural environment. "We may coax, persuade and reason," he wrote, "we may preach and scold and threaten; we may pet or lead or drive; we may cuff or kick or censure—most of which are likely to be ineffective in bringing out the most precious values of a boy." In his years of teaching Rust had plenty of chances to employ all of these tactics and measure their success. His own children recalled him as something of a disciplinarian; his youngest son, Quentin, said that when it came to doing chores, "it was his way or the highway." But, aiming for his ideals, Rust urged adults to "so shape [a boy's] opportunities and environments that he may develop into his afterself, the man he might become, the best there is in him."[5] Rust was not willing to concede that "bad seed" inevitably produced delinquents; he aligned himself with the forward-thinking educators who believed that the child's surroundings could be structured for optimum results. His progressivism was not out of line with the Mormon belief that a community of like-minded individuals could shape the future of every young person in its membership.

As a reference to his own abilities as a guide, Rust gave George Fraser's name to Berolzheimer and Koehler. In May they stopped by Fraser's Manhattan law office; Fraser reported back to Rust that "they are tremendously keen on making the trip with you and were most concerned to get from me some arguments to use on their parents so as to obtain permission."[6] Fraser cautioned Rust that the boys were "wholly inexperienced" and that he should probably take along an assistant. Dave made tentative plans to hire a man, but wound up bringing only his son Jordan, who at sixteen was old enough to help wrangle the horses and be a companion for the boys. On July 5, 1919, Dave and Jordan set out west from Kanab with two extra riding horses and a pack mule, heading for Zion Canyon, where they would meet their guests. Whatever these young men were made of, it would soon be tested in the incredible slickrock wilderness they would be entering.

Two days' riding brought Dave and Jordan to Springdale, a tiny community at the southern edge of Little Zion's great canyon. The town's role as the gateway to Utah's most popular national park was still in the future, for Little Zion was only then emerging from obscurity. Six weeks before Dave and Jordan arrived, Senator Reed Smoot introduced a bill to expand what was (as of 1918) Zion National Monument into a national park. The bill would become law that November, and southern Utah would at last have its own tourist draw to compete with the Grand Canyon and Yellowstone. Already a few tourists were checking out the immense sandstone canyon, lured by the comforts promised at the new Wylie Way camp in the valley.

On the morning of July 8, leaving Jordan in Springdale to look after the horses, Rust hitched an auto ride up to the Wylie camp to meet the boys and help them pack necessities for the trip. His first impression was dubious. "When I saw them I tried to talk them out of it," Rust recalled later. "The Navajo country was the wildest place in the world."[7] The boys would not be dissuaded, however; Charles especially was determined to have a go at it.

Like many well-educated young people, Berolzheimer and Koehler kept journals of their travels. These they collected in a series of scrapbooks, imprinted with the official seal of their own secret society, the "4000 by 2 Club." Two volumes of these journals describe their western trips in 1919 and 1920, when they returned for another adventure with the Rusts.[8] The boys took turns writing each day's entry. Since Dave did not keep records of these trips, their journals provide an invaluable picture of two of his longest journeys.

Dave decided that they did not have time to explore Zion's sights; he was anxious to get started on their desert trek. Taking the boys back to Springdale, he and Jordan loaded their packbags, got their guests saddled, and headed for the East Fork of the Virgin River, climbing out of the canyon via a rough, precarious route called the Old Shunesburg Trail. If this leg of the trip was to be a gradual introduction to the land, the boys must have wondered what they were in for. Charles's photos show them leading their horses up the steep crossbeds of the Navajo Sandstone, headed for the rim of Parunuweap Canyon. They made a dry camp on a ledge below the rim. The next morning, thirsty and with no morning meal, they climbed on, leading their animals until they reached easier ground. One narrow defile in the sandstone was tight enough to hang up the mule in midair by its pack bags. Arnold wrote that "to cheer us up Mr. Rust began telling us pleasant stories of how men had lived for days and days with no water at all."

They reached Kanab the next day. Dave put his guests up at the "Hotel Highway," which Dee Woolley owned and Will and Sarah Rust operated. The boys enjoyed a picture show that evening—their last taste of civilization for more than two weeks. Dave needed most of the next day to pack for the trip. The few settled outposts along the way would have little in the way of supplies, so he had to make sure they took enough tinned and dried food to supplement the mutton he hoped to procure. He would have to make whatever field repairs were needed to the packsaddles, camp gear, and other essentials. With waterholes uncertain and many miles apart, they would make do with a few one-gallon wooden water kegs and a larger keg for the animals.

Finally, at six, they left town, striking southeast toward the low shoulder of the Kaibab Plateau, some twenty miles distant. They followed the new Grand Canyon Auto Road part of the time, but when it suited them they wandered through the sage-covered flats and washes that led gradually upward. Riding out of the day's heat, they continued under a full moon until nearly midnight.

The next morning's climb to the summit of the plateau took only a few hours. The scene that greeted them at the edge of the East Kaibab monocline would have thrilled any young man who had read of the lonesome desert wastes. Here the mountain dropped off abruptly, not in a sudden cliff, but in a graceful swoop reflecting the dramatic flexing of the earth's crust. At the foot of the monocline lay the stone-dry House Rock Valley, bounded on the north by the long line of the Vermilion Cliffs. Charles and Arnold excitedly recognized this as one of the scenes from Zane Grey's *Heritage of the Desert*.

As they followed the wagon road beneath the cliffs, they could see how the desert sloped gradually to the southeast, where a meandering trench sunk into the limestone flats showed the course of the Colorado River. Marble Canyon, as it was known, presented a formidable barrier to travelers and could be headed only at Lees Ferry, where the cliffs relented for a short distance. This destination, with its little ranch oasis, was a full day away. Beyond Marble Canyon, the Echo Cliffs appeared to block further progress, but Rust knew of a trail that surmounted them to reach the broad Kaibito Plateau and the beginning of Navajo country.

The House Rock Valley was the domain of the Grand Canyon Cattle Company, which used the desert flats as a winter range fenced in by the awesome topography. Other homesteaders were beginning to settle at the few waterholes in the area, but it would be another nine years before a proper auto road would bridge the Colorado. Dave made sure that Charles and Arnold got a close look at the buffalo herd that was maintained by Uncle Jim Owens, the government hunter. Numbering up to a hundred animals, they were descendants of bison that Buffalo Jones had brought to the desert for his catalo breeding experiment, which had proved not to work as the calves they produced were sterile.[9]

The Southwest's "monsoon" season was beginning as the intense heat of the desert drew up moisture from the Gulf of Mexico. Cooled by an afternoon thunderstorm, the party made it past Soap Creek, a short tributary to the Colorado that offered a slim trickle of water. Past this they made a dry camp and were able to reach Lees Ferry the next morning, the day's heat already building. This historic crossing had been used for over fifty years by the Mormon explorers and settlers of the region. It was named for John D. Lee, who arrived in 1871 under an unofficial exile from Utah owing to his role in the 1857 Mountain Meadows massacre. Since 1910 the ferry had been operated by Frank and Jerry Johnson, sons of a local settler, under a contract to Coconino County, Arizona.[10] The Johnson brothers were gracious hosts to the few travelers who showed up.

Lees Ferry lay at an altitude of just under 3,200 feet. Here the sun baked the earth to dust, and the ranch's shady cottonwood trees were a blessing to those who ventured this far. There would be little else to relieve the rigors ahead. Rust had crossed the Colorado here with the Frasers in 1916 and with Donald C. Scott that April. George Fraser had taken an interest in the site's rich history of settlement, mining, and occasional outlawry, but Berolzheimer and Koehler were more interested in a cooling dip in the Colorado and the fresh food offered at the ranch.

When Rust had come through in 1916 he was at the limit of his familiar geography, and he had enlisted a Navajo guide to lead the way to Richardson's trading post at Kaibito. This year he had already been to Navajo Mountain with Donald Scott and felt he could make the journey eastward unassisted. On July 15, after ferrying the outfit across the Colorado, he carefully picked a route up through the steep slopes of the Echo Cliffs. On the climb they found an enormous petrified tree stuck in the cliff—"five and a half feet thick by fifty or sixty long," observed Arnold.

That evening, after huddling around the campfire in the rain, Dave cobbled together a crude shelter out of the tarpaulins he used to cover the packs. They awoke the next morning to a refreshed world. The rain meant that the sandstone waterpockets that dotted the Kaibito Plateau would be full, and Dave delighted in showing the boys a catchment where they could do laundry and get a bath. The trail to Kaibito Spring was easy riding, offering few diversions except for a small sandstone arch Rust remembered from his previous trips. Here the boys met their first Navajo, riding up from his cornfield to greet them. More Indians were hanging around the trading post, loafing or doing their business, to the great interest of Charles and Arnold. They purchased some silver rings and were treated to a roping demonstration (with Charles as the lassoee) by a friendly Navajo youth.

It is not clear why Rust passed up a visit to Inscription House ruin, a part of Navajo National Monument located twenty miles east of Kaibito. Instead, he chose the same route he had taken with George Fraser, threading through the wild breaks of Navajo Creek and climbing to the Rainbow Plateau south of Navajo Mountain. Here they met a party of student archaeologists led by Dr. Byron Cummings, which was excavating artifacts at the so-called Red House and Yellow House ruins at the southwestern foot of the mountain. Cummings had been a professor of classical languages at the University of Utah, but had turned his interest toward the prehistory of the Southwest and was famed as the codiscoverer of Rainbow Bridge. In 1915 he accepted a position as the director of the Arizona State Museum. Rust was surprised to find among Cummings's party a cousin of his whom he had not met before.

All this travel, taxing as it must have been, was a prelude to the main event—a climb of Navajo Mountain, followed by a descent into the canyons that held Rainbow Bridge. The former was the unmistakable landmark visible from almost any vantage point in the central canyon lands. Charles Bernheimer, an explorer from New York City who first visited the region in 1920, described the mountain as "massive and majestic, the commanding, long-distant object of this region. It fascinates, it hypnotizes, for the eye is constantly drawn toward it."[11]

Navajo Mountain's magma pool had failed to break through the overlying sedimentary layers, which remnants still fully cloaked the mountain, unlike in the Henry Mountains, where igneous dikes were exposed in jagged ridges. The Henrys were the locale of G. K. Gilbert's pioneering studies of this type of mountain building, which he termed "laccolites," or laccoliths as they are commonly called today. Herbert Gregory, in his landmark 1916 study of the geology of the Navajo Reservation, determined that Navajo Mountain was of the same type.

Rainbow Bridge, on the other hand, was so hidden among the convolutions of canyon at the mountain's northern base that it was not formally discovered until 1909. The bridge owed its existence to the tilted and exposed layers of Navajo Sandstone north of the mountain that were subjected to greatly accelerated erosion from the gradient thus created. The mountain itself is a storm-maker and created much of the precipitation that historically funneled down Bridge Creek and carved the elegant canyon and its namesake bridge. This relationship is also recognized in Navajo spirituality, which joins Navajo Mountain and Rainbow Bridge as sources of precious rain.[12]

The Anglo discovery of Rainbow Bridge forms an exciting and contentious chapter in the exploration of the Colorado Plateau. The accounts of Byron Cummings and William Douglass jockeying for the first glimpse of the bridge, and the acrimonious and rather pointless debate that continued for years over which of the two first reached it, indicates the importance that some explorers placed on the question of priority. One scholar, Stephen C. Jett, has presented a carefully documented claim that John and Louisa Wetherill actually visited the bridge in 1908 but kept quiet about it.[13] Most scholars, including Jett, point out that the Paiutes and Navajo who lived in the area, and probably prehistoric inhabitants as well, long knew of the bridge and attached their own meanings to the formation.

Rust wasted no words on such issues. He took the long view and placed equal emphasis on native, Spanish, Mormon, and government explorers when recounting the history of the region for his clients. His own guiding in the region deserves more mention than it has received, for he was leading parties to the bridge well before it became a popular destination.

Early tourist parties to the bridge used the Rainbow Trail, blazed by John Wetherill and Nasja Begay in 1909, which skirted the north side of the mountain to Bridge Creek. Rust and the Frasers followed this trail with Nasja as their guide in 1916. Dave, though, had other plans. Heeding the irresistible urge to climb Navajo Mountain, he led the boys up the trail on the southeastern side of the mountain to War God Spring, where they made camp in a cool aspen grove. Here he proposed a novel route to the bridge—over the summit and straight down the north face of the mountain. It would save circling back around to the traditional trail that came in from the northeast, but they would have to descend a slope of unrelenting steepness and no small danger. The following year the north face turned back no less a guide than John Wetherill and his companion, Charles

Bernheimer. Bernheimer noted that "the north side has no slope at all, only sheer drops. It was impossible."[14] To take two untried young men on it, as well as his own son, spoke of Rust's confidence in their abilities.

The next morning they packed up and left the horses at the spring, traveling light with little food and no blankets, for they knew that Bridge Canyon would be plenty warm. The face of the mountain had an overall angle of about thirty degrees, steep enough to require careful footwork the whole way down. They didn't actually need ropes; the danger was not that they would pitch over a cliff, but that one of them might stumble on the loose rocks and break a leg. To get an injured person back up to the top and down the horse trail on the other side of the mountain would be a major undertaking. If Rust were the one hurt—at age forty-five his joints were not quite as elastic as they had once been—he would have to depend on the boys to get him out. As always, he exercised caution and saw to it that the boys did, too, and they reached the upper forks of Bridge Canyon that afternoon, tired but whole.

That night they camped just upstream of Rainbow Bridge. Watching from their bivouac, Arnold observed "the slender semi-circle of sandstone flung almost across the cañon." Though the bridge was public knowledge by then, they could share in the sense of personal discovery that they had truly earned. The next morning they continued the short distance down the canyon to the foot of the bridge. Rust thought he could see a way up onto its top, so after getting out the rope, they scrambled up and exulted in their commanding perch. After gingerly climbing back down, they bathed in Bridge Creek, took pictures, and shared what little lunch they had brought. Then they retraced their route out of the canyon labyrinth. After following Bridge Creek and the Rainbow Trail for a few miles, they tackled the vertical-mile climb back up the mountain.

Anyone who has guided teenagers in the outdoors knows the inescapable rule for keeping them going: feed them, feed them, and feed them some more. But Rust had brought short rations for their quick excursion to the bridge. The boys' description of their meals reads like a recipe for a vision quest, not a strenuous mountain climb. They finished the last of the food—"two cans of lunch tongue, a package of raisins, and some corn bread"—on the way up the mountain. It says a great deal about their inner fortitude that they were able to make the climb at all. Too tired to charge up the face of the mountain, they made their way slowly and rested often. They stopped short of the summit for another spectacular bivouac, keeping a fire going against the cold. There was certainly no wilder place in the

Southwest to watch a sunset. Ridge by ridge, the red rocks far below glowed carmine red and sank into shadow. The thin air at close to nine thousand feet would have displayed stars in a profusion unimaginable to someone from the misty eastern seaboard.

The next morning they breakfasted on the crumbs of corn bread in the meal sack and headed over the summit to their camp at War God Spring. Rust's quick-and-light approach worked well with a couple of young, agile men, where it might not have suited an older client. He certainly saw no need to outfit a huge expedition such as Charles Bernheimer brought in 1922 on his western approach to the bridge. Bernheimer employed two guides (John Wetherill and Zeke Johnson) and two wranglers, and he reserved two riding horses for himself. All this required eighteen pack horses and mules and three-quarters of a ton of oats for feed, not to mention dynamite for blasting a new trail through the rock cleft they called Redbud Pass.[15] True, the archaeologist Earl Morris accompanied the party, and his excavations of ancient Puebloan sites required extra packs, but theirs was an expedition of an altogether different order. Rust supplied his trip from one pack mule, a "minimum impact" approach for the time. Though this may partly have been motivated by his inveterate economy, a small pack string took less feed, water, and effort to manage in rough terrain.

In today's world of well-mapped wilderness, it takes some imagination to get a visceral sense for the scale of this country. Atop Navajo Mountain, they were almost fifty miles from the nearest dirt road, and they were heading still farther in. The route ahead lay across the northward-draining canyons that ran down to the San Juan River, forty miles eastward across the grain of the land to Monument Valley. Rust had gotten good and lost while attempting this journey in 1916; this time he had better maps and a sense of where to go, and they completed the traverse in just two days.

This wild landscape was the ancestral homeland of the San Juan Paiutes, but increasingly the Navajo were expanding westward into the region.[16] The U.S. Government, following its usual approach to Indian affairs, had established and then rescinded various reservation boundaries, nominally awarding the territory around Rainbow Bridge to the Paiutes. Rust and his party chanced to meet Old Nasja, the father of the guide Nasja Begay, near his farm in Piute Canyon. The younger Nasja, unfortunately, had died in 1918 from the influenza epidemic that had taken many of the Paiutes in the area. In any event the landscape was not heavily populated, and the native people were simply another aspect of the Old West that Charles and Arnold had come to see. There were only a few years left before automobile tourism would bring numerous visitors to the region. In 1924 the Richardson brothers would open Rainbow Lodge on the south side of Navajo Mountain, stealing a march on John Wetherill, who was using the new trail to Rainbow Bridge that he had blazed with Charles Bernheimer around the west side of the mountain. With two guide services circumnavigating the mountain, visitation to the bridge climbed steadily, and new roads were built northward from the Tuba City–Kayenta "highway."

Monument Valley was also getting on the map. Charles and Arnold had planned their trip on the strength of W. H. Hopkins's article describing his pioneering auto trip in 1917, but many others would soon follow. George Fraser, in fact, was out exploring the ruins in Tsegi Canyon that summer with George Bird Grinnell, traveling mostly by auto. While the landscape itself would change little in the coming years, its sense of abiding wildness was surely diminishing.

Still, in this country the traveler was utterly dependent on his mount, and Rust was becoming alarmed at his own horse, which had taken ill back on the Kaibito Plateau and was steadily growing worse. A dry camp on the journey to Monument Valley didn't help matters. They were relying on water pockets, a few of which they found the next morning, but it was not a place to take lightly. They paused in Monument Valley only long enough to take in the views. Low on supplies, they headed north to Spencer's trading post on the San Juan River at Goodridge, the site of present-day Mexican Hat, Utah. The boys were glad to be past the days of meager meals and alkaline water, though their journal expresses wonder at the marvelous rock formations and numerous physical challenges they had encountered. If there was any doubt left in Rust's mind about their endurance, it was resolved by now. Years later, he recounted how the cowboys in Springdale joked about Charles's slight frame, adding simply that of the three boys he took on this trip, Charles was the only one never to propose turning back from any objective.

Riding east from Spencer's trading post, the party arrived in the town of Bluff, which Charles described as holding only a dozen families compared with its earlier population of three hundred. They put up at a resident's home and enjoyed plates and plates of ice cream, made with fifty pounds of ice garnered from the local store.

Rust wanted to show the boys Natural Bridges National Monument, located fifty miles to the northwest via a relatively easy ride along Comb Wash. Leaving Bluff, they set out for this destination. Once again, afternoon rains gave relief from the heat, and after camping near the wash they made their way up into the piñon-juniper forests of Cedar Mesa.

Theodore Roosevelt designated the three massive natural bridges in upper White Canyon as a national monument in 1908, the first such monument in Utah and one of his many conservation enactments. Few parties came to this area specifically to see the bridges, as it was a long pack trip from either Blanding or Bluff. This was evidently Rust's first visit to the area, as it took some time for him to locate all three bridges in their hidden canyon setting. The Edwin, or Owachomo, bridge could be seen from the rim just above Armstrong Canyon, a tributary of White Canyon; they rode down to it that first evening and climbed onto its flat top. The next morning, riding along the rim approximately where the current monument loop road is located, they searched for a way into White Canyon proper. Leaving the horses behind, they scrambled down the steep cliffs and ledges of the Cedar Mesa sandstone, shinnying down trees and uncoiling the rope where necessary to reach the bottom. Rust scouted up a wrong fork—possibly Deer Canyon—looking for the Augusta (Sipapu) bridge. In his equable manner, he told the boys, "The only thing to do is to explore the canyon, and if the bridge is not there—why then it's in the other canyon."

They opted to head down White Canyon to see the Caroline (Kachina) bridge, climbing it as they had the Edwin, and returned to camp up through the cliffs. Another roped descent the following day took them to the Augusta, which they also climbed, completing their tour of the bridges. The boys by now were used to scrambling around on the slickrock, and they counted the adventure as good as any on the trip so far. Their climbing abilities enabled them to visit and photograph a set of intriguing prehistoric structures, known today as Horsecollar Ruin. This feature had been excavated in 1907 by a party led by Byron Cummings, but the site received little publicity until monument custodian Ezekiel "Zeke" Johnson came across it in 1936 and began showing it to visitors.

The history of the Anglo discovery of the White Canyon bridges is less dramatic than the Cummings-Douglass "race" to Rainbow Bridge, reflecting the incidental way in which cattlemen and prospectors often chanced across such features. One story holds that the Glen Canyon gold prospector Cass Hite first located the bridges with a Paiute guide in 1883, calling them the President, the Senator, and the Congressman. Zeke Johnson credited a cattleman named Emery Knowles with discovering the bridges while looking for strays. Word of these spectacular features spread among prospectors and stockmen in the area, including James A. Scorup of Bluff, who saw the bridges in 1895. In 1903 Scorup led Horace J. Long of the Hoskaninni Company, the Colorado River gold-dredging scheme formerly owned by Robert Brewster Stanton, to the bridges. Long sent his field notes to his boss, W. W. Dyar, who wrote a description of the marvels for *Century Magazine* in 1904. This launched public awareness of the bridges, aided by a short piece quoting Dyar's article that appeared in the September 1904 issue of *National Geographic Magazine*.[17]

Further publicity came from an article published in *National Geographic* in 1907. It's author, Edwin F. Holmes, visited the bridges in 1905 under the sponsorship of the Salt Lake Commercial Club. The article featured paintings of the bridges by the Salt Lake City artist H. L. A. Culmer, who accompanied the party. This group named the Edwin bridge in recognition of Holmes's sponsorship of the expedition. (The Scorup-Long party had named the Caroline bridge after Scorup's mother and the Augusta for Long's wife.)[18] Soon after the monument was designated, they were given the Hopi names Owachomo, Kachina, and Sipapu, by which they are called today. Many Utahns, however, Rust included, kept to the previous names.

In his *National Geographic* article, Holmes raised the possibility of some kind of protective designation for the bridges: "From all that is learned of this wonderful country, it is believed that its preservation and care should be undertaken by the United States Government, as in the case of the Yellowstone Park, so that roads may be opened and these greatest of the world's natural bridges made accessible for the tourists from our own country and from all over the world, who would flock thither were the road made better."[19]

This appears to be the first instance of anyone recognizing the national park potential of the Utah canyon lands. Holmes, like most travelers who wrote about the West's natural wonders, seemed intent on rendering the White Canyon bridges accessible to touring automobiles.

Natural Bridges, however, was to be another of the prototypical monuments of the Southwest, a tiny set-aside protecting some distinctive oddities of nature. The intent was simply to prevent appropriation by would-be entrepreneurs or defacement by casual visitors; there was no thought given to protecting the surrounding lands. Roosevelt's initial proclamation set no boundaries for the monument; these were added in a subsequent presidential proclamation in 1909.

Despite Holmes's call for improved access, it would be another ten years before vehicles could grind over Comb Ridge and drop down past the prominent twin buttes known as the Bears Ears to reach the monument. Pack trains, for the moment, would offer the only means for tourists to see the bridges and poke around its ruins. Zeke Johnson, a Blanding prospector and cattleman, had been guiding parties into the area as early as 1908 and relied on guiding fees to supplement his minimal Park Service salary. (For years, like Walter Ruesch at Zion, his pay was exactly one dollar a month.) At the time of Rust's first visit in 1919, there were no signs or booklets anywhere to inform tourists of the bridges' existence, and they remained a noteworthy destination embedded in a nearly trackless canyon system. As the *National Geographic* advised, "No person should think of going into this region without having thoroughly studied all the conditions. The few guides that have been there have a very limited knowledge of the country, and the main and side canyons so cut up the country that a party may easily become lost."[20] While Rust indeed had limited knowledge of the area, he had long experience with finding his way in the canyon country, and a few false starts up side canyons were nothing to fear. For him, the country was perfectly accessible.

Dave and the boys were nearing the end of their backcountry sojourn. Another day's ride would take them to Blanding and thence onward by automobile to Mesa Verde National Park in southwestern Colorado. As Dave led the way up out of White Canyon toward the Bears Ears, Charles paused to look back over the country they had traversed:

As we were looking at the yellow sky in the West, we noticed a small looking mountain rising above out of a flat looking country. How far we had come from the great Navajo Mountain was difficult to realize. But it was easy to understand how the Indians had once worshiped it and I could well imagine a lone Indian in my place looking with wonder at this lonesome monster rising from the level plain in the dusk and surrounded by a golden crown of light from the setting sun.[21]

It had been an amazing passage for Berolzheimer and Koehler. The two youths had come through a mostly uncharted wilderness, and their guide had not pampered them. Rust told an interviewer years later that "it was a rough trip and I made it rougher."[22] Great adventures make a lasting impression on young men and women, and there is nothing like riding or walking over a long, difficult trail to get a sense for the land—and to discover one's capabilities. Rust knew this from his own youth, and he could see the same slow transformation happening to his son and their two young friends. Charles and Arnold, though they came from wealthy families, had chosen the most rugged adventure they could find, one that would expand their horizons like no other.

One final treat awaited the party at Mesa Verde. This renowned concentration of ancient Puebloan ruins had been designated a national park in 1906, and since the ruins were accessible by vehicle, they attracted considerable tourist traffic. There was even a Wylie-style tent camp opposite Spruce Tree Ruin. Rust and the boys spent several nights there and were fortunate to meet Dr. Jesse Walter Fewkes, a noted archaeologist who was working at Mesa Verde. Dr. Fewkes consented to give a lecture to the assembled tourists, and afterward Dave introduced himself and the boys. When Fewkes heard that they had just crossed the Navajo Reservation on horseback, he invited them on a personal tour of the ruins the next day.[23] In these early days of the national park system, natural history was sometimes explained directly by renowned scholars, there being as yet no ranger-naturalists staffing the park. Later during this tour, while they were inspecting a recently discovered kiva, one of Dr. Fewkes's men uncovered a buried jug and showed it to the party. That evening Charles wrote in his journal of his fascination with "these ancient inhabitants of our country, who surpassed the other Indian races of their time and future time, in art, architecture, and other cultures which make up a high civilization." One can hardly imagine a more exciting form of learning. Rust certainly would have taken pride in showing the wonders of his home country to these eager and articulate young men.

Following their tour of Mesa Verde, Dave and Jordan said goodbye to Charles and Arnold, who caught a ride to Ouray, Colorado, for the train home. That fall they would begin their college studies, Arnold at Cornell, Charles at Harvard. Dave and Jordan returned to Blanding to retrieve their horses and pack stock. Reaching Bluff, they were told that a rancher had killed a Navajo and that tensions on the reservation were high. Rust was advised not to return that way. "It was very touchy," Jordan recalled. "But my dad said, 'Hell, I have to get home,' so we traveled by night and it was pretty hairy for a while."[24] Sticking to wagon roads to make time, they reached Kayenta on August 9, where they overnighted at John and Louisa Wetherill's trading post and again met Byron Cummings, who was staying there. Bypassing Rainbow Bridge and Navajo Mountain, they returned home without incident. The family's welcome and Ruth's bountiful table provided a pleasant end to their weeks in the desert regions. The Rusts would see more of Charles and Arnold in the coming years; indeed, Charles would become a close friend of the family. The journey west had fulfilled their expectations and more. The desert truly was a place to stretch one's wings.

The next morning Dave was up with the twilight arch, chiding the rest of us who were bent on a little beauty sleep. But the scene was worth the early effort: a new glory is shed across the canyon by the eastern sun, and we reveled in its magnificence. As the morning sun illumines the colossal south canyon wall its promontories lengthen and its recesses deepen greatly.

J. CECIL ALTER
Through the Heart of the Scenic West (1927)

OF ALL THE SCENIC WONDERS of the Southwest, the Grand Canyon and Zion Canyon seemed destined from the first to become stars of the National Park System. Both canyons possessed the requisite grandeur and breathtaking beauty that Americans could take pride in. Legislation to create a Grand Canyon National Park had been introduced at intervals since 1882, but was stymied by opposition from prospectors and miners who feared the loss of their claims. President Roosevelt's declaration of a relatively small Grand Canyon National Monument in 1908 was not to be the last attempt to protect this greatest of canyons. President Taft recognized Zion Canyon in 1909 by proclaiming a miniscule Mukuntuweap National Monument; it did not have such high resource values that stockmen, prospectors, or timber men objected to its being set aside.

Monument designation conferred a degree of protection and recognition upon these scenic marvels, but none of the monuments in the Southwest were adequately funded, and few were staffed with so much as a single caretaker. Many, in fact, were simply temporary expedients; farsighted individuals in government and private business often saw the Antiquities Act of 1906, under which the president could unilaterally establish national monuments, as a holding action until sufficient support could be mustered to get national park legislation through Congress. This body was often beholden to local politicians and their backers in the resources industries.[1] While many of the early national monuments in the Southwest, such as Chaco Canyon and El Morro in New Mexico (established in 1907 and 1906, respectively) and Montezuma Castle in Arizona (1906), were set aside to prevent private exploiters from carting off archaeological relics, this concern was less of an issue for either Zion or Grand Canyon. Much of the impetus for protecting these areas, and especially for converting them into national parks, came from the mainline tourist industry of the day—the railroads. The Santa Fe Railway had a strong interest in the South Rim of the Grand Canyon, where its El Tovar Hotel was the premier tourist destination in the region. The Union Pacific, through its regional subsidiary, the Salt Lake Route, saw much promise for tourism at Zion and the North Rim. Both companies were willing to invest in large hotels and other infrastructure, and they had access to powerful senators and congressmen. National parks, with their aura of grandeur and significance, could be advertised to the touring public more easily than could any of the national monuments. The railroads' influence, together with the support of local businessmen, provided the needed boost for park legislation. By 1919, when Congress passed park bills for Zion and Grand Canyon, the course of park development at Zion and the North Rim was settled, even though it would be a few more years before significant numbers of tourists would arrive.

Rust had missed an opportunity to get in on the ground floor of the tourist business in 1915, when J. H. Manderfield of the Salt Lake Route was looking for someone to ferry visitors across the Arizona Strip to the North Rim. Now more experienced entrepreneurs like the Parry brothers and the Wylie Way company were accommodating the growing numbers of sightseers. With both Zion and the Grand Canyon gaining the national recognition (and centralized control) that park status conferred, Rust's wilderness world was about to change dramatically.

Although by 1919 Rust was no longer directly employed by the Grand Canyon Transportation Company, he still had a stake in its facilities. These consisted of his Bright Angel Creek trail, the tramway over the Colorado River, the camp at the mouth of Bright Angel Creek, and the Woolley cabin on the Kaibab Plateau, which served as the staging point for the entire operation. At first these facilities had required permits only from the Forest Service, which, before the Park Service took over, managed all of the surrounding lands including Grand Canyon National Monument and the adjacent Grand Canyon Game Preserve on the Kaibab Plateau.

The Forest Service typically had close ties to local residents, and its field personnel on the Kaibab (and there were few of them) rarely tried to exclude working people. Rust told the story of how in 1908 he needed to pasture some sheep on the Kaibab to provide mutton for his tram crew. The local supervisor objected, saying he didn't want sheep running within the game preserve. Rust pleaded that he had to feed his men. The supervisor relented, telling Rust, "All right, but be sure when you kill one that the animal has wool on it and not hair."[2]

Such informal relationships sufficed in the early days of Forest Service administration. But Tim Hoyt, a founder of the Transportation Company who later worked for the Forest Service's regional office in Ogden, noted in 1910 that a park bill had been introduced that would include lands north of the Colorado River. He urged Dee Woolley to secure his rights: "I suggest that you get in an application for the occupancy of the ground needed and cinch Fuller [Catalo] Spring at once and any other that may be needed and then if the Park is created it may have the effect of giving you the ground floor even if the Forester's permits are cancelled." Acting on this tip, the company in April 1911 obtained special use permits from the Forest Service for both the Woolley cabin in Fuller Canyon and Rust's Camp on Bright Angel Creek.[3]

With relations generally cordial between the Transportation Company and the Forest Service, getting annual renewals for these permits presented no particular problem, so neither Woolley nor Rust took extra precautions to safeguard their investment in the trail and tram. In fact, they supported the creation of the park: in 1911 Woolley's son Bert, who worked for the Forest Service in Washington, sent him a map of one of the proposals that had been introduced by Senator Flint of California. Woolley and Rust looked over the map and gave it their blessing, even suggesting that the park boundary be set farther north at 36° 30' N. latitude. This would have included De Motte Park, "*which by all means* should be included in the Nat'l Park," Woolley wrote.[4]

Park designation certainly called attention to the North Rim, which had been Woolley's goal all along, but his company had no rights to the land on which it had built its improvements. Unlike Rust's Camp, the tourist cabins and hotels at the South Rim were located either on mining claims of various degrees of legality, or on the Santa Fe Railway's twenty-acre depot at Grand Canyon Village. When Grand Canyon National Park was finally created in 1919, the new federal managers had no obligation to continue issuing occupancy permits, and ownership of the trail, the tram, Rust's Camp, and the Woolley cabin passed to the government. The supervisor of the Kaibab National Forest wrote to Rust on March 31, 1919, informing him that the company's special use permit had been "transferred to the closed files" and suggesting that he take up the matter with the Park Service. He noted that the bill establishing the park provided for concessions for accommodation or entertainment of visitors, which "shall be let at public bidding to the best and most responsible bidder."[5]

Neither Woolley nor Rust had enough clout to protect their investment from federal takeover, and they apparently did not pursue any sort of concession arrangement with the Park Service. Curiously, Rust inquired whether there might be a position available as the superintendent for the Kaibab section of the new park, but was told that no separate position would be filled. He then applied to be superintendent of the entire park, but this job was filled through regular agency channels.[6] Rust would have made an effective ranger for the Kaibab, had he chosen to pursue a career with the Park Service. But the job would have meant more summers away from his family, and by then he had built strong connections to the community in Kanab. He did not appear to be terribly serious about pursuing a park job.

In 1921 the Park Service decided to replace Rust's tram with a footbridge, which would offer the only realistic means for large numbers of travelers to cross the river. The work crew made use of the tram's main cable during the bridge's construction. The tram cage was cast aside on the north bank and notice was sent to the Woolley family to remove it. No compensation was offered.[7] The following year the Park Service granted a concession to the Fred Harvey Company to build a permanent tourist camp on Bright Angel Creek, which would become today's Phantom Ranch. Rust's Camp was by then little used and was being called Roosevelt Camp in honor of the former president's visit in 1913. (Rust had earlier told Ellsworth Kolb that this was "certainly a big improvement in nomenclature.") A writer for *National Geographic Magazine*, visiting the bridge that spring, made use of the discarded tram cage as a framework over which to drape her tent.[8]

Rust's trail and tram may simply have been too primitive to appeal to the Park Service, which saw a grander future for its holdings, involving not dozens but thousands of visitors. The agency was looking for well-capitalized concessioners who, as park historian Michael Anderson noted, "would supply visitor accommodations, employee housing, groceries, meals, utilities, supplies, souvenirs, and entertainment."[9] No longer would a handful of colorful miners, trappers, hunters, and other small-time outfitters provide their unique services in the park's backcountry.

That the new agency took a liberal approach to tourism is shown by its willingness to consider another proposal for a cable tram—this one spanning nearly the entire canyon. In 1916 an engineer from San Francisco named George Davol came up with the notion of a passenger tramway that would speed tourists from the South Rim to a point below the North Rim and back, avoiding the need for the long, tiring trail ride down to the river. The cable would be strung in sections anchored to various inner-canyon buttes, totaling (in one proposed alignment) 21,400 feet—giving tourists an awe-inspiring view of the inner gorge without actually having to set foot in it. Davol enlisted support from the Santa Fe Railway and even got Acting Park Service Director Horace Albright to support the idea. Stephen Mather, however, once he resumed his duties in 1919, was not persuaded, and the idea died.[10]

Rust blamed the Union Pacific Railroad for pressuring the Park Service to evict his company; with what accuracy is not known. The Utah Parks Company, the railroad's tourism subsidiary, was not created until 1923, and it did not acquire the Wylie camp at Bright Angel Point until 1927, paying the Wylies twenty-five thousand dollars for their facilities and proceeding to build a grand tourist lodge nearby at the rim.[11] It seems unlikely that the railroad would have been intent on acquiring Rust's trail and the Woolley cabin as early as 1919. More likely the whole operation, never profitable, had simply run its course. Dee Woolley was seventy-three years old when the park was created and no longer took an active interest in his venture. Always sanguine, he saw his company's work as just one more step toward fulfilling his longtime dream of bringing the world to the North Rim country. That it was not profitable seemed to matter little to him. Rust later reminisced about the tourist venture with Ruth's sister Mary Chamberlain (who was known publicly as Mary Howard); he told her that Woolley "felt that some person or company more experienced than himself in caring for the tourist, someone with more capital, should be induced to come to these scenic spots and establish permanent accommodations, such as was being done at the time in other parks." Rust told Chamberlain that Woolley actually encouraged the Wylie Way company to locate at the North Rim, arranging for a Wylie representative to tour the area with Governor Spry during his 1916 visit.[12]

Rust characterized the whole Grand Canyon trail and tram project as simply another of Woolley's interesting avocations. "Your father was a business man on one side and a hobbyist on the other," he told Chamberlain. "I was his assistant hobbyist. The Grand Canyon Transportation Company should have been called the 'Woolley Hobby Company.'" By this time he could afford to make light of his years of effort constructing the trail and tram, but the loss disturbed him. Referring to the cottonwoods he had planted at his camp, he said, "these trees are my green memorial: the only thing left of my work. When the government took over, everything was destroyed. Woeful work." And as late as 1930 he expressed dismay over the whole affair to his young friend Ned Chaffin, suggesting that he took the confiscation of his tram and camp personally.[13] The project may have been a hobby for Dee Woolley, but Dave had put his body and soul into it.

Rust never returned to see Phantom Ranch or the Park Service's new suspension bridge. In 1920 he took the archaeologist Neil Judd partway down Bright Angel Creek, intending to visit the ruins near the mouth of the creek, but they were stopped by high water.[14] This was as close as he came to revisiting the site of his and Dee Woolley's dream. Now there were new places to explore. With his tourist venture at the Grand Canyon over, Dave would not look back. Henceforth he would derive his satisfaction as a guide—and what money he could—by leading one party at a time into the vastness of the Colorado Plateau.

With the Grand Canyon off the table, Rust turned his attention to the many possibilities for trips in the lands to the north and east. He returned to the Navajo Reservation in the spring of 1919 with Donald C. Scott—a trip made memorable by an awesome sunset atop Navajo Mountain. Upon returning from this outing, Rust received an invitation from George Fraser to tour the Indian reservations of northern Arizona and New Mexico. Fraser had arranged to travel with an acquaintance of his, the noted outdoorsman and conservationist George Bird Grinnell. Fraser told Dave he could not employ him as guide for this trip, since he was not familiar with the territory, but instead invited him along as their guest. By then, however, Dave had agreed to lead Charles Berolzheimer and Arnold Koehler through the Navajo country. Fraser and Grinnell made most of their trip by auto; the two parties nearly met each other at several points along the way.

Fraser's brand of travel remained resolutely adventurous. As much as any of Rust's clients, he sought the kinds of activities that, as historian Hal Rothman put it, "truly pitted individuals against themselves, people against the rough, cold realities of the American West in a genuine quest for experience and understanding."[15] Fraser's interest in the native peoples of the Southwest probably exceeded Rust's. While neither man exhibited any of the romanticism toward Indian life that characterized some of the early tourists, Fraser brought his habitual deep curiosity to his travels, and managed to visit many of the now-famous Indian pueblos and archaeological sites in the Southwest. Rust seemed to hold more of a prejudice toward the Navajo and Paiutes that he met on his travels in Arizona. His apparent low regard for the Southwestern tribes hardly differed from the attitude of many of his fellow Westerners.[16]

Political affairs again drew Rust's interest in the fall of 1919, when he ran for and won a position on the Kanab town board.[17] One of the recurring issues facing the board was the town's water system. Kanab derived its culinary supply from a spring in Hog Canyon north of town, which Dee Woolley and others had tapped in 1909 following a flood that took out the sand dam on Kanab Creek. The pipeline from the spring was privately owned and continually broke down. Finally, in 1920, the board decided to build a new water system at a cost of forty thousand dollars—a major expenditure for a town of a few hundred inhabitants. The board also enacted a one-mill levy to fund a city library, a civic improvement dear to Dave's heart.[18]

Rust and Fraser again explored the possibility of a Colorado River trip in 1920, this time to include Fraser's second-oldest daughter, Ann. Besides Glen Canyon, Fraser wanted to boat down the Green River to its confluence with the Colorado, returning upstream to Moab. This adventure, popularized today as the Memorial Day "Friendship Cruise," foundered when he was unable to make arrangements with anyone who had a power boat. But Fraser also wanted to see new high points as well. In June he suggested that they start from Lees Ferry on horseback, head up the Paria River, and "work over to Fifty Mile Mountain and follow that to its south east end where we can get the view you and I have so long speculated about."[19] This promontory directly overlooked Glen Canyon and a wilderness of sandstone canyons between the Kaiparowits Plateau and Navajo Mountain. Once again, though, Dave had already planned to take Berolzheimer and Koehler out into some of that same country. He invited Fraser to join this trip, but his friend demurred, telling him that "the choice of a companion to take into the 'wild' should be made advisedly, like matrimonial contracts."[20] In the end Fraser opted to take Ann on a motorcar tour of Arizona, visiting several national monuments, the South Rim of the Grand Canyon, and the Hopi villages. The river had to wait.

The year 1920 saw two milestones for the Rust family. Ruth's father, Edwin D. Woolley Jr., passed away at his home in Kanab on July 20. He was seventy-four years old and had served for twenty-five years as the president of the Kanab

LDS Stake. Neither Dave nor Ruth set down their thoughts, but his loss must have been deeply felt. "Uncle Dee" had been a mentor to Dave and had helped steer him toward his work in tourism promotion. It seems clear, too, that some of Woolley's enthusiasm for the Grand Canyon rubbed off on Dave. Not many Utahns of Woolley's time felt as strongly about the value of scenery, or understood that the North Rim was a wonder deserving of worldwide attention.

A happier event took place that November, when Dave and his brothers and sisters gathered in Manti to celebrate George S. and Eliza Rust's sixty-fifth wedding anniversary. It was the first time in thirty years that the entire family was reunited, for they had scattered throughout Utah, and Julia Rust had moved with her husband to a homestead in Alberta. Laura Rust, who lived in Riverton, Utah, met Julia's train in Salt Lake City and accompanied her to Manti. George B., Orion, and Roy Rust came from their homes in Utah's Uinta Basin, while Dave and Ruth drove up from Kanab with Will and Sarah. The latter two couples referred to themselves as the "Big Four," and Ethel Jensen, who was living with the elder Rusts in Manti, recounted the family's boisterous reunion.[21] Dave especially enjoyed telling jokes and sharing stories of his outdoor adventures, as well as roughhousing with his grandnephews and nieces. The following day the family participated in a formal service at the Manti LDS temple. George Rust called the occasion "the happiest day of my life" and told of how he had come to understand the heavy price of his long quest for gold. He died on June 18, 1922, at the age of eighty-eight. Will Rust traveled to Manti to be with him during his last days.

George Fraser waited only until the second week of January 1921 to begin planning his next excursion with Dave. This was to be a month-long trip to Bryce, Zion, and the North Rim, and would include Fraser's wife, Jane, and their daughters Ann, age nineteen, and Jane ("Jane Jr."), age seventeen. Though this was intended to be a less arduous trip than Fraser's previous excursions, Dave still eschewed the tourist amenities in these parks. He met the Frasers on June 13 at the Denver & Rio Grande station in Marysvale and took them by car to Bryce Canyon, where his riding horses and mule were waiting. He had along his old horse "Indian," who had proven too slow for George Fraser in 1915 during their High Plateaus traverse; this animal made a placid mount for Jane Fraser. To accommodate their extra gear, Rust brought a light wagon instead of packsaddles. They began with a leisurely ride along the summit of the Paunsaugunt, taking in the views of the Bryce amphitheaters and visiting the natural bridge midway down the plateau. After making several forest camps in the East Fork of the Sevier River, they headed west toward Zion, camping on the east rim of the main canyon and also above Orderville Gulch.

Fraser had long wanted to traverse the East Fork of the Virgin River through Parunuweap Canyon, having been turned back from the lower part of this spectacular narrows on his 1914 trip with Rust and George Fraser Jr. John Wesley Powell named this gorge in 1872 for a Paiute word meaning "roaring water canyon." That September, Powell, Steven V. Jones, and Joseph W. Young forced their way through the deep, quicksand-prone defile. Powell described the adventure in his 1875 book *Exploration of the Colorado River*, inexplicably changing the year it took place to 1870. "After spending some hours in breaking our way through the mass of vegetation and climbing rocks here and there," he wrote, "it is determined to wade along the stream. In some places this is an easy task, but here and there we come to deep holes where we have to wade to our arm pits. Soon we come to places so narrow that the river fills the entire channel, and we wade perforce."[22] In 1921 Rust and the Frasers left their wagon on the plateau and rode down into the canyon, camping in and exploring at least part of it. Fraser did not keep a journal of his family's trip, so whatever obstacles and delights they encountered in Parunuweap are not recorded.

Returning to the high country above the East Fork, they traveled eastward over the dunes to Kanab. Here Ruth welcomed the Frasers to their small home and set out a fine dinner. Then it was on to the Kaibab. Rust led the party west to Powell Plateau, both men's top destination in the Grand Canyon. Fraser wanted to complete the exploration he had begun in 1914 by riding to the southernmost tip of the plateau at Wheeler Point, which gave a spectacular close-up view into the Granite Gorge of the Colorado River.

Further adventures awaited on the eastern end of the Kaibab, where they took in the views from Skidoo Point (Point Imperial) and Atoko Point. Rust even arranged a one-day mountain lion hunt near Bright Angel Point. Leaving the Kaibab, they rode down to Dave's farmstead at Pipe Spring. Continuing west and north, they rode over the shoulder of Canaan Mountain to the former site of Shunesburg on the Virgin River. In this latter ride George Fraser once again got to duplicate one of the journeys Clarence Dutton described in his *Tertiary History*, reaching the same point beneath Smithsonian Butte that gave such a superb view of the Towers of the Virgin.[23]

Their trip covered 489 miles by horseback (Fraser, with his customary exactitude, kept a daily log) and for an easy family outing, they managed to get into some secluded corners of the region. Rust was deeply pleased to be back in the field with his old friend as well as to meet more of Fraser's family. (This time he was able to be back home for the birth of his eighth child, Quentin, on August 12.) Fraser enjoyed the outing, too, even though it was not as adventurous as those he and Rust had taken in the preceding years. "I went on this journey with considerable trepidation and rather meagre anticipation," he wrote to Rust afterward. "I thought we would be handicapped by the wagon and was fearful we might encounter such discomforts as would neutralize the ladies', especially Mrs. Fraser's, pleasure. But you had everything planned and adjusted so perfectly that they and I never once could find or think of anything we would have changed." He concluded his letter with a fine tribute to his friend: "To see the country with one who understands and enjoys it, and shares in one's enthusiasms is a privilege and a delight." Ruth Rust, too, enjoyed meeting the Frasers whenever they visited Kanab. Jane Fraser sent the Rust family a special Christmas package that year, containing gifts for each of the children and "24 napkins for her large table which harbors so many guests!" Ruth described their families' relationship as a "friendship above price."[24]

The two men continued to exchange pleasantries through the mail, such as when Fraser objected to the state's campaign to limit smoking: "I note the Utah Legislature has passed a law prohibiting the sale, etc. of cigarettes, and apparently also prohibiting smoking in public places. I wish you would obtain an opinion from the attorney general as to whether Powell's Plateau is a public place within the meaning of this statute." Or, when Rust was assembling his outfit for his Colorado River voyages, Fraser offered a suggestion: "As to a vessel to operate on Glen Canyon, the Shipping Board has a number which can be bought. What would be wrong with the 'Leviathan'? You could get her for a price."[25]

In 1921, following several years of postwar expansion, the nation suffered a depression brought on by a sharp drop in the price of agricultural commodities. The downturn hit Kanab residents hard, causing the town's only bank to close its doors. George Fraser somehow heard of this and understood the difficulty it would cause his friend. In late August he sent two $250 checks to Rust, "both or one of which you might accept as a loan until things clear up."[26] Years later, Dave recalled Fraser's generosity in an unpublished essay he called "My Best Neighbor."

Without mentioning Fraser by name, he told what his help had meant, extending the concept of neighborliness across the continent:

> This genuine neighbor of mine is a lawyer (not a priest, or Semite) and he lives the Law of Leviticus (19-18) toward his fellow men, with the compassion of the Good Samaritan. When my bank suspended, & he found me "stripped" & "half-dead" financially he relieved my embarrassment by extending a substantial loan without request. No one around me offered support—I didn't expect help; but this friend heard that I was "wounded" and cared for me. And the big value was not in the money advanced (and the money was certainly needed) but the stimulant the kindness gave my soul which will cheer me forever.

The depression of 1921 seems to have further soured Rust on the Republican Party. In September 1924, in advance of the national election that would re-elect Calvin Coolidge, Rust wrote a rather vitriolic campaign piece that was adopted at the state Democratic convention. In it he decried the "betrayal of the people through corruption in office among high officials," referring to the scandal-plagued administration of Warren Harding, who had succeeded Woodrow Wilson in 1921. While the "rank and file of the Republican party" had voted for these officials "only through good faith and party zeal," Rust felt that the Republicans were to blame for bank failures, mine closures, bankruptcies, and mortgage foreclosures in southern Utah's counties.[27] Honesty and integrity were common themes in Rust's writings, and he held public officials to a high standard. In his later years Rust would find reason to switch parties again, but during the 1920s he would continue his maverick position as a Kane County Democrat.

In the fall of 1921 Rust was re-elected to the Kanab town board. Although this was a partisan position, the board was concerned more with such issues as public health and safety than with party platforms. When the board convened in January 1922, Rust was voted its president, the equivalent to the town's mayor.[28] It was a proud moment for the Rust family. He passed along the news to George Fraser, offering that it was not exactly a high office in such a small community. Fraser wrote back at once with his congratulations, refusing to make light of his friend's election:

It is very well and commendably modest to refer to your offices jocularly, but the fact is that the holding of a public office in a community like yours carries greater import with respect to the individual than it does in a large city. In a small town, every man is known to and by his neighbors. His actions, affairs and relations with his fellows are an open book closely scrutinized. Therefore, when an office of confidence and trust is reposed in any man, it carries with it a real personal endorsement. As a friend of yours, I am highly gratified at this recognition of your capacity and other qualities by the people who know you best.[29]

Fraser's beautifully worded letter is a testament to the esteem in which he held his friend, as well as his lack of condescension toward the townspeople of rural Utah. The disparity in wealth between the two men mattered little to them when placed alongside their shared interest in the Colorado Plateau and the bond they felt from their adventures.

Among the issues Rust and his town board dealt with was whether to grant a license for a pool hall; he corresponded with acquaintances in Salt Lake City about the effect such establishments (whether officially licensed or *sub rosa*) had upon the youth. The board also sought to stem the spread of influenza, which was still extending its reach into the rural West after the devastating outbreak in the eastern states in 1919. The board appointed a quarantine officer who was to maintain a closure on the road west of Fredonia.[30]

During this time Rust became interested in locating mining properties to supplement his farm income. He looked at buying a claim in the once-productive Silver Reef district west of Toquerville, and sent some ore samples to Fraser to have them assayed. Fraser reported the somewhat discouraging results back to Dave and politely declined his invitation to throw in on the project. Dave then tried to interest him in an old mine at Toroweap where he had purchased a share, but Fraser knew all too well what was required for such a venture to be successful: "I have seen so much money lost in mines, and quite recently in the misfortunes of a friend of mine, who was buried in the Kaibito Desert Copper Mine enough to keep you and me comfortable the rest of our lives, have had a good illustration of how costs eat up values in remote places, that my faith in such speculations is very slim."[31] His letters to Dave betray a little irritation with these proposals, but as a friend he felt obligated to respond, and he carefully explained how the location of the claims and their low mineral values would preclude success. Dave evidently still had some of his father's prospecting blood in him, for he continued to stake or buy the occasional claim for years to come.

In his position as mayor, Rust continued to promote the economic interests of southern Utah, which sometimes seemed to be neglected by both the state and national governments. In August 1922 he gave a talk to the Salt Lake Commercial Club to boost his twin interests of tourism and better roads. Roads were essential not just to bring in visitors, but for exporting agricultural products. With his Pipe Valley ranch and his guiding business, Rust had a direct stake in both tourism and agriculture. He told the Commercial Club audience that the North Rim of the Grand Canyon would become one of the top tourist destinations in the West once a "first class" highway was built there, connecting it to the other national parks of the region.[32] The Park Service had already taken up the idea of linking the western parks by road; in 1920, Director Stephen T. Mather dedicated the National Park to Park Highway, a 4,700-mile long route that connected twelve parks in seven western states.[33] Grand Canyon and Mesa Verde were key stopovers along this route, but the emphasis was still on the South Rim; the North Rim and Zion National Park could be reached only by poor connecting roads, via the primitive Colorado River crossing at Lees Ferry.

Rust, however, drew the line at a more ambitious proposal that would have put the North Rim and the Kaibab Plateau on the national map. In 1921 the writer Emerson Hough, after visiting the southwestern parks in Director Mather's company, penned an influential essay for the *Saturday Evening Post* called "The President's Forest." Hough, a conservationist who also wrote for George Bird Grinnell's magazine *Forest and Stream*, had noticed the effects of decades of heavy livestock grazing on the flora of the Kaibab. He proposed to include most of the Kaibab outside of Grand Canyon National Park in a large wildlife preserve. "And why not take the cattle and sheep out," he wrote, "and throw all this messed-up, impractical, complicated business into one new and distinct management whose one task shall be the preservation of a noble refuge as it was left by Nature? One thing is sure: if this be not done, our Kaibab wilderness and its wild life are doomed."[34] Hough, who had earlier helped to persuade the government to protect Yellowstone's bison herds, echoed a frequent complaint of those who felt an affinity for wild nature. He concluded his article with an impassioned plea to protect the Kaibab's forests and wildlife. "Where, then, is adventure now to be had?" he lamented. "Where is there a wilderness? I do not know."

Utah senator Reed Smoot, who had earlier sponsored legislation to create Zion National Park, introduced a joint resolution in Congress to enact Hough's plan for a "President's Forest." The proposal would have placed the Kaibab off-limits to lumbering, mining, and livestock grazing, although the land would remain under Forest Service control. Mather even secured the cooperation of the Grand Canyon Cattle Company, which was willing to vacate its grazing interests on the Kaibab for the sake of the new preserve.[35]

Rust would have none of it. He saw the move as tantamount to a giant expansion of Grand Canyon National Park. He told his Commercial Club audience that livestock grazing did not mar the forest or otherwise interfere with its attractiveness to tourists. Whether he stood to lose summertime grazing privileges for his small herd at his Pipe Valley ranch is not known; more likely he was representing what he saw as the best interests of southern Utah's citizens. Moreover, he probably still felt the sting of the Park Service's takeover of his Grand Canyon trail and tram.

Concern about the use of the Kaibab forest was not limited to outsiders such as Mather and Hough, however. As early as 1913 a committee of the Salt Lake Commercial Club, themselves boosters of a tourist highway to the North Rim, called on District Forester E. A. Sherman to "stop the leasing of lands in the Kaibab forest for cattle grazing and that this district be set aside as a game reserve." The group felt that "the lack of flowers and vegetation on the Kaibab" conflicted with its future as a recreational attraction.[36]

The notion of a "President's Forest" preserve saw no more success than the Forest Service's earlier plans to introduce railroad logging to the plateau. For decades to come, most of the Kaibab Plateau would remain open to the Grand Canyon Cattle Company. In 1927, the northern boundary of Grand Canyon National Park was expanded to take in Little De Motte Park, where the present North Rim entrance station is now located. Park officials proposed an even larger expansion in 1930, taking in more of the Kaibab Plateau as well as lands to the south and east, but nothing came of this move.[37]

Around 1922 Dave and a fellow Kanab cowboy named Charley Mace took Dave's friend J. Cecil Alter out to Dutton Point, a trip Alter chronicled in his book *Through the Heart of the Scenic West*. Alter was not especially attracted to pack trips—he felt that an automobile was a perfectly adequate way to get to Point

Sublime and such places—but Dave insisted that greater sights lay farther west on the Kaibab. Alter depicted Rust as an engaging travel companion, leading the party through the plateau's disorienting topography. "A classic theme for an artist to paint would be 'The Guides at Fault,' as Dave and Charley sat deep in their saddles contemplating the beautiful but bewildering maze of timber all around and wondering which way to go.... 'We better keep to the west of the ridge,' Dave counsels. 'We can add five miles very easily by getting too far north.' And thanks to the lost trail, Dave brought us onto the balcony of the brilliant and deeply gouged Shinumo amphitheater."[38]

If Rust lost the trail at times, he made sure to err in favor of staying close to the canyon's rim, so that his friends could enjoy views into the immense basins the river's side canyons had carved out of the plateau. Powell Plateau, an isolated peninsula beyond Muav Saddle, was one of his favorites. There he would present the great eastern view from Dutton Point, then cross the plateau to sample the western perspective, where the Colorado made a northward run through Middle Granite Gorge. Isolation and the absence of springs still limit visitors to a handful at these magnificent overlooks.

Alter described how Dave could relieve the rigors of the trail with his cheerful humor. After days of putting up with scummy, tadpole-filled waterholes on the typically dry Kaibab, Rust led him to a fresh, cool spring near Muav Saddle. Dave spat out the clear water, saying, "it has no body to it." Later, while watching the sunset from Dutton Point at the edge of the Powell Plateau, they could hear the braying of wild burros on the slopes far below them. Dave said that these were merely the calls of unfortunate tourists who had failed to make it back over Muav Saddle before dark.[39] Even then, tourists were considered to be several notches beneath real adventurers, and Dave clearly felt allegiance to the latter group. If anything, he probably would have preferred to spread his bedroll right there at the edge of Dutton Point, with as little as possible between him and his canyon, ready to greet the sunrise and another day of exploration.

> What could be finer than to awake with the warm sun peeping
> over the canyon walls, the cool water of Harris Creek nearby,
> and Mr. Rust engaged in cooking a delicious breakfast of fried
> beans and boiled mutton? It was not long before we started
> our way down-stream, towards the Escalante River. The can-
> yon grew narrower and steeper, its red sides rising above to
> a height of four hundred feet. The canyon twisted back and
> forth, forming little sand benches and at other places, run-
> ning under the cliff. We splashed through the water at these
> places, with the red sandstone eaves roofing our trail.[1]
>
> CHARLES BEROLZHEIMER
> Journal entry, August 14, 1920

EARLY IN 1920 Arnold Koehler took a break from his studies at Cornell to pay another visit to George Fraser at his downtown Manhattan law office. Over lunch, the two adventurers compared their experiences crossing the Navajo country. Fraser was impressed with the unorthodox route that Koehler and his friend Charles Berolzheimer had taken to Rainbow Bridge. "I inferred you put it up to the boys pretty hard and did them a world of good," he wrote to Rust afterward. "You certainly put over a rough one in walking from the summit of Navajo Mountain to the Arch and back. I should think your experience of the heat of the Rainbow Plateau would warn you against such an effort."[2]

Evidently neither young man felt that Rust had unduly challenged them, for they were eager to have another go at the canyon wilderness. Charles, immersed in his studies at Harvard, wrote to Rust in March, saying that "every time I look at the picture of Navajo Mountain or at one of my Rainbow Arch pictures, I take in a deep breath and imagine myself to be breathing the dry desert air instead of the damp air of Cambridge. And my own bed seems harder to sleep in than the sandstone at the foot of Nonnezosshe."[3]

The two young men would soon have occasion to savor the southwestern atmosphere again. In August 1920 they were back in Utah, ready for another adventure with the Rusts. This time Dave planned to investigate the Escalante River region south of the Aquarius Plateau as well as tour some of the Utah High Plateaus. Dave and Jordan headed out from Kanab with their pack mule and riding horses for the seventy-mile trip north to Bryce, leaving the animals under Jordan's care at the Forest Service ranger station while he borrowed a car to meet Arnold and Charles in Panguitch.

Bryce Canyon at that time was under the jurisdiction of the Forest Service. Although national monument designation was three years away, tourist traffic was picking up; the Syretts' lodge and tent camp near Sunset Point had opened that summer to cater to visitors. Rust and the boys preferred to rough it outside the ranger station. Charles, Arnold, and Jordan enjoyed the view of the multi-colored pinnacles in the amphitheater of Bryce Canyon, and hiked down to the canyon bottom while Dave began readying gear for the trip. Back on the rim, the boys could see Navajo Mountain far to the southeast, a reminder of the views they had worked so hard to achieve the year before.

Closer to hand was a lookout point that Rust definitely did not want to miss: the ten-thousand-foot-high southern end of the Table Cliff Plateau, also known as Powell Point. Reaching the point involved a short descent and overnight stay at a ranch in the Tropic Valley to the east of Bryce, then a long climb up the western rampart of the plateau. The Powell Survey established a triangulation station here in 1875, and the master view it gave of the Paria amphitheater and points beyond told why. Charles observed that the view from the summit was partly obscured by haze (probably from distant forest fires), but even so, they could make out the Kaibab Plateau and Mount Trumbull on the Uinkaret Plateau, more than a hundred miles away. The party spent a chilly night at the point, setting fire to a large tree to announce their arrival to the residents of Tropic (the "leave-no-trace" outdoors ethic was still some years away).

As much as Rust enjoyed his panoramic overlooks, he understood that scenery alone did not hold young people's attention for long. He thought he could come up with a little bit of adventuring for Charles and Arnold. Looking east from Bryce with their binoculars two days before, they had seen a small arch in the cliffs below Powell Point. Now, having reached that promontory, they scrambled down the side of the cliff, where there was no trail and the steep, crumbling sedimentary layers afforded minimal footing. Arnold found the going pretty scary, but he wrote that "Charles was in his element. He went skipping blithely along as though there was a sidewalk under his feet. He was so light that the rocks hardly slid at all."

They reached what was actually a double arch or window, which they named Spectacle Bridge. From this vantage they enjoyed the sight of another graceful span carved from red sandstone on a nearby ridge, which few travelers took the trouble to see. The climb up was just as arduous, and Rust held Arnold by a rope in a few places. They returned to Powell Point and rode off in search of water, a campsite, and bed.

One of the advantages of touring in the Aquarius country was the small towns found in every major valley, which enabled the traveler to relax and reprovision every few days. Such amenities as drugstore soda fountains and movie theaters had been absent on the Navajo Reservation the year before, but in the town of Escalante, a day's ride east from Table Cliff, the boys enjoyed the chance to rest up. Dave was planning to head out into the desert again, hopefully clear to the tip of Fiftymile Mountain. This was his first trip into the Escalante River country since his 1897 trek into Glen Canyon.

They were heading into another immense wilderness. Almon H. Thompson of the Powell Survey led the first topographic reconnaissance of this region in 1872, a great traverse from Kanab to the mouth of the Dirty Devil River, where the party retrieved a boat left during their Colorado River voyage the year before. Trying to find a route eastward from the upper Paria River drainage, they crossed a divide and followed a little stream through a pleasant grassy valley. Farther down, however, the stream carved into a sandstone anticline. Their Utah packer, Pardon Dodds, told them they were on the upper reaches of the Dirty Devil, so, skirting the river gorge, they reconnoitered to the south. The stream, Thompson soon observed, debouched far to the south, and could not be the Dirty Devil. They had, in fact, come across the Escalante River, the last major stream to be placed on the map of the Lower 48 states. Thompson called the tributary to the river they had found "Rocky Gulch," and later, "False Creek"; it is today known as Harris Wash.[4]

Backtracking to the north, Thompson's party climbed the Aquarius Plateau and made their way to its eastern edge, where they got a good look at what they called the "Dirty Devil Mountains." Within a few years Powell would name them the Henry Mountains after his friend Joseph Henry, the Secretary of the Smithsonian Institution.[5] Thus they stitched together the last piece of the Colorado Plateau's topographic quilt. Thompson and other members of the Powell Survey returned in 1875 to begin mapping the region. They published the first topographic sheets of the Escalante basin and the Henry Mountains starting in 1886.

Rust and his outfit of 1920 were one of the first sightseeing parties to get into the Escalante canyons. Prospectors and oilmen were starting to examine the region, and cattlemen knew it well enough, but it would be almost another thirty years before the river and its storied side canyons and arches would be featured in a major magazine.[6] The topography posed severe barriers to travel. The geologist Herbert Gregory faced this problem in 1915 when he began his investigations of the area for the U.S. Geological Survey. As he reported in his landmark book *The Kaiparowits Region*, "the recognized 'ways of going' may be called roads only for want of a better name. They are in reality trails with alternating stretches of sand, bare rock, and steep inclines over which with few mishaps a skillful driver may conduct a strongly built, lightly loaded wagon."[7]

In the early 1900s the citizens of Escalante and Boulder Town searched for routes to take wagons between their villages, blasting out dugways in the sandstone and filling in hollows in the tortuous canyons surrounding the Escalante River. One early route descended into Phipps Wash and emerged at the river downstream from the present-day Highway 12 crossing at Calf Creek.[8] Soon after, a new route was located that dropped off of the crest of the Escalante anticline at what locals called Head of the Rocks, just north of where the modern highway descends into the canyon. The continuation to Boulder followed benches between Sand and Calf creeks. This road became an alternative to the so-called Boulder mail trail, a mule track that led across the slickrock to the north of the wagon road, descending into and out of the narrow defile of Death Hollow. All of these routes wandered painstakingly through the almost-continuous cliffs of Navajo Sandstone that guarded the river, and none permitted easy passage for a wagon and team.

For the traveler heading south, a relatively easy route lay over the long benchland that stretched fifty miles to the southeast from the town of Escalante to the historic crossing of the Colorado River at Hole-in-the-Rock. Rust chose this route rather than head directly up onto the Kaiparowits Plateau. They were heading into yet another of the Southwest's vast and not very well charted outbacks. The wagon road they were following dipped in and out of wash bottoms, skirting minor escarpments in the pale Entrada Sandstone. Most of the way was easy riding across the surface of the weathered red Carmel Formation, dotted with piñon and juniper trees. Above them rose the long escarpment of the Straight Cliffs, which terminated in the bulk of Fiftymile Mountain overlooking Glen Canyon.

Their immediate concern was water. There was a slim flow in Harris Wash, but farther south the side drainages, which headed in the dry cliffs to the west, contained nothing but sand and clay. They made it as far as Coyote Hole in the upper reaches of Coyote Gulch, but the "black, rotten water" at this feeble spring was barely enough for the horses. Rust left Charles and Arnold there, and taking Jordan, scouted the cattlemen's trail that led up through the cliffs. Although there were supposed to be a few springs scattered along the top of Fiftymile Mountain, it was a long, uncertain route, and the haze in the atmosphere promised to dilute the view from the end of the plateau. Reluctantly he and Jordan returned to camp and led the boys back to Harris Wash and good water.

Today's hiker, after following the popular and increasingly verdant route down Harris Wash to the Escalante River, might marvel that this canyon was once the principal road from Escalante through the Waterpocket Fold. Charles Hall, a member of the 1879–1880 Hole-in-the-Rock party, discovered that just upstream from the mouth of Harris Wash, another canyon led up to the crest of the Fold. This canyon was named Silver Falls for the lovely drapery of desert varnish adorning its sheer cliffs. Hall's route crossed the Fold via a convoluted sandstone canyon the settlers called Muley Twist, which emptied out onto the barren plain of Halls Creek. This wash led down to a ford at the Colorado River, where Hall ran a ferry for a few years.[9] This was the closest thing to a road across the Fold.

With the advent of the Glen Canyon National Recreation Area in 1972, cattle grazing was curtailed within Harris Wash, and dense willow stands and numerous beaver ponds began to encroach on the trail. In Rust's time the canyon bottom was grazed nearly bare. Wagons, and later trucks and even automobiles, were taken over the route, the drivers prying out flood-washed boulders as needed. As they followed the canyon, Rust and the boys enjoyed seeing the small ruins and granaries perched in the cliff walls, which overhung dramatically in a series of grand bends as they approached the Escalante River. Crossing that stream, the road continued up Silver Falls Canyon toward the Waterpocket Fold. When they reached the first ramparts of the Circle Cliffs, Rust veered north, passing near a dry well that the Ohio Oil Company had drilled below Wagon Box Mesa just that year. Once again they were out of water, and after a day's ride of more than twenty miles they had to make a dry camp. Arnold's journal entry the next morning indicates their discomfort:

> Dry camping with dry horses does not come under the head of amusements. So when Mr. Rust woke us up at four and got the horses together there was not a dissenting note in the whole party. Even Charles jumped right up and

got dressed. The most important question, of course, was where to get water. The map that one of the Escalante people had drawn for us showed water only in Circle Cliffs Valley, twenty miles away, so we had to get there. In the chill gray of the morning we started. It was not nearly sun up yet, and we only had eaten a few raisins and prunes. All in all it was a very woe begone party. On our way to the valley we found a dried creek bed which had horse tracks going up it. Mr. Rust thought there might be water up there, so we followed it up to the head without success.

They made their way north among the buttes and hummocks that rose in the interior of the Circle Cliffs Upwarp, the exposed heart of a giant anticline. The Wingate Sandstone cliffs that ringed this amphitheater were cut through by stream courses that usually carried no water. With considerable effort and anxiety they searched the dry cliffs for signs of a spring, eventually finding some rockbound pools near a feature called the Lamp Stand, a small pinnacle that rises north of today's Burr Trail. Rust did not often get into such scrapes, but this was unfamiliar territory, and unlike the local cattlemen he did not know the location of every waterhole. They were probably in no real danger—Dave knew how far you could push things if you had to—but it was a trial nonetheless for his young friends.

After this welcome refreshment it was time to climb west and north onto the cooler and greener Aquarius Plateau. Rust had seen little or none of the Aquarius before his 1915 High Plateaus trip with George Fraser, but the huge, forested tabletop, especially its eastern part known as Boulder Mountain, was becoming one of his favorite destinations. He liked to call it "a perfect flower-land" and a "rendezvous for poets," marking Dutton's claim that on its summit "the explorer... forgets that he is a geologist and feels himself a poet."[10] To reach it, they chose a route up the southeastern flank of the mountain, climbing out of the piñon-juniper woodland of the Circle Cliffs and into the lovely ponderosa pine forest that swathed the middle slopes. Aspen groves along the trail soon beckoned for a halt, and at a small lake the party stopped for lunch and a bath. Charles's delight in reaching the forest inspired this little paean:

How glorious it is to have all the water you want! Yes, it is a great treat, but only after a desert trip, where the value of it is realized; where it is lacking— where it is always the elixir to be sought for and cherished.... We have been over such a trip; we have come to the place where water is plentiful—where

Graduation portrait, Richfield High School. *Courtesy of Blanche Rasmussen.*

Dave (left) and his brother Will in camp, probably during their 1899 prospecting adventure in the Henry Mountains with Nathaniel Galloway. *Courtesy of Blanche Rasmussen.*

Edwin D. ("Uncle Dee") Woolley Jr. (left), Utah Senator George Sutherland, and Utah Governor A. L. Thomas on the Kaibab Plateau, 1905. Woolley arranged for a string of notables to see his North Rim country, which he felt was ready to become a tourist Mecca. *Courtesy of the Edwin Dilworth Woolley Photograph Collection, L. Tom Perry Special Collections, Harold B. Lee Library, Brigham Young University, Provo, Utah.*

The first passengers to ride the Rust tram across the Colorado River. Dave recorded their names as "Rose Evans and Lida Belveal, two young ladies from El Tovar and Los Angeles." An unidentified crewman of the Grand Canyon Transportation Company accompanies them. *Courtesy of Blanche Rasmussen.*

Rust's Camp in Bright Angel Canyon. A spartan precursor to today's Phantom Ranch, the tent camp was located near the present-day mule corrals on the east side of Bright Angel Creek. Note the stone fence and garden area. *Courtesy of the Edwin Dilworth Woolley Photograph Collection, Brigham Young University.*

Dave Rust in the Inner Gorge of the Grand Canyon, on an upriver excursion from Bright Angel Creek with Emery Kolb in February 1909. Photo by Emery Kolb. *Courtesy of Blanche Rasmussen (also in Kolb Collection, NAU PH568-865).*

Unidentified (but brave) passenger riding the lumber cable to the top of Cable Mountain, Zion Canyon, 1912. *Courtesy of Blanche Rasmussen.*

Early auto excursion to Bright Angel Point. *Courtesy of the Edwin Dilworth Woolley Photograph Collection, Brigham Young University.*

Ruth and Dave at home in Kanab, 1907. Children from left: Jordan, Richard, Emma. *Courtesy of Blanche Rasmussen.*

Dave and Ruth Rust at the new Grand Canyon Lodge on the North Rim, September 1928. The Park Service invited the Rusts to attend the dedication of this spectacularly situated lodge and the nearby North Kaibab Trail, which replaced Rust's trail down Bright Angel Canyon. The tourist future of the North Rim was now assured. *Courtesy of Blanche Rasmussen.*

George Fraser Jr. in the Zion Narrows, North Fork Virgin River, July 1914. *Courtesy of Dorothy Shore.*

The Frasers (George Sr. and Jr.) enjoy a view from the North Rim of the Grand Canyon on their 1914 trip with Rust. *Courtesy LDS Church Archives, Rust Collection.*

George Fraser near the summit of Mt. Marvine, a high point on his 1915 High Plateaus trip with Rust. Fraser's Alpine experience as a youth helped him surmount this rather breathless pitch. *Courtesy of Dorothy Shore.*

Charles Berolzheimer, Rust's companion on several long pack trips, on a snowy morning on the Aquarius Plateau, August 1920. *Courtesy of Blanche Rasmussen.*

Breaking camp below the Aquarius, August 1920. *Courtesy of Blanche Rasmussen.*

J. Cecil Alter (left) dropped off George Fraser and his daughter Sarah in the 100-degree heat of Hanksville, en route to their Glen Canyon voyage of July 1930. *Used by permission, Utah State Historical Society, all rights reserved.*

Glen Canyon, July 1930. Rust pilots Sarah Fraser in his King canvas boat. *Courtesy Special Collections, J. Willard Marriott Library, University of Utah.*

Dave Rust, George Fraser, and Jerry the mule, 1930. *Courtesy of Blanche Rasmussen.*

Motoring down Capitol Wash in the Waterpocket Fold was a chancy undertaking in the 1920s and 1930s. The route remained in use until a paved highway was opened along the Fremont River in 1962. *Courtesy of Blanche Rasmussen.*

Dave at prospector's cabin, Hite, Utah. *Courtesy of Blanche Rasmussen.*

An Escalante cowboy admires the "Honda" (Broken Bow) Arch in Willow Gulch, a tributary of the Escalante River, on Rust's trip with Dodge Freeman, May 1941. Rust called it "one of the three best bridges of the 6 seen on trip." *Courtesy LDS Church Archives, Rust Collection.*

George Fraser (sitting), Dave Rust (right), and unidentified person at the Powell Survey monument on Mt. Dellenbaugh, Shivwits Plateau, Arizona, 1930. *Courtesy of Blanche Rasmussen.*

Nelson Rust with Dave's canvas canoes in Glen Canyon, near the Crossing of the Fathers. Note inner-tube life ring in stern. *Courtesy LDS Church Archives, Rust Collection.*

Expansive views toward Gregory Butte greeted Freeman and Rust when they climbed out of Glen Canyon on their Colorado River voyage in 1939. *Courtesy LDS Church Archives, Rust Collection.*

The long trail ahead: Dave Rust and Dodge Freeman take a break at a corral on the Horse-thief Trail during their 1935 Orange Cliffs circumambulation. *Courtesy LDS Church Archives, Rust Collection.*

Dave Rust and Emery Kolb at the South Rim, December 11, 1945. The two Grand Canyon pioneers met around 1907 and became lifelong friends. *Courtesy of Blanche Rasmussen.*

canteens or kegs need never be filled—the Aquarius Plateau—the mountain down whose green aspen-covered sides run a hundred streams in and out of myriads of little lakes.

Rather than push on for the summit of the plateau, which was ringed by volcanic cliffs, they descended again into the Boulder Creek drainage, heading for the hamlet of Boulder Town and an overnight at Francis Lyman's ranch. Food was next on the young men's minds, and a campfire dinner at the Lymans, consisting of potatoes, eggs, onions, milk, and cream, completed the day.

Lyman was willing to show the party the way back up the mountain, following a faint trail up the East Fork of Boulder Creek past some small lakes and beaver ponds. As they rode through a soaking cloudburst, Lyman warned them that the late-summer "monsoon" season was on them, and to be prepared for wet weather from now on. The boys didn't realize how completely the change in elevation would alter the weather. As they reached the summit of the plateau near Horseshoe Lake, nearly eleven thousand feet high, the wind blew raw and they eagerly sought the warmth of their beds.

Arnold and Charles both noted how appreciative Francis Lyman was of the beauty of the mountainside. Often on Rust's trips, local people professed disbelief that someone would want to ride through the wilderness simply for the fun of it. With George Fraser, Rust got used to saying that they were "just prospecting around"; on this trip, the story was that they were looking for oil—the buzz of the current year. Charles wrote that Lyman was one of the few who understood their scenic quest. He "seemed to derive the utmost pleasure in showing us the different beautiful spots among which he has spent the greater part of his life."

That morning, riding over the gentle summit of the plateau toward Spectacle Lake, the boys took in the pleasant scene. "Every few hundred yards a new lake or pond appeared," Charles wrote, "some surrounded with tall spruce trees, others edged with rocks or long marshy grass, from its mirror-like surface. One serene body of water after another, one grove of long green grass surrounded by dark trees after another, one wide flat after another covered with grass cropped short by the sheep; black boulders of all sizes; these things did we fully appreciate and enjoy, as we rode along." Rust, busy with camp chores, never put down his own reactions, but he must have taken great pleasure in his young friends' enjoyment of the Aquarius. Here was a fine example of one's environment exerting a gentle pull in the direction of appreciation and betterment.

Riding out from camp they soon came across a herd of three thousand sheep—just one of many herds that made up the sixty thousand sheep grazing on the Aquarius that year.[11] Dave needed to restock the larder, so he located the foreman and procured a lamb for seven dollars, which he proceeded to butcher. Charles was fascinated and photographed the whole process. Arnold investigated the sheepherder's tent, noting that its library included books on Latin grammar and plane geometry. Many of these sheepmen were students trying to keep up their education. The herder invited them to afternoon dinner, consisting of "bread, jam, honey, lamb's liver, kidneys and heart, and rice," much to the boys' enjoyment.

The Aquarius, true to its name, provided the party with plenty of water—though not necessarily in the form they anticipated. On August 20 Dave and Jordan awoke to find the walls of their tent pressing in on them, weighted down with three inches of snow. They shook off the tent and roused Arnold and Charles, who were decidedly surprised by the sudden transformation of the plateau into a gleaming winterscape. But the high-altitude sun soon melted the snow, and they continued on after more views.

Dave wanted to show the boys the panorama from Bowns Point, arguably one of the finest in the entire Colorado Plateau. Arnold decided to stay in camp with Jordan, however, so Dave and Charles rode the several miles to the point. This cliff, named for the cattleman Will Bowns who operated the Sandy Ranch east of the Waterpocket Fold, sticks out on the southeastern edge of the Aquarius, giving a commanding view extending from the Henry Mountains, around through the broken-up Escalante canyons, to the wide, mysterious Kaiparowits Plateau. The rains had cleared the atmosphere, and in the distance the towers of Monument Valley and even the hump of the Kaibab Plateau could easily be seen. Closer at hand, at the foot of the sheer cliffs at the plateau's edge, the dark greens of spruce and pine and lighter-green aspen provided a pleasing contrast.

Earlier explorers had also discovered that this vantage offered a superb overview of the country. In 1866 a detachment of Utah's territorial militia under Captain James Andrus traveled over the summit of the Aquarius on an expedition nominally intended to locate the mouth of the Green River. Franklin B. Woolley, an older brother of Dee Woolley, kept the log of the expedition and recorded this description of the view at or near Bowns Point:

At noon on Sunday Oct. 2d we came suddenly out on to a high bold promontory of the S Eastern edge of the mountain overlooking the country to N.E.E. and SE and South. In some directions probably for a distance between one hundred and two hundred miles. Immediately under us and down the black volcanic precipice forming the South Eastern face of the mountain and more than a thousand feet below are three small lakes surrounded by groves of timber beautifully Situated.... Below these lakes again, down under another precipice to the S.E. is the Colorado Plateau. Stretching away as far as the Eye can see a naked barren plain of red and white Sandstone crossed in all directions by innumerable gorges similar to those mentioned above. Occasional high buttes rising above the general level, the country gradually rising up to the ridges marking the 'breakers' or rocky bluffs of the larger streams. The Sun shining down on this vast red plain almost dazzled our eyes by the reflection as it was thrown back from the fiery surface.[12]

Woolley's description is notable for mentioning the "Colorado Plateau" three years before John Wesley Powell and his men boated down the Green and Colorado rivers. Powell initially used the term to denote the Coconino Plateau south of the Grand Canyon instead of describing the entire region surrounding the middle stretch of the Colorado River. The Andrus party approached no closer to the confluence of the Green and Colorado rivers, which they could see was locked in a maze of canyons off to the east. Instead, they headed northwest across the Aquarius to Otter Creek and Grass Valley. Woolley took note of prospects for future settlement in the area, and found conditions favorable in a place they named "Potatoe Valley"—the site of the town of Escalante.

Rust wanted to linger at Bowns Point, but the afternoon rains were beginning, so he led the way back to camp. Jordan had built a good fire, dried their wet blankets, and showed Arnold how to construct comfortable beds of spruce boughs, so all enjoyed a restful night despite the cold.

It was time to leave the high country and head down to warmer regions for resupply. They picked their way down from Bowns Point on a steep and treacherous sheep trail, reaching the aspen belt under the cliffs, and continued down Tantalus and Temple creeks (now called Oak and Pleasant) toward the Waterpocket Fold. At the old Eph Hanks ranch on Temple Creek—a property that later became the Sleeping Rainbow tourist lodge—they got a good meal, pasturage, and stories from Rust's old friend Benjamin Baker.

After spending the night at Baker's ranch, the party headed north along the western edge of the dramatic Waterpocket Fold to the Fremont River. At the village of Junction (now called Fruita) they enjoyed the season's fresh apples from its cliff-bordered orchards. They rode downriver and managed to locate Hickman Natural Bridge, then unnamed, which several townspeople had told them about. In a few more years some local residents would recognize that the Navajo Sandstone domes rising above the Fremont could attract tourists, and began to talk up the idea of a "Wayne Wonderland" national park. Charles, the outsider, at once recognized the beauty of the Waterpocket Fold: "These cliffs did not resemble any we had ever seen before. They wound in and out, making huge amphitheaters, at times broken by a deep canyon. And, above all, intertwined and interlocked with the cliffs and immense canyon walls, rose magnificent temples in red or white, steep pinnacles or beehive domes, or any of a great variety of grand looking spectacles."

He may have appreciated the scenery, but Charles was not exactly on to the ways of the locals. The owner of the ranch where they were having lunch took an interest in Charles's horse:

"That's a nice horse you've got there," pointing at Bullets. Ever do any trading?"

"Oh sometimes."

"I've done trading but I always get beat: I always get beat—yes, I always get beat." Which remark fixed the mental capacity of Mr. Mulford in our minds.

Fortunately for Charles, he did not own the horse he was riding, so he did not try to match wits with the canny gentleman.

Rust led the party farther up the Fremont River to a camp beneath Chimney Rock, a striking monolith at the western entrance of present-day Capitol Reef National Park. On their last day in the wilderness, Dave took the boys on a long detour up onto Thousand Lake Mountain for a final view of the canyon country. On the way they stopped in Torrey, a few miles west of camp, where Dave was surprised to find a fellow he had met on the Colorado River a quarter-century before. Taking a turn at the journal, Rust remarked on the memories that welled up from his boyhood; apparently he had not been back since leaving for Fredonia. "It was like a dream to find a familiar face in a once very familiar strip of country. All day I have been turning over bygone pages of life's diary."

Then it was up the long southern slopes and ledges of the mountain. Like its companion plateaus, the Fishlake and the Aquarius, Thousand Lake Mountain rose to over eleven thousand feet—"the altitude intoxicates us and makes the animals hot," Dave noted. As they climbed he observed that "all around us are peaks and towers of red and white—in fact all the primary and secondary colors and all other possible shades of color intermingled—such as would overwhelm the color photographer or the painter." Many of Rust's landscape descriptions took note of the variegated colors found in the sandstones, shales, and limestones of the Colorado Plateau; for one who was not an artist he seemed to derive particular enjoyment from noticing the bold reds of the Wingate and Moenkopi rocks and the gentle pastels of the Chinle and the various Cretaceous and Tertiary formations.

The trail was steep, but ahead lay one more of his "lookoffs," and Dave could not resist. At last they reached the summit of the plateau. Here was yet another grand panorama, as fine as the others they had witnessed on the trip. He sketched out the view:

> From the southeastern point we look down upon the colored world—a hundred miles of the Waterpocket Fold stretching from the San Rafael to the Colorado. The Henry Mountains are plainly outlined and the Elk Ridge [beyond the Colorado in the Abajo Mountains] is dimly seen through the haze. The Dirty Devil River loops away to its destination and all the mesas, temples, strips of red and blue deserts and deep red gorges so varied and numerous that we are puzzled and hypnotized. Lakes are under us all round the "second jump" of the mountain. Arnold asks where the thousand are. We conclude that the explorer who named the region "saw double" or possibly fainted in an attempt to make an accurate count. The towns of Torrey and Teasdale are tiny green patches nestled in the nooks far below. Sheep bells and a couple of herders draw us away and we cross the plateau to the only spring—a "drop down" for the last night in the woods. Lamb chops, new potatoes in cream, the world's prize winning honey and hot doughgods filled up our gaunt features and a bed of spruce boughs took us into a sleep undisturbed by mosquitos or other undesirable creatures.

A tough climb, a grand view, a dutch-oven dinner, a bed under the stars—of such things are perfect days made.

In the trips of these two summers, Rust had taken Arnold and Charles to the best viewpoints he knew, pointing out the great landmarks of the Colorado Plateau from many vantage points. Charles and Arnold, for their part, had shown that they could take on the toughest trails in the region, push through hundred-degree heat in search of water, and keep warm in the chilly deluges of the Aquarius. Hardship and beauty were somehow associated; they had earned their views. For a teacher like Dave, watching them tackle the challenges of travel and camping in rough terrain brought a lot of satisfaction.

Back down in the Fremont Valley the next day, Rust pastured his horses and cast around to find someone to take them to Manti and the rail station. Most everyone was at work with the harvest, but they managed to find a young man who could take them in his father's Model T. They left the next day. The stress and worry of the trip were over, and Dave enjoyed some light moments with the boys. Finding a pair of elk antlers discarded by a hunter, he hid behind a haystack and got the boys' attention with his best impression of a bugling elk. After mounting the antlers to the car's hood ("Fords are hornery creatures," Arnold observed), they took off on a bumpy road across the rolling highlands of the Awapa Plateau, bound for Fish Lake. At this long, glacially scoured lake they spent the night at a small fishing resort, Dave and the boys taking rowboats out to try their luck. Later that evening they kept the other guests up with an improvised hootenanny. For Dave, this wasn't guiding; it was more like a family holiday. They stayed over another day so Arnold and Jordan could fish, but Charles was willing to accompany Dave to visit one more vantage point. The two climbed easy trails up to the Fishlake Hightop, where they enjoyed lunch with a pair of sheepherders. Back at the hotel, Arnold and Jordan had made the acquaintance of "two beautiful Loa girls," in Charles's words, with whom they went for a row on the lake. The day ended with the charming scene of everyone sitting around a campfire singing old Scotch ballads. Perhaps it really was a more innocent time.

On August 27 they arrived in Manti, the antlers still mounted on the Ford. Rust helped Charles find a carpenter to make a crate in which to ship them home, then went to call on his parents. For the benefit of their guests, George Rust recounted some of his experiences crossing the plains in 1847 and the first hard years in the Salt Lake Valley. Finally it was time to say goodbye to Charles and Arnold, who boarded the train for Salt Lake City and the comforts of the

Hotel Utah. They would return in three years to enjoy another adventure with the Rusts, this time in the very different ambience of Glen Canyon on the Colorado River.

While Dave had missed his chance in 1920 to take in the view from the end of Fiftymile Mountain, he found a chance to remedy this two years later. George Fraser had been corresponding with Dr. Raymond C. Moore of the University of Kansas about his geological investigations on the Kaiparowits Plateau; Moore was working with Herbert Gregory of the U.S. Geological Survey on a study of the economic geology of the region. Fraser was intrigued with this seldom-explored section of the canyon lands, and wrote to Rust in May to propose another expedition.[13] The chance to witness the hawk-like view from the end of the plateau was too much to pass up. They made plans to rendezvous in Richfield in early July—once more braving the heat of midsummer.

Fraser again brought his daughter Jane to Utah for what would be a much more strenuous outing than the previous year's. Rust brought Jordan to help wrangle the animals. A drive over the Fishlake took them to the Torrey valley to collect Dave's riding stock. They attended the Fourth of July festivities at the Teasdale town hall: "Young Coleman Snow acted as master of ceremonies," Fraser recorded, "with the assistance of Miss Brinkerhoff, teacher at Glendale, who resides here. She invited Rust and me to speak. I made Rust accept but declined myself, because I was fearful lest I might tread on the Mormons' toes. As soon as I found how the performance was going, I exceedingly regretted my refusal.... A very dignified, serious performance, entirely devoid of any religious suggestions or significance, and purely patriotic throughout."[14]

Their horseback journey took them over the Aquarius Plateau and across Death Hollow. After climbing Canaan Peak, the highest point on the Kaiparowits, they traversed under the shale slopes beneath Powell Point on the Table Cliff Plateau. Camping in a pleasant, spring-fed meadow, Fraser wrote that "the amphitheater in which this camp 18 lies is grander and more pleasing and impressive than the exposures on the Paunsaugunt. Above us is a natural bridge in the pink limestone, which overlies heavy bed of shales."[15]

After overnighting in Tropic, they began the most severe part of their trip—the Last Chance Creek desert at the foot of the Kaiparowits Plateau. Their goal was to follow the route used by the Dominguez-Escalante expedition of 1776–

1777 to reach the Crossing of the Fathers in Glen Canyon. This was dry, rugged country, but the group negotiated the slickrock trail, climbing through a notch in a ridge at Gunsight Butte and descending to the Colorado River at Kane Creek, near the historic crossing. Rust at that time did not appear to know the location of a set of steps that Escalante mentioned in his diary, by which the party descended over icy rocks to the river. These were located a mile downstream from Kane Creek at a side drainage that would later be named Padre Creek.[16]

The return leg involved climbing to the crest of the Kaiparowits Plateau, an immense tableland looming above Glen Canyon. Here they met Raymond Moore, who was doing his season's field work. He would publish his findings as part of Herbert Gregory's 1931 report *The Kaiparowits Region*. At the southern tip of the Kaiparowits, the plateau narrowed to a bold prow overlooking Glen Canyon, affording the grand viewpoint that Rust and Fraser anticipated. Directly below them the Colorado River threaded a course through Glen Canyon, while only fifteen miles to the southeast rose the great bulk of Navajo Mountain, which the two men had climbed in 1916. Between the two high points lay some of the most broken and difficult topography in the West.

Descending eastward from the Kaiparowits via a cattlemen's trail in Collett Canyon, the foursome ended their pack trip with a long ride underneath the Straight Cliffs to the town of Escalante. They arrived on July 27 to find a three-day celebration of Utah's Pioneer Day still in progress. They watched horse races and wrestling and boxing matches; an amateur theater presentation that night was "very creditably done," Fraser noted.[17] Between the July 4 celebration in Teasdale and this event, they had been out in some of the least inhabited country one could still find in America.

The Frasers returned to Richfield in a hired motorcar, following the Birch Creek–Escalante Canyon route that climbed over the divide between the Table Cliff and Aquarius plateaus. At the time, this was the only road connecting Escalante with the rest of the world. In a recap of the journey that he sent to Rust, Fraser wrote that "the flivver kicked a good deal at the hills and never would have negotiated the pass but for the generous assistance from a crowd of husky boys returning after celebrating the 24th." The local villagers' hospitality seemed boundless. "At Widtsoe, Mr. Montague and his wife awaited us, and we were transferred to their machine. We lunched with them at Coyoto and had difficulty in refusing their cordial invitation to stop for a week. You know what Widtsoe is."[18]

In the coming years the two families continued frequent exchanges of news. Ruth sent the Frasers jars of her homemade preserves at Christmas, and George Fraser reciprocated by sending a pair of expensive Zeiss binoculars to Dave. He wrote: "I hope it arrives in good order & that it will serve through (the rest of?) your declining years if not as a beacon at least as an aid to vision." Rust no doubt appreciated the gift, but even more he must have felt the benediction of a friend who could feel free to rib him about his age.

Still another hallmark of their friendship came in 1923, when Jordan Rust was looking at pursuing a college education. At the time, he was taking classes at the Dixie Normal College in St. George, but he was interested in broadening his horizons, perhaps by attending Brigham Young University in Provo, as his father had done. At the conclusion of their 1922 trip to the Crossing of the Fathers, Fraser suggested that he be allowed to underwrite part of Jordan's tuition. He took up this idea again in a letter to Jordan the following April, urging him to think beyond the borders of Utah. "In many ways you would get a great deal out of a year or two in Provo; probably you would have more enjoyment there than anywhere else, but it seems to me that [Brigham] Young would be for you very much what Harvard is for a boy living in Cambridge—disadvantageous because its atmosphere and association brings nothing new and hence lacks the broadening influence of an environment different from what one is accustomed to." Fraser was careful not to disparage the Utah school, but he advised Jordan to look at Harvard, or at least Stanford, where Dave had attended years before. "My belief is you will do more for yourself, your family and your people later on," he wrote, "if you jump into strange waters than if you follow along the lines of the familiar." [19]

In the end, Jordan chose to go to Palo Alto. Fraser offered a three-thousand-dollar loan without any conditions of repayment, saying only that Jordan not inform his father about it. Dave found out, of course, but he did not stand in the way of the generous offer. Jordan wrote years later that he could not have attended Stanford without it. [20] It was an amazing kindness from a friend, one that Jordan never forgot.

Fraser and Rust enjoyed reminiscing about their trips even though they were not able to join up in the field. A favorite topic was which scenic viewpoints were the best in the region. In 1925 Fraser took up the issue over lunch in New York with the geologist Herbert Gregory: they "instantly agreed on Navajo Mountain as No. 1, with Table Cliff, Tantalus, the south-east tip of the Fifty Mile Mountain and Mt. Ellen in the second class."[21] Fraser, a book collector, sent Rust copies of some of the classic texts of the Southwest's explorers, including a volume from the Wheeler Survey and the U.S. Geological Survey's Second Annual Report, containing some of Clarence Dutton's preliminary work on his *Tertiary History*. Dave sometimes found occasion to return the favors, such as when Fraser requested a letter of introduction to Utah senators Reed Smoot and William H. King, with whom Fraser wanted to work out some change in legislation affecting his railroad investments. Usually, though, Fraser's wealth and standing ensured that most of their exchanges would be to Dave's benefit. The new clients that Fraser referred formed a significant part of his business. Still, their warm letters suggest that it remained a friendship of equals. "Anyone is justified in deriving satisfaction from a friendship which persists between any two who have journeyed in the rough together," Fraser offered in response to a complimentary letter from Rust. "My own satisfaction is the greater because there is no one whose good opinion I value more highly than yours."[22] This from a man who hobnobbed with the cream of New York society.

Dave missed his companionship. In 1925 he lamented to Jordan that Fraser appeared to be in too poor shape to make any further trips into the backcountry. "He begins to doubt if he will ever hit the trail with us again," Rust wrote. "You know, this cuts me to the bone for I like to be with him very much."[23] But he had gained a great deal from George Fraser's acquaintance, including an approach to guiding that emphasized close contact with the land and its inhabitants. The Dirty Devil cowboy had forged an unusual connection to this proper, well-spoken New Jersey gentleman. Their friendship, and the wonders they had seen in the backcountry, would continue to have a major influence on Rust's life and career.

12 | *Return to Glen Canyon*

The trip down the river seems like a delightful dream. I see that powerful current sweeping along by the cliffs. I hear your songs and see your figures in the distance dwarfed by the magnitude of the towering rocks. The trip altogether was so much more impressive than I had imagined possible that I will make no comparisons. It is unique.

J. P. PROCTOR
Letter to Dave Rust, 1925[1]

At about 3:30 we left the cheery town of Hyte and started on our 150 mile trip down the Colorado River where we expect to be the only living human beings, without much chance of being disappointed.

JORDAN RUST
Journal entry, July 20, 1923[2]

GLEN CANYON, the Colorado River's easygoing middle reach, began in the tailwaters of the boat-eating maelstrom of Cataract Canyon and ended at Lees Ferry, just above the dangerous rapids of Marble Canyon. Between these barriers the Colorado's muddy flow swept past long, tapestried walls of sandstone, giving boaters time to admire the changing panorama. There were minor rapids where the river broke over bedrock ledges or ran into boulders ejected at the mouths of canyons, but early-day river runners found Glen a welcome relief from the fearsome drops and holes of Cataract. John Wesley Powell, who led the first recorded traverses of the canyon in 1869 and 1871, initially gave two names to this stretch of the Colorado: Mound Canyon, for the bald-head sandstone domes in its upper section, and Monument Canyon, for the turreted, massive buttes lower down.

Were it not for the difficult stretches that bracketed it, Glen Canyon might have seen considerable river traffic even before Powell's day. As it was, the canyon probably drew more use during the mining boom of the 1880s and 1890s than in the first half of the twentieth century. Set in a vast, roadless wilderness, no easy routes led down to the canyon. Other than at major side drainages such as Crescent Creek, Glen's sheer sandstone walls presented a challenging obstacle, as the Mormon emigrants to Bluff discovered at Hole-in-the-Rock during the winter of 1879–1880. Even as late as the 1930s, the fords at Dandy Crossing and Halls Crossing were the only reasonable routes to take horses and stock across the river; automobile traffic had to wait until the Hite Crossing ferry began operation in 1946. Highway engineers bridged the river below Lees Ferry in 1929, but this left a long, roundabout route for travelers in south-central Utah.

Lake Powell, which began to fill in 1963, transformed Glen Canyon into one of the most celebrated vacation destinations in the West. The lake's deep, cliff-rimmed waters draw thousands upon thousands of motorboaters, water skiers, and Waverunner pilots. Its 160,000-acre expanse of blue water has come to symbolize the gulf between those who appreciate the power of the internal combustion engine to take them closer to nature's wonders, and the smaller number who look back to the days when oars and paddles, and the skill to use them, were the outdoorsman's essentials. The latter were Dave Rust's tools when he launched his Glen Canyon guiding business in 1923, bringing the first regular tourist traffic to that stretch of the river. Over a span of nearly two decades, he introduced dozens of clients to the joys of floating peacefully down the ever-changing canyon. This great river, with its endless stone walls always rising above, lodged in his mind early and never seemed to leave.

The gold rush that Cass Hite kicked off in 1883 brought hundreds of miners to Glen Canyon, but few of them took much interest in the canyon as scenery. Rust was an exception. Drawn to the river in the fall of 1897 with his brothers Will and Orion, he saw something there besides the possibility of a paying gold placer. In his essay "Boating on the Colorado" (1901), which drew on his experiences during two seasons on the river, he noted that "hard work seems less hard when one's mind is employed by pleasant thoughts." Some significant part of his time in the canyon appears to have been occupied in just such musings, staring up at Glen's golden walls, its mysterious and inaccessible cliff dwellings, its brilliant cloud-lit sky.

Dave's friend and literary mentor, Harrison R. Merrill, understood the close connection Rust felt to Glen Canyon. Merrill chose it as the setting for a 1929 article about Rust in *Improvement Era*, the Mormon youth publication he edited. Merrill depicted Dave working his placer claim as a young man, sweaty and bare-chested, halting to rest and admire the cliff walls above him. Dave proclaims to his brother Will that "this is a wonder river and a wonder canyon," and that someday people will pay good money to enjoy its scenery. "People ought to see this country," Dave declares, "and by cripes, I'm going to help them see it."[3] Merrill may have embellished Rust's sentiments, but he was probably accurate in tracing the origin of Dave's notion to work as a guide to those early years in Glen Canyon.

Rust tried to interest George Fraser in a Glen Canyon voyage soon after their first pack trip in 1914, and he rowed Fraser and his son a few miles upriver from Lees Ferry in a borrowed rowboat during their 1916 Navajo journey. But it was not until the summer of 1923 that he was able to launch a real trip into the river he called the "Silvery Colorado." The occasion was a third visit by Charles Berolzheimer and Arnold Koehler, the young Ivy League men who had accepted the challenge of traversing the Navajo country in 1919 and the Waterpocket Fold in 1920. By now they were good friends with Dave and his son Jordan and were ready to try something new.

Rust outfitted the trip by purchasing two collapsible canoes made by the Kalamazoo Canvas Boat Company. He was already familiar with these craft, having used one belonging to the Grand Canyon Transportation Company at Bright Angel Creek in 1908–1909. Fourteen feet long, stiffened by steel ribs running fore and aft as well as circumferentially, they came with a twenty-two-ounce canvas duck fabric that was stretched over the assembled frame. A waterproofing solution applied to the canvas completed the job. Designed as portable fishing boats for North Country lakes and streams, they were hopeless in big rapids but could handle ordinary waves and minor riffles. Outfitted with oars instead of paddles, the boats proved light and maneuverable and could carry hundreds of pounds of gear. (Rust preferred the control that oars gave him, though he sometimes carried paddles for his passengers to use.) The little boats could even handle the imposing sand waves that the Colorado often threw up unexpectedly in high water. Rust found that these waves were best taken on sideways instead of bow-first. Glen's rock-ledge drops proved more problematic, especially at low water levels, for the canoes could not take much of a scraping on the shallow shelves that spanned the river at several points. Despite being advertised as "puncture-proof," the boats were anything but. (Frederick Dellenbaugh recounted similar difficulties with these ledges during Powell's 1871 expedition, even though they were using wooden boats.[4])

Though his boats lacked the durability and cargo capacity of larger craft, they were quite adequate for Rust's low-key trips. He was already used to packing light for his long horseback journeys, and most of his kit could be adapted for use on the river. The boats' portability was their greatest advantage; they could be packed up with Rust's other duffel and shipped at modest cost with the U.S. Mail from Kanab to Hanksville. There he had arranged to transfer his gear to a mule-drawn wagon to be driven down to Hite at the head of Glen Canyon.

The greatest obstacle to floating Glen Canyon wasn't the river, but the arduous trek getting there. In the 1920s Hanksville seemed like the end of the earth. A county road connected it to the town of Green River, but this primitive track offered sixty miles of dust, dirt, sand blows, and gumbo. To the west of Hanksville, State Road 677 led to Torrey and the central Utah valleys, and while it was an official state route, it had some shortcomings. Instead of boring straight through the Waterpocket Fold along the Fremont River, the route of the modern Highway 24, the original route jogged south to enter Capitol Wash, a twisting, steep-walled, boulder-choked defile that had originally been cleared out by Wayne County pioneers, George Rust among them. Prone to flash floods in the summer, a traverse of Capitol Wash could be as hairy as any rapid in Glen Canyon. There also was the notorious Blue Dugway west of Caineville, a treacherous cut through a barren Mancos Shale hillside where one could easily lose a wagon in wet weather.

From Hanksville, Glen Canyon lay another fifty miles to the southeast. Not until the 1930s was there a usable auto road beyond Granite Ranch, sixteen miles south of Hanksville. Once at the head of Crescent Creek (later called North Wash), there were still miles of quicksand-laden wash bottom to negotiate before reaching the river. Faced with this lengthy trip to Hite in the summer of 1923, Rust chose a more appealing alternative: a horseback ride down the canyon of Trachyte Creek, the route used by most of the original Glen Canyon gold rushers. But first, obeying his desire to see as much country as possible, he would take Jordan, Charles, and Arnold on a roundabout horse-packing trip, making their way to Hanksville in leisure and seeing some high country until their boats arrived with the mail.

Dave and Jordan left Kanab on June 26, riding for three days up to the little village of Widtsoe, located just north of Bryce Canyon. Here they arranged pasture for their horses and hitched an auto ride north to Richfield, where they met Charles and Arnold at the Denver & Rio Grande station. Returning to Widtsoe, they set out on an unhurried tour of the Aquarius Plateau, revisiting some of the high country they had seen in 1920. Even Jordan was impressed with the Aquarius, writing in his journal that "this day will never be forgotten because of our renewal of acquaintance with the most enchanting country in the world."[5]

After crossing the Aquarius and the Waterpocket Fold, they reached the King Ranch on the west slope of Mount Ellen on the evening of July 8. This was the old George Coleman property where Rust and the Frasers had spent a pleasant evening in 1915 during their High Plateaus traverse. Over the next three days they replicated parts of that earlier journey, camping at eleven thousand feet in a saddle along the summit ridge of Ellen and enjoying a "fine ham" provided by a sheepherder. Then they climbed up to the glorious viewpoint atop the highest peak of the long ridge, where they took in "the great view," as Rust called it, with "clouds & storms around to make atmosphere the very best."

As a sidelight they indulged in some hard-rock prospecting, an idea Dave had never quite given up. On July 11 he took the boys down to Bromide Basin on the steep eastern slope of Mount Ellen, where they found the old prospect holes he had dug with Nathaniel Galloway in 1899. Here Dave placed new claim notices, ever hopeful that his diggings would one day prove out. Then they descended the steep northeast face of the mountain. "Down Bowl Creek we slide, rip and tear, making things descend pretty fast," Jordan wrote. (Bowl Creek was the earlier name for Bull Creek, the major drainage on that side of the mountain.) After another night and a hot breakfast at a friendly ranch, they pulled in to Hanksville to find that their boats had arrived safely.

Amid preparations for the river trip, Rust found time to arrange a social gathering. He still knew folks in Hanksville, so he sent out a call for anyone interested to meet at the assembly hall that evening for a dance. To the accompaniment of harmonica and organ, the townspeople enjoyed an evening out with the visitors from back east.

As it happened, a physician from New York named William Robinson was also touring through the region on his summer vacation. Robinson published an idiosyncratic newsletter he called *Critic and Guide*, a sort of wellness magazine of the day, filled with suggestions for leading a healthy and moral life. In an article modestly titled "The Editor and His Uniquely Glorious Trip," he described the curious scenery he had seen coming through the Waterpocket Fold: "I was wondering why nothing has been written and why so little is known about this wonderful canyon country between Torrey and Hanksville. If the Government adopted this region as a National Park, advertised it, improved the roads, people would be flocking to it. Because, I repeat, there are few regions in the world to surpass this in extent and grandeur."[6]

Hanksville itself made less of an impression on Robinson. Its austere setting left him wondering why God had set these people down in such a bleak place. But his account of the scene that evening at the assembly hall suggests that the townspeople could put on a lively show:

> At first there was only one dim lamp, that struggled but failed to overcome the darkness in the Hall, and the people danced more by touch than by sight; but soon two more lamps were brought in, and you could distinguish the faces of the partners.... The farmhands, and cowboys, who were at first a bit backwards, soon overcame their shyness, came in and joined the dance "and a good time was had by all." The college boys danced well—our college students do not permit their studies to interfere with their pleasures, which is quite right, and they enjoyed themselves as well as at any of the fashionable dances in New York.

Even though their boats had arrived, Dave and his compadres were in no hurry to get to the river. He arranged with a local man named Hall to take their gear to Hite, then led his crew back up to the Henrys to continue their wanderings. Exploring above Bromide Basin, Dave located another hard-rock claim. ("Locating," in miner's parlance, means staking the boundaries of a claim, typically by enclosing written notes in cans placed in rock cairns.) "Hope it turns out as in Nev. days of 49," Rust noted in his journal, referring to the gold-rush days of the Sierra Nevada.

Rust was in his element. Wandering around country he knew from his youth, spending evenings at friends' ranches or at sheep camps up in the timber, doing a little prospecting for fun—this was free and easy living, spent in the company of three young men whom he trusted to handle themselves. Up in the Henrys the cold, clear snowmelt streams rushed down from high meadows; ponderosas gave lunchtime shade and tall grass kept the horses happy. When one tired of life in the open, there waited life back home in Kanab, with family, responsibility, and a position of respect in the community. All this helped to cast a warm glow over their vagabond's life in the hills. Dave got along well with Charles and Arnold and enjoyed their lively intellects. (He worked Jordan a little harder.) On July 14,

Bastille Day, they celebrated by singing the Marseillaise, in French. They took turns reading an essay on money—apparently Emerson's "Wealth"— "apropos the mining venture." Later that day Dave left Jordan and Arnold at their shady camp while he and Charles, always the more adventurous one, climbed up to a high ridge to view the desert scene to the east. After returning to camp Dave suggested that they visit a herder's outfit he had seen lower down the slope, thinking they might buy some meat. They returned in time for dinner, carrying a whole mutton. Life seemed pretty good.

Five more days were spent getting to the river. Not all of this time was lost in pleasant dreaming; it rained steadily as they traversed southward underneath Mount Pennell and they were glad to dry out at a goat herder's fire. Feed for the horses was scarce at times, and one day all three boys were sick with colds and stomach pains. ("Even Jerry cinch sore," Rust wrote, referring to their pack mule.) Nevertheless, they took time to see the sights, scrambling up the steep, rocky slopes of Mount Ellsworth in the Little Rockies to savor fine views in all directions, including straight down Ticaboo Canyon to the Colorado River. That route seemed too steep, so they returned ten miles north to Trail Canyon, following this cobbled wash to Trachyte Canyon. They were again in desert country, and as they lost elevation the heat once again enveloped them. Trachyte Canyon, fortunately, held a running stream, and farther down canyon they poked up an interesting side drainage (now named Woodruff Canyon) to enjoy its cool narrows and a small waterfall.

Finally, on July 18, they reached the river at the old mining camp of Hite. Rust noted that only three dilapidated cabins remained there, one of them occupied by a Tom Humphries, a long-time placer miner and genial storyteller who was only too glad to have company. Though Hite was no longer a busy hub for Glen Canyon's gold miners, the site still served as a stopping point for travelers using the river crossing that Cass Hite had located in 1880. He named a shallow stretch above the mouth of White Canyon "Dandy Crossing," for it was one of the few feasible places to get through the cliffs and across the river.

Other than Humphries, the town site was abandoned. On the morning of the nineteenth, they rode up the river to Crescent Creek to collect their boats, and continued on to the mouth of the Dirty Devil, where they could look into the great gorge of the Colorado as the river emerged from Cataract Canyon.

It was time to get going. Dave let the boys launch the boats and float down to Hite, but they missed the landing and all hands had to get wet lining them back upstream. Both boats had punctures to repair—possibly Dave had purchased them used—which along with the labor of packing occupied them well into the afternoon of the next day. At 3:30 p.m. on July 20, they set out into the muddy waters of the Colorado. Rust piloted the lead boat and Jordan the other, with Charles and Arnold as passengers most of the time. That evening they made it to Good Hope Bar, where Dave had worked in the summer of 1898. There came the inevitable problems to deal with on this shakedown trip:

> Arnold & Jordan have trouble breaking oars. We took an extra ash from Dandy [Crossing]. On account of broken oars (and uncertain ability) I tow their boat over Trachyte rapid. The Ticaboo rapid gave us a lot of kick—each boat paddled through canoe fashion. A good deal of the time the hind boat was cross wise. Rained at bedtime.

Gregory Crampton, who compiled a history of Glen Canyon, described these rapids as dropping about five feet in half a mile, producing fast water at low river levels but no major hazards.[7] Still, this was Rust's first run on this stretch of river with his new boats, and he was not about to take any chances. The rocks and boulders that had flooded into the riverbed at the mouths of Trachyte and Ticaboo canyons required careful maneuvering to avoid tearing the boats' canvas fabric. Hitting one of these rocks the wrong way with an oar could easily break them, as they discovered.

Most of the time, though, the Colorado flowed in a broad, steady current, broken only by eddies, boils, and light riffles. Dave described it on another occasion as "muddy beyond description, a thick milk porridge." He showed the boys how an egg disappeared when dropped in a cup of the fluid. "You have to learn to like the Colorado," was his advice. Drinking the stuff, though, was another matter, and side canyons with pockets of clear water were especially welcome.

Dave decided his boats needed names. He chose to name his after John Wesley Powell and Jordan's after G. K. Gilbert, "since we have studied the records of these great explorers on our trip." His own journal refers to Powell's original name for the upper stretch of Glen:

Cool breeze, sprinkle, as we float down the graceful bends. An extraordinary panorama-movie. In reality, the shapes & carvings, & weatherings are countless and full of interest & variety, in fancy, there is unlimited opportunity for personification. "Mound" canyon sure enough—the river walls are deep red & usually sheer, the top wall has all sizes of hogans for a roof. And the variety in clouds blends to make the sweetest coloring.

Solitude—not a man on the river (they say) from here to Lee's Ferry. At Tickaboo [*sic*] ranch yesterday, we might have seen a Mr. Carpenter, but his reputation and a mile walk persuaded us to pass on. So we must put up with our own (meagre) company for 10 days. Our 14-foot specials are riding fine, but the oars are a complete humbling.

Rust could consult several books as a guide to Glen Canyon; the most detailed of these was Dellenbaugh's *A Canyon Voyage* (1908), which he had read years ago in the Grand Canyon. Powell's *Exploration of the Colorado River* (1875) mentioned only a few specific features in Glen Canyon, such as Music Temple and the Crossing of the Fathers. Rust also brought along the set of river survey maps that the U.S. Geological Survey had published in 1922. With these publications and his own knowledge of the river from his two mining forays in 1897–1898, he was able to stop at the most notable points of interest in Glen Canyon. These included Moqui Canyon, where the group inspected several ruins, but found them to be "of rather ordinary type." They were disappointed to find little flowing water in this side canyon, and what there was had been "polluted by cows." That fall, a National Geographic Society party led by Neil Judd and John Wetherill would spend four days in this canyon, conducting the first scientific excavations of its ruins.[8]

They moved on to find more interesting sights. Commemorating Utah's Pioneer Day on July 24, they pulled over below the historic Mormon wagon road at Hole-in-the-Rock. Climbing up the extraordinarily steep defile, they inspected the route the Bluff colonists had chiseled out to get their wagons down the cliff. Rust was impressed at this engineering feat—"one side of wagon must have rested on faith (other on rock trail cut)."

Below the mouth of the San Juan they stopped at one of Glen Canyon's most outstanding features. Dave had not been here before, but Powell's book promised a worthwhile stop. Dave's journal shows his delight and wonderment:

2 miles N.W. [from the San Juan] at the turn we come to Music Temple by Powell's description. Sure enough the most musical place we've ever seen. Everybody tries his voice. Too far from boats to carry stuff so we sleep on white sand in San Juan county & the Piute Reservation. This is exquisite architecture!! The Temple is not an auditorium but a music palace. More than expected. Should like to bring Miss Poll- or some other singer here. Feature this with Rock Cr. Rainbow trip. Try to find names of explorers but cannot. —feel the solemnity & sacredness of place.

On July 26 they pulled over to the south bank to take one of the more strenuous hikes of their trip—a long side canyon leading to Rainbow Bridge. A mile up the canyon they found a narrow "subway"—a section of overhanging walls that Rust described as "splendid." Farther on were several pools that they had to swim, one of them more than fifty feet long. Jordan recorded that they "walked and walked and walked up the narrowest canyon in the world." But after hiking more than seven miles they caught a glimpse of Navajo Mountain, and from its position realized they were following Oak Creek instead of Aztec and Bridge canyons. Tired and hungry, their shoes giving out, they turned back. "It was a forlorn and footsore party that reached camp that night at about 10 o'clock," Jordan wrote.

The next morning they floated a short distance around a bend to the mouth of Aztec Creek, negotiating a "heavy rapid." The leader of the 1922 U.S. Geological Survey party had painted the canyon wall here with the helpful sign "BRIDGE CANYON—T. C. WIMMER" to assist future visitors. Jordan's and Arnold's shoes had given out, so Dave and Charles set off up the canyon, carrying only a package of currants, figuring they would find water on the way.

By now Dave had visited Rainbow Bridge three times via the overland route— once in 1916 with George Fraser and twice in 1919 with Donald Scott and with Charles and Arnold. On this visit he noted that "the Arch still remains the magnificent single piece of rock carving." On the way up they met two Navajos heading for the river, so Dave asked them to encourage Jordan and Arnold to make the hike. But their tripmates were too tired, and after waiting in the shade of the bridge for a while, Dave and Charles headed back, stopping to enjoy a "delicious bathtub" near the junction of Aztec and Bridge canyons.

More waves and small rapids awaited as they drifted down to the Crossing of the Fathers. Rust grew nervous as he watched the second boat turn sideways and flounder in the waves, and he resolved to tow it if they encountered any more rough water. But no serious incidents occurred. Charles, in fact, was a good swimmer and easily stroked across the river at one smooth reach.

The Crossing of the Fathers, or *El Vado de los Padres*, as Dave generally called the historic ford, had become one of his favorite stops. He had first visited the ford in December 1897 on his way downriver from his mining camp to spend Christmas at the town of Pahreah.[9] In 1922 he and Jordan had led George Fraser and his daughter Jane overland from the Paria River to search for the crossing used by the Dominguez-Escalante party on November 7, 1776. This time he and the boys set up camp on the long sandbar by the crossing, and early the next morning retraced the old trail used by native peoples for centuries, climbing far enough to gain views of Navajo Mountain and nearby buttes. Dave did not record whether they found the steps that the Dominguez-Escalante party had chiseled into the rock near the mouth of what was later called Padre Creek.

They reached Lees Ferry and the end of Glen Canyon on July 29. Rust was surprised to find the place "thickly populated"—their little party happened to emerge from Glen just as another U.S. Geological Survey expedition was assembling, this time to descend the Grand Canyon. Directed by Claude H. Birdseye, chief of the survey's topographic division, and cosponsored by the Southern California Edison Company, this expedition was the last of three conducted from 1921–1923 to map potential hydropower dam sites along the Colorado. Its personnel included Rust's old friend Emery Kolb, who was on shore with his wife and daughter; E. C. LaRue, the leading advocate of Colorado River hydropower; and Lewis Freeman, who would chronicle the expedition in his book *Down the Grand Canyon*. Frank Dodge, a rodman (surveyor's assistant) with the party, rowed across the river that evening to visit Rust's camp. Jordan and Arnold walked down to the ranch at Lees Ferry, where Frank and Jerry Johnson gave them some welcome bread and fruit.

The next morning they crossed the river to visit with the rest of the surveying party. Rust shared his extensive knowledge of local river history, including the travails of the Escalante party and the Mormon pioneer John D. Lee.[10] The Geological Survey crew set off down Marble Canyon that morning, leaving Rust to take his group back to Kanab. His little tourist party had thoroughly enjoyed the beauties of Glen Canyon, and it was a bit ironic that they concluded their voyage by meeting the outfit that was laying plans to flood the canyon.

Rust's first river expedition convinced him that such trips could be made for profit, and that Glen Canyon's stunning scenery and historical points would interest visitors. But it would take decades for this stretch of the Colorado to get on most tourists' agenda. Dave, as usual, did not advertise his river-guiding service, and many decades later, few books on the river's history even mentioned his trips.[11] As with his overland outings, he relied on word of mouth to gain clients.

If Rust returned to the river in 1924 he kept no record of it, but in 1925 he made two voyages down Glen Canyon, both in the heat of midsummer. During the first ten days of July, he guided Dr. Frank R. Oastler of New York City and his wife, Maude, from Hite to Lees Ferry.[12] Dave's daughter Emma was along, and she and Maude Oastler became the first women known to have floated the length of Glen Canyon. Frank Oastler was a well-known surgeon on the faculty of Columbia University, and later served on the National Park Service's advisory committee on education in the parks. The Oastlers were touring the Southwest at the behest of Park Service director Stephen T. Mather, who had asked them to scout for possible new parks and monuments. George Fraser, once again, had referred the couple to Rust. Before meeting Dave for their river trip, the Oastlers engaged his fellow guide, Zeke Johnson, to show them some of the country around Natural Bridges National Monument, where Johnson served as custodian.

Following their survey of Cedar Mesa, Johnson brought the Oastlers down White Canyon to the Colorado River opposite Hite, where they awaited Rust's arrival with the boats. Jordan drove Dave and Emma to Hanksville in their Willys-Knight car and returned to Kanab, where his friend Charles Berolzheimer was once again staying with the family. Dave and Emma rode with the freight wagon directly down Crescent Creek. It took two and a half days of hard, dusty traveling from Hanksville to reach the river. A loose wagon tire came off as they started out, so Dave wedged it back on and devised some shims to hold it in place. Bacon grease served to lubricate the axle. At the river's edge, elevation 3,600 feet, he wrote with his usual understatement that "we notice the heat." He rendezvoused with the Oastlers on July 1, crossing the river to camp at the old Hite town site.

Emma had accompanied her father on a pack trip across the Paunsaugunt, Table Cliff, and Aquarius plateaus in 1924, and was used to sleeping on hard ground and riding twenty miles or more in a day. The river presented new difficulties, however, as Emma recounted for a family history:

I never did learn to swim so Dad put a life jacket on me and tied a rope around my waist and put me in the river to see if I could stay afloat in the swift water. Was I glad that I was never dumped out. Dad couldn't swim either. What a pair we were. Kanab had no swimming pool.

The river was very smooth most of the time until we came to the rough water, where we had to either run the rapids or portage around them. That was done by carrying the boats and all of the supplies down past the rapids on shore.... We camped on the sand bars or beaches. Mrs. Oastler slept in her tent. I just made a bed in the sand and put my sleeping bag down and made do. I was always tired enough to sleep anyway. All of the glens were so inviting along the way and we usually found springs of clear water.[13]

As on his first trip in 1923, Dave stopped at Hole-in-the-Rock, Music Temple, and the Crossing of the Fathers, as well as taking the party on the twelve-mile hike to Rainbow Bridge. Jordan drove the shuttle to Lees Ferry on July 10 to meet the river voyagers. Dave finished the excursion by taking the Oastlers to the North Rim, where they visited Point Sublime. Rust's brief journal for the trip recorded no major difficulties such as the broken oars that they experienced during their shakedown voyage in 1923. The main problems were those presented by the long distances and harsh conditions of a summertime trip in the desert. Heat, wind, and sun were the ordinary hazards of life on the river, but such inconveniences probably detracted little from the scenic delights of the trip. Twelve years later, Maude Oastler wrote to Rust following the death of her husband, offering her memory of the voyage: "It seems only yesterday that we were all going down the big river, and you were singing 'Flow Gently Sweet Afton' and suddenly we were in the Rockledge rapids and I nearly broke my teeth chewing a prune pit."[14] Floating for days down the wide, roiling stream, hiking up shady side canyons, making camp on the Colorado's broad sandbars—all this would have imparted a pleasant atmosphere to the trip.

Rust's second trip that summer took place from July 24 to August 3. His clients were another medical couple, Dr J. P. Proctor and his wife, Elizabeth Ritchie. Proctor was a noted ophthalmologist then living in Santa Fe, where he was studying the incidence of trachoma, an eye disease, in Native American populations. Ritchie had been Dave and Emma's guest on their High Plateaus pack trip of the previous summer. They also arrived at the river courtesy of Zeke Johnson. The voyage was plagued at times by strong winds and sandstorms, and the midsummer heat proved excessive, but they enjoyed fine campsites and made side hikes to Hole-in-the-Rock and Rainbow Bridge. Camping near the mouth of Last Chance Creek, Rust strolled along the sandbar by moonlight, reminiscing about a similar night in 1897 when he ran a stretch of the river with his fellow miner, Ed Meskin.[15]

When they reached Lees Ferry, Jordan and Charles were standing on the ferryboat to greet them. "Ice-cream & other refreshments for dinner—a great feast," Rust noted in his journal. Civilization, sparse as it was at Lees Ferry, must have seemed welcome after ten days of camping in the sand.

Following their trip the ferryman at Lees, Jerry Johnson, took Dr. Proctor and Mrs. Ritchie to the El Tovar Hotel at the Grand Canyon. Johnson was impressed with Rust's clients: he told Rust that "when we arrived at our destination the Doctor asked me what my bill was, and He just doubled what I had told Him." Dr. Proctor also wrote to Rust from El Tovar, expressing his satisfaction with this unusual vacation. "The success of the trip was due to you and I'll never forget your unceasing efforts for our comfort."[16]

The river guides that followed Rust in subsequent decades took highly individual approaches to boating the Colorado. Norman Nevills, Rust's immediate successor on the river, sought to give many of his trips an exploratory theme, ranging from scientific discovery to locating natural bridges. In more recent years many outfitters working on the remaining stretches of the river have emphasized comfort and luxury, with wine and cheese served on riverside tables; others, such as Ken Sleight, who began floating Glen after World War II, became knowledgeable about the many fascinating side canyons on the river and encouraged their clients to explore them, rather than lie around camp.[17] Rust belonged to this school, promoting an active adventure despite the heat and windstorms that could make his summertime ventures fairly taxing. His river trips offered an early glimpse of a river canyon that in the coming years would make a lasting impression on more and more Americans. As with his overland trips, Rust was well ahead of the times. After World War II, many others came to realize that Glen Canyon offered an extraordinary experience, and starting in the late 1950s until the floodgates on Glen Canyon Dam closed, they set off from Hite in droves. By then, the ripples that Dave Rust's canoes had left in the current decades ago had bounced off the riverbanks and faded away.

AUG. 3—Start at 6 and breakfast at 8:30 at first water on North Wash. On then 3 hrs. to shady cliff in Crescent Canyon abt. half way to Hog Cr. We have sampled Chocolate, Vermilion, White, Grey, Blue, Yellow, Pink, Volcanic Black, Cliffs—now we are in the Orange, with oranges for refreshment. Very cool considering the season....

AUG. 4—Down to Hite and on to good camp below 2 Mile. Cake, oranges, pineapple, spuds, ham, jam (apricot) whole-wheat bread, etc. on food bill today. Five Blue Herons greet us already. The Coconino & Moenkopi have run under and the Chinle makes the valley. Delightful sleeping place, cool enough.

From Rust's 1927 Glen Canyon journal

IN THE FALL OF 1925, with his two Glen Canyon voyages of the summer behind him, Rust approached Utah governor George Dern, with whom he had served in the state legislature, to try the river. Dern was interested in seeing potential dam sites on the Colorado, so he had his personal secretary, Oliver J. Grimes, make the necessary arrangements. When it became clear that the governor could not take time from his schedule that fall, they looked to next spring for the outing. Dern had already been planning an auto trip to Toroweap with Chauncey Parry of Cedar City, and the governor asked Rust whether all of them could make that trip together instead of going on the river. Although Dave knew Parry, who was a principal in the Utah Parks Company, he stuck to his plan, pointing out that they could easily take in the view from Toroweap after they got off the river. Besides, he asked Dern, "Glen Canyon is practically all in UTAH, while the Grand Canyon at Toroweap is all in Arizona. I wonder if that should not incline us to make sure of the exploration of *our own* first?"[1]

In what Rust termed a "curious coincidence," Parry stopped by Kanab to visit Rust as the governor's letter lay on his desk. They agreed to throw in together for the river trip, Parry to act as Rust's assistant. Rust purchased a third canvas canoe to accommodate the extra two members of the party.

In April 1926 the governor's party rendezvoused at Moab for a preliminary power-boat cruise on the Colorado, running twenty miles downstream to inspect a proposed dam site. Afterward they drove to Hanksville to meet Dave for the ride to Glen Canyon. Joining Dern, Grimes, and Parry was Glen M. Ruby of

Denver, a mining geologist and friend of Dern's who nominally came as a representative of the governor of Colorado. Rust led them down the Crescent Creek route to Hite, motoring as far as Granite Ranch and proceeding from there by wagon. It would be another seven years before the first automobile would make the journey to the river.[2]

Grimes, a publicist who in 1918 had expounded on the wonders of Bryce Canyon, wrote a series of articles on the voyage for the *Salt Lake Tribune*. He described the scenery at Rust's usual stops, including Music Temple, Hole-in-the-Rock, and the Crossing of the Fathers. Governor Dern contributed his account to the Salt Lake City *Deseret News*.[3] A former miner, Dern was particularly interested in the old prospects along the river, and he recounted a visit with William Carpenter, the only remaining placer miner in Glen Canyon, whom Dave had declined to visit in 1923 for the sake of his young charges. Dern described Carpenter as "an old, long-haired bewhiskered prospector, a typical forty-niner, of ragged, unkempt appearance," though he "seems to have had some education and a good deal of intelligence." At Good Hope Bar, where Dave had once worked, Dern marveled at the old water wheel, dilapidated buildings, and rusted machinery. "All are mute evidence of the blasted hopes of men," Dern wrote. "The quest for gold leads them to the most remote and desolate places, and frequently, as in this instance, their faith was not well founded and their work and money was wasted."[4]

At Bullfrog Rapid, one of the more exciting spots on this stretch of river, Dern observed how Chauncey Parry "rode it standing up in his boat, stripped to the waist, waving an oar and yelling 'ride 'em cowboy.'" Most of the trip was uneventful, but a few miles above Lees Ferry, Grimes's boat got in trouble in a series of sand waves. They had enjoyed riding the "rollers" earlier in the trip, but these were curling over and breaking. Rust and Dern, in the lead boat, rowed closer to shore and avoided the worst of them, but Grimes and Ruby, following in the next boat, headed into the rough water. Rust turned his boat around to face the men and calmly observed to Dern, "those fellows like the big ones better than I do."

Grimes and Ruby made it over the first large waves, but then they hit one that Grimes described as a "roaring monster," which flipped their boat end-over-end. Rust recalled later that they "looped the loop backwards."[5] Grimes grabbed the gunwale of his boat and tried to right it, but the next wave washed it from his grasp. "In the next thirty seconds or less," Grimes wrote, "three other big waves smashed me in the face and my lungs felt the need of fresh air." Though apparently neither man was wearing a life preserver, they managed to stay afloat. Rust tried to row back to them, with Dern standing in the canoe, ready to throw the life ring. It was Parry who made the rescue, however, coming up in the third boat. He helped haul Grimes and Ruby out of the river, but their canoe sank and was lost.

The incident was fearful indeed, but Rust faulted Grimes and Ruby for not staying close enough to him to avoid the sand waves. It was the only time that one of his boats spilled. Other than this mishap, Dern and Grimes enjoyed the trip and described the scenic features of Glen Canyon in glowing terms. Climbing out of the canyon at Hole-in-the-Rock, Grimes wrote of being "overwhelmed by the splendor of the inspiring panorama unfolded to us." His description of the long vistas in all directions reveals their surprise and wonder as they emerged from the shadowed cleft:

> Bare tawny and orange rocks, emphasized by rounded knolls, occupied the foreground and blended into an undulating and gently sloping plain of orange sand to the west. Dimly on the northwestern horizon rose the hazy bulk of Boulder mountain or Aquarius plateau; to the north the peaks of the Henry mountains formed a jagged skyline, some dark and threatening, others scintillating in their snowy caps; to the south the massive form of Fifty-mile mountain or Kaiparowits plateau, swam in a sea of lavender haze.... To the east there rose almost perpendicularly the orange wall of the canyon, broken in but a single place, and through this break, flanked on each side by massive sandstone pillars, were faintly discernable the wheel ruts of the old immigrant wagons on their way to the San Juan. It was a humble and thoughtful little group that stumbled over rocks and sand dunes back to the river.[6]

Rust would feature this climb on nearly every subsequent river trip, combining as it did spectacular scenery with a connection to recent Mormon history. Although he could claim no relatives among the 1879–1880 Bluff colonists, it was a saga told often in southern Utah, exemplifying almost unbelievable perseverance in this difficult environment.

Less well known was the desperate effort of the Dominguez-Escalante party in the approaching winter of 1776 as they searched for a way across the Colorado. This party of Spanish friars and explorers looked first at the mouth of the Paria, then upstream at a river ford long used by Indians, later given the name Ute Ford. Rust showed Governor Dern and his party the steps cut in the sandstone ledges near the mouth of a small side canyon (later named Padre Creek) that had enabled the expedition to bring their horses down over rain- and ice-slick rocks to the river. Grimes's photograph of the governor on the steps was reprinted in his *Salt Lake Tribune* article.

Some confusion attended the location of these steps in the ensuing years. The U.S. Geological Survey's 1922 river map showed the Crossing of the Fathers about a half-mile upstream at Kane (Cane) Creek, which led Utah historian Charles Kelly to unsuccessfully scout that site for the steps in 1932. His party rented Rust's canvas canoes for use on the river, but they evidently did not ask him how to find the steps. (Although Rust had long known of the Indian ford, he never recorded when he located the actual steps.) The next year Kelly heard from George C. Fraser, who had searched for the location with Rust in 1922. Fraser informed Kelly, "I think you will find Escalante's route was through the canyon immediately below the Ute ford. There are still visible in the slick rock on the trail into that canyon, cuts such as might have been made with a hatchet. You will remember Escalante's description of the slippery descent to the river."[7]

Despite this clue, Kelly did not locate the steps for five more years. In 1937, his friend and fellow river runner, Dr. Russell Frazier, heard from a local cowboy that there were steps cut in an unnamed canyon a short distance below Kane Creek. Wasting no time, Kelly and Frazier took a motorboat upriver from Lees Ferry and "after some searching we found them—a long series cut in the north side of the little canyon enabling horses to reach the rim above."[8] After some examination, however, they decided that these could not be the real steps. Returning that fall on a horseback expedition over Gunsight Pass, Dr. Frazier located another set of steps in a small drainage they called Padre Creek that better fit Escalante's description. Their "discovery" was played up in the Utah press, with the *Deseret News* running a front-page headline announcing the find, complete with a map and photographs of the explorers.[9] Frazier and Kelly appeared to take credit for the discovery, telling the newspaper that "these steps alone, which have never been discovered before by any historian, are sufficient proof that Escalante crossed at this point."

Kelly and Frazier returned to the site in 1938 on a motorboat trip starting from Dandy Crossing. A noted guest on their trip was Julius Stone, a man with a long connection to the river. Stone had invested in Robert Stanton's failed mining venture in 1898 and had floated the Colorado in 1909 with Nathaniel Galloway. The goal for their current trip was to place a plaque at Padre Creek commemorating the Dominguez-Escalante expedition, and also to authenticate some historic rock inscriptions they had heard of, including the dates "1534" and "1642" supposedly inscribed on a wall opposite Lake Canyon.

The older of these was particularly enticing, for it would have documented the earliest Spanish *entrada* in the region, predating by six years the arrival of Garcia López de Cárdenas at the rim of the Grand Canyon. Kelly and Frazier thought the only party that could have made this inscription was that of Cabeza de Vaca, whose party of Spanish shipwreck survivors may have crossed through New Mexico and Arizona before reaching Mexico City in 1536. In an article he wrote for the *Saturday Evening Post* describing their trip, Kelly admitted not finding any sixteenth-century inscriptions, but to him the "1642" date at Lake Canyon appeared to be genuine. He realized, however, that there was no corroborating record of any Spanish explorers venturing into the area at that time.[10]

When Rust floated Glen the following year with his young friend Henry Dodge Freeman, he noted that the 1642 inscription did not seem to be genuine. Reaching the Crossing of the Fathers three days later, he wrote in his journal that he was "happy to note that Dr. Frazier et al. figured out the same *ford* I located with Geo. Fraser, Gov. Dern & several other partners years ago." It was characteristic of Rust not to call attention to his earlier knowledge of the crossing. As he told river historian Dock Marston in 1949, "we sought no publicity or notoriety, just quiet enjoyment." His companion on a 1938 voyage, Dr. L. F. H. Lowe of Princeton, wrote to Kelly after reading his *Saturday Evening Post* article and offered, dryly, that "Mr. Rust spoke at some length [during their trip] about the inaccuracy of the accepted location of El Vado, of his own reading of Escalante's journal, and of his finding of the chippings in the rock which you mention."[11]

Near the end of the governor's trip, the party examined the proposed Glen Canyon dam site above Lees Ferry. Dern was satisfied with the location from an engineering standpoint; the rock walls appeared strong enough to anchor a mammoth dam. But he gave the overall concept less than a ringing endorsement: "I think the Glen canyon dam and reservoir would be of limited permanent benefit to Utah. We would get some benefit from the money spent in construction, because a good deal of Utah labor would doubtless be employed, but this is a temporary benefit.... [L]ittle or no Utah land could be irrigated from the reservoir."[12]

Dern realized that "a lot of the beautiful glens and beauty spots" would be submerged under the reservoir, but that "more scenery would be gained than lost by making the lake." Though Rust wrote little on the subject, he generally shared this viewpoint. To him, as well as to the government surveyors, hydropower development on the Colorado represented the inevitable march of progress. He supported economic activity that might better the lives of local people, such as dams, mines, and improved roads. Earlier that year, after Herbert Gregory had told him about his survey of the mineral prospects in the Paria River drainage, Rust indicated his approval of developing that river, too: "Hope the coal and possible reclamation projects may bring industries into that barrenness, which at present is a straight diet of scenery. You remember, there is only one house left in the Pahreah, the same house where we [Dave and his brother Will] danced on Christmas, 1897. The valley where the town once flourished(?) would look better as a reservoir, and the Clark Bench between the Paria and the Wahweap has plenty of good land."[13] No matter what scenic and historic points of interest the Glen Canyon dam might inundate, there was simply nothing to discuss. The completion of Hoover Dam in 1935, widely heralded as a milestone in the nation's development, was only the first step in harnessing the Colorado to the needs of man. A Glen Canyon dam and reservoir, its boosters believed, would logically come next.

Adventures in Glen Canyon continued to be an important part of Rust's guiding program for the remainder of his active career. He stated in his later memoirs that he led about one trip a year down Glen, though he took notes only on trips he made in 1927, 1937, 1938, and 1939. He continued to try to interest clients in his combined horseback and boat journey, the approach he had pioneered with Berolzheimer and Koehler in 1923. This was his preferred way to experience the variety of the Plateau Province, ranging from eleven-thousand-foot high alpine tundra to the sun-baked rocks at Lees Ferry, a mile and a half lower down in the province's giant staircase.

A summertime trip in 1927 with three Ivy League students was typical of these far-ranging journeys—a month-long horseback tour from the Arizona Strip to the Henry Mountains, capped by a voyage down Glen Canyon. Henry G. ("Harry") Bartol Jr. and Benjamin Sturges were eighteen-year-old students set to enter Harvard that fall; a third friend, twenty-one-year-old Gilliat Schroeder of Yale, joined them for the horseback portion of the journey.[14] Harry Bartol's father was a Wall Street stock broker whose family was listed on New York's social register, yet a thorough adventure out West was precisely what his son had in mind. Phillip Rollins, a well-traveled friend of the family, had written to a Union Pacific agent that spring to find a suitable guide for the young men. "Because of my abiding respect and affection for real Westerners," he wrote, "I am anxious that the first impression received by young Bartol shall be such as comes from true Westerners and not from the hybrid type that, working at dude ranches, feels compelled, because of the inaneness of the dudes, to fill them with 'bunk.'"[15]

The Union Pacific agent referred Rollins to Rust, who presumably was not of the hybrid type, whatever that might mean, and was certainly no dude rancher. Dave wrote back to the agent, offering to take the youths on a breathtaking adventure covering a huge, mostly pristine territory:

> One of the best programs in this entire region is about as follows: Start horseback and packmule trip at Bryce say July 6, ride north-east to Table Cliffs (over 10,000 ft. elev.) great southern and eastern lookoffs, over forest trails north and down to primitive town of Escalante, over rough trail across Dead Man Gulch and up Bear Creek to top of Aquarius Plateau (Powell National Forest and one of the most charming) to the eastern tip for what Dutton called "Unsurpassed Panorama" views of the Escalante Basin and the Dirty Devil Basin, across the Water Pocket Fold on an old trail followed by Thompson and Dellenbaugh in 1872 to the Henry Mountains, climb Mt. Ellen to survey region and possibly climb Mt. Ellsworth overlooking the Colorado. This horseback trip will require about twelve days riding an average distance of about 20 miles per day. Now I suggest that we drop the land-ponies and take the water-ponies [his boats] which will meet us at the Crescent Canyon junction with the Colorado. About seven days will carry us to Lees Ferry 170 miles through Glen Canyon with Rainbow Arch and Cliff Dwellings and other interesting features enroute. From Lees Ferry we can automobile back to Bryce or Cedar City, one or two days.[16]

Henry Bartol accepted Rust's offer, sending the boys into what must have seemed a wilderness. Rust and his son Milton met the young men at the rail terminus in Cedar City on July 2, returning to his Pipe Valley ranch where they collected his horses and pack stock. A ride east to Kanab and onward to the Paria River sampled the wide-open desert below the Vermilion Cliffs. Following the river upstream, they began the magnificent climb up into the Pink Cliffs of the

Paunsaugunt in what is now Bryce Canyon National Park, where they enjoyed the luxury of Ruby Syrett's park cabins. Then it was eastward to Powell Point on the Table Cliff Plateau for an "extraordinary view—fog, clouds, great color scheme," he noted.

Dave's trips often featured a progression from overlook to overlook, for he reserved his greatest admiration for the panoramas to be found atop the rimrocks and peaks of the Southwest's canyon lands. Rust collected scenic views the way some of his friends in southern Utah acquired horses: he was never quite satisfied that he had found the very best among all the possibilities. He learned to examine cliffs, mesas, and canyons with a practiced eye, always searching for the vista that surpassed all the rest. Whether it was a dramatic wall of Wingate Sandstone, streaked with desert varnish, a colorfully banded exposure of Chinle shale, or a barren desert expanse surrounding an imposing Entrada tower, he knew all their varieties—the shades and moods of a fantastic landscape.

He had perfected this routine with George Fraser in 1914 and 1915. On subsequent excursions he would bring his guests out to the brink at one of his favorite lookouts, typically in late afternoon when the shadows were lengthening, and introduce the panorama like a concert impresario, sweeping his arm across the great spectacle of mesas, buttes, hidden canyons, and sunlit rimrocks. There they would spend hours piecing these elements into an understandable whole. He would pull topographic maps and geologic reports out of his packbags so his clients could learn how the folds, faults, anticlines, and grabens gave the forces of erosion room to work. Whether from Brian Head, Table Cliff, or Bowns Point— the highest level of the Grand Staircase—the lessons of the earth's evolution could not be mistaken.

A rough descent off of Powell Point with the Bartol party led to what Rust called the "Jurassic Plateau"—the great expanse of Navajo Sandstone slickrock between Escalante and Boulder. The haphazard trail through the petrified waves of sandstone skinned and lamed several of his horses, but a hospitable rancher in the latter village permitted them to rest and re-shoe the stock. The party met a local dairyman who packed his cream to Boulder for mail shipment over the mule trail to Escalante. This enterprising fellow made more than a hundred dollars a month, Rust noted, despite the circuitous route to market.

A climb up onto the Aquarius Plateau took the party to more of Dave's favorite viewpoints, including Bowns and Tantalus (Chokecherry) points, thence down into the rough eastern breaks of Boulder Mountain and through the Waterpocket Fold to the King Ranch. More climbing brought them to the summit ridge of Mount Ellen, where they had to dig out hollows for their beds in the stony slopes. Fresh lamb for dinner, obtained from a nearby sheepherder, compensated for the discomfort of their high perch. "Animals very stiff and tired. Boys are certainly good sports," Rust observed.

As in 1923, their wanderings were far from over; Dave took the party down from Ellen to reach the welcome orchards of Fruita on the Fremont River, where they spent several days resting up and viewing the rock art and geological features along the river. Then it was back onto the Aquarius for still more views, including a night spent at Bowns Point: "on top of S.E. Salient to get great view and the clouds & storm combine to make it extraordinary." They journeyed across the plateau to Widtsoe, where they arranged a ride for Gilliat Schroeder back to Cedar City, and turned south for Kanab and Dave's home. There they would collect his boats and at last head for Glen Canyon.

As lengthy and demanding as their travels had been thus far, Rust's party would encounter its greatest difficulty on the road to Hanksville. Reaching Torrey by auto on July 31, Dave hired a truck to transport their river gear. Then the rains began: "August 1—Eph. Jorgensen arrives with Dodge truck at 5:30 and we pack up and leave without breakfast by 7 A.M. Motor to Notom for breakfast-lunch and on to Caineville by 12 M. Wait for storm to pass then—five miles of terrible mud. Stick in wash after working road for 2 hrs. Birdie Curfew-Gifford helps us out with yellow team. Road extremely rough from recent rains to say nothing of fresh mud. To Hanksville for late bread and milk supper & bed in the hay." At Hanksville the party switched to more reliable transport: "With Fred Giles as teamster and 2 saddlehorses we start for Granite at 12:15. Five hrs. cool ride, supper and rest at Granite, a 2 hrs evening drive till after dark completes the day."

By the time they set out from Hite on August 4, they had already seen a major swath of the Utah high plateaus and desert. But Glen Canyon offered an amazing contrast to all that the boys had seen thus far. Within the week Rust had allotted for the trip, they could take hikes up fascinating side canyons and inspect interesting historical features from the canyon's mining days. Later river explorers would bring to light many of Glen's less-obvious side canyons, giving them names such as Hidden Passage, Iceberg, Twilight, Grotto, and Dungeon, but there is no record of Rust ever visiting them. He typically explored Moqui and Lake canyons, which sheltered some remarkable ruins, including an unusually well-preserved dwelling in Lake Canyon that was later named Wasp House. While exploring this canyon with Bartol and Sturges in 1927, he encountered one of the canyon country's chief hazards:

> AUGUST 6—Our boatlets carry us through Wingate and Navajo canyons to mouth of Lake Canyon for good camp-site. We tied very near the mouth, put spuds to cook and sauntered up Lake Cr. above water falls and were returning to camp when a wall of mud and rocks and debris jumped over the falls with tremendous rush and noise. Terrific shock and surprise! We ran for camp to try to save boats and food and beds. We won by a close margin—Harry & I having to cross ahead of the mad flood. Saved everything except my hat which was left on the Creek bank as we started our walk, and a pin of an oar. Very fortunate and thankful. Moved everything to safe quarters—river rose over a foot so other side canyons must have contributed. The wall of the flood in Lake was indicative of some broken reservoir above Kinsabe. We had no warning whatever. It might have been very critical, even a tragedy.

Lake Canyon had seen a great flood in 1915, when a natural dam forming a good-sized lake, called by the locals "Pagahrit," had burst open. Conceivably Rust may have witnessed a repeat of this event on a smaller scale, although ordinary flash floods in the canyons could easily produce such volumes.

Two days after escaping from Lake Canyon, they made the long hike to Rainbow Bridge, Rust and the three boys sleeping out under the arch just as he had done with the Frasers in 1916 and with Berolzheimer and Koehler in 1919. The next day they climbed the ledges above the arch, where Rust let Bartol and Sturges down onto the span with a forty-foot rope. It was not an inch too long, Rust noted. The boaters reached Lees Ferry on August 11. "So the trip seems to be over," Dave concluded his journal. "A very delightful swing with an unusual program of experiences. Strenuous and instructive." Rust itemized his costs for the Glen Canyon portion of the adventure as $540, including $200 for his and Milton's time and $225 for transport from Kanab and return. Wear and tear on the boats came to $70, while supplies for the trip amounted to only $45. It was still a hefty outlay, and far exceeded what an average tourist would pay for a Utah Parks

Company bus-and-hotel package to Zion, the North Rim, and Bryce Canyon. But his itinerary was a world apart in its degree of immersion in the countryside.

⌒

Mudholes and flash floods such as Bartol and Sturges experienced, and the risk of capsizing a boat, were an expected part of a real canyon adventure. Safety was always paramount to Rust, however, and his river ventures required extra precautions. His passengers did not always wear life preservers (he felt the kapok vests of the day could be a liability when soaked), but he kept an inflated automobile inner tube in each boat, attached to a line for use as a rescue float. He was never one to let his guard down; while his guests often camped under sheltering ledges above the river, Rust made it a habit to sleep by the boats, ready to move them to higher ground if the river rose suddenly.

He had witnessed the power of this stream during his Grand Canyon venture as well as during his mining days. In his 1901 essay "Boating on the Colorado," he recounted floating Glen Canyon with several fellow miners who deliberately took their boat into a set of sand waves that were forming as the river swung next to a vertical wall of sandstone. "As each wave dashed against the boat and echoed among the bluffs, my heart jumped with corresponding pulsations, until I could have offered my own funeral prayer," Rust wrote in the ornate style of the period. "The boys said I was pale, and they laughed heartily, but it was a dry, unmirthful time for me."[17]

If, as his daughter Emma said, he could not swim, such experiences would have indeed been frightening. So he took no chances running Glen's riffles and small rapids, towing the second boat in some cases and even lining some of the larger rapids on occasion. Later parties rarely took such precautions, but most of Glen's voyagers used sturdier craft than Rust's. By the time rubber rafts were introduced after World War II, Glen's rapids had receded in most people's minds to minor obstacles offering a pleasant bounce or two.

The river could still display awesome power, as a group Rust guided in the fall of 1929 discovered. Dr. Frederick J. Pack, a professor of geology at the University of Utah, engaged him to take a party of six acquaintances, mostly scientists, down Glen Canyon. Pack had explored widely around Utah and was known for his discoveries of dinosaur fossils. In 1921 he discovered and named the Goblet of Venus, a remarkable balanced rock near Natural Bridges National Monument. He was a partner with A. L. Inglesby in the "Intelligencer" tour company, a bus service that took tourists on guided trips through Zion and other Utah parks, and he sometimes accompanied the tours as an erudite guide to the scenic rock formations of southern Utah. Two physicians with an interest in the outdoors joined him for the Glen trip, including Dr. Howard A. Kelly, a distinguished member of the faculty of Johns Hopkins University. Kelly, age seventy-one, was typical of many of the gentleman explorers of his time, with wide-ranging interests including entomology, mycology, and astronomy.[18]

This was one of the larger groups Rust would take into the backcountry. He planned to use just his three canvas canoes, without a second boatman or one of his sons as a helper. A photograph in the *Deseret News* showed the seven men ready to depart Salt Lake City, under the headline "Brave Treacherous River for Science."[19] "Thrills and dangers aplenty await these men," the article went on. Rust, however, had no intention of subjecting any of his clients to undue hazards, as the men learned.

Rust met the group in Hanksville on September 5. Dr. Pack and his party drove down through Capitol Wash, encountering slippery conditions due to recent rains.[20] Stormy weather could persist for days in the autumn, with the normally dry sandstone slopes shedding water like a sheet of glass and setting every wash to flowing. The group made it to Granite Ranch the next day, where they waited for the freight wagon loaded with their gear to catch up. From there the group proceeded by mule. Since Dave did not have enough animals for everyone, they took turns walking, making it a long two days to the river. When they reached the river they found it in flood. "Great trees in the form of driftwood were passing down the river in rapid succession," Dr. Pack noted. "The river had expanded its width to about 1500 feet, and was running at an estimated velocity of twenty to twenty-five miles per hour." Running it was impossible under such conditions.

They determined to wait out the rise. The next day the river came down several feet but was still well above its normal level. On September 9 the men explored around the mouth of the Dirty Devil, upstream from Hite, but on returning to camp they were surprised to find that Rust had disassembled the boats and was packing up to leave. "This, at first, was a great disappointment to most of us, since we had come a long way and had looked forward to the adventure for several months," Dr. Pack wrote. "Our better judgment, however, convinced us that Mr. Rust was right, and that a trip on the river under existing conditions would be extremely hazardous." Dr. Kelly, though an experienced outdoorsman and an avid canoeist, was relieved to be spared the risk of running the swift current.

Rust must also have been disappointed, but he knew how dangerous high water and floating snags could be for his fragile "boatlets." His usual caution prevailed. Dr. Pack's account suggests that Dave was not given to consulting with his clients before making decisions he knew were necessary; safety, as always, trumped any other consideration. There would be no "thrills and dangers" on his trips if they could be avoided.

Rust never took paying passengers anywhere but Glen Canyon, and thus did not expand his business into a truly modern guiding venture. Charges for his trips ranged from $200 to $250 per person for a typical ten-day float, which in the 1920s and 1930s was steep enough to deter casual tourists. Nor did he promote his venture in any systematic way; as with his overland trips, most clients came to him via word of mouth. River guiding never was very lucrative for Dave, but after his retirement from teaching in 1928 it formed a welcome supplement to his meager finances.

⌒🦅

The birth of the modern river-guiding industry on the Colorado and Green rivers is generally credited to two individuals: Norman Nevills of Mexican Hat, Utah, and Bus Hatch of Vernal, Utah. Nevills got his start taking customers down the San Juan River in 1936, branching out to include Cataract Canyon and the Grand Canyon.[21] As with many other parties, he floated Glen Canyon as an adjunct to these more thrilling canyons. Hatch gradually got into the guiding business during the 1940s on the Green and Yampa rivers. Both men, but particularly Hatch (Nevills died in 1949), benefited by the postwar explosion of interest in river running that was aided by the use of military-surplus rubber rafts. These craft made even major rapids runnable to ordinary adventurers with a little training and experience.

Rust played only a small role in what would eventually become a major economic enterprise in the towns of Moab, Bluff, Vernal, and Green River. He belonged more to the tradition of the guide than the tourism promoter; he had no desire to take large parties down the river. As with his horseback trips, he was most comfortable in the company of one or two interested and aware outdoorspeople, to whom he could show the geologic and cultural wonders of the river corridor. Rust called his little boats "water-ponies," a term that Powell had over-heard an Indian apply to his wooden boats. It fit Dave's as well, for he used his craft as transportation, not to seek whitewater thrills. The river's magnificent sur-roundings were the reason to be there, the boats merely the necessary means. If Dave did not exploit the full commercial possibilities of the Colorado River, it was because he had a different vision: as with all of his trips, he was looking at the land. Taking direction from the nineteenth-century scientist-explorers who had opened the Plateau Province to modern inquiry, he saw meaning not just in the river corridor, but in the entire Colorado Plateau. In this he anticipated by many decades the tremendous flowering of interest in the region that finally took off in the 1970s.

14 | *Unusual Campout Excursions*

When your appetite for the Wilderness prevails and
you feel that you must get away from the surfeit of society into the solace of solitude, away from the cushions
and other conveniences for a few days or a few weeks—
let your requirements be known by night letter, or other
communication, to DAVE RUST, Kanab, Utah.

Dave Rust (1925)[1]

AT A TIME WHEN RUST and his clients were seeking
more intimate contact with the wildest sections of the Plateau Province, more
and more Americans were indulging in a great romance with automobile touring. The passion for mobility gained speed in the years following World War I as
roadworthy machines became more affordable and the nation's transcontinental
roads improved. The West's scenic wonders were an increasingly popular destination; by 1923 visits to the Grand Canyon topped the one hundred thousand
mark. While many tourists still arrived at the South Rim by rail, more than a
third of them braved the highways in their automobiles. The newly improved
road to the North Rim was also beginning to draw motorists. Seven thousand of
them came in the summer of 1925 to visit Bright Angel Point, Cape Royal, and
Point Sublime—places that only a decade before saw perhaps a dozen visitors in
a week's time.[2]

Tourism at Zion and Bryce lagged far behind the South Rim, but in an effort
to improve access, the Park Service opened a better road up Zion Canyon in 1925.
An enlarged campground midway up the canyon at The Grotto accommodated
the independent tourist. For those who wanted a packaged experience, the bus
touring concession operated by the Parry brothers of Cedar City was dropping
off tourists every day at both parks. The colorfully eroded amphitheater carved
into the Markagunt Plateau at Cedar Breaks also attracted visitors, although they
had to negotiate a steep road built in 1921 up to the plateau overlook. The Utah
Parks Company, a tourism venture set up in 1923 by the Union Pacific Railroad,
built a rustically decorated lodge near the rim in anticipation of growing traffic. National monument designation at Cedar Breaks waited until 1933, owing to
a jurisdictional dispute between the Park Service and the Forest Service, which
initially controlled the land. Bryce Canyon, too, came in for improvements as it

transitioned from a national monument to a full-fledged national park in 1928. The Utah Parks Company's lodge and cabins near Sunset Point drew increasing numbers of independent auto tourists as well as hosting its own bus tours.[3]

All this expansion of roads, campgrounds, gasoline stations, and roadside cabins presented Rust with clear opportunities—if he wanted to pursue them. Although he had lost control of his Bright Angel Creek trail, tram, and river camp following the creation of Grand Canyon National Park in 1919, he might have recouped the loss by following the lead of his brother Will, who opened a tourist lodge at De Motte Park on the Kaibab Plateau in 1922. Will and a partner had renovated an old ranger cabin and built six new ones from native spruce logs, adding more as traffic to the North Rim grew.[4] Dave and Will were close companions and had worked together in various mining and stock-raising ventures; it would have been a natural course for them to partner in a tourist business. But Dave was too footloose to be pinned down at a resort, even one as attractively located as Will's. Increasingly he was taking his guiding business in the opposite direction from the mass market. Where the automobile had democratized travel, he turned toward a select group that wanted a more primitive encounter with the outdoors.

Rust was in no way tied (as the resort owners and tour operators were) to the region's handful of national parks and monuments. He realized, as did few others at the time, that the Plateau Province ought to be experienced in its entirety, not merely as a collection of scenic wonders. No tour package or set itinerary could give his clients a sense for the scale of this country, nor offer the kind of open-ended, wandering excursion that Rust favored. All of his guests enjoyed a unique outing tailored to their interests, roaming freely through country Dave knew well and often venturing into unfamiliar canyons and mesas as well. No commercial tour outfit cared to compete in this kind of travel, but his trips nonetheless appealed to the minority of adventurers who sought a more authentic approach to the Southwest.

Rust was also coming to the realization that the pace of travel was important, too—that you missed something while speeding from park to park in a comfortable tour bus. Occasionally he would take his guests to a scenic destination by auto, but even then he would inject his own style into the trip, spending leisurely afternoons at vista points and making low-key tent camps somewhere off in the woods. It was not an approach calculated to make money, but rather one that would allow his clients to fully experience the landscape and the camaraderie of small-group travel. For this, he appeared willing to give up the chance to make his mark in the tourism business.

Dave still faced the problem of how to draw new clients to his time-consuming and somewhat expensive mode of travel. A typical worker in an eastern manufacturing plant could not afford a train ticket west, let alone the cost of a guide and horses.[5] Even a middle-class white-collar worker might make only $3,000 in a year. He could take his family on a modest vacation—perhaps to a gathering place in the country like New York's Chautauqua—but a long horseback trip in the Southwest was out of the question. The Frasers' trip with Rust through the High Plateaus in 1915 cost $550 for a month in the field, plus hundreds more for rail fares. Even charging only ten dollars a day for his services, Dave was limited to guiding the decidedly well-off.

Although he had some of the grandest scenery in the world to offer his clients, Rust spent little time promoting his business. He was well known to the residents of southwestern Utah from his service in the state legislature and on various committees promoting the Good Roads program, but outside of J. H. Manderfield with the Salt Lake Route, he had few contacts in the world of organized travel. He lacked the resources of a Fred Harvey Company or other large enterprise that could commission color brochures and take out advertisements in magazines. All he could do was place a few lines in regional publications such as the *Good Roads Automobilist*—although this had been enough to catch Charles Berolzheimer's eye and lead to one of his finest trips.

But there was something unique he could offer his guests—an experience that was focused on the land, not on the comforts of travel. In the spring of 1925, as he had ten years earlier, he tried to put his program into words for use in a prospective publicity brochure. Titled "Unusual Campout Excursions," it began with an overview of the canyon lands section of the Colorado Plateau:

> That Strip of Wonder-Land across from the corner of southwestern Utah to the corner of southwestern Colorado—between Zion National Park and Mesa Verde—is the most enchanting portion of the Plateau Province in America (according to Powell, Dutton, and their fellow geologists), and the abiding place of unsurpassed view-points, deep canyons, painted deserts, monument valleys, natural bridges and thousands of other curious rock-

shapes, which cannot be approached except by the help of a saddle-horse and pack-mule as did the early explorer.

He was right about needing horse and mule. Outside of the national parks, the "wonderland" of which he wrote was the most isolated, least traveled part of the Colorado Plateau. The state highway maps of Utah for that period depicted a region extending forty or fifty miles on either side of the Colorado River that was utterly devoid of roads. Unsurfaced byways that would be considered primitive by today's standards led to the towns of Escalante, Hanksville, and Mexican Hat—and there they ended. From Moab to Lees Ferry, along 230 miles of the Colorado River, there was not a single vehicle crossing. Rust had been through much of this country on horseback or by canoe, and in the next decade he would check out most of the rest of it.

Any trip with Dave Rust involved climbing trails to high vista points from which one could inspect the intriguing landforms of the region. Around this time he began to compile a mental list of what he called his "Fourteen Points"—an informal roster of scenic lookouts that he added to or subtracted from as time went on. The title was a play on President Woodrow Wilson's plan for postwar world peace, but Rust used his version to ponder what were the best vantage spots in the canyon country. The list was somewhat malleable and was the source of much discussion with his well-traveled clients as they discovered new vista points. The key was their breadth of view over the surrounding landscape. One had to choose from a surfeit of superlative rims and mountain peaks. He listed five in his prospective brochure: "In the Plateau Province of Utah, the southern tip of the Paunsaugunt, Table Cliffs, the eastern tip of Aquarius, the top of Pine-valley Mountain and the top of Ellen peak in the Henry Mountains are among the most commanding viewpoints of the world—offering to him who will linger and look the supreme classics in scenery."

His friend Harrison R. Merrill took notes on this topic during a 1924 auto excursion out to the Toroweap promontory in the western Grand Canyon, itself a worthy member of the list. He included Rust's scenic picks in an article he wrote for the Salt Lake City *Deseret News*.[6] Dave placed the view from "Lookout Ridge" on Navajo Mountain at the head of the list, followed, surprisingly, by the summit of Mount Ellsworth in the Little Rockies. The latter was the relatively obscure crag located east of the Henry Mountains that he had climbed on his 1923 river trip; it offered fine views into Glen Canyon. Dutton Point on the Grand Canyon's Powell Plateau came next; it was perhaps Rust's favorite place to stare out at the Canyon's buttes and temples. The Grand Canyon also offered the dramatic sheer cliffs of the Toroweap, Bright Angel Point, and the seldom-visited prow of Cape Final at the eastern end of the Kaibab Plateau. The aforementioned views from the Aquarius Plateau, Table Cliff Plateau, Pine Valley Mountain, and Mount Ellen were included. In 1924, his trips with George Fraser still in mind, Rust included four overlooks he had first visited with his fellow connoisseur of geology: the east rim of Zion Canyon, the west rim of Moonlight Creek in the northern Navajo Reservation, Thousand Lake Mountain, and the southeastern edge of the Kaiparowits Plateau. Any person who paid a visit to each of these peaks and promontories could boast that they had gazed over the bulk of the Colorado Plateau. Few people besides Rust could say they had—perhaps only the geologist Herbert Gregory was as familiar with the region in all its splendor.

As much as he loved his expansive viewpoints, Dave had much more he could offer his clients. With his wide-ranging experience, he knew that he could lead them out into an incredibly diverse backcountry. His 1925 publicity blurb featured one of his favorite excursions, a horseback and canoe adventure (today it would be called "multisport") that he had pioneered two years previously with Berolzheimer and Koehler:

> Scout RUST offers an unlimited variety of programs: Long or short to match your convenience; up among the flowers and spruces of the High Plateaus or down in the bare rock region or happy combination of both; a suitable repertoire for each season and each month of the whole year, through altitudes ranging from 2000 to 11000 feet above the sea. Perhaps the most thrilling excursion he has to offer for the season of 1925–26 is a boating voyage 170 miles through Glen Canyon (Colorado River) from the Dirty Devil to the Paria.

As with the brochure he wrote in 1915, he never got "Unusual Campout Excursions" into circulation. The expense of printing and distribution was beyond his limited budget. It was his reputation, more than any advertising, that garnered new clients and kept old ones coming back. An attorney, businessman, or physician whose work kept him tied to the city wanted to be sure that his family's vacation time was well spent. Dave's clients spread word among their friends and assured them of their guide's competence and good nature.

Each of the best-known guides in the region had his own style. John Wetherill of Kayenta was known for his quiet competence out in the far reaches of the Navajo Reservation; Zeke Johnson of Blanding made friends with his exuberant heartiness and his predilection for tall tales. Rust was the most intellectual of the three. "The fact that I'd been to school didn't hurt me in being a guide," he told an interviewer. "Even my knowing Shakespeare intimately didn't do me any harm, for I could talk him, too. Many horse wranglers could doubtless have done better at making trail and so on, but my own wide experience came in and has come in good around the campfire at night."[7]

While he liked to expound on Plateau geology and history, he also learned much from his well-placed and educated clients. "Do you know everybody in Boston?" Donald Scott asked Rust in 1928. His wife, Louise, had just attended a party at which several of Rust's former clients, including the scientist George Agassiz, were present. When she mentioned that she had recently been on a trip with Rust, Agassiz "fairly jumped out of his chair" to recount his rugged adventures with Dave through the headwaters of Zion in 1909.[8]

Most of Dave's clients probably understood what they were getting into. Many of them were world travelers who had dealt with hardships in exotic places. They had little interest in a plush tour package. Sheer adventure was part of the attraction; a long horseback ride in the American Southwest promised a definite break from one's comfortable routine. These men, women, and young people may have come out West with their own idea of what they would find, but Dave wanted to show them the country as it really was.

Dave had no truck with Wild West-style entertainments, fancy showmanship with horse or rope, or the other trappings of the Buffalo Bill crowd. The skills he displayed with horse or rope were those he had learned as a young man in the Dirty Devil hills. These he employed simply to get a job done. Life on the trail meant rounding up the pack stock before breakfast, filling the water kegs (often a laborious, cup-by-cup process at desert seeps), packing the mules, and setting off on dusty and occasionally hazardous canyon routes and washes. The next camp might be twenty miles or more distant in a landscape hardly conducive to rapid travel. The summer sun was unrelenting down in the slickrock country; often-times hot winds would blow out of the southwest all day and into the evening, stirring sand into the blankets and the evening stew. With luck, Dave would find a sheltered camp next to a running stream, and all would enjoy a heavenly sleep under a canopy of rustling cottonwood leaves.

While Rust's trips usually ventured into some pretty inhospitable terrain, he tried to deflect thoughts from sore muscles by making long lunch stops and ar-ranging for relaxed evenings. As every outfitter knows, a good meal and pleasant conversation around the campfire can induce a happy state of mind in footsore and saddle-weary guests. Camp fare was usually simple: bacon, biscuits, or oat-meal for breakfast, a stew and beans for dinner, or a roast leg of lamb when one could be procured from a sheepherder. Dessert might be spoonfuls of sourdough fried in bacon fat and served with honey. Tinned goods, crackers, and a pot of jam often sufficed for lunch en route to the next viewpoint. Only the barest luxuries got stowed in the pack-bags—perhaps a tin of salmon or tomatoes. The gourmet refections of today's pampered clientele would have come in for some ribbing back then.

Dave included one treat in his larder that was calculated to leave his guests with a good impression when they ended a trip, as they usually did, with a long, hot, dusty ride back to civilization. "I always brought a couple-three-four lemons and put them in the bottom of my pack-bags," his niece, Nora Mickelson, re-called him saying. "On the last day of the trip, I'd get the coolest water I could, then I'd make lemonade. That was my advertising."[9]

Rust's connection to the eastern elites led to an inquiry in 1927 from Robert H. Stewart of the Raymond & Whitcomb Company, a Boston travel agency that for decades had arranged posh railcar tours to the West for its wealthy clients. Stewart wanted Rust to set up an outing for Larz and Isabel Anderson, one of the city's most prominent couples. Stewart emphasized that "this will be quite an outfit, requiring a cook and cookee, sufficient pack animals or automobiles to take care of tents, provisions, etc." Rust took the assignment, although it involved auto touring instead of his usual horseback explorations. He arranged to hire two passenger cars and a truck, along with three drivers and a Swedish cook he knew in Kanab. Isabel Anderson wrote an account of the trip for the *Boston Transcript*, which gives the flavor of one of Rust's more genteel outings.[10]

The Andersons took the Salt Lake Route to Cedar City via a branch line from Lund that had opened in 1922. Rust met them there and led the entourage up onto the Kolob Plateau west of Zion Canyon. "We came into the 'parks' of the uplands," Anderson wrote, "clean flat tops of pasture land framed in by dark evergreens, where flocks of sheep ranged with their herders camped with covered wagons." Continuing north to Cedar Breaks, they took in the view from "Perfection Point," evidently Rust's name for one of the rim's magnificent overlooks. Bypassing the Union Pacific lodge, they continued to a camp he had chosen in advance. Typically for Dave, it featured the best views—Anderson described it as "perhaps the finest site we have ever enjoyed. It was far off from the regular tourist camping place, on the very rim of Cedar Breaks, with a screen of fine spruce behind for a windbreak. Tents had been put up and the cook stove was sending out its cheery supper smoke."

Leaving their chilly night's camp (Anderson and her husband hardly slept), the party continued east over the lush, spruce-edged meadows of the Markagunt Plateau to the Sevier River valley and up to Bryce Canyon. The party opted for warm cabins that night. They spent only the next morning at Bryce, then drove on south to the Grand Canyon, most likely stopping at Will and Sarah Rust's Hotel Highway in Kanab, which they operated in addition to their tourist camp. Views from the North Rim provided a fitting conclusion to the trip. The Anderson's trip did not lead to a continuing relationship with Raymond and Whitcomb, which might have provided more such clients. Generally, Rust's tours were too primitive for most of the company's cultivated, upper-class clientele, who, according to historian Earl Pomeroy, "cherished its prearranged comforts, and returned to the train after each brief sortie into the unprotected world beyond with a sense of home-coming and gratitude."[11]

Rust's journals, moreover, give no indication that he found the trip with the Andersons especially rewarding. Automobile touring held no particular interest for him, especially when a big, unwieldy outfit had to be coordinated. He enjoyed occasional motor jaunts with a friend or two out to North Rim viewpoints such as Toroweap or Point Sublime, but even on these trips he was aware of the limitations of auto travel. On his 1924 Toroweap excursion with H. R. Merrill, Dave planned ahead for possible breakdowns, scrounging around Kanab for extra water jugs. "Others tried to convince our guide that it was unnecessary to load the car down with water," wrote Merrill, "declaring there would still be water in the water pockets and reservoirs of Toroweap Valley." But they found the entire region dry except at one wash, where a "famishing stream of oily looking water" allowed them to top off their radiator. Nearing the end of the long drive, their young driver cowboyed his Dodge into a fast run, to Rust's concern: "'Be careful my wild one,' Dave cautioned. 'If you lose a wheel here you may find a 75-mile walk warm and tiresome.'"[12] His horses and mules were still the more reliable conveyance, and he preferred watching the scenery go by at an animal's pace. He would use the machines where necessary, but his heart was still in the wilderness.

Other entrepreneurs would bring auto tourism to fruition. In 1927 the Utah Parks Company bought out the Parry brothers' bus tour operation, which had been shuttling visitors from the rail station at Cedar City to Zion, Bryce, and the North Rim.[13] The company added tours from the Denver & Rio Grande terminus at Marysvale and featured overnights in its park lodges and cabins. Even as the railroad consolidated its operation, however, private citizens were finding that the automobile allowed them the freedom to travel on their own schedule, camp where they felt like, and keep expenses down. While the Union Pacific resisted this form of tourism—it refused to advertise in California precisely because that was where many of the so-called "sagebrushers" came from—the free-ranging auto tourist was the wave of the future.[14]

Rust's wilderness trips stood in marked contrast to the tourist-lodge experience in the national parks. By 1929, after the Union Pacific had opened its lodge at Bright Angel Point, the Utah Parks Company offered a five-day bus tour of Zion, Bryce, the North Rim, and Cedar Breaks for just under ninety dollars.[15] Some writers encouraged independent-minded tourists to make the journey on their own. C. C. Presnall, a Park Service naturalist at Zion, suggested that motorists in Salt Lake City make a weekend trip to the Utah parks, taking advantage of the new highway tunnel at Zion's eastern entrance which had opened the way between Zion and Bryce. His proposed itinerary sounded even more rushed than the railroad's: "Leave Salt Lake City as early as possible Friday afternoon, drive 268 miles to Cedar City for the night, then drive to Bryce (90 miles) for luncheon Saturday, stopping an hour or so at Cedar Breaks en route. Saturday afternoon join the guided auto caravan that leaves Bryce Lodge daily at 2:30 to see all the major views along the rim drive, 38 miles round trip. Then 90 miles to Zion, arriving in the cool of evening in time for a late dinner and dance."[16] The contrast with Rust's pack trips could not have been more complete.

In the coming years Dave would compare these two modes of travel in his own writings, promoting his leisurely style of exploration. Zion and Bryce offered amazing scenery, to be sure. But he could put together an incredible itinerary through mountain, desert, and river—often in a single trip. His clients would experience the country at a measured pace as they rode across the Paunsaugunt and the Aquarius. From the plateau's eastern edge at Bowns Point or Tantalus Point, they could look out over the Waterpocket Fold toward the peaks of the Henrys and know that they would need two more days of hard riding to get there. The mountains and canyons that were everywhere visible were not just a scenic backdrop; they were waypoints on an unforgettable trip that brought out the complexity of the Plateau Province.

In September 1928 Dave's friend Emery Kolb, with whom he had boated during his Grand Canyon days, arranged for a joint adventure in Glen Canyon. The occasion was a visit from Kolb's longtime friend W. Louis Johnson of New York City, with whom Emery had hunted mountain lions on the Kaibab.[17] A friend of Johnson's named George C. Hollwith accompanied them. It was the first extended river trip Dave and Emery made together. Dave kept no account of the trip, although the four men jotted their names in the visitor register at Rainbow Bridge. This was Dave's eighth visit to the bridge, while Emery counted it as his third. By this time more than a hundred people were making the overland trip to the bridge each year, many coming from the new Rainbow Lodge that had been opened south of Navajo Mountain in 1924. Few visitors at that time approached from the river.

Although the national parks were a relatively small part of his overall itinerary, Dave was honored to be invited to the dedication of the new Grand Canyon Lodge at Bright Angel Point in September 1928. This dramatically situated rimside hotel was the Union Pacific's answer to the El Tovar, and its opening marked the arrival of the North Rim as a prime tourist destination. A large party of dignitaries, including Park Service director Stephen T. Mather and his assistant, Horace Albright, attended.[18] The presence of Heber J. Grant, president of the LDS Church, signified the importance the North Rim and its tourist business held for Utah. Whatever ill feelings Dave still harbored toward the Park Service and the Union Pacific must have been outweighed by his pride in having helped develop tourism at the rim. Dave, accompanied by Ruth, also joined the party at Bryce Canyon, where this scenic marvel was dedicated as Utah's second national park.

☙

With more time available during the off-season, Rust decided in the fall of 1928 to run once again for election to the state legislature. Unlike in 1916, when he ran for the Utah House of Representatives, he took on the much larger state senate district. This included major parts of Garfield, Iron, Beaver, Millard, and Sevier counties as well as his home in Kane County. His opponent was William T. Owens Jr. of Panguitch, the seat of Garfield County. Running on the Democratic ticket in 1928 was an uphill battle, unlike his successful (if casually conducted) campaign for state representative in 1916, when President Wilson's coattails aided the Democrats. Dave gained an endorsement from one of his former colleagues in the legislature, J. F. Tolton of Beaver, who had served as Speaker of the House during the 1917 session. Tolton praised Rust for his "far-sightedness and his ability to analyze questions," as well as his courtesy toward his fellow members. "I learned to trust in your diplomacy to help steer matters which came before committees," he wrote, "and was never disappointed in the results of your conclusions." Tolton's support was not sufficient to carry the election, however; while Rust led among voters in Kanab and adjacent areas, the more populous northern part of the district went solidly Republican.[19]

Remarkably, before the election was even held, the Rusts had decided to leave Kanab. Dave and Ruth had long wanted their children to attend Brigham Young University in Provo, and they felt they could help make this happen if they lived close to its campus. That September, Ruth's brother Roy Woolley and his wife Viola, who lived in Provo, decided to move and offered to sell their house to the Rusts. Dave and Ruth seized the opportunity. The family packed up its belongings with little preparation—Blanche Rust, who was nine years old at the time, learned they were moving only the night before they left.[20] The Rusts kept their home in Kanab well into the following year, and Dave kept a presence there, but at least some voters probably felt that he was no longer strongly committed to Kane County's affairs.

The move to Provo amounted to an early retirement for Dave. He would never resume a full-time career as an educator, although at one point he taught some high-school-level English classes through BYU. He turned his attention to his guiding work, which he was increasingly basing out of his friend Jim Pace's ranch at Torrey. Provo was more convenient to Torrey than Kanab had been, as well as being easier for most of his clients to reach via connections in Salt Lake City. Rust had sold his ownership in his ranch at Pipe Spring in 1927, giving them some funds toward retirement. He was also trying to dispose of his interest in a mine near Toroweap in which he had invested in the early 1920s.

One of Rust's grandsons, Joseph Rust, believed that the move may additionally have been motivated by the changing situation in Kanab. Dave no longer worked in the schools nor held elective office. The passing of Dee Woolley meant that new leaders had emerged in the community.[21] But he never set down his reasons for the move. He and Ruth kept close ties with their friends and family in Kane County and made visits at least once or twice a year; often these were combined with Dave's trips, especially when he needed to arrange a pickup at the end of a Glen Canyon voyage.

Dave's long experience with the Colorado River brought an unusual opportunity in the fall of 1929, the result of a federal court action that came to be known as the Colorado River Bed Case. For several years the state and federal governments had been granting competing leases to oil drillers on the Colorado downstream from Moab.[22] Both entities claimed ownership of the river bed and thus the right to issue leases and accrue royalties. The question hinged upon whether the Colorado, Green, and San Juan rivers were navigable, and hence subject to state jurisdiction. The Feds brought suit against the State of Utah to settle the title to the bed of the river. The matter came before the U.S. Supreme Court, which appointed a special examiner to hear the case at a series of hearings held in Los Angeles, Salt Lake City, and Denver starting in September of that year. The federal government paid for Dave to attend the Los Angeles hearing as one of its witnesses.

The court also subpoenaed many of Dave's longtime river-rat friends and gold miners whom he had known from his Glen Canyon days. At the hearings he enjoyed the chance to relive Glen's history with many of its participants, including Zeke Johnson, Lou and Arth Chaffin, Bert Loper, and others. Rust's own testimony focused on his experiences in running Glen during various water conditions, as well as relating his story of crossing the Green River in 1891. He answered questions succinctly, sometimes amusingly so, as when he was asked how he had navigated upstream in Glen Canyon in the 1890s:

Q: How did you operate the boat up there—how did you get it up?
A: "By hard work."
Q: Well, what do you mean, hard work?
A: "Rowing and towing."[23]

While his testimony formed only a small part of the lengthy hearings, he was the only person who had regularly taken passengers down Glen. While he was clearly "navigating" the river, he did not minimize its difficulty, telling the court that "in the first place, I have a responsibility to make the trip safe; one reason why I have selected a small boat which is easily managed, quickly managed, to avoid the sandbars and the shoals and the whirlpools, the wind waves and the sand waves which we sometimes encounter." He noted that he had "been driven ashore by the wind a number of times, occasionally have to wait over three or four hours for the wind to go down so that we can go on safely."[24]

The federal government had believed that Rust and his fellow prospectors and river-runners would show how hard it was to use these rivers. Rust's experiences seemed to show otherwise. The examiner tried to zero in on the small size and shallow draft of Rust's canvas canoes, which clearly did not represent normal commercial boat traffic. But in the end, the court ruled that nearly all of the Green and Colorado rivers within Utah were navigable, and thus belonged to the state. Only Cataract Canyon was held to be unrunnable for ordinary boats and would retain federal sovereignty.

Among the river veterans participating in the case was Frederick Dellenbaugh, whom Dave was pleased to meet in Los Angeles that September. As a young man Dellenbaugh had taken part in Major Powell's 1871 expedition down the Green and Colorado rivers, as well as his subsequent surveys of the Plateau Province. In later years he had become something of an expert on the region's history. Rust had been corresponding with him about such matters as the location of the Crossing of the Fathers and A. H. Thompson's exploration of the Aquarius Plateau. In October, Dellenbaugh traveled to Salt Lake City for a further round of hearings in the case. During a break in the proceedings he and Dave joined Bert Loper, who lived in town, for a drive to Provo to interview some other Glen

Canyon old timers. Rust invited his friends to lunch at his home, and their conversation would have conjured up many other characters and incidents from the Colorado's early days.[25]

Dave had kept up a correspondence with George Fraser in the years following their 1922 excursion to the Crossing of the Fathers, but for years Fraser, busy with work, was unable to make any trips to Utah. He continued to travel in Europe, and sent Dave a "wish you were here" postcard from Egypt in 1928, where he and Jane were touring the Nile by boat. In the fall of that year he invited Rust to meet him in La Junta, New Mexico, where he was inspecting some ranch lands he owned. "It has been too long since we met," he wrote, "and I can think of nothing that will give me greater pleasure than to put in a day or so with you."[26] He offered to pay Rust's bus fare to come down for a visit. Dave was pleased to make the trip, one of the few times that he ventured outside his home territory.

In 1930 Rust at last fulfilled his dream of taking Fraser through Glen Canyon. Dave had brought up the subject almost every year since their first overland journey in 1914, even though he did not acquire his own boats (nor any real experience in river guiding) until 1923. Perhaps Rust's inexperience weighed on Fraser, for unlike on their horseback trips, once they were on the river he might not be able to count on Rust's seeming ability to get them through any difficulty. By 1930, though, Dave had become an experienced guide to that stretch of the Colorado. Fraser, moreover, was no longer feeling very fit for a long saddle trip. The river offered a way to see the country without undue exertion.

In April 1930 Fraser had dinner in New York with Frederick Dellenbaugh and Clyde Eddy, the latter of whom had boated the canyon in 1927 on a movie-making venture. Eddy showed them his exciting pictures of running rapids in Cataract Canyon and the Grand Canyon, but both he and Dellenbaugh would have made it clear that Glen Canyon was perfectly safe, and well within Fraser's capabilities. It was enough to convince him to make the trip. He sent Dave a check for a thousand dollars to cover expenses, and urged him to hire another man "to avoid overwork."

At one point their old friend J. Cecil Alter of Salt Lake City was to have joined them, but he bowed out of the trip. To pilot the second boat, Rust obtained the services of Bert Loper, one of the legends of the Colorado River. Loper knew Glen intimately, and from about 1909 to 1914 had lived at the mouth of Red

Canyon, a dozen miles downstream from Hite. Pearl Baker, who knew Loper late in his life, described him in her book *Trail on the Water* as "a big man, athletic, powerful and quick, with the competent manner and air of command common to that type. He was pleasant company, with a good story or a tuneful song in his fine baritone voice adding to the enjoyment of any campfire."[27] Loper knew the river's currents from hard experience, having made an epic upriver slog in the winter of early 1908 from Lees Ferry after becoming separated from his companions, fellow prospectors Charles Russell and Ed Monett. His 160-mile upstream journey to Cass Hite's cabin at Ticaboo Canyon is surely the most grueling odyssey any person has had in Glen Canyon. Loper was an able counterpart to Rust, and his skill and experience ensured a safe trip for the party.

Fraser brought along his youngest daughter, Sarah, age eighteen. She had been eager to accompany her father after having listened to her older sisters talk about their magnificent adventures on horseback out West. "This was all sort of magical to me," she recalled. "My sisters would pack all these fascinating clothes and things, then they'd come back and talk of riding their horses; I was so jealous of them... I couldn't wait to be old enough to take a trip with him."[28]

The Frasers arrived in Salt Lake City in early August. Cecil Alter offered to drive them down to Hanksville to meet Rust and Loper; on the way, they stopped by Fruita to check out the petroglyphs at the Oyler ranch and hike to Hickman Natural Bridge. The heat at Hanksville was tremendous, and they still had two days' ride to the river, where it promised to be even hotter. Once they launched into the Colorado, though, the daytime breezes and a river to splash in made the journey tolerable.

Sarah Fraser described how Dave and her father explored up and down the river's side canyons like two old prospectors, talking about the geology of the canyon and thoroughly enjoying each other's company. Dave pulled over at all of his favorite sites, including Music Temple and the Crossing of the Fathers, where Sarah waded and swam across the river ("the water was heavenly," she recalled). She was disgruntled, however, to be left behind when the men stopped by the camp of the prospector William Carpenter—he favored going without clothes, and Rust could not persuade him to put on any for the sake of their lady guest.

Sarah found Bert Loper to be a fine companion. As he maneuvered their canoe downstream, he told stories about his years on the river. He had left the river with "five dollars less than when he went in," he told Sarah, "and that was what most gold rushing was about."[29]

George Fraser had wanted to stay on the river and continue through the Grand Canyon, according to Sarah, but her mother was loath to see them take on such a risky trip. Rust was not equipped to guide in the Grand Canyon, in any event. Instead, the foursome took out at Lees Ferry, where Jordan met them in Dave's Willys-Knight. They spent a day resting in Kanab at the home of one of Ruth's relatives, sleeping in the orchard to avoid the heat. Then they drove out to Toroweap, one of their favorite viewpoints, and westward toward the Shivwits Plateau (Loper appears not to have accompanied them on this part of the trip). Fraser had long wanted to climb Mount Dellenbaugh, the plateau's seven-thousand-foot-high summit, which afforded yet another of the grand lookouts that he and Dave so enjoyed. Dave hired some horses from an area rancher rather than cart his own down from Torrey. Reaching this summit was the culmination of all of Fraser's journeying in the Colorado Plateau since 1914, fulfilling his ambition of seeing the region as Powell's scientists had surveyed it—"from the Pink Cliffs to the Parashont," as Fraser put it.

Sarah photographed her father as he sat atop a stone survey monument that Powell's men had erected on Dellenbaugh, glassing the far view, with a satisfied-looking Rust surveying all. They knew the Plateau region from every angle, and each appreciated the scene as much as any human could. Their thoughts must also have turned to the three men from Powell's 1869 expedition who had quit the river at Separation Rapid, only to meet their deaths soon after, either at the hand of some Shivwits Indians or possibly from suspicious Utah townspeople. In recent years a rock inscription on Dellenbaugh bearing the words "Dunn" and "1869" has been publicized,[30] but none of Rust's party recorded finding any historical markings.

George and Sarah concluded their 1930 trip by driving to the Bay area and southern California, Sarah at the wheel. On their return to New Jersey, they stopped by Provo for a visit with Dave and his family. Fraser expressed his appreciation by letter after their return: "You certainly gave us a great time. We enjoyed every minute and incident of the trip, and are everlastingly grateful to you for all your trouble and interest and your care of us, but most of all for your good company."[31] This trip proved to be Rust and Fraser's last journey together; Fraser's health was declining and he would make no more primitive journeys in the Southwest.

It is not hard to put in mind the picture that Sarah Fraser described of her father hiking up the Hole-in-the-Rock trail with Rust in 1930—the two men making their way up the steep, rocky path above the Colorado River, stopping to examine the juniper logs sunk into holes in the sandstone for wagon supports, and turning around to admire the view across the canyon to the north face of Navajo Mountain. Sweating in the heat, but determined to get to the top, they puffed up the last few yards to the plateau where the domes of the Henry Mountains came into view. Off to the southeast, far beyond the Colorado River's canyon, stretched the wide expanse of the Navajo Reservation. Perhaps they recalled the time they got lost above the rim of Moonlight Canyon in 1916—in a time when even the most experienced travelers could lose their way. That incident stood out among all their many adventures, for, as George Fraser once wrote of his friend, Dave was seldom out of his reckoning.

The chief resource of Southern Utah, we are almost ready to admit, is the "Scenery." And along with this scenery of plateaus, canyons, cliffs, towers, temples, monuments, natural bridges, desert valleys, are sprinkled the ruins of the homes of a prehistoric people—the Basket Makers and the Cliff Dwellers. These ruins are ours to protect, ours to preserve but not ours to exploit and sell for selfish purposes.

DAVE RUST
"Preserve the Ruins"

AS ANGLO SETTLERS and cattlemen took possession of the deserts of southern Utah in the mid- to late 1800s, they could see all around them the work of a vanished race: carefully built stone dwellings tucked under inaccessible cliffs; smaller, mud-plastered structures that suggested the homes of a diminutive people; mysterious paintings and etchings decorating sandstone walls. Sometimes an agile cowboy took the trouble to climb the cliffs or creep along scary ledges to explore inside these structures. For a reward he might find a beautifully formed and decorated pot or bowl buried in the dust, perhaps a woven basket or sandal, or even the mummified remains of some ancient burial.

The cliff dwellings resembled the pueblos of the Hopi and Zuni Indians, so it was supposed that the ancient people had been ancestors to those tribes. Some Utahns called them "Mokis" or "Moquis," a name they used for the Hopi people, and the small masonry structures we now know to be storage cists were often called "Moki houses," as if people might have curled up inside them. There was even speculation that the Toltec tribes of Mexico had long ago made their way north into Arizona and Utah, so there were occasional references to "Aztec" ruins. The leavings of a more primitive race known as the Basket Makers lay deeper down in some sites. Science and folklore mixed together in the popular understanding, lending a fascinating allure to the vanished peoples of the canyon lands.

Rust had long taken an interest in the prehistoric remains that could be seen throughout the region. In 1906, while working on the Grand Canyon trail and tram, he and his men looked over a small ruin they had come across on the north side of the river near the tram anchorage. Major Powell and his men had seen it while stopping at Bright Angel Creek on their 1869 voyage. With George Fraser in 1916, Dave had examined a shattered dwelling at the base of Navajo Mountain, and they noticed other structures in alcoves while on their way east to Monument Valley. Three years later, visiting Mesa Verde with Charles Berolzheimer and Arnold Koehler, Dave enjoyed meeting Dr. Jesse Walter Fewkes, who was conducting the first systematic excavations of the park's great pueblos. And in 1920 he accompanied Neil Judd, a protégé of the University of Utah archaeologist Byron Cummings, on a foray down Bright Angel Canyon. They explored ruins in the upper part of the canyon and in a tributary called Phantom Creek, but high water in Bright Angel Creek stopped them from reaching the river.[1]

Later in his guiding career, Dave liked to take his river trip guests up Moki and Lake canyons to view cliff dwellings along these drainages. But he had not yet had a chance to take part in actual research and rub elbows with the scientists he so admired. Once again it was a referral from a former client that opened up a new avenue of discovery. In May 1927 Rust received a letter on the stationery of a Boston law firm, inquiring whether he could outfit an extended excursion with the aim of locating new archaeological sites. The writer was William H. Claflin Jr., an attorney with an interest in the prehistory of the Southwest. He was acquainted with Dr. J. P. Proctor, with whom Rust had boated down Glen Canyon in 1925, and who had suggested Rust as the best guide for such a trip. Claflin and his wife gave financial support to Harvard's Peabody Museum of American Archaeology and Ethnology, where he had the official capacity of Curator of Southeastern Archaeology and sometimes conducted his own field investigations. He also traveled extensively in the Southwest, dating back to 1912 when as a young man he visited the ruins in Jeddito Valley in northeastern Arizona.[2] In 1923 he had excavated sites in Tsegi Canyon on the Navajo Reservation under the museum's auspices. Like Cummings, he made a mark in an age when nonspecialists could carry out important research.

Claflin had ridden after mountain lions with Uncle Jim Owens on the Kaibab in the early 1900s, and on one of these trips he had briefly met Dave and his brother Will. Claflin told Rust, "I have always wanted to go into the country lying northwest of the Colorado River, bounded, roughly, on the north by the Freemont [*sic*] River, then swinging southwest to Henry Mountain, Circle Cliffs, Escalante River and the Kaiparowits Plateau region."[3] He and his companion, Raymond Emerson, a grandson of the writer Ralph Waldo Emerson, wanted to scout this region for "cliff dwellings or ruins."

This was exactly the sort of trip that Rust was best qualified to lead. He offered his services at the rate of twenty to twenty-five dollars a day, including a helper and his saddle horses and pack mules. He told Claflin that "I regard this region as intensely interesting from the Aquarius and Henry Mountain high look-offs for form and color panoramas or in detail as we ride across the mesas and down the canyons.... The cliff ruins are very primitive and not to be compared with the San Juan region. You may find these very primitive features to your liking. I believe it is a field that has not been scientifically explored for Cliff-Dwellers or Basket Makers."[4]

Rust alluded to some "very interesting burials" that had been found recently near Torrey by his friend Ephraim P. Pectol, a grocery-store owner who had been scouring the cliffs of the Waterpocket Fold for prehistoric treasures. The previous summer Pectol caused a local stir when he displayed three large, well-preserved buffalo-hide shields that he had unearthed in a cave east of town.[5] Pectol added these spectacular finds to his already considerable collection.

Rust met Claflin and Emerson in the fall of 1927 for a rough-and-ready survey of the region between the Aquarius Plateau and the Colorado River. He brought along his son Milton, at age twenty-one an experienced hand with horses, to serve as wrangler. Not all of the trip involved archaeology; after meeting at Bryce Canyon, they spent three days hunting mountain lions on the Paunsaugunt Plateau. His clients insisted on living the simple outdoor life, telling Rust to bring no canned goods—they could get by on bacon, coffee, biscuits, and such game as they could scare up. "At our first meeting," Rust recalled, "Bill had taken me to one side for a warning, that I must not say anything to Ray about Ralph Waldo Emerson. It seems that a surfeit of compliments had been thrust upon the nephew [actually grandson] of the famous American essayist. Another stipulation eliminated titles and surnames, we were to address each other in camp as Ray and Bill and Dave and Milt."[6] His clients clearly wanted to enjoy a bit of frontier democracy, where family background meant less than one's horsemanship and congeniality.

Dropping off of the Paunsaugunt, the four men made their way east past the muddy flow of the Paria River, following the stockmen's trail beneath the Table Cliff Plateau which led down to the town of Escalante. After buying supplies and socializing, the group set out for the rugged slickrock of the Escalante

River drainage. Dave took them down Harris Wash to the river and up the other side via Silver Falls Creek, following the same route he had taken with Berolzheimer and Koehler in 1920. This time they stayed on the old wagon route across the Waterpocket Fold that had been pioneered by Charles Hall in 1881, winding through the bends of Muley Twist Canyon and emerging from the Fold in the desert of Halls Creek. They continued south down this barren drainage to the Gene Baker ranch near the Colorado River and another welcome stopover.

They saw a few prehistoric granaries along Harris Wash and elsewhere along their route, but little to warrant a major investigation. Whether to find more promising sites, or simply for adventure, Dave decided to take the group directly west from the Baker Ranch on a cattle trail that led up onto the crest of the Fold. He wanted to get to its southern tip for a view out over Glen Canyon, so he led the men on what he later called "the roughest four days we had ever tackled." The crest of the Fold formed a broad ridge at just over five thousand feet in elevation, but traveling along it was anything but smooth. Innumerable slickrock domes, deep clefts, and incipient watercourses combined to make the topography confusing; in places the bare sandstone slopes were difficult going for a horse. As they neared the trench of the Colorado River in Glen Canyon, the crest became a rocky maze sliced crosswise by joints and fractures, forcing them to hunt for a way through the jumbled terrain. But the view from the southernmost promontory of the Fold was well worth the effort: directly below them, at the base of a sixteen-hundred-foot dropoff, the river flowed past an abandoned meander that looped six miles around to the south. Known as "The Rincon," this dry channel represented an ancient course of the Colorado, probably during Pleistocene time when the river carried heavy runoff from Rocky Mountain glaciers. Rising above this feature was Wilson Mesa, across which the Bluff emigrants had struggled during the winter of 1880 as they emerged from their terrible crossing at Hole-in-the-Rock. While Dave's scenic detour might have been off the topic of archaeology, the rarely witnessed sight was magnificent.

The group returned to the Baker Ranch and retraced their way toward Escalante, carrying "a bag of pottery and other artifacts, the only trophies of the trip." They made a side trip up to the village of Boulder, where Rust had heard of a promising site on the north edge of town. Here they found stone chips and pottery fragments scattered on a limestone knoll that hinted of ancient habitation. Despite the disappointing results from the rest of their trip, Claflin and Emerson must have been satisfied that the country north of the Colorado harbored some interesting prehistoric ruins, for the following spring Claflin proposed a more ambitious undertaking—a five-year survey of the central Utah canyon lands for archaeological remains, to be undertaken by the Peabody Museum. He and Ray Emerson would fund this program, which would for the first time bring experienced archaeologists into a region that had been largely overlooked.

The Boston men were impressed with Rust's competence as a scout, and recommended that the Peabody Museum hire him as packer and chief guide for the expeditions, since the country to be surveyed had few roads and presented severe logistical difficulties. S. J. Guernsey, the museum's assistant director, finalized plans in April 1928. The museum was willing to pay Rust eighteen dollars a day—less than he had asked for, but Guernsey felt that the museum personnel were used to horses and so Dave would not need a wrangler.[7] The first summer's program would outfit out of Escalante and investigate the ruins at the town of Boulder, thence working its way north into the Waterpocket Fold and the region around Torrey.

Before the museum fielded its first team to begin actual excavations in Utah, a student who had recently enrolled in Harvard's graduate anthropology program decided to have a look at some of the potential sites. This devotee was none other than Donald C. Scott, with whom Rust had made his memorable climb of Navajo Mountain in 1919. The two men had continued their acquaintance over the years and had joined up for another pack trip in May 1925. Scott was hardly a typical graduate student; he had risen far in the publishing world and in 1922 had joined with a group of investors (among them Franklin Delano Roosevelt) to buy the *New York Evening Post*.[8] Archaeology, however, was his passion, and by 1928 he had the means to pursue it. He told Rust that he wanted to "make a careful reconnaissance of some area not previously covered by archaeologists," taking notes for a subsequent Peabody Museum party to make a complete excavation. He admitted that "although I am very far from knowing enough to sit down and grub out any one site with completeness, still I should like to make a test trenching wherever it seemed promising and to keep a record of the broken pottery and other relics which were found."[9] He was particularly interested in investigating Pine Alcove Creek, the name Powell's men had given to Bullfrog Creek, a tributary of Glen Canyon.

Dave met Donald Scott and his wife, Louise, at the Denver & Rio Grande station in Richfield on April 12, 1928. They motored south to Escalante, where they met Milton, who had already recruited their pack stock from a local rancher. The foursome left for the backcountry of the Waterpocket Fold via a wagon road that had been pioneered by a cattleman named Sheffield, which snaked out toward a wedge formed by the Escalante River and Harris Wash. Along most of its length, the river was protected by continuous cliffs, but Rust knew of a sand slide that breached the walls and led down to the mouth of Silver Falls Creek, shortcutting the usual Harris Wash wagon route. They reached the Baker ranch on Halls Creek on the twentieth.

Rust was happy to be back at the river, even without his boats. Here they could explore the prehistory of Glen Canyon in greater detail than he had been able to on his river trips. Wading in the shallows at times, they worked their way upriver past the mouth of Hansen Creek to Smith Fork, the site of a notable petroglyph panel. It was crowded with both lifelike and abstract representations: bighorn sheep, humanoids with bow and arrow, spirals, jagged lines. Farther upriver, they located several fine rock art sites in Trachyte Canyon. Part of Scott's goal was to photograph these sites while Louise made drawings; this collection, now at Harvard's Peabody Museum, formed the first comprehensive record of rock art in Utah.[10] Back at Hite, they camped by the cabin of the prospector William Schock and then made their way upstream to Crescent Creek, their exit route from Glen Canyon. They spent the better part of two days investigating a variety of rock art displays in this canyon, including, Dave noted, a "pecked snake with mouth open over 10 feet long near painted man (Basket-maker) about 5 feet high."

Rather than follow the wagon road north to Hanksville, Rust opted (as he often did) for the scenic route, climbing over the Henry Mountains to the King Ranch west of Mount Ellen, thence north along the edge of the Waterpocket Fold to Notom and the Fremont River settlements. At Fruita, a garden spot in the heart of the Fold, they stayed with Michael Valentine Oyler, known as "Tine" around town, whose ranch Dave called "one of the most charming and interesting spots in S. Utah, a veritable museum of Archaeology." He was referring to several rock art panels found on the north end of Oyler's property, where sandstone cliffs rose directly above the Fremont River. These spectacular panels, which were still not well known outside of the local area, displayed an amazing variety of figures, including petroglyphs depicting bighorn sheep and imposing god-like humanoids, the meaning of which still invites much speculation.

On May 7 they rode up to Torrey to visit E. P. Pectol at his informal museum in the back of a grocery store he ran. Seeing these priceless artifacts in the hands of a private collector may have presented a dilemma for a trained archaeologist like Donald Scott. Passage of the Antiquities Act of 1906 made it illegal to collect prehistoric artifacts from the public domain without the federal government's permission. This law, however, was routinely ignored by local people. Pectol had gathered the artifacts out of curiosity and admiration, not for resale, but he, like most other private collectors, did not keep accurate records of their provenance. His collection thus had limited scientific value. Men like Pectol, however, knew where more collecting sites could be found, and so were invaluable informants to researchers. Probably Scott politely gathered what information he could use for the museum's studies. Eventually, the National Park Service required Pectol to give up some of his best items, an ironic outcome since he was one of the early proponents of a national park in the area.[11]

The Rusts and the Scotts had been in the field for a month and had covered close to a hundred and fifty miles of tough desert terrain. Donald and Louise had come a long way for this opportunity, though, and they wanted to explore further before returning to Cambridge. Within the vast expanse of southern Utah's canyons and plateaus were potentially thousands of prehistoric sites, and the more exacting work that would follow under the Peabody Museum's sponsorship needed a focus if it were to be successful. The Scotts' reconnaissance was crucial to point the way for further work.

After checking out ruins and rock art sites near Hickman Natural Bridge and in Cohab Canyon, now popular destinations within Capitol Reef National Park, Rust took them south to Temple (Pleasant) Creek, which sliced down from the eastern edge of the Aquarius Plateau through Navajo Sandstone cliffs. "Horses very happy," Rust wrote as they camped at a choice, well-watered site. He showed the Scotts some rock art sites near the Floral Ranch, a secluded property that had been settled in 1878 by the pioneer Ephraim Hanks. For more than a hundred feet along a great curving wall of sandstone, unknown artists had inscribed figures of bighorn sheep, coyote- or wolf-like creatures, and looming, god-like beings bearing horns and headdresses. The wall overlooked a wide, grassy flat that must have been an excellent camping place for early wanderers. G. K. Gilbert had mentioned these "picture-writings" in his 1880 *Report on the Geology of the Henry Mountains.*

Farther upstream in the canyon they located a promising site under an overhang, but it was "too scary to get closer than 100 feet," Rust observed. He would return to this site with a Peabody Museum crew that summer. The party then proceeded over the shoulder of the Aquarius to Boulder Town, where they stayed with a rancher Rust knew. They took another look at the mound site north of the village that Claflin and Emerson had investigated, and the Scotts agreed it would be worth a further look by the follow-up expedition.

A still more remote destination awaited the Scotts' exploration that May. After riding over the mail trail from Boulder to Escalante, and enjoying a Tom Mix movie at the town's theater, Rust and the Scotts made arrangements to head up onto the Kaiparowits Plateau, a dry, unfriendly region that dominated the skyline to the south. Dave had been to the southern edge of the plateau with George Fraser in 1922, but few whites other than some of the local cattlemen had been there. Dave employed a young Escalante man named Kenneth Griffin to help Milt wrangle the stock, and on May 18 the party set out on the old Hole-in-the-Rock road underneath the long, banded wall of the Straight Cliffs. Along the way they revisited a natural sculpture collection that he had seen with Berolzheimer and Koehler in 1920. Rust called it "the best little Garden of statues & natural bridge—a hawk had his nest & one young bird in top of one. So we name it Eagle Garden." Today the locality is known as Devil's Garden, site of a small but gracefully sculpted span called Metate Arch.

Rust planned to reach the Kaiparowits by climbing through a break in the Straight Cliffs, which formed the eastern rampart of the plateau. On top was an extensive tableland lying above seven thousand feet elevation, called Fiftymile Mountain, where scattered springs made camping possible. This piñon- and juniper-dotted plateau, cold in winter and hot and dry in summer, seemed an unlikely place for early peoples to inhabit, yet in hidden overhangs they found small granaries and dwellings. They located an "extraordinary cliff house" under the rim, which they reached with the aid of a hundred-foot rope. There was time for only a brief reconnaissance of the plateau; later researchers discovered that the Kaiparowits held hundreds of prehistoric sites, including the remains of many stone houses scattered over the plateau's high country. These were often mere outlines in the ground and eluded the Scotts' quick traverse.[12]

To conclude their brief stay on Fiftymile Mountain, Rust took the Scotts out to the eastern tip of the plateau, which presented another sweeping panorama of buttes, mesas, and canyons. The view encompassed White Mesa and Square Butte to the south, Navajo Mountain and Monument Valley to the southeast, and the San Juan River gorge and the Abajo Mountains off to the east. Glen Canyon and the Henry Mountains to the northeast completed the scene. For Dave, no trip was complete without a careful examination of the distant view. It was as if he needed to place himself within the Plateau Province, to refresh his sense of where he stood.

Finally, they dropped off of the Kaiparowits to explore some side canyons of the Escalante River. "When I am on the canyon rim I hanker to go to the bottom," he wrote on a subsequent trip with Donald Scott, yet "when I am at the bottom of a canyon for any length of time, I want to climb to *rim*."[13] He felt some elemental urge to constantly seek new points of view.

Ken Griffin knew of some ruins in Davis Gulch, so he led Dave and Donald Scott on a long evening's ride to investigate, while Milt and Louise stayed behind at their camp at Cave Seep underneath the Straight Cliffs. After skirting the upper narrows of Davis Gulch, Rust, Griffin, and Scott zigzagged down to the canyon bottom on a stock trail that had been chiseled into the sandstone. Farther downstream were notable cliff dwellings, granaries, and rock art panels. They found "a very interesting Kiva 8-1/2 ft in diameter, partly covered. Ken had called it a 'well.'"[14] The journey back to camp lasted well past dark, "finding our way back by moonlight through the rattlers to a dead camp fire," Donald Scott recalled. "Milt and Louise seemed to have taken it for granted that we would probably never come back."[15]

The party rode to Escalante to conclude their six-week survey of the canyons. Dave took the Scotts on an auto tour out to the Grand Canyon as a sort of frosting on the cake; he noted that they had to cut and remove forty trees off of the road to Point Sublime.

While the Scotts' trip was basically a scouting expedition, it pointed the way for subsequent Peabody Museum expeditions, particularly at the Boulder Mound site. The first of these was led later that summer by a twenty-four-year-old Harvard student named Noel Morss. Like Donald Scott, Morss would go on to a career in the business world. His work in the Southwest, however, established his reputation among archaeologists, based in large part on what he discovered during this trip. It was not his first visit to the region; in 1927 he had worked on the northern Navajo Reservation and visited Forbidding Canyon near Rainbow Bridge.[16]

In early July Rust met Morss and his assistant, Robert Sanderson, in the town of Escalante. Dave's young friend Harry Bartol came along to help wrangle the stock and to participate in the excavations where he could. Their first goal was to excavate the Boulder Mound site that Rust had visited on his two previous scouting expeditions. This turned out to be a rich locality, with the remains of two masonry pueblos and additional underground pit houses, all buried in sand that had drifted against the limestone knoll. Morss and his crew found abundant evidence of habitation, unearthing three adult male skeletons along with pottery jars and bowls that had evidently been included with the burials.[17] Subsequent investigations in the 1950s and later showed that the village had been established around 1150 A.D. by the so-called Kayenta Anasazi, and was home to as many as two hundred people. Although it was a far outpost of this culture, artifacts found at the site show that its residents traded with people from Mesa Verde and other centers of Kayenta life in northern Arizona. The site was abandoned by about 1250 A.D.[18]

From Boulder the party moved over the eastern shoulder of the Aquarius to Temple Creek, where Dave took another look at the overhang that he and Donald Scott had been unable to reach in May. This time he was able to lower Morss and Sanderson on a rope to investigate what turned out to be a freestanding storage structure. A nearby cave yielded a variety of stone and bone tools, an interesting moccasin, and "a large collection of clay figurines."[19] The moccasin, along with others found during this expedition, appeared to be unique; it was crafted from the hide of a bighorn sheep, still with its hair, and sported a dewclaw at the heel. Only woven sandals made from yucca and other fibers had been found in the cliff dwellings of the Puebloan peoples; this was further evidence of a culture different from the cliff-dwellers.

Rust led them north underneath the cliffs of the Fold to Torrey, where Morss examined E. P. Pectol's extensive collection. He noted in his report that "considerable interest in the local antiquities is taken by the inhabitants of Torrey, so that the immediate neighborhood has been thoroughly prospected."[20] Pectol's buffalo-hide shields, he believed, were of "comparatively recent" origin.

At this point Rust had other obligations—perhaps another party to take out, although he did not record this—so Morss continued his explorations with

Clarence Mulford, a Fruita resident, as guide. Morss spent a week excavating a large cave in Fish Creek Cove, a sagebrush-dotted amphitheater south of Torrey. Situated at the base of the Aquarius Plateau yet close by the Fremont River, the site offered early inhabitants a wide variety of environments for hunting, foraging, and raising crops. Abundant rock art decorated the sandstone walls, and the cave yielded more sheep-hide moccasins, pottery, and an unusual wicker-roofed dwelling.

Morss returned to Utah in 1929 for a follow-up trip to unearth more evidence of what appeared to be a distinctive ancient culture. Traveling without Rust, who was engaged with another Peabody Museum expedition, he examined sites in the Nine Mile or "Minnie Maud" Canyon near Price, Utah. This canyon is often referred to as the "world's longest art gallery," with more than a thousand identified prehistoric rock art sites.[21]

Morss's investigations in 1928 and 1929 led him to conclude that he had uncovered a culture with significantly different lifeways than the pueblo-building peoples centered in the Four Corners area. In his 1931 report on his Utah explorations, Morss proposed the existence of a "primitive, peripheral culture, of which the outstanding original features were a primitive type of moccasin and elaborate clay figurines."[22] Their dwellings used a mixture of wood, wicker, and clay, and in general they did not appear to be as settled as the pueblo-builders south of the Colorado River. They did not appear to be "an integral part of the main stream of Southwestern development," yet he noted that "the originality shown in many details of their culture makes it difficult to think of the Fremonters as merely a backward Southwestern tribe." While Morss did not formally name the new culture, they came to be called the "Fremont," as distinguished from the culture that would come to be called the Anasazi.[23] Morss did not necessarily perceive them as poor relations of the Anasazi, offering that "the absence of the superficially impressive features of Southwestern culture, architecturally durable houses and colored pottery, does not necessarily indicate that they were not, on the whole, as well fed, clothed, housed, and generally comfortable as their Pueblo II counterparts."

For the next several years, the Peabody Museum's archaeological expeditions constituted the bulk of Rust's guiding work. The museum fielded a second expedition in 1929 (independent of Noel Morss) under the direction of Henry Roberts, another graduate student at Harvard. This was a wide-ranging foray covering more of the Fremont River–Waterpocket Fold country, but also venturing out into the San Rafael Desert and the cliffs above the Green River. Joining Roberts was Alfred Kidder Jr., the seventeen-year-old son of Dr. A. V. Kidder, who had conducted earlier archaeological expeditions for the Peabody Museum in the Southwest. The expedition engaged a Hanksville man, Les McDougal, to assist Rust in navigating the Robbers Roost country and the region west of the Green River known as "Under the Ledge," which was still somewhat unfamiliar to Rust.

As they were scouting this country, they rode into the backcountry camp kept by Ned Chaffin and his two older brothers, Faun and Clell, at Waterhole Flat. The brothers were away branding cattle at the time, and they returned to camp that evening to find strangers standing by the fire. After some discussion, Henry Roberts hired Ned to help them scout archaeological sites in the vicinity. This led to hard feelings when McDougal was let go. "Faun got madder than hell," Ned recalled decades later. "He flipped his lid. And he called old man Roberts some unpolite names and one thing and another. And said he sure didn't think by me going with 'em, they was going to let Les go. 'Cause he hated to take Les' job away from him."[24] This was the height of the Great Depression, and a job with an outfit like Peabody paid good wages—Faun Chaffin knew that McDougal had a family to feed. But Roberts stayed with Ned Chaffin, who knew the cliffs, alcoves, and all-important water holes in the country they were exploring.

The archaeologists spent weeks searching the inhospitable country beneath the Orange Cliffs for prehistoric sites. Dave got out the rope to gain access to hard-to-reach caves and cliffs. He also had plenty of work managing the camp and the pack stock in what he described as a "poverty-stricken" terrain.[25] Their work paid off with several exciting finds, including a large, intact pot located in an unlikely-looking cave, a medicine bundle buried in a cliff dwelling, and a buffalo robe.

An oil wildcatter working in the area had told them about a good pictograph site in Horseshoe Canyon, a long defile sometimes called Barrier Canyon because of its lengthy, sheer cliffs; so, following a recently constructed oil exploration road, they entered the canyon and soon were rewarded with several excellent displays of prehistoric art. The most striking of these was a few miles upstream, above a shelf of rock on the west side of the canyon. Rust described it as containing "no less than 20 square-shouldered, ornamented, painted figures grouped with numerous other unique figures. The greatest gallery I have seen."[26] Some of the figures were as large as a man, though they lacked limbs and showed a distinctive ghostlike appearance. Smaller figures bearing staffs, and still smaller depictions of bighorn sheep, adorned the wall, all painted with a vivid hematite. They stood in contrast to the figures along the Fremont River at Fruita, which sported arms and legs. They are now thought to be the work of an older culture than the Fremont called the Archaic. Some rock art in Horseshoe Canyon, painted in what is called the "Barrier Canyon style," has been thought to be 6,000 to 8,000 years old, but in 1994 a radiometric study of a paint fragment from the site showed it to be no more than 3,800 years old.[27]

The elongated torsos of some of the figures were elaborately decorated; anyone studying them would realize that they were the work of artists with a feeling for beauty and symbolism, not mere savages. But not all who enjoyed these fabulous paintings felt that they should remain in public view; the oilman who had told them about the site mentioned that he thought he might saw out some of the figures and take them home with him. Fortunately he was otherwise occupied and so the "Great Gallery," as it is called today, remains one of the finest rock art displays in the world.

Rust outfitted another Peabody Museum crew in the summer of 1930. This time he brought his pack string past the Green River to Moab, where on July 25 he met Henry Roberts, who was once again in charge of the archaeological investigations. Donald Scott Jr., a student at Harvard, was part of the crew this year, along with his father, who had assumed the duties of assistant director of the Peabody Museum the previous year. This was new territory for Dave, and he employed a Moab man, Len Woodruff, to find trail. They rode down the east bank of the Colorado to Indian Creek and explored the rich leavings of the Puebloan culture in that basin and southward. For five days they scouted in Beef Basin, Ruin Park, and Salt Creek, collecting pottery, baskets, and other artifacts. Ruin Park, in particular, was notable for its standing masonry structures located in open fields rather than underneath alcoves. These had been built during the culmination of Puebloan culture in the Utah canyon lands, before the climatic or social changes that led to their abandonment by about A.D. 1300 throughout the region.

The explorers also searched for hidden sites in the maze of canyons above the Colorado. The Moab newspaper reported that "a few ruins, which are very inaccessible, were entered for the first time by the explorers, who gained entrance by being let down on ropes." Lacking time, the team conducted no excavations. Donald Scott Sr. developed chest pains midway into this trek—Rust noted that he was so ill he had difficulty holding onto his horse—so the crew headed to Moab so he could return home.[28]

On August 10 Rust, Roberts, and Donald Scott Jr. reassembled in Green River to continue work in the Waterhole Flat area of the previous year's expedition. Two more Harvard students, Waldo Emerson Forbes and James Dennison, joined them; Dennison was the son of Henry S. Dennison, a business acquaintance of Donald Scott, Sr. The country south of Green River town was still tough to get into; "after getting stuck," Rust noted, "busting a fan belt and a hind spring along with puncturing gas tank we arrive at the hospitable Biddlecome Ranch." Dave had sent the pack animals ahead with another man to Flint Spring, where on August 13 they descended into the benches of Under the Ledge to meet up again with Ned and Clell Chaffin. The crew made further excavations in several caves they had located the previous year. Dave listed their finds as including "6 ears of corn wrapped in bark—also some pieces of feather-cloth!" He took considerable pleasure in these scientists' work, and enjoyed their stimulating company around the campfire. In those days the average Utah native had at best a rudimentary knowledge of the previous inhabitants of the land. These recent archaeological investigations had not filtered into public knowledge, and the complex organization of Fremont and Puebloan societies was still only dimly understood.

After finishing the month of August with excavations under the Orange Cliffs, the party moved up to Horseshoe Canyon to excavate a site they had noted the previous year, located about a mile downstream from the Great Gallery. Donald Scott Sr., who had recovered from his illness, rejoined the group. "Horseshoe Shelter," as they called the site, contained several small rooms in which were found projectile points and clay figurines similar to those that Noel Morss had found in the Waterpocket Fold. At that time, the extent of the newly identified Fremont culture was unknown; over time their artifacts (notably a characteristic style of coiled gray pottery) would be found over a wide area of central Utah and even into the Great Basin of Nevada and Idaho and parts of western Colorado.

Rust's final expedition with the Peabody Museum took place the following summer, bringing to a close a rewarding association with the museum's scientists. Their work for 1931 focused on the Book Cliffs region north of Green River town, Ninemile Canyon (Minnie Maud Creek), where Noel Morss had surveyed in 1929, and still farther north and east in the Uinta and Green River basins. Jim

Dennison and Waldo Forbes returned, along with another young Harvard graduate student, John Otis ("Jo") Brew, who directed the fieldwork. Donald Scott Sr. again joined the group, which with assistants and wranglers (including Dave's son Nelson) came to ten men. Dave wrote his recollection of the expedition some years later:

> The program was to cover the Tavaputs plateaus and the canyons of the Green River between the East and the West. Some time was spent on Hill Creek (East) and considerable more time was spent in the Minnie Maud (West) where we found numerous pictograph galleries and where we dug out a pure Basket-maker burial in cave site number 31. To complete the survey almost to the Wyoming line, we explored Ashley river canyon and Jones Hole on Green River above Split Mountain canyon. Numerous other spots were checked and sampled. To finish off a most interesting summer full of fun and study and exercise, we went fishing on the head of the Uinta river and Chain Lakes with a climax climb to the 13500 foot top of Mt. Emmons for an unsurpassed panorama of the regions explored.[29]

This lengthy trip was Brew's introduction to packing in rugged country, and he later credited Dave for guidance: "you set me on the right track in the west, providing both inspiration and precept."[30] He was determined to learn to ride, "even if it killed him," in Donald Scott's words. Fortunately, as Brew recalled in 1971, Rust "provided intimate knowledge of the country, the horses, and the mules; and his saddle mules were the smoothest-riding and best-trained quadrupeds I have ever met up with."[31] The two men kept in touch after the Peabody Museum finished its work in Utah; in 1938 Brew invited Dave to visit him at the pueblo ruins at Awatovi in northern Arizona's Hopi country, where he was conducting an excavation.

Donald Scott also complimented Rust's ability as guide for these expeditions: "As you know, most 'guides' cannot appreciate that we have to cover the country for our archaeological purposes almost regardless of conditions and a good many expeditions have suffered because they have been steered off on to the easier trails and better water and browse by the local talent.... [A]mong your many gifts not the least valuable is your understanding of this need and your willingness and determination to put the outfit through if it is not utterly impossible—and sometimes then."[32]

As a result of his five-year association with the Peabody Museum, Rust developed an even stronger appreciation for the scientific worth of the Colorado Plateau's archaeological resources. Around this time he wrote a short essay titled "Preserve the Ruins," in which he foresaw the value to tourism of leaving prehistoric structures and artifacts unimpaired. "It might be expected," he wrote, "that the people who live in Southern Utah will not need to be forced to obey the law of preservation with respect to these ruins which may become such a great asset in connection with the wonderlands around us. It is rather to be expected that we will have the sympathy and vision to handle with regard our sacred inheritance." While he never published the essay, he likely imparted his views to his guests in the field, and discouraged them from pocketing artifacts.

Education and enforcement, however, barely slowed the incidence of vandalism and thoughtless collecting. This was a time when few people saw prehistoric sites as anything more than curiosities or as sources of valuable artifacts for one's collection. Although the Antiquities Act made unauthorized collecting illegal, there was essentially no enforcement outside of the national parks and monuments. In Utah, committed individuals such as Zeke Johnson at Natural Bridges National Monument might keep an eye on things and track down a pothunter where they could, but he could patrol only a tiny corner of the canyon lands region.

The Peabody Museum's program in Utah during the period 1928–1931 seems to have left a mixed legacy, at least in the region north of the Colorado where Rust accompanied them. Of the four main expeditions he guided (not counting the two preliminary scouting trips with Claflin, Emerson, and the Scotts), only one published study resulted—Noel Morss's landmark 1931 paper on the Fremont. Neither Henry Roberts nor Donald Scott published their findings from their expeditions, although their work was carefully recorded and preserved in the museum's files. J. O. Brew, who accompanied Donald Scott on the 1931 expedition, went on to conduct an important series of excavations at Alkali Ridge in southeastern Utah beginning that same year.[33] And the Scotts' extensive photographs and drawings of Utah rock art were the basis for Polly Schaafsma's 1994 book, *The Rock Art of Utah: A Study from the Donald Scott Collection.*

Noel Morss's Fremont culture has been carefully studied and outstanding new sites discovered in a broad region across Utah and its bordering states. Our knowledge of the ancient inhabitants has increased many fold, with new interpretations of how they survived the challenges of the canyon and plateau environment. Scholars disagree, however, on whether they were a distinct group of people or merely a collection of groups with shared characteristics, some semi-nomadic, others more settled.[34] Whatever the interpretation, the Fremont left behind evidence of a complex society, one in which people felt the need to make clay figurines, artistic pottery, and ornate, imposing rock art. Though they did not construct breathtaking cliff palaces like their neighbors to the southeast, they successfully occupied the demanding landscapes of the northern Colorado Plateau and adjoining Great Basin for more than a thousand years. Even the seemingly inhospitable Escalante River basin turns out to have been a major locus of habitation. The picture that is slowly emerging of these peoples shows a tremendous resourcefulness amid the Plateau Province's harsh environment. More than one researcher has drawn comparisons to our current—and rather intensive—use of the landscape, and has asked how long it can be sustained.

The Fremont of south-central Utah seemed to have melted into the background by about 1300 A.D., owing to obscure causes that may have included environmental changes, attacks from neighboring cultures, or the availability of better conditions to the south, where drought was not as severe. Ongoing studies will also shed light on the fragile environmental conditions still found in the region, as well as the continuing effects of climate change. Science has made the former peoples much more than a curiosity or a mysterious backdrop on which to drape our imaginings; their story may tell us much about our own chances to inhabit the Colorado Plateau.

16 | Monuments in Sandstone

> On a Utah map, with the Utah-Arizona border as a base,
> draw a line to scale 125 miles north approximately through
> the towns of Bluff and Moab, thence west 125 miles, thence
> south to the base 125 miles, and you thus describe an area of
> over 15,000 square miles, more than one-sixth of the total
> area of the state of Utah.... This region is unsurpassed in
> variety of mountains, high plateaus, lakes, deep canyons,
> temples, towers, strips of genuine desert, bare-rock por-
> tions painted in all the combinations of fantastic coloring.
>
> DAVE RUST
> "I Came Out of the Wilderness"

AFTER COMPLETING the last of his archaeological ex-
peditions with the Peabody Museum in 1932, Rust again had to face the prospect
of supporting his family without steady employment. He and Ruth had four children living at home, ranging from Nelson, age eighteen, to Helen, their last child,
who was born that June. At times they also offered room and board to other
young relations who were studying at Brigham Young University. Only through
strict economy—some of the children remembered it as penury—were Dave and
Ruth able to maintain their household. Around this time Rust wrote a short essay
titled "If I Were Rich," observing that "there is a homely saying, 'No disgrace to
be poor, but mighty inconvenient.'" He felt, perhaps a little wistfully, that "not-
withstanding the frequently quoted parable of the camel and Lazarus, a rich man
may have an opportunity with a beggar to get into the kingdom of heaven and he
will be quite as cool and free from torment." His outlook was probably colored
by his travels with men and women whose economic station far surpassed his; yet
out on the trail, where life was stripped to the essentials, they rode as his equals.
Rust, in his own words, valued "integrity and unselfishness" above all else; money
always seemed to be secondary.

Despite his relative poverty, the freedom to travel with his eastern clients
counted for much. Although the Depression had hit the country with full force,
there were still families of means who could afford to spend their vacations in the
wilds of the Southwest. As before, Dave relied on his former clients to spread the
word about the Utah canyon country and bring him new business. Friends such
as George C. Fraser, Bill Claflin, and Donald Scott could hardly be surpassed as

well-placed agents. Rust did not always specify who referred his various clients, but adventurers with connections to Princeton and Harvard continued to head west to see his favorite territory. In 1933 he led a trip over the Aquarius Plateau and into the Henry Mountains for a party of six young women from New York, Rhode Island, and Maine, including Libby Sturges, the sister of the young man who had accompanied Rust in 1927. Some of the women also went down Glen Canyon with him that summer. He kept no record of these trips, however.

His favorite journeying companion, George Fraser, was not able to return to Utah owing to work and family commitments as well as declining health. While he and Rust continued their correspondence, they would not meet again. Fraser's last letter to Rust, dated June 27, 1935, spoke of their long acquaintance dating back to the day in southern Utah when they first met:

> Twenty-one years ago tomorrow, George and I, with very tender feet, embarked on our Western voyage of discovery, with little more idea of where we would fetch up than had Christopher Columbus.
>
> That we did not spend forty years in the wilderness was due to the modern Moses of mathematical mind who met us at Toquerville with two horses to carry three of us. But that is the smallest part of our obligation to him. He calloused our feet and opened our eyes and took us on high mountains whence were revealed prospects beyond previous narrow concepts, that gave abiding stimulations and started unending trains of thought.[1]

As always, Fraser generously credited Rust for the success of his Colorado Plateau trips. In fact, Fraser had a very clear idea of what he wanted to see when he first set out for Utah; it was a happy coincidence that Rust shared his love of geology and knew many of the places he wanted to explore.

In October 1935, while flying to the Southwest on business, Fraser took ill unexpectedly with heart pains. At a stop in Dallas he was taken to the hospital. George Fraser Jr. telegrammed Rust with the news and expressed hope for his father's recovery. Jordan Rust was traveling in the eastern U.S. at the time with his wife, Edloe; they caught a plane out to Dallas to see how their friend was faring.[2] Unfortunately, they were not able to see him—the hospital staff mistakenly sent them after someone else with the name of Fraser who had recently checked out, and once they returned to the hospital they were informed that visits were limited to family members. Jordan was keenly disappointed not to see his friend and benefactor, but he and Edloe stayed in Dallas for several days and spoke with members of his family.

George Fraser passed away in Dallas on November 15. The news undoubtedly hit Dave hard, for he counted Fraser as one of his closest friends. He did not put down his thoughts in his journal, but he did pass along the sad news to their mutual friend, J. Cecil Alter. Alter offered his condolences by letter, telling Rust that he "could not at any time ever reach the beautiful tribute of praise and affection I read of him in the letter you wrote." He went on to say, "I know what Uncle Dee meant to you. His going from your life was like filling up the Grand Canyon. Fraser's going must be like the loss of all the books and maps of the country. Under the circumstances of such a beautiful friendship between you and him, you will forgive me for the pride I feel in having been instrumental in bringing you together."[3]

Theirs had indeed been a remarkable friendship. Fraser and Rust had not only put in many weeks together on trails through some of the roughest country in the West, but they had shared and built upon their mutual interest in geology and history. It was a rare experience for a Utah native who had been brought up in the most rustic surroundings to be on close terms with a man of George Fraser's experience. Fraser's journals and letters occasionally indicate his impatience with men of his own station who did not appreciate the wider world. Instead, he found an improbable bond with someone out in Utah who understood the deeper joys of travel.

George Fraser's passing was part of an end to an era—the generation of Victorian explorers who brought with them a unique, highly informed approach to travel. More and more of Dave's clientele were younger men and women who had read stories of the Southwest's open spaces and were eager to have their own adventures. Jim Dennison's experience with the Peabody expeditions in 1930 and 1931 seemed to have given him a taste for the desert, and in 1932 he returned to work with J. O. Brew on Alkali Ridge in southeastern Utah. These trips piqued interest among members of his family back in Massachusetts, and in the summer of 1934 he made plans to return to Utah with his father, Henry S. Dennison, his sister Mary, and her husband, David Stickney. He wrote to Rust that he wanted to "disappear into the loneliest, ruggedest, most beautiful part of your wonderful state for about 10 days.... My principal desire is to get in some desolate, riotous canyon country and just meander around, climbing into granaries, messing in cave-dust, and exploring wild places. I want to be free to go off for a day at a time, while the others do what they want to."[4]

Jim's father was president of the Dennison Manufacturing Company of Framingham, Massachusetts, a paper and office products firm. Henry S. Dennison was known as a progressive employer who had set up an unemployment insurance program to help workers he had laid off during the Depression. In the years that followed, he hired and became a mentor to a young economist named John Kenneth Galbraith, who would go on to have a major impact on the nation's economic policies.

Jim Dennison wrote to Rust that spring to make arrangements. He assured Rust that his father, while sixty years of age, was a "driver" and was ready for any adventure. Concerned that his family and friends enjoy the experience—and perhaps to relieve Dave of some of the work—he suggested that Dave bring along a camp cook. Rust's reply showed his usual good humor: "Must we have an expert cook (a creature hard to find who can adapt to camping on a wild trail). Please be frank about this matter. Do you suppose that if I put on my cleanest appearance and did my very best with the dough-gods we could make out for such a short trip?"[5]

On July 11 the Dennisons made their way to the Jim Pace ranch south of Torrey, Utah, where Rust now based his operation. Pace had been a student of Dave's at the Loa High School in 1896, and had offered to board Dave's horses in his scenic fields below the ramparts of Boulder Mountain. (Rust could not have paid him much for this privilege; probably Pace made use of Dave's stock at times.) At the ranch, the Dennisons found Dave and his son Milton, sans cook, shoeing horses in preparation for the trip. Then they began the climb up into the cool, shady aspen and spruce groves that made the Aquarius Plateau such a welcome summertime destination. As always, Dave took them to his favorite lookoffs, beginning with Donkey Point on the north side of the plateau. Here they gazed across at the deep-red Moenkopi cliffs that rose above the Fremont River valley and formed an elegant base for Thousand Lake Mountain. To the northwest rose the high Fishlake Plateau where Dave had herded sheep as a youth. Farther north could be seen the summit-points of Mount Terrill and Mount Marvine, mementos of his long journey in 1915 with the Frasers. Off to the northeast lay the mysterious, heavily dissected uplift of the San Rafael Swell, topped by curious blocks of sandstone reaching to seven thousand feet in elevation. Its southern reach was cut by the innumerable small canyons of the Moroni Slopes, the outwash of which petered out in the gray desert north of Caineville. The Swell was one of the few places in southern Utah that Rust had not explored in depth.

Though they were gazing across at Thousand Lake Mountain, that name seemed more appropriate for the plateau on which they stood, for on the Aquarius, myriad small lakes and tarns occupied indentations left by a Pleistocene icefield. The eastern block of the Aquarius was also known as Boulder Mountain, for as the ice melted, it deposited basalt boulders all over its summit and flanks. Groves of spruce and subalpine fir filled sheltered nooks on the summit plateau, while much of the surface was still tundra-like, displaying lovely alpine heather and grasses.

Heading south from Donkey Point, the party rode across these flower-decked parks at over eleven thousand feet to Horseshoe Lake and the meadows along Pleasant Creek at the plateau's southern rim. Views here were compromised by the dusty atmosphere stirred up by a strong southwest wind, so they continued on to Bowns Point at the southeastern tip of the Aquarius, which offered perhaps the best view of all—one that Rust had celebrated many times since his first visit there with George Fraser in 1915. This overlook disclosed an entirely different scene. The peaks of the Henry Mountains dominated the middle distance, with the smaller, rocky summits of Mounts Holmes and Ellsworth rising beyond; past these peaks, tapestried Navajo Sandstone cliffs outlined the gorge of Glen Canyon. In this era before power-plant haze, they could see far beyond to the Abajo and La Sal mountains, even to the westernmost peaks of the San Juans in Colorado. Completing the view off to the southeast, across the deserted mesas of the San Juan River, rose the spires and buttes of Monument Valley. While the latter exhibited perhaps the most impressive results of erosion, in reality the entire region was a monument to the ceaseless forces of nature. The earth appeared to be undergoing a long cycle of denudation, exposing the thousands of feet of sediments and windblown dunes that had slowly accumulated during Mesozoic time.

Dropping down off the east face of the plateau, Rust led the group down to the old Ephraim Hanks ranch on Temple (Pleasant) Creek, stopping on the way for a swim in Bowns Reservoir. In back of the ranch they had a look at the remarkable petroglyph gallery that Dave had visited with Donald Scott and Noel Morss in 1928. Rust's journal for July 18 suggests the easy enjoyment of life on the trail: "Milt has long chase for horses. Jim explores for ruins. Mr. D & David find natural bridges. 'Lady' Mary & I do work around camp. Mulligan stew of mutton, beans, 2 doves, onion. Jim returns tired & thirsty, came over plateau above camp & I helped him find way down. On to Frisky Spring via Dry Cr. trail."[6] This was an unstructured approach to guiding that assumed a degree of independence and curiosity among his clients—there was no need to ride herd on this crew. As they circled back across the Waterpocket Fold to the southern slopes of the Aquarius, they enjoyed many of the amenities that Rust made sure to include in his program: fresh milk and mutton at sheepherders' camps; fishing in the clear streams that tumbled off of the plateau; a calf-roping demonstration at a cow camp; exploring for ruins and natural bridges; and conversations with the stockmen and ranchers whose homes and summer camps they passed.

Dave had planned a grand dessert for their final day in the high country. When they reached the Table Cliff Plateau at the western end of the Aquarius, ten days out from Torrey, they put up camp, enjoyed dinner, and set off south along the narrow neck of the plateau in the fading light. A bright, nearly full moon rose over the rims to the southeast. When they reached the brink at Powell Point, ten thousand feet up in the clear air, the pink, buff, and grey cliffs below them were brushstroked in soft moonlight. The canyons and mesas of the Paria Amphitheater were only faintly suggested, but Rust knew what was out there. As he had first witnessed in 1915, the view extended clear to Monument Valley and even to Vishnu Temple on the Grand Canyon's North Rim. His friends were enthralled—few places in the world could offer such an encompassing scene.

Following their evening at Powell Point, Rust led the Dennisons west off of the plateau to Pine Lake, where he had arranged to meet Jim Pace with auto transport for his guests. Dave and Jim, along with Dave's youngest son, Quentin, trailed back across the Aquarius to the Fremont valley, a three-day ride. "Another great campout excursion comes to happy end," Dave noted in his journal.

Their wanderings covered perhaps a hundred miles through forest and canyon, and the viewpoints they reached disclosed dozens of landmarks that Rust knew by heart. From the Grand Canyon to the Green River—the core of the Colorado Plateau—he understood the lay of the land as few others did. Most of its high peaks and plateau rims were familiar. He had located hidden springs, alcoves, and graceful stone bridges in canyons far from any road. For the benefit of dozens of men and women, as well as some eager youngsters, he had read the words of Powell, Dutton, and Gilbert and helped them understand how the landscape had come to be made.

Clarence Dutton, trying to describe these scenes in his 1880 *Report on the Geology of the High Plateaus of Utah*, fell back to quoting the pioneer geologist

J. S. Newberry, who had investigated the region in 1859: "Though valueless to the agriculturalist, dreaded and shunned by the emigrant, the miner, and even the adventurous trapper, the Colorado Plateau is to the geologist a paradise. Nowhere on the earth's surface, so far as we know, are the secrets of its structure so fully revealed as here."[7] Rust could take pride in showing these vistas to those who had never experienced the great openness of the Southwest.

As Rust's horizons expanded, his approach to guiding was changing as well. No longer was he seeking tourists by the trainload; his Grand Canyon trail venture belonged to the past. Nor was he interested in shepherding visitors around in buses, an approach that his friend Chauncey Parry had originated at Zion and Bryce. At the Grand Canyon, Rust had been a tourist booster in Dee Woolley's mold, devoting years of his life to improving the transportation infrastructure so that the average tourist could enjoy the region's scenic wonders. As a civic leader in Kane County from 1912 to 1928, he had taken the lead in lobbying for better roads to southern Utah's national parks. By his sixty-first year, though, he had crafted a much more personal approach to the Colorado Plateau. He valued these river gorges and lonely mesas for their remoteness—for the adventure of getting to them—as well as for their scenery and geologic interest. These were not trips he could market widely to the public, nor did he try. He had learned that there were men and women who prized the experience of discovering wild places in small, intimate groups, and who were willing to endure the discomforts and uncertainties of desert and mountain travel. Eager to take on a more genuine kind of exploration than was possible with any tour group, they found Rust ideally suited to their needs, and he found them to be the congenial and stimulating companions he craved.

All that was lacking in this arrangement was widespread fame or a large cash flow, and these had never been Dave's priority. What held his interest most was the simple act of looking at a landscape. In the popular imagination this was often derided as merely viewing scenery, but Rust saw something in the distant view that, he felt, could enlarge one's life. Like many who have felt a strong connection to the natural world, Rust believed that the quest for magnificent vistas could have a profound influence on the human spirit. He addressed this theme in a 1929 article for *Improvement Era* titled "Fleeing to Zion—for Scenery."

He began the piece with a grand conceit, comparing modern-day tourists to the exodus of persecuted Mormons from Missouri and Illinois to their Zion in the West. The growing numbers of tourists were, in Rust's time, "speeding like the wind over railways and highways—and airways" to visit the scenic lands of southern Utah. While many Mormons would have found the metaphor a bit of a stretch, Rust was not beyond employing a fanciful image. He observed that these thousands of visitors "return as swiftly as they come.... What do they carry away with them? What is the value of scenery?" His answer drew on his wide reading: "In one of the oriental Bibles it is recorded that if we have but two cakes we should sell one and buy a narcissus; for the cake simply feeds the body while the narcissus feeds the soul. Perhaps these many travelers are feeding their souls. Perhaps the sunshine of open spaces has destroyed some of the germs of prejudice. It is difficult to measure the influence of classic literature or classic paintings or classic music—or classic scenery." Here was Rust's mature realization that our reaction to beautiful places has a moral aspect, a quality the visitor must cultivate. "The man who climbs a mountain or crosses a desert or looks into a deep-carved canyon," he continued, "should return from such experiences with genuine values; if he does not return definitely enriched, then he is not worthy to be called 'traveler.'"

He returned to this theme in his unpublished essay "Genuine Travelers," written within a year or two of "Fleeing to Zion." In it he advocated intellectual preparation to appreciate the geology of the desert environment: "Someone has referred to the strip of wonderland across the Plateau Province between Zion Park and Mesa Verde as the land of perpetual sandstone. But all the other rocks are here in proper relationship, from the tertiary to the granite, decorated by volcanic cones and lava caps, books in stone of all ages so plain that he who runs can read—if he knows the language."

This quest gave his work as a guide a definite context. When he took men, women, or young people into the backcountry, he did more than find the trail and cook the biscuits. As an educator, he set the stage for learning—by leading his clients to choice lookoffs or through tortuous canyons, then allowing them some time for contemplation. At the right moment, he would reach into his pack bag for some inspiration to share with his guests. Harrison Merrill, a professor of journalism at Brigham Young University and an editor of *Improvement Era*, witnessed Dave's deft hand at this during the trip they took to the Toroweap overlook in 1924:

> That morning before breakfast I got a hunch that will help me and many others who visit the Grand Canyon. As I walked around one of the cars I found Rust reverently unwrapping a large book.

"Now come and let's see what Dutton says about it all," he said.

I sat beside Mr. Rust on the running board of the car facing Vulcan's Throne and the army of volcanic cones that swarm over the Uinkaret Plateau west of the valley while he read the description of the country written by Captain C. E. Dutton, a member of the geological survey who had made an extended study of the region in which we were. Although the report was written in 1881, I question if there ever has been or ever will be a finer description of the Toroweap district.[8]

It was a scene he repeated often. Rust once referred to his geologist-hero as "the Prophet Dutton," elevating him to a worthy niche in his personal pantheon alongside Powell and Gilbert. These geologists understood the call to aesthetic appreciation. Dutton expressed this most often, working architectural, literary, and artistic images into his landscape depictions. Rust, too, tried to view the canyon country with an artist's eye. Using another favorite analogy, he wrote in "Fleeing to Zion" that the Plateau Province "is a land of many colors—the very strongest of reds and blues and yellows, with all possible varieties of shades and combinations—an immeasurable art gallery whose landscapes cannot be copied on canvas."

Rust's attachment to the classically trained explorer-scientists of the Colorado Plateau was a bit out of step with the times. The writings of Dutton and Gilbert never reached a popular audience, and other, less scientific writers such as John C. Van Dyke, Charles Lummis, and George Wharton James did more to define the region in the popular imagination. By the early 1920s novelists such as Zane Grey were coming to the fore as interpreters of the Southwest, aided by movies set under the Vermilion Cliffs of Kanab and the towers of Monument Valley. To his credit, Grey worked strong and evocative descriptions of the Utah and Arizona canyons and plateaus into his novels. He took advantage of worldwide interest in the American West, as well as created some of the icons that helped to perpetuate its mythic allure. He was a useful intermediary between East and West, stoking the imagination of the prospective traveler and suggesting to western hosts what the tourist might want to see. Wild Indians, dusty cowboys trailing herds of longhorns, gunfights—all these became part of the tourist West. Westerners learned to cheerfully supply these thrills, with varying degrees of staging.

Rust, however, had a different program. He wanted to show his guests the Colorado Plateau he knew, both its landscape and its people. Appreciating the underpinnings of these landforms was essential for the traveler. One of his favorite books, *The Scientific Study of Scenery* by the British geologist John E. Marr, urged readers to study the geomorphology of the mountain and desert regions of the world. It was, Rust wrote, "a book I heartily commend as a guide for every traveler. That sounds like preparedness, perhaps, but we don't go fishing without hooks and bait."[9] It was not an approach calculated to appeal to the masses, and Dave's style of travel would remain out of fashion until much later in the century, when a new generation of guides and educational programs would revive it under the rubric of "eco-travel."

While Dave was fashioning his highly individualized approach to guiding, many Utah residents were just beginning to appreciate the value of this region for tourism. Traditionally reliant on agriculture, Utah faced the double whammy of the Depression coupled with the return of a persistent, severe drought. In 1934 the town of Hanksville recorded just two and a quarter inches of rain—an appalling amount even for a region used to dryness.[10] With its rangelands withered and its desert waterways gullied, Utah suffered a steady erosion in wages. The villages at the edge of the Colorado Plateau were especially hard hit, forcing many residents to return to the primitive, self-sufficient way of life of an earlier generation. For some wage-earners, federal relief programs, including the Works Progress Administration and the Civilian Conservation Corps, provided the only jobs available.

A handful of civic leaders in the towns around the rim of the canyon lands recognized the need to diversify beyond crops and cattle. They realized that the desert sands that proved so stinting of grass held another kind of wealth: scenic beauty, abundantly displayed and potentially useful. Many residents of the towns along the Fremont River knew there were worthy scenic features hidden in the cliffs of the Waterpocket Fold; a photograph of a lovely natural bridge near Fruita was in circulation as early as 1914.[11] The realization was not universal, and it took farsighted people such as Rust to point out the possibilities. But tourists continued to get in their automobiles and seek out these strange rock monuments and canyons. While traffic to Utah's national parks peaked in 1931, and had slackened close to 20 percent by 1933, visitors to Bryce Canyon still numbered more than thirty thousand annually, and nearly fifty thousand came to Zion.[12] Local businessmen understood that this traffic signified demand for gasoline, food, and lodging.

In Wayne County, which lacked any designated parks or monuments to attract visitors, it remained for two local men to publicize the Fold country. Starting in the early 1920s Joseph Hickman, principal of the Wayne County High School in Bicknell (and for whom that natural bridge would later be named), along with his brother-in-law E. P. Pectol, began a campaign to designate a state park in the heart of the Fold. Hickman was elected to the Utah legislature in 1924 and set about raising support for the area, which local people were calling the "Wayne Wonderland." He succeeded in establishing a state parks commission, intending that his proposed "Capitol Reef State Park" be the first.[13] (Capitol Reef was another local name given to the dome-like monuments of Navajo Sandstone that rose high above the Fremont River.)

In July 1925 Hickman, Pectol, and other supporters organized a weekend celebration in Torrey for the park-to-be. Residents hung a banner proclaiming "Welcome to Wayne Wonderland" over a bridge on the road leading down to Fruita. Hundreds of people drove from Richfield, Loa, and neighboring towns to hear the guest speaker, Governor George Dern. Dern acknowledged the great scenic wonders of the area, but he emphasized the need to build new roads to bring in tourists. Rust attended as a guest of Pectol, whom he had known from his Caineville days. His son Jordan and their friend Charles Berolzheimer, who was spending the summer with the Rusts, were along, helping Dave ready his boats and supplies for a second Glen Canyon voyage that month.

The state government, however, lacked funds to establish such a park and build the necessary facilities. At first, Hickman and Pectol envisioned a small set-aside of only 160 acres, but they and others speaking at the 1925 celebration clearly believed that the federal government would soon get involved and establish a national park. The Park Service, however, was unaware of the area's scenic features; there was simply too much uncharted land in south-central and southeastern Utah, and the few on-the-ground staff such as Zeke Johnson at Natural Bridges had their own bailiwicks to patrol.[14]

The death of Joseph Hickman in a boating accident on Fish Lake just a few days after the Wayne Wonderland celebration was a setback for the park's sponsors, and the idea languished for several years. Leadership for the project fell to Pectol, who was the local Mormon bishop and a capable organizer. In 1928 he came up with county funds to hire a Salt Lake City photographer named J. E. Broaddus to document Capitol Reef's scenic attractions. Broaddus had visited the area in 1926 and wrote several articles extolling its beauty over the next few years. "There is so much in Wayne county that years will be required to discover [it] all," he proclaimed in the *Salt Lake Tribune*. "But the beginning has been made.... And this year for the first time the new wonderland will welcome hundreds if not thousands of those who quest always for the unique, the beautiful, the undiscovered."[15]

Park Service involvement did not come until 1931, when Pectol and other civic boosters met in Loa with Thomas Allen, the superintendent of Zion and Bryce national parks, to lay out their ideas. Their meeting had the desired effect, for the following year Roger Toll, the Park Service's point man for assessing proposed new parks, paid a visit to the area. Toll was superintendent of Yellowstone National Park, but he also toured the western park regions during the Depression years as his agency sought new lands to add to its system. Among the places it was considering were the Kolob Canyons west of Zion National Park, the prehistoric dwellings and rock art sites in Nine Mile Canyon that had interested the Peabody Museum's archaeologists, and minor sites such as a group of pictographs in Johnson Canyon east of Kanab. Toll visited all of these in the fall of 1932, and after a second visit in 1933 he recommended that the Park Service establish a monument in Capitol Reef, as well as add the Kolob Canyons to Zion National Park.

Two more years of wrangling over boundaries and grazing rights would follow, however, before President Roosevelt would designate Capitol Reef National Monument, taking in thirty-seven thousand acres centering on the most spectacular central part of the Waterpocket Fold.[16] Tourist visits remained light, however, given the poor condition of the roads and the absence of lodges and tour bus services such as existed at Bryce and Zion.

The monument, in fact, hardly covered all of the worthwhile features in and around the Waterpocket Fold. To the north and east lay the rough, barren hills and washes of the Middle Desert and South Desert—country Rust knew from his youth and through which he had taken George Fraser and his son in 1915. Here they had viewed the stunning Entrada Sandstone temples that rose hundreds of feet out of the desert floor. The Park Service did not even know about these features until 1945, when Charles Kelly, the custodian at Capitol Reef, visited them along with Frank Beckwith, a newspaper publisher and desert aficionado from Delta, Utah. Kelly, not knowing of Rust's trip with Fraser, speculated that no one other than the local cowboys had ever been there. (In fact, recent scholarship has shown that the exploring party of John C. Fremont passed by the monuments during the winter of 1853–1854.)[17] Kelly told higher-ups in the

Park Service of his discovery and suggested that Cathedral Valley be added to the monument. A Park Service party came in 1950 to examine the area, but the proposal languished, once again, due to concerns about existing grazing rights and possible mineral values. Cathedral Valley was eventually added to the monument in 1969, along with a large extension to the south that took in more of the Waterpocket Fold.

A few knowledgeable outsiders also saw that the canyon systems of southern Utah and northern Arizona contained many other magnificent examples of erosional geology. Among them was Frank Oastler, who boated down Glen Canyon with Rust in 1926. Before meeting Dave at Hite, Oastler had toured Cedar Mesa with Zeke Johnson, where he was particularly taken with a gorge on the southern edge of the Abajo Mountains called Arch Canyon. It boasted numerous Puebloan ruins as well as its namesake arches high up on sheer canyon walls. Oastler served on a Park Service committee to promote educational activities within the parks, and apparently knew Director Mather personally. He recommended that Arch Canyon be considered as a new national monument, telling Mather that "it would be a shame to have it get into the hands of the exploiters." [18]

Other prominent easterners had their own visions for promoting the Plateau Province. Charles Bernheimer, the New York explorer who had extensively toured the Navajo and San Juan country with Zeke Johnson and John Wetherill, had been pressing Park Service officials since 1928 to create a Navajo National Park stretching from Rainbow Bridge far to the east and north. His proposal took in Monument Valley, the Goosenecks of the San Juan River, Arch Canyon, and the White Canyon natural bridges—all of the country he had been exploring since 1920. In the spring of 1931 Miner Tillotson, the superintendent of Grand Canyon National Park, visited Bernheimer's proposed parklands along with Roger Toll. The men were impressed with the area's cliffs, mesas, and canyons and made a favorable recommendation. Albright himself visited the region the following year, but jurisdictional disputes over the Indian lands involved scuttled the proposal. [19]

Nor did anything come at first of the other early park ideas. As late as 1933 no one in the Park Service, at least publicly, was seeing the interior of the Colorado Plateau as anything more than a collection of geologic curiosities. That was about to change. Within a year the agency, seemingly out of the blue, would begin to promote a much grander agenda for the canyon lands, one that would carry it— and a sometimes unwilling public—into the modern era of park expansion.

I'll expect to see you down there soon. It's a great place—a
vast wilderness of mountains, canyons, natural bridges, caves,
lakes, deserts, cliff dwellings, streams and overall awe-inspiring
panoramic views that well deserve being called a Park. A Wilderness Park of constantly changing delights and thrills.

DAVE RUST
Interview, KSL Radio, about 1936

A TYPICAL EVENING at one of Rust's backcountry
camps involved finding water and firewood, cooking the beans, laying out bed-
rolls, and seeing to the horses and pack mules, with time left over for conversation around the campfire. Usually Dave would find a quiet moment to make a
brief entry in his notebook highlighting the day's adventures, although on some
of his trips in the early 1930s he seems to have omitted the practice. Thus he did
not record the year in which he met an unusual young man from Chicago who
was interested in exploring some of the farther recesses of the canyon country.
Henry Dodge Freeman was a geology major at Princeton; his father, Charles Y.
Freeman, was a prominent Chicago attorney who served on the board of the
Commonwealth Edison Company. Coming from a family of such means gave
Dodge the wherewithal to make extended vacations in the Southwest during the
Depression years.

Despite his position of privilege, Dodge's ambitions ran to the rustic, and like
many adventurous Ivy Leaguers he was drawn to the Southwest. In 1933 he joined
a unique government project that was making archaeological and other scientific investigations in the northern Navajo Reservation. Known as the Rainbow
Bridge–Monument Valley Expedition, this project was the brainchild of Ansel F.
Hall, a Park Service naturalist and chief of its Field Division. He engaged dozens
of college students for the project's summer-long studies.[1] Freeman's job was to
assist with mapping and drawing charts of the group's archaeological excavations.
Several of the participants went on to careers in the canyon country, among them
Freeman's coworker at the map table, Norman Nevills, who became one of the
first commercially successful river guides on the San Juan and Colorado rivers.

Freeman met up with Rust around this time, nominally in order to do fieldwork for his senior thesis at Princeton, a survey of the vanadium and uranium

deposits of the Colorado Plateau. In it he stated that these deposits "from the economic standpoint may not at the present time warrant a great deal of attention."[2] (They would in a few more years.) Freeman's real interest, however, was to live the life of a cowboy in the Wild West. Tall, lean, and handsome, Dodge looked the part. He idolized Butch Cassidy and dedicated his thesis to this "Last of the Great Outlaws, Beau Ideal of Road Agents." Rust held no brief for any outlaw—he called Cassidy the "Chairman of the Appropriations Committee"—but he was willing to show Dodge the country. So began a long friendship between men separated by almost two generations, yet who shared a common passion for the backcountry.

Dave kept notes during four of their excursions from 1935 to 1941. The first of these was their most remarkable journey, a huge loop around the heart of the Utah canyon lands.[3] Their trip circled the Orange Cliffs in what is now Canyonlands National Park and took them through some of the most remote pockets of wild country left in the Southwest. Typical of Rust's later trips, it was a wide-ranging ride from viewpoint to viewpoint, with stopovers at lonely ranches and small towns to reprovision.

Dave met Dodge in Kanab on August 2 for a preliminary auto excursion down the seventy-mile dirt track to Toroweap, followed by a climb of Pine Valley Mountain north of St. George to enjoy another of Rust's "Fourteen Points." After a stop at Zion Park, where they chatted with the geologist Herbert Gregory at the park lodge, they headed for the Waterpocket Fold country and the start of their main adventure. Dave had arranged to move his horses, normally boarded near Torrey, to Milo Curtis's Sandy Creek ranch south of Notom. The Curtis family offered the hospitality of dinner and beds, and the two travelers made ready to leave on the morning of August 8. Dodge rode Rust's blaze horse "Pissant," with Dave leading three pack horses. Their route took them up through the austere, otherworldly rims and mesas flanking the western slopes of Mount Ellen, but instead of climbing to the summit they headed north into the painted shale hills along Sweetwater Creek. Traversing around the trailless north side of Mount Ellen, they cut along steep, loose sidehills in a convoluted badland. As darkness fell, they made camp in a wild hollow miles from the nearest habitation.

Rust never minded a touch of civilization on his backcountry trips, so after a stop at Dugout Spring, one of the few waterholes in this barren landscape, they rode on down the dry hills and washes to Hanksville. Here they paid a visit to the Albert Weber family, who ran a boarding house and café for ranch hands and the occasional passerby. While Rust's horses got hay and water, the tired riders enjoyed lunch and an afternoon rest. Their hosts took them to Hanksville's newest attraction, an artesian well dug two years previously by the federal Drought Relief Service. Rust called it a "marvel," remembering how his family had relied on shallow wells in the alluvium at Caineville.

That night a thunderstorm brought a little rain—always welcome in a place that rarely received more than six inches in a year. Around midnight the clouds parted to reveal the moon, three days past full and encircled by a rainbow. One can picture Dodge's excitement as they stood outside the Webers' home that night—here he was in this desert hamlet, more than a thousand miles from Chicago, about to head out into still wilder country: the mesas and box canyons of the legendary Robbers Roost, where Butch Cassidy and his gang had hidden out just forty years before.

From Hanksville the trail stretched eastward over a gently rising plain displaying wind-scalloped dunes of red sand. Ten miles from town they reached the sandstone rim of the Dirty Devil River canyon at the head of the storied "Angel Trail," a primitive stock trail that led down over steep waves of slickrock to the river and the mouth of Robbers Roost canyon. The route had been given its name by one of the local cattle rustlers, who felt that wings were needed to surmount it.[4] The Roost canyons, in turn, headed in a cluster of narrow box canyons far to the east—a natural hideout with few exits. Although it was a major side drainage, its sandy bed offered no water, and the river carried only gray silt. "We dig in gravel for drinking water but it is bitter so horses and men suffer," Rust wrote. At midnight he heard the restless animals setting out and got up to head them off. They could somehow sense that good water was not far away. Next morning, heading downstream around a long bend, all hands reached Angel Spring, a trickle at the base of a sandstone cliff that gave them their first decent water since Hanksville.

It took Rust two hours to locate the eastward continuation of the Angel Trail, which led up out of the river canyon to the Biddlecome ranch on Roost Flats. The ranch was now run by Joe Biddlecome's daughter, Pearl, and her husband, Frank Baker. To Dodge, this outpost looked like the real thing. He relished the chance to ride out with Frank after his horses while Dave repaired the packsaddles and shod his own mounts. Dodge got to watch Frank demonstrate his cowboy skills by roping a coyote—no mean trick.

Rust was now back in the country he had explored a few years earlier with the Peabody Museum crew. In the upper part of Horseshoe Canyon, Dave found a "splendid campsite with grass plenty and good water." Dodge hunted strays with Frank Baker farther down in the canyon; he thought he might come back that fall to stay with the Bakers and try his hand at cowboying.

With the horses rested and fed, they were ready to head out on one of the most spectacular trails in the West—the long, sunrise-facing escarpment of the Orange Cliffs. Leaving the head of Horseshoe Canyon, they followed the old outlaw trail that led southeast along a steadily narrowing isthmus, overlooking Millard Canyon to the northeast and the upper forks of Happy Canyon to the southwest. Reaching the brink of the Orange Cliffs, they plunged down a canyon that the local cowboys called the North Trail, which led down through the towering Wingate cliffs to the benchlands of Under the Ledge. At Waterhole Flat, miles to the south, they stopped by the camp of Ned and Faun Chaffin, Dave's friends from the Peabody trips who were still running cattle in this inhospitable country. Years later, Ned told a Park Service interviewer that "you just as well been on another planet as to be down on Waterhole Flat in those days.... You couldn't hear a train whistle. You never saw a plane fly over. You never saw anyone."[5]

Dave continued to quest after views, so he led Dodge up to Red Point, where they witnessed a "great panorama in exceptional land and sunlight combination." After camping at another of his old Peabody sites, Rust led Freeman out to the rim of Cataract Canyon, where the Colorado frothed and stormed down its narrow gorge, fifteen hundred feet below. He knew there was no way across this chasm, but to him, a view was always worth a detour. Heading for the mouth of the Dirty Devil, Rust made camp at a place he called Sand Dune Pockets, half a mile from the brink of Cataract Canyon. As the view opened up to the southwest, they were delighted to witness an "overwhelming spectacle of candlestick & other buttes with Navajo & Kaiparowits & 5 of Henry Mtns. as background."[6] Camp felt welcome after days of hard riding: "water and grass good," he noted. "Beans and doughgods & tea and jam taste just fine. *Appetites.*"

Reaching the mouth of the Dirty Devil River, they encountered quicksand that made for a difficult crossing. Safely negotiating this hazard, the men passed Dandy Crossing and continued to Hite, where they were greeted by its sole occupants, Arth and Phoebe Chaffin. Their work had transformed this ramshackle abandoned village into a small oasis. Arthur L. Chaffin (Ned Chaffin's uncle) purchased the property in 1932, returning to the river he had known three decades previously during his gold mining days. (In the early 1900s, after doing some sluicing himself, he had opened a sort of mini-mart for prospectors at the

old Stanton mining property at Camp Stone.) Chaffin possessed no small me-
chanical talent—he and his brothers had built roads for some of the oil companies prospecting around Hanksville, and he turned his improvisational genius to
the barren landscape around Hite. Before long he had set up an irrigation system
that fed a small orchard and garden. Over the years, according to his friend Harry
Aleson, Arth and his wife cultivated "figs, pomegranate, Siberian dates, peaches,
apples, pears, plums, cherries, almonds, walnuts, grapes, cantaloupe, watermelon,
alfalfa, corn, strawberries, currants, and most every vegetable grown in the U.S."[7]
In the coming years Arth Chaffin would work with scraper, pickaxe, and pry-bar
to improve the rocky track down North Wash, completing an automobile route
from Hanksville to the river. He lobbied the state government to install a ferry
crossing on the Colorado, which he ran from 1946 to 1964, when Lake Powell
flooded him out.

The little oasis under the cliffs at Hite made for a welcome break. "Breakfast
& lunch at Chaffin table—melons both kinds by the dozen," Rust wrote. He and
Dodge tried a sample of Arth's homemade peach brandy, as Freeman later recounted to the river guide, Ken Sleight.[8] All this was a fine repast after a week of
beans and sourdough. That afternoon Arth ran his motorboat back up to Dandy
Crossing and helped the men cross their horses, leading each one by a rope they
held firm from the boat. Then they set off to explore the country east of the river,
which Rust had only rarely visited.

For more than thirty-five miles, Rust and Freeman followed the sandstone
benches above White Canyon that led up to Natural Bridges National Monument, located in the upper forks of the canyon. Afternoon thunderstorms produced several flash floods for their entertainment, but fortunately their camps
were well above the streambeds. They stopped by Zeke Johnson's tent on the rim
overlooking the Edwin bridge but found him away, probably repairing trail or
guiding visitors somewhere in the monument. Seven hundred travelers would
brave the primitive road from Blanding to the monument that summer—twice
the number of a few years ago—but these intrepid motorists were still only at the
edge of the wilderness. Few of those arriving by car would see the country as Rust
and Freeman had.

Without stopping to tour the bridges, they headed up onto the high country
that overlooked Cedar Mesa. On August 25 they climbed one of the Bears Ears,
the twin turrets that rose to the east of the monument, for what Rust called "one
of the superior viewpoints of the Plateau Province." Leaving their horses to graze

in a meadow below the Ears, they hitched a ride into Blanding with a Forest Service truck driver. Here they bought supplies and returned to their rested mounts early the next day.

Still more views awaited as they rode north along Elk Ridge. Horse Mountain, an otherwise unimposing high point at the northern terminus of the ridge, offered the most spectacular vantage. Rust called it "one of the sweeping glorious panoramas of the west—or the world. Rain & clouds & sunset combined to perfect the view." At just over nine thousand feet, this peak offered a commanding view of the tortuous landscape they would be passing through on their way north to Moab. Below the Wingate cliffs that rimmed a great eroded basin lay a looping series of shallow canyons cut into the Cedar Mesa sandstone. To the west the trench of the Colorado River was visible, and beyond that rose the Orange Cliffs—the rampart they had descended twelve days before. The men spent the night in a meadow below the summit, climbing back to the top before dawn so they could witness the sunrise edging across the landscape. "*Feast* on views from 5:30 to 10 o'clock," Rust wrote the next morning.[9]

Leaving the Abajos, they dropped down to the high desert at Beef Basin, reaching Ruin Park and its interesting collection of ancient Puebloan masonry towers, which Rust had first visited with the Peabody Museum archaeological expedition in 1930. After spending the night, they continued north into the series of deep, dramatic canyons called the Grabens, the product of a slow pulling apart and collapse of the earth's crust as underlying salt and gypsum formations dissolved or flowed out. These canyons trended north toward the confluence of the Green and Colorado rivers, but instead of proceeding to this geologically significant overlook, Rust turned east to find a way through a puzzling labyrinth of pinnacles called the Needles. After investigating several dead-end canyons, they camped for the night at one of the few seeps in the area.

Rust's journal for August 31 documents a typical day on the trail as they headed out of the Needles and continued north into the Indian Creek drainage:

> Horses come to water before six so we up & catch em and prepare breakfast of doughgods, coffee, bacon and grape-fruit. Start at 8:30 and reach over an extremely winding route Squaw Flat about 10:30. Grass burnt up. So we trudge on to Cave Spring. Good water at old campground, and 1/2 bale of hay to offset Russian thistle for the ponies. Take picture in cave.... Potatoes and gravy and prunes-apricots cooked for lunch. Pants nearly gone. Must

reach Moab soon. Find some grass near cave, so we loiter until late afternoon then head north till we strike better feed for the night. Camp on rim
of Ind. Creek canyon. No-see-ums bad. Had to apply salt water to bites at
midnite.

The winding course of Indian Creek took them down to the Colorado River,
which they followed on a tiring ride upstream to Kane Spring Canyon. Along
the way they inspected the oil rigs that had been stationed on both sides of the
river during 1925–1927, and that had aroused much excitement in Moab and the
region. (This oil boomlet occasioned the dispute over lease royalties that brought
about the Colorado River Bed case in which Rust had testified in 1929.)

On September 4 they reached Moab. After a brief rest in town, during which
Rust got a haircut, read mail from home, and visited the editor of the local newspaper, they decided to sample the high country of the La Sal Mountains to the
east. Their goal was a climb of Mount Peale, at 12,700 feet one of the highest
summits of the range:

4th—Drive with Geo. Wash. Johnson in Ford "A" to his ranch near La
Sal. Milk for (OK) supper. Sleep cool on lawn. Sent our tired horses back to
Spr. below Grand river narrows by Len Woodruff.

5—With 2 fresh h's and 1 pack mule we climb Mt. Peale for sweeping
lookoff and luscious camp at Cold Spr. See 2 big buck deer. Nearly ran into
swarming bees on road up. Rained at midnight.

6—Baited horses with flour to catch 'em. Pretty stormy all around so
we decide to drop back to Johnson ranch. Showers like April on way down.
Model "A" to Moab with Arden Johnson.

7—Wrangled the ponies, wrote letter home, hobnobbed with old timers, supplied and pulled out at head of 7 mi. canyon for camp. Fred Strong
of Moab joins our expedition.

The most scenic portion of their six-week journey was over. Their return
route took them westward on the Horsethief Trail, which reached the Green
River at the mouth of Mineral Canyon. This trail had been used by rustlers in
the late 1800s to drive animals stolen from ranches around the La Sals into the
Robbers Roost canyons. Like the outlaws before them, Rust and Freeman forded

the shallow river, leaving Fred Strong to return home, and followed Horseshoe Canyon back into the Roost country. This completed an amazing 250-mile-long loop, not counting the bends and twists in the trail. All that remained was the long ride back to Hanksville, which they undertook by moonlight. The tired riders reached the Webers' yard at 3 a.m. on September 14. Dodge caught a ride to Torrey the next afternoon, leaving Dave to take the horses back to their winter pasture.

Their expedition was reminiscent of the long journeys Rust had made with George Fraser twenty years before. With Fraser no longer able to make such trips—he passed away that fall, to Dave's surprise and deep sorrow—Dodge Freeman came to be his frequent companion in the field. Dodge would return to Utah three more times to explore more of the canyon country with Dave, reliving scenes from the Old West with one of its more interesting practitioners.

During their trip Rust and Freeman had heard stories circulating about a Park Service plan to establish a new national monument in the region they had just traversed. Such talk was nothing new; Rust knew about the proposal for a Wayne Wonderland national park, and in the ten years since the festival at Torrey in 1925 this idea had expanded considerably. Originally conceived as a 160-acre state park, local boosters were now thinking of a national park or monument as large as 360 square miles in the Waterpocket Fold country, which would attract tourists and lead to needed highway improvements. The Utah State Planning Board, a Depression-era agency charged with cooperating with the federal government in recovery efforts, supported the idea, and the Park Service was seriously considering the proposal.[10]

But something even bigger was afoot. Earlier that summer a group of Park Service officials had chartered a light plane to fly from the Grand Canyon to Moab, taking a few turns around the Orange Cliffs region. They returned a few weeks later to hire a power boat for a quick trip down the Colorado to check out the scenic features along the river. Fred Strong, who operated a river boat that serviced the oil rigs downstream from Moab, was their pilot. The group included Miner R. Tillotson, the superintendent of Grand Canyon National Park, and four other agency staffers with backgrounds in geology, wildlife, and landscape architecture.[11] Also along was Rust's old friend Emery Kolb. Very possibly Strong or Kolb told Rust the substance of the park officials' conversations.

Tillotson, in fact, had his eye on a much larger parcel of land than just the Wayne Wonderland or even Arch Canyon and Cedar Mesa. His investigations around Moab were part of what appears to be a "more or less clandestine fact-finding mission," according to authors Maxine Newell and Terby Barnes. In their book *The Untold History of Utah's Grand Staircase–Escalante National Monument*, they attempt to piece together the origin of the largest Park Service proposal ever made within the 48 States—the enigmatic Escalante National Monument of the mid-1930s.

As first presented to the public in June 1936, the Escalante National Monument would have covered nearly seven thousand square miles of the Utah canyon country—nearly four and a half million acres stretching along more than 250 miles of the Colorado River from Moab to the Arizona line, and a hundred miles of the Green River above its confluence with the Colorado. Nearly all of the terrain that Rust and Freeman covered in their six-week pack trip would have been within the monument, with a lot left over. Most of Cedar Mesa, the canyons of the Escalante River, the Henry Mountains, and the entirety of present-day Canyonlands National Park were included.

Most historians ascribe the monument's origins to Harold Ickes, Franklin Roosevelt's enterprising Secretary of the Interior, who was something of an empire-builder and was friendly to new park proposals. Newell and Barnes, however, after reviewing some Park Service files that were about to be discarded at Canyonlands National Park, believe that the concept arose in response to a letter from a Denver petroleum geologist named Harry A. Aurand. In March 1934 Aurand wrote to Roger Toll, outlining six areas in southern Utah and northern Arizona that he felt might be of national park caliber. The list was a curious mix of familiar landmarks such as the "Monumental Valley" on the Utah-Arizona border, and places less well known, including the Kaiparowits Plateau, the Goosenecks of the San Juan River, and Dark-Woodenshoe Canyons. Aurand even threw in a rock formation he called Muffin Butte, located near Grand View Point north of the confluence of the Green and Colorado rivers.

Toll endorsed Aurand's ideas and forwarded his letter up the line, where the concept seems to have snowballed into a much grander proposal. By the end of 1934, Arthur Demaray, the associate director of the Park Service, broached the idea to Secretary Ickes of an all-encompassing monument to set aside the greater part of the canyon lands region, instead of a number of smaller designations around individual landscape gems. Ickes gave the concept his blessing on January 23, 1935, leaving the Park Service to draw up the particulars.[12]

By May 1935 the agency had set a tentative boundary for the monument. It stretched well into Arizona, covering the Vermilion Cliffs and the House Rock Desert west of Lees Ferry, and included most of the Kaiparowits Plateau. It omitted the main peaks of the Henry Mountains, however, and much of the southern Waterpocket Fold country.[13] Following Tillotson's field review that summer, the Park Service revised the proposal, locating it entirely within Utah and covering 6,968 square miles of the public domain. The proposal was twice the size of Yellowstone National Park, taking the concept of land protection into entirely new territory. The Utah State Planning Board gave the concept a largely favorable evaluation in a report prepared by its director, Ray West, in May 1936. Creating a huge new park, West felt, would mean a windfall in federal dollars, including "the expenditure of large sums of money for the construction and maintenance of roads, bridges, lodges, stores, etc., all of which can be more satisfactorily carried on by the National Government than by state or private individuals."[14]

The families who ran cattle and sheep in the region, though, felt threatened by this huge expansion of Park Service authority. Looking out for their interests, the regional director of the federal Grazing Service, J. Q. Peterson, convened a meeting in Price, Utah, in June 1936 to solicit their views. J. M. MacFarland of the Utah Farm Bureau spoke for many of them: "We can't afford to set aside this land for a few bobcats and wildcats.... If you turned the tourist loose in that big area you would have to turn out the National Guard to find them." Charles Redd, a prominent San Juan County rancher, objected that even if existing grazing rights were grandfathered in, federal regulation would mean the eventual demise of his livelihood: "[T]he record of the Park Service is not very promising to the livestock industry because they are not satisfied as long as there is a sheep or cow left.... This is just a little harder rap than we can take without putting up a battle."[15]

Redd was not opposed to bringing in more tourists, and referred to the efforts of Blanding residents to improve the road to Natural Bridges. He bolstered his concern about the Park Service's intentions by mentioning a letter he had received from a "friend in Chicago" who had made a number of trips out to this region. This traveler expressed concern about turning the canyon country into a tourist destination with developed roads leading everywhere.

The writer, in fact, was Dodge Freeman. Redd's testimony quoted from a letter Freeman had written to the Moab *Times-Independent* that would appear in the paper two days after the hearing. Freeman may have met Redd during his stopover in Blanding in August 1935, and could have sent him a copy of the letter, or the paper's editor, Loren Taylor, might have passed it along. Freeman's letter referred to his 1935 pack trip with Rust during which they had heard rumors about a new national monument. He feared that such designation would diminish the region's sense of true wilderness—a quality he did not associate with national parks and monuments. "To me," he wrote, "the charm of the wilderness along the Colorado rests far more in its inaccessibility and freedom from trodden paths than in its admitted wonderful beauty. I often asked myself last summer whether I would get the same sense of pleasure and enjoyment I got riding through that country on horseback if I were to go through by motor bus or auto with a lot of rubberneck tourists ogling around and making inane remarks—I trust you can satisfy yourself as to the answer that came to me!"

The National Park Service during the 1930s was indeed a supporter of developed tourism, and was heavily involved in building roads into its holdings, including long, winding "parkways" such as the Blue Ridge in Shenandoah National Park and the Going-to-the-Sun Highway in Glacier National Park. There was even discussion within the agency of a proposal to build a road across the Grand Canyon, from the South Rim to the North Rim, all the way down to the river and up again.

Rust also held a dim view of the Park Service after what he regarded as the confiscation of his Grand Canyon trail and camp. He had grown to have a more elitist view of tourism, in which he saw the Colorado Plateau as a place of wonder that demanded—and rewarded—real physical and intellectual effort. Some of his attitude seems to have rubbed off on Freeman, who in his letter to the Moab paper outlined an alternative concept of setting aside public land: "What a pity it would be to destroy this [wilderness]—even to touch it. Why shouldn't the government take steps to preserve such a territory by forbidding roads to enter it, just as it takes steps to create national parks for the opposite reason.... [I]sn't it time to move toward a new policy of creating so-called primitive areas whereby those few people who choose to can recreate for themselves the individuality and, to be trite, ruggedness of those who have gone before us?"

Not long after the Escalante monument proposal surfaced, Rust offered some of his thinking about the region in an interview with a Salt Lake City radio station.[16] He described the Utah canyon country as a "wilderness park," but he stretched its boundaries to some fifteen thousand square miles, taking in everything from the town of Green River south to the Arizona border. He had in mind a wild region that dwarfed most people's conception of a national park. "Our present twin parks, Zion and Bryce, are simply choice samples of Utah scenery in comparison to this vast and varied region in the southeast quarter of the state which is contemplated as a Wilderness Park, a region large enough to blanket all the other national parks in America."

To Rust, this region was "unsurpassed in variety of mountains, high plateaus, lakes, deep canyons, temples, towers, strips of genuine desert, bare-rock portions painted in all the combinations of fantastic coloring." One of its chief attractions, he felt, was its undeveloped rusticity: "There are no paved roads, not many roads of any kind, in fact, and the wild trails are rough even for a pack-mule. No cities, only a dozen villages and a scattering of ranches. There are only about 5,000 people in the entire area, and this includes sheep-herders, horse thieves, and Indians.... If you want to get away from the contamination of society, away from the predatory automobiles, away to complete freedom, you may find here a vast solitude where you may wander for weeks without meeting a human being."

Rust did not mention the Escalante proposal by name; he was less concerned about the political status of his "wilderness park" than with how people ought to see it. By this time he was committed to the kind of open-ended, individualized travel that gave his clients the time to let their mind and senses fully comprehend the landscape. He had no patience for what he called "see it and run" tourists. "The importance of speed is exaggerated," he wrote in his essay "Genuine Travelers," which he wrote around this same time. "Do you rush through an art gallery of masterpieces? Quite as absurd to race through scenic masterpieces." In this he parted company with his friends in southern Utah who saw parks primarily as a means of boosting tourism. As someone who had heralded the coming of automobiles to the North Rim in 1909, he now saw a need to put on the brakes.

By no means, though, could Rust be counted among the ranks of conservationists who by the mid-1930s were becoming more visible within the nation's land-management agencies. The primitive areas that Dodge Freeman alluded to were just then being established on the national forests around the West, under the instigation of such visionaries as the Forest Service's Bob Marshall, Arthur

Carhart, and Aldo Leopold. If Rust supported the Escalante National Monument in concept, as his interview suggests, he gave no indication that he actively lobbied for it or for any other protective designation within the canyon lands. His distaste for the Park Service lingered, and his ties to the Utah ranching community were still strong. Some of his clients, notably Dr. Frank Oastler, were active conservationists—Oastler had lobbied for new parks such as Glacier and Isle Royale as well as Utah's Arch Canyon—so Rust had at least been exposed to their perspective. His thoughts lay more in the cultivation of the individual. To him, a "genuine traveler" ought to take an active interest in the landscape, but he felt no particular duty to agitate for its preservation.

Some of Rust's friends and acquaintances in the civic clubs around southern Utah were willing to buck the stockgrowers and endorse the Escalante monument. The Lions clubs of Moab and Green River, in particular, favored the plan, seeing it as a means for attracting tourists and obtaining badly needed federal roadbuilding dollars. The Moab Lions' resolution stated that the monument "would create another famous tourist playground within the state similar to Zion, Bryce Canyon and Grand Canyon."[17] These civic clubs' concept of the monument was akin to a giant billboard, advertising their local scenery and whisking tourists into heretofore inaccessible regions. This was exactly the kind of plan that Freeman and Rust feared. But the few voices within the Park Service calling for a wilderness withdrawal could not carry against this current. By 1940 Director Arno Cammerer was talking with Utah state leaders about creating a national recreation area rather than a national monument. Such designation would allow grazing, hydropower development, and mining to continue, while giving impetus for new tourist roads.[18]

The discussions between the Park Service and Utah state officials eventually dissolved into what historian Elmo R. Richardson called "personal antagonisms and mutual distrust."[19] And with the country gearing up to fight another war, new parks in the West dropped off of the Roosevelt administration's list of priorities. The Park Service continued to debate within its own ranks what, if anything, could be accomplished in southern Utah. Capitol Reef was established as a national monument in 1937, but no park proposals made any headway until well after the war. A proposal for a Canyonlands National Park emerged in the 1950s under the leadership of Bates Wilson, then superintendent of Arches National

Monument, but congressional enactment waited until 1964 and a more favorable climate in Washington.

The spotlight that shone on the canyon country following the war was perhaps what Dodge Freeman feared most. His remnant of Butch Cassidy's Old West would melt away in the new era of automobile tourism and hydropower development. Energy extraction, too, came to the fore following the war as uranium prospectors swarmed over the canyon lands—an ironic update to his geologic studies in the region. But the extent of these developments was unknown in 1935. When Rust and Freeman rode into Hanksville at the conclusion of their grand tour around the Orange Cliffs, no one truly understood how radically the face of the canyon country would change. Adventurers like Dodge Freeman would have only a few more years to experience the joy of traveling through these primitive and untrammeled open spaces.

In answer to the question why he had come by way of Richfield
and Wayne County to reach the Colorado, Mr. Rust gave one
of his smiles, just a little difficult of interpretation, and said
"this trip is for pleasure," intimating in his following remarks
that we who live nearest to the area little appreciate its great
scenic worth and future possibilities as a tourist attraction.

"Party Equips Here for River Trip,"
Richfield Reaper, July 7, 1938

RUST'S JOURNEY WITH DODGE FREEMAN in the
summer of 1935 cemented a friendship that would lead to more outings in the
coming years. Several of Dave's children recalled how these trips helped to soften
the loss he felt from George Fraser's death.[1] Dodge's youth and adventurous spirit
suited Dave, who in his seventh decade was still able to ride little-used trails and
spend long days in the saddle. But until their next expedition, Rust had other clients who had heard of his unique backcountry travels and wanted him to outfit
a trip. In 1936 a Vermont industrialist named Ralph Flanders got in touch with
Rust about taking his family on a horseback excursion. Flanders was the head of
several machine tool companies and served on President Roosevelt's War Production Board during World War II. He would go on to a career in the U.S. Senate, where he was noted for his introduction in 1954 of a resolution censuring
fellow Senator Joseph McCarthy.

Flanders enjoyed traveling, and each summer he offered his children the opportunity to choose some exotic destination. (Perhaps it was no coincidence that
he knew Philip Berolzheimer, who had offered the same choice to his son Charles
in 1919.) Flanders's daughter Nancy loved to ride horses, so when her turn came
she proposed a trip out West. "We looked over a map of the country," Flanders
wrote in his book *Senator from Vermont*, "and concluded that the most remote
area—farthest from railroads, highways, and habitations—was to be found in
southeastern Utah north of the Colorado River, or on the headwaters of the Salmon River in Idaho."[2]

Flanders consulted another business friend, Henry Dennison, who had ridden with Rust in 1934. Dennison recommended the Utah trip for a spirited adventure and suggested that Dave be their guide. The Flanders arranged to begin

their excursion in Torrey on June 28. Dave's youngest son, Quentin, came along as wrangler. He was fifteen at the time but was already an experienced rider. Fritz Hopf, a cousin of Charles Berolzheimer who was staying with the Rusts that summer, also joined the party.

Their first day involved a twenty-four-mile ride through Capitol Gorge, turning south down the Notom road to the Sandy Ranch. "Nancy, an experienced rider, stood it well," Flanders recalled, "but it was an ordeal for a soft tenderfoot like her father. After the first day everything seemed easy." Dave wanted to ride up onto the Aquarius above the Wildcat Ranger Station in time to see the summer's sheep herds being driven up to the plateau's summit. Flanders found this sight captivating: "[A]s the flocks (ewes and lambs) poured over the edge at the top of the trail and spread out grazing the verdure, we could think of nothing after those toilsome and deadly deserts but of the redeemed souls entering on the heavenly pastures."

Flanders remembered seeing the peaks of the Henry Mountains—"a range of burnished silver," he called them—from his train car on a westward journey earlier in the century. Rust was only too happy to take him there. They made their way back through the Waterpocket Fold and across the benches above Sandy Creek. "Woe betide the man without a guide in that country," Flanders wrote. He remarked how, after Rust told them they would reach a spring within a few hours, he emptied the stale water from his canteen. "Never will I forget the stern rebuke from Dave Rust," he went on. "The man who, in the desert, pours out water before he can refill his canteen is potentially a suicide himself and an accessory to the murder of his companions." Rust was overdramatizing their situation, but it is interesting that he felt no compunction about upbraiding his wealthy client. Flanders was on Rust's ground, and the old desert hand knew the rules for safe conduct.

Quentin was not as enthralled with the trip. "I hated every minute of it," he recalled.[3] Riding an old, slow horse at the end of the pack string, he ate dust all day and found the scenery scant compensation. He had to get up at dawn each day and bring the horses in by breakfast, a tough job when the animals were disposed to wander in search of feed. Flanders felt that Dave was pretty hard on the boy, but one incident redeemed Dave in his mind. When they were camped high in the Henry Mountains, a young sheepherder approached the group and asked if they had seen his horse. Quentin at once rode out with the boy to help him locate it. As his son sped off, Rust proudly announced, "[T]here goes an Eagle Scout."

"That one comment wiped the slate clean of debits and left a good balance of credit for the disciplinary father," Flanders wrote.

They returned to Torrey via a long ride along the Dirty Devil (Fremont) River and the Waterpocket Fold. Stopping for lunch in one of the settlements along the river, Flanders observed a scene from the Old West: an extended Mormon family—"grandfather and grandmother, sons and daughter with wives and husbands, and grandchildren aplenty" had gathered around a corral to watch two of their older boys break a horse. "Life seemed simple and easy—no worry, no hurry" to the easterner. He had not lived through the Dirty Devil's floods.

Flanders later told Rust that his trip was "one of the most delightful recollections of my life." In another letter written in 1961, he contrasted his experience wandering the mountains and plateaus on horseback with another view he had had of the Utah desert: "You will be interested in knowing that in flying in a chartered 707 Boeing plane from San Francisco to Washington a year ago I found that we were going a hundred miles or so away from the Henry Mountains. I asked the skipper to fly me over them. The Aquarius Plateau, the desert and the saddle of the two peaks were in full view of the cockpit. What a difference! The pack train trip was memorable; the jet plane view was simply interesting."[4]

In late June of 1937, Rust took the John S. Chafee family from Rhode Island on a two-week pack trip over the Aquarius Plateau to Table Cliff Plateau and Powell Point.[5] Chafee was a principal in the Brown & Sharpe Manufacturing Company of Providence, a machine tools firm, and may well have been referred by Ralph Flanders, who was in the same business. Joining Mr. and Mrs. Chafee were their son John, who would go on to a career in the U.S. Senate, their daughter Janet, and a young friend. Dave brought Walt Smith of Torrey along as wrangler. After enjoying the view from Powell Point, the elder Chafees returned as far as Escalante, where Rust arranged for a car to take them to Torrey. Rust and Smith rode back with the youngsters. They set out down the Escalante River, which quickly canyoned up east of town. Cattlemen often used this scenic stretch of the river to take their herds down to the benchlands in the Circle Cliffs, and the sandy trail, stripped clear of most vegetation, offered easy riding.

As they proceeded down the canyon, a thunderstorm that was building up over the Aquarius let loose on them—a "glorious downpour," Rust noted—and soon they could see they would need to pick up their pace. As the rain slid off the sandstone slabs above Death Hollow and Sand Creek, these streams quickly swelled into minor torrents. Soon the river rose as well, and the riders enjoyed the thrill of keeping ahead of the flood. The canyon was not so narrow that they couldn't have waited it out at almost any point; Rust would never have put his charges at any real risk. Still, it gave the three young men a good story to relate back home.

In his last years of guiding, Dave grew increasingly interested in the canyons of the Escalante River, which along its winding, hundred-mile course from the town of Escalante to the Colorado cut into three of the classic Mesozoic strata of the Plateau country: the billowing white domes of the Navajo Sandstone, the slabby, water-laid ledges of the Kayenta Formation, and the greatest cliff former, the glowing red Wingate Sandstone. Impassable cliffs guarded the river in most places, except at side canyons or where huge sand slides banked up against the walls. Cowboys from Escalante and Boulder knew the routes, but tourists came nowhere near the area. Escalante folks had driven automobiles down to Hole-in-the-Rock as early as 1934, and that same year the geologist Edwin McKee and his wife made a trip into the river canyon, but a National Geographic expedition that reached Wahweap Creek in 1949 would claim discovery rights, titling their report "First Motor Sortie into Escalante Land."[6]

The Civilian Conservation Corps built a gravel road between the two towns across the upper canyons of Sand Creek and Death Hollow in the early 1930s, but this route—the so-called "Hells Backbone" road—hugged the edge of the Aquarius at over eight thousand feet and was snowed in each winter. Not until 1940 did the state highway department finally bridge the river at Calf Creek, joining for the first time the towns of Escalante and Boulder with a year-round road.[7] And these settlements were merely outposts at the edge of an even more remote region.

In the mid-1930s word of a mysterious disappearance put the Escalante canyons into the pages of newspapers across the nation. The story of young Everett Ruess, the California wanderer who trailed off into Davis Gulch in November 1934 and was never seen again, became one of the canyon country's most durable legends. That anyone could vanish so thoroughly within one of the 48 States made for a sensational story. The following summer the Associated Civic Clubs of southern Utah asked Rust to keep an eye out for the lost youth while he was out on his trips. He and Dodge Freeman talked about "the young artist who disappeared" on their 1935 excursion, and Dave knew some of the cowboys in Escalante who had taken part in the search. It was time to see what those canyons held.

The occasion was another visit by Freeman in July 1937. This time he brought along an acquaintance from Princeton, Dr. L. F. H. Lowe, a professor of Romance languages. A Boulder, Utah, rancher and packer Rust identified only as Mr. King joined them.[8] On July 17 they headed out from his ranch on horseback, taking the "lower road" south from Boulder that led toward the sheer Navajo Sandstone walls overlooking Calf Creek, a pretty, cottonwood-lined perennial stream. The road—more properly a track cut into the slickrock—skirted this impassable canyon on the west, dropping more than a thousand feet down to the Escalante River. The next day they followed the road up out of the river canyon to an open benchland stretching south to Harris Wash. Following the primitive Sheffield track back to the river via a handy sand dune, they camped in a stretch of canyon that is still seldom visited today.

After following Harris Wash back up to the western benches, they continued south for several days almost to Hole-in-the-Rock, where they looked for a route down to the river east of Davis Gulch. Another sand dune provided the way where it breached the tall Wingate cliffs above the river. After following the Escalante to its mouth, they backtracked and spent another difficult day searching for the so-called Black Trail that crossed the Waterpocket Fold, named for a local cattleman who had inscribed his name in an alcove along the way.[9] It was a long, slow route that took anything but a straight line through the sandstone knobs and fissures. Their canteens ran out in the middle of the afternoon; Freeman recalled that it was "all bare rock and blind going…. [W]e damn near pooped out, both horses and men, on account no water at all."[10] At a dry camp overlooking Halls Creek, Rust opened tins of grapefruit and tomatoes for the thirsty crew. By the time they arrived at Baker's ranch, they had been twenty-six hours between water sources—a lot to endure in the heat of midsummer.

After a rest at the ranch, the outfit returned via the old Hall road through Muley Twist canyon, a well-known and easier route that brought them back to the Escalante River. A last day's ride up the south fork of Wolverine Canyon and west to Boulder Town completed their journey—"a corking program," as Rust described it. He would return four years later with Freeman to revisit parts of their route, making the trip in late spring when the heat was more bearable.

Professor Lowe returned in July 1938 with another Princeton student, Harold Hartshorne, to float Glen Canyon.[11] Rust and his son Nelson drove to Richfield to meet them. While in town, Rust stopped by the local newspaper to give an interview, which was about as far as his publicity efforts went. He told the paper that he intended to make this something of a history voyage, with stops at Halls Crossing, Hole-in-the-Rock, El Vado, and other interesting sites. No man knew Glen's history better. "To walk out over the trails on either side, to reflect upon all we have read of their romantic history, to take pictures, to view the cliff dwellings and pictographs—this is what we want from the trip," Rust told the editor.[12]

The river displayed its past at many points. Besides the ancient cliff dwellings they saw in side canyons, there was abundant evidence of more recent human interest in the river. At Hansen Creek they talked with three Japanese prospectors who were still trying to make the placers pay. They stopped at Robert Stanton's gold dredge, mired in the sands of lost dreams—dreams that Rust had shared in a more modest way. They drifted on down to a landing below Hole-in-the-Rock and climbed up its steep steps to admire the view. Rust took photographs for his friend Chauncey Parry, who had a notion of building a tourist lodge here. Rust mentioned that he might drop off passengers at the base of a tramway which Parry hoped to build—a tourist future for Glen Canyon that never came to pass, at least at that site.

After crossing the river to explore the continuation of the old Mormon trail to Bluff, they floated down to Music Temple, always one of Rust's favorite stops. He was disturbed to find that the notes in the visitor register had been removed, and he took note of recent footprints on the sand. These they knew to be from an expedition led by Norman Nevills that had launched from Green River, Utah on June 20. Back in Richfield, the newspaper editor had mentioned that this expedition was overdue at Lees Ferry; Rust's group would hear more of Nevills's trip once they got there.

The hike to Rainbow Bridge was nearly mandatory on Rust's trips. They read the register below the bridge, took pictures, and returned in late afternoon, taking advantage of the canyon walls' shade. That evening they were surprised by two hikers who emerged from Aztec (Forbidding) Canyon. They were Joseph Ruetz, a student at Notre Dame, and Louis Miller of Washington, D.C., and they had spent the last month exploring the rugged country around Navajo Mountain. When they showed up they were wearing "worn foot-ball togs," according to Rust (Ruetz went on to a career as football coach at Stanford). He gave them an old pair of pants for patches, and took them in his little boats down to the mouth of Navajo Creek.

At the Crossing of the Fathers (Rust preferred the Spanish *El Vado*), Dr. Lowe was not feeling well, so they landed on the opposite shore and took photographs.

Rust's journal hints at his displeasure at missing this historic site: "We do not go into Vado Cr. on account of mud, & the Col. (Lowe) thinks it too strenuous to walk half mi over rocks from Cane Cr. to examine steps cut in trail by Padre Escalante so we move on to some shady lunch spot."

Their last day on the river was spent in leisurely fashion, taking advantage of the current to make good time on the river. Rust's journal gives a sense of the delight many river runners have experienced on an uncrowded, unhurried river:

JULY 17.—Sunday Up & away at 7 A.M.—two hrs. run past Navajo Cr. to Sentinel Rock at Mouth of Wahweap. Pulled in the shade for swim & fig newtons and rest. Encountered few sand waves. The water swift as usual only more so. Drifting is fast enough for our purpose. Thousands of Mud-wasp dwellings plastered on wall of the great Rock. I'm sitting now in the shade of the Rock which is pictured in Dellenbaugh's Canyon Voyages & I'm reading the description of El Vado in that book, p. 148. Good place for lunch & rest. I read to crew God of Open Air.[13]

Clouds come over after long stop in shade. Wind comes up—we row against head wind for five miles then drift quietly down the deepening gorge to Lee's Ferry by 5:30 PM. Make camp below rock houses as usual and spread out on the bar for a cool night.

At Lees Ferry they learned that the Nevills expedition had reached there on July 8, exchanged two crew members, and gone on into Marble Canyon. They also read some newspaper accounts of the "missing" expedition and of their own trip. Whatever public notice Rust received of his voyage, it had been inadvertently eclipsed by Nevills. Rust's fellow river guide had been taking guests down the San Juan River for several years and had decided to expand his operation by mounting a scientific expedition on the Green and Colorado rivers. Among his passengers were two women botanists, Elzada Clover and Lois Jotter, who became the first women to run the Grand Canyon.

Unlike Nevills's later trips, in which he actively sought publicity, this trip stumbled into it. Nevills had planned to take nine or ten days to float through Labyrinth, Stillwater, Cataract, and Glen canyons, and had told the press he expected to arrive at Lees Ferry about the Fourth of July. When he did not arrive, newspapers across the nation ran stories speculating that disaster may have befallen them. "Anxious over Fate of Canyon Expedition" headlined an Associated

Press story in the *New York Times* on July 4, 1938. It said that "torrential rains" had made the river especially dangerous and that veteran river runners were offering "gloomy predictions" of Nevills's chances. Local papers ran front page stories for days, painting the Colorado as a fearsomely dangerous foe. Lois Jotter later described the media's reaction as a "feeding frenzy."[14]

Rust had told the Richfield paper that in view of the recent storms, Nevills was probably only exercising appropriate caution by laying over a day or two. He acknowledged that the party faced real hazards: "Cataract Canyon has about 50 miles of the meanest water in western America, rock studded and grasping for victims in a storm." But the Nevills party had encountered difficulties even before they reached Cataract. High water had created strong eddies at the confluence of the Green and Colorado, causing one boat to be swept away and stranding its crew on shore overnight. They recovered the boat, but another flipped in a rapid farther down Cataract. These mishaps, along with time spent collecting plants, put the party behind schedule. On July 7 a Coast Guard airplane was dispatched from Texas to look for the missing party. It located them about twenty miles above Lees Ferry and dropped notes to the boaters, observing their hand signals indicating that all was well.[15] Nevills arrived at Lees Ferry the next day, nine days ahead of Rust, and other than running short on food, his party was unharmed.

These were still the young days of Colorado River running, and the press saw the Nevills trip as good copy. They even worked Rust into the story, with some accounts depicting his trip as a rescue mission. Professor Lowe found this irritating. The following spring he wrote to Charles Kelly, who had also made a 1938 Glen Canyon voyage: "In case you noticed a fairly widespread and ridiculous press account last July stating that we had gone in search of the Nevill [*sic*] expedition, please discount it. We made no such statement, obviously could have had no such intention, and regret the false publicity given to [a] simple pleasure trip."[16] Rust's party had put on the river on July 8, below Cataract Canyon, just as Nevills was reaching Lees Ferry.

In the years that Dodge Freeman had been exploring the canyon country, he had not yet floated down Glen Canyon, so Rust sought to remedy this in June 1939.[17] They led off their three-week excursion with a pack trip from Torrey to the top of Thousand Lake Mountain, descending eastward down the Hartnet desert and on to Caineville. After taking a break in Torrey, Dave arranged for a truck to take them down the long North Wash route to Hite, where they arrived on the twenty-first, in time for lunch with the Chaffins.

Rust was growing increasingly interested in the river's history. He had participated in a small part of it himself, and he had met or known of many of his fellow Glen Canyon gold miners. On this trip they chanced to meet Bert Loper at Smith Fork, who was guiding two geologists, Ralph Miller of Columbia University and Charles B. Hunt of Yale.[18] (Hunt's study of the geology of the Henry Mountains region was published in 1953 as a U.S. Geological Survey Professional Paper.) The men talked about old days at Hite, and Rust's brief notes of the encounter mention Loper's story of catching "two fat fish" at this locality in 1908—which, Rust wrote, had "grown bigger ever since."

While floating the river, Dave and Dodge pulled over to inspect several old mining camps and paid a visit to Loper's former cabin at Red Canyon. Farther downstream, Rust and Freeman attempted to locate the old Mormon wagon road leading southeast from Halls Crossing, but storms and erosion over the years had erased traces of the path. At Lake Canyon they looked at the "1642" date and other inscriptions that had fascinated Charles Kelly and Russell Frazier the year before, but concluded that the writing was much more recent.

Dodge's young legs made him a willing explorer, so he and Dave trekked up to the rim at Oak Creek, Meskin Bar, and at a point several miles below the Crossing of the Fathers. Future Glen Canyon enthusiasts would spend much of their time exploring the river's amazing side canyons, but Dave, ever seeking new vantages, reveled in the views he found atop Glen's cliffs. On either side of the river was an enormous bare-rock landscape, punctuated by huge monoliths such as Gregory, Tower, and Gunsight buttes. To the south and east, the blue-gray bulk of Navajo Mountain dominated the skyline, while Navajo Point at the southern tip of Fiftymile Mountain towered four thousand feet to the north of the river.

Their trip ended at Lees Ferry on June 29, where they met Archie Hansen, a highway engineer, who offered the two men a welcome beer—"good and cold," Rust noted—and drove them to the Marble Canyon Lodge a few miles up the road for dinner. (These were still the days when a river trip pulling into Lees Ferry generated some interest, and informal hospitality on the part of the region's inhabitants was the rule, not the exception.) The next morning Rust and Freeman were out on the highway at 5 a.m. to await the bus from Santa Fe, which arrived hours later. Back home, Dave had his photographs of the trip enlarged for Dodge, and his journal records his anticipation at the next trip they were planning—a journey into the southern Waterpocket Fold and Moody Canyons of the lower Escalante River.

Under Rust's guidance, Freeman was getting as thorough a picture of the region as anyone could, with the possible exception of the government geologists who had been combing the canyons and mesas for decades. Their summer 1940 program involved a change of plans, postponing their Escalante trip for a visit to the high country of the Aquarius and Paunsaugunt plateaus. Rust's notes for this excursion were brief, although he observed that the Aquarius was "bleak from drouth" and feed was poor at some of the ranches they stopped at along the way. Following the Boulder mail trail across Death Hollow to Escalante town, Rust found the "trail very dim.... Rained as we were crossing Canyon, great spectacle."[19] After exploring the Paunsaugunt they returned to Torrey via the Aquarius, staying high to avoid the desert heat. The notes Dave wrote each night at camp reflected long days in the saddle and camp chores that kept them busy into the evening. He would have a bit more to say on his final wilderness journey the following year.

By the spring of 1941, Rust had been guiding visitors throughout the Colorado Plateau for more than three decades. Now sixty-seven years old, he would make one last pack trip with Dodge Freeman, revisiting the Escalante River canyons they had explored in 1937, and extending their wanderings farther out onto the southern end of the Waterpocket Fold. Early May would be a more opportune season for this venture; they had no desire to repeat their cottonmouthed experience crossing the Waterpocket Fold in the July heat.

Rust prepared for the trip by visiting Dr. Eldon Beck, a botanist at Brigham Young University who had recently been working in the Escalante River region. Rust paid particular attention to Dr. Beck's photos and notes of several natural bridges in these canyons. He had none, however, of Gregory Natural Bridge, a span that had managed to elude public attention far longer than Rainbow Bridge. A few Escalante stockmen knew about it, but the narrows of Fiftymile Gulch (or Soda Gulch, as they called it) discouraged travel through the canyon. A person on foot could get through a tight passage a mile or so above the bridge, but not cattle or horses. The geologist Herbert Gregory may have seen the bridge in 1918 when he was scouting the country for his report on the Kaiparowits Plateau, but he chose not to mention it in his journal. When his report was issued in 1931, he located it incorrectly in Fortymile Gulch and called it the "Fortymile Bridge." William Chenoweth's USGS survey party located the bridge in 1921 while checking out tributaries to the Escalante River that would be flooded by his proposed Glen Canyon Dam.[20]

The bridge attracted no further attention until Norman Nevills decided to feature it on a 1940 Green-Colorado River expedition. To build excitement and perhaps to attract customers, he played up the bridge as if it were virtually unknown, and hinted that his expedition would make the formal discovery. Nevills even suggested that it might be larger than Rainbow Bridge.[21] His party made measurements of the bridge's opening, and although it fell short of Rainbow Bridge, they were able to place it among the great sandstone spans of the Colorado Plateau.

For his trip with Dodge Freeman, Rust drove down to Escalante to make arrangements with his packer, Junius Wilson, who would set out ahead of them. Dodge joined Dave a day later, bringing a movie camera and 2,500 feet of color film with which to record the adventure. Dave's last backcountry journal[22] is worth presenting here in full, cryptic jottings and all, for it conveys the informal character typical of his trips, where he might have a destination in mind but the route could be serendipitous. Dave and Dodge were true wanderers, used to each other's company and eager to see new places. With only sketchy maps and descriptions from local cowboys, they were prepared for a bit of adventuring, come what may.

Dave's journal shows them heading down the familiar route south from Escalante to Willow Tank, a waterhole in upper Hurricane Gulch. From there it was an easy ride down the sandy wash of Hurricane to where it joined the wondrous meanders of Coyote Gulch, one of the most beautifully incised canyons of the entire region. This they followed to the Escalante River, where they were treated to a view of Stevens Arch, a magnificent span cut in a sandstone fin high up on the east side of the river, silhouetted against the sky. They followed the river downstream to Fiftymile Gulch (Rust calls it "The Fifty"), which they followed several miles upstream to find Gregory Bridge. After taking in this sight they returned to the river, rode back to Willow Gulch, and climbed back out to resupply at their cache at Willow Tank and head up onto Fiftymile Mountain.

From Dave Rust's 1941 journal (explanatory notes are in brackets):

MAY 4 (SUNDAY)—Dodge & Jim arrived Escalante 4 p.m. We had lunch at Minnie's with Beckers "coffee" then overtook Junius Wilson & the packs at fence 30 mi. down desert for first camp-site. Eight animals: 1 mule, 2 black saddlehorses, 1 pinto, 1 brown mare, 1 yellow horse & 1 bolly bay, 1 white saddlehorse.

MAY 5—To willow tank for lunch & make cache. Then into Coyote Gulch & down 4 miles to camp #2. First taste of mosquitos for an hour about dark. The climate perfect. Water warm enough for bath.

MAY 6—I go back to cache for more food & we go about 4 mi. to Coyote Arch [now called Jacob Hamblin Arch] which does not span creek. Lovely spot. Creek could easily be changed to go through Arch. Camp at arch so as to get pictures next morning.

MAY 7—Another arch spanning the gulch (stream) about 3 mi down canyon [now called Coyote Natural Bridge]. Have to leave stream bed along left bank to avoid falls, then near Escalante River have to shelve to right to reach river. Camped near outlet on Coyote Cr., good pasture in sand slope. Glorious arch seen north near mouth Stevens Canyon [now known as Stevens Arch].

MAY 8—Navigate river down to Willow Gulch, medium high water, some quick-sand. No difficulty. Interesting necktie bend via trail on right. Make camp mouth of Willow Cr. (Gulch). Put up fence across creek to hold horses.

MAY 9—Down river about 4 mi. to mouth of Fifty Gulch and up the gulch about a mile to great arch which spans creek. Massive and impressive. Note in a monument by Nevills boating party of 1940 calls it by some Navajo name meaning The Beautiful. Lunch under arch & take pictures from every angle. This must be the "Gregory" bridge named as an afterthought by Nevills. Moki steps up right wall of cañon below arch. We go up creek (gulch) about 1 mile, as far as animals can possibly go. Junius cuts some steps & ascends part way to top of arch. Could not reach top.

MAY 10—Take many pictures then retreat about 1 mi. to Es. River & up river 10 crossings to Willow Gulch then up gulch thru very narrow places & past honda arch, one of three best bridges of the 6 seen on trip. Go to cave corral for camp not halting for lunch. An easy day from Cave Corral to the "Gregory" Arch via Willow & the R. Splendid scenery all the way. Escalante "punchers" camped at Cave—Alma Liston, Neal Liston, Gail Bailey, Usher Spencer. Conversations ad lib. Wood scarce & water limited.

MAY 11—Junius & I go to Willow tank for cache. Some oats disturbed by mules, otherwise unmolested. Dodge goes with Bailey toward river for cattle. Dinner at 4 P.M. Kentucky ham, etc. Checked gulches from Willow tank to Cave.... Gail Bailey stayed with us overnight.

MAY 12—We climb Kaiparowits and camp on the Top. Sky somewhat murky so not good for color movie. Windy. Wild cattle tracks. Looking back over the Waterpocket-canyons coming into the E.R.: Stephens, Cow, Fence & one unnamed shorter canyon. Campbell soup, Kentucky ham, tea, honey, doughgods for dinner. Dodge & I walk out to extreme point but no good for pictures.

May 13—Up early & Dodge goes to rim for pictures, June wrangles while I cook ham, hot-cakes, tea, spuds. We decide to wait till noon for better picture conditions. Pulled back to base camp at Corral Cave in 4 hrs, 5 P.M.

This far into their trip they had still not reached the most difficult stage of their explorations. After dropping off of Fiftymile Mountain, Rust, Freeman, and Wilson made their way along the Black Trail that followed the benches between Davis and Clear creeks back to the Escalante River. From here they crossed the river and climbed up onto the Waterpocket Fold. They could not find a way into Bowns Canyon, a short tributary of the Colorado that headed from the crest of the Waterpocket Fold. (Rust later told river historian Dock Marston that this canyon was named for a "prehistoric cowboy," presumably Will Bowns.) They returned via the Moody Canyons, a series of three dramatic, Wingate-cliffed gorges tributary to the Escalante River that cut the Waterpocket Fold farther north. Dave's journal resumes:

May 14—Direct to Escalante River via No-See-Um trail (Black trail) 10 AM to 3:30 P.M. No trouble. A dinner of beef C. soup, ham & Pictrics beans, canned peaches, tea, crackers, doughgods, butter. Dodge took movie of the trail dropping down.

MAY 15—Out on top of Water-Pocket region over "bald-heads" to a wild camp at water holes. Six hours run. Much time spent looking for trail into Bown Canyon. Good view on brink of Colorado. Found no trail off so went north on west side. After dinner Dodge goes down trough to jumpoff of short canyon which puts into E.R. about 1 mi. up stream from 50 Gulch. And he goes to rim of Fence canyon which enters E.R. at "necktie" bend. I climb east bald-heads to explore.

MAY 16—Across east bald-head ridge via pass to head of Bown then abt. east to rim of Long Canyon. Then north along rim to easy crossing and on to east rim of Water Pocket for grand lookoff from point which shows very wide swing (toward Halls Crossing) of the region. Retreat over 1 mile & make camp about 2 P.M. at crossing of Long Canyon. Started this morning at 8. I walk down gulch about a mile to where it jumps off about 500 ft. into canyon with small stream, pasture horses in bottom. Big tank of difficult to reach water 1/2 mi. below camp.

To monument point (maybe high point) of Water Pocket in 6 hrs. Tanks of water & good pasture for animals near high bald-head. After dinner Dodge hits trail toward Moody following 2 horse tracks not over 9 mos. old. I stroll east rim to look into two deep colorful gorges which cut Navajo & Wingate & Chinle & into Moenkopi—typical erosions of east Waterpocket. Saw cowboy horsetracks so hope to find way into Moody (Emery King calls it Middle Moody).

MAY 18 (SUNDAY)—Explored for trail off into the Moody. Followed horse-tracks north about 6 miles then off north-west of round mesa, timbered, into rough canyon, a leader into branch of Moody. Turned cold & windy and snowed 2 or 3 in. during night. June pitched tent for him & Dodge. I stayed out comfortably in bag. Cold enough. Dodge ran thorn in ankle, rub with turpentine.

MAY 19—Cold & foggy and some hail—we go into Moody over very rough trail including one jumpoff over 100 feet drop. [Dodge Freeman noted later that they spent half a day piling up rocks to make it down one dropoff.] Good camp in the open near corral. We are not certain whether we are in the East Moody or a branch of Main Moody. (Emery King, May 26, says we are in Middle Moody. The East, or as he calls it South, can be reached from corral over pass.)

MAY 20—To the E. River and up river about 6 miles nearly to mouth of Collet [Twentyfive Mile Gulch]. Good pasture on bench. Cliff ruin. Dodge rides into quicksand & bogged down, got camera stuff soaked. Little pack mule stuck also & had to be dugout. Horse came out with less work.

MAY 21—Up Collet to bend above 25 mi. water then high ridge N. of road to Tank Corral for fine finish camp. Fresh rain water in tanks. Secure pasture in canyon below. Cliff ruin in cave high up from bottom of Collet (about 4 mi. from E.R.) Seems inaccessible from top or bottom. Saw two other ruins on trip, one near Coyote arch & one in E.R. at horsepasture below mouth of Collet.

MAY 22—Ride into Escalante 15 mi for noon, starting at 7:30. No-see-ums not pleasant as we neared town.

Changed packs from ponies to the Durant then Dodge joined me in a racing ride to Richfield via Panguitch. Road through Kingston canyon washed out. Some car trouble delay. Put up at Johnston Hotel & had good bath & retired on twin beds. Tomorrow we saunter to Provo. The great trip is over.

Although Dodge Freeman's movie camera was ruined in his encounter with the Escalante River's quicksand, he carried home wonderful memories of his trip with Rust. He later told the riverman Ken Sleight that the Escalante River canyon "perhaps has no equal for beauty anywhere." He held an "unforgettable memory" of "flushing a pair of snowy egrets from a fern-lined bower in 50 Mile Canyon at the point where it boxes up above Gregory Arch."[23] In an added loss, Dodge's still photographs of his trip, both color and black-and-white, were damaged when the basement of his home in Lake Forest Park, Illinois, was flooded. After returning home from their trip, Dave noted in his journal that Dodge "had a lasting experience by getting his saddle horse and the pack-mule stuck in quicksand. Wet his valuable camera and lenses and some film. We dug 'em out in about an hour. Such vicissitudes make choice items in a trip."[24] Despite his sanguinity, a full photographic record of their wild excursion would be priceless today.

When Dave and Dodge rode back to Escalante that May, they were leaving behind a landscape that still eluded most people outside of Garfield County. Norman Nevills's trips down the San Juan and Colorado were bringing more outsiders into the region, but in the minds of most Americans, southern Utah was principally the home of Zion and Bryce parks, and not much else. Some local people were curious about the Escalante's concealed wonders, and in September 1941 Dave noted that a party of seventy automobiles made the sixty-five-mile trip down the dusty track from Escalante to Hole-in-the-Rock.[25] There they met some of the descendants of the Mormon emigrant party of 1879–1880 who had retraced the trail westward from Bluff. No one other than cattlemen and oil company geologists, though, had any reason to venture off this track into Dave's "mysterious region." And with the gathering worldwide conflict, backcountry explorations for pleasure would soon be curtailed. At the age of sixty-seven, Dave was riding home from his last wilderness trip, closing the book on a half-century of travel in the far corners of the Colorado Plateau.

19 | The World Open to View

Yesterday received colored films from Dodge Freeman—now we can have a show ala Escalante. I am thinking back on the various Christmas days—in the Hartnet 1887 alone, Koosharem 1883, Pahreah 1897, Blake City 1891, Kanab 1902, Stanford 1903.... Life is an accumulation of interesting experiences—hope the next probation will be equally interesting.

Dave Rust
Journal, December 25, 1941

America's entry into World War II effectively dried up Rust's possibilities for further desert excursions as the demands of war-related work and restrictions on travel kept potential clients from visiting the Southwest. Gas rationing was extended to the entire country by the end of 1942, further limiting tourism. Dave's journal gives little indication that he was ready to hang up his saddle, although long days in the desert and nights spent on a thin mattress must have become a bit harder for a man of his age. Even with a wrangler to look after the stock, and a young, experienced client such as Dodge Freeman, the backcountry was a demanding place to visit. On his birthday in March 1941 he noted that he had "only 3 years more to go to 70," and that he "must depend on variety of memories for most of my fun." Two months later he would guide Dodge on a demanding tour of the Escalante canyons, so his wistfulness for bygone adventures was perhaps a bit relative. But, as he noted a few years later, "decrepitude is creeping up on me." To preserve some of those memories, on New Year's Day of 1941 he began jotting down items of note from his life.[1]

He also used his free time during the war years to indulge his love of books. In his journal he recorded a wide variety of literary interests: among his readings that year were Lin Yutang's *Importance of Living*; the journals of John Burroughs, whom he had met in the Grand Canyon in 1909; a biography of Joan of Arc—"one of the most touching figures in human history," he wrote—and, closer to home, a biography of Brigham Young. On April 13 he commemorated Jefferson's birthday by starting James Maslow Adams's *The Living Jefferson*, writing that the founding father would be "one of our 'house guests' for a month." He read an article in *Life* on Hinduism, which prompted him to read both the *Ramayana* and the *Mahabharata*. "The man who hasn't the habit of reading is imprisoned," he noted. "He should have a favorite author—a literary lover—and then change that lover occasionally." The youngster who had chafed at the lack of books in Caineville now had time to explore the world of letters.

Spiritual topics continued to interest him, and his eclectic reading reflected his wide interest in other religions. While he never appeared to waver in his fundamental belief in the tenets of Mormon theology, he remained something of a maverick, and like a good Zane Grey hero, he rode his own trail. Dan Duncan, the autobiographical cowboy Rust sketched out for his projected novel "The Queen of the San Rafael," was no believer in "rusty religious dogmas."[2] Duncan "prayed with his eyes open"; for him (and presumably Dave), inspiration was as likely out in the wilderness as in church. Rust looked outward, searching for what the far hills might disclose.

He also dreamed about floating the Colorado. Reading Julius Stone's *Canyon Country*, the account of his epic voyage on the Green and Colorado with Nathaniel Galloway, "takes me back to 1909, when I was invited to accompany them but on account of pneumonia early that spring concluded it wise to decline though I wanted to go." He never took on the Colorado's major rapids, and so did not make it into the history books as one of the river's explorers, even though he was the first guide to operate regularly in Glen Canyon.

Early in the war years he expressed his dismay to his son Jordan that he might never go down Glen Canyon again, and that his saddles might remain unused. Jordan replied that "maybe the real strenuous stuff is behind you, but there are plenty of diverting and interesting things left to do." He suggested that once the war was over the two of them "take a spin around the rocks in a Helicopter or some such contrivance and get a different perspective."[3] Jordan owned a light plane and had once arranged to have his parents take a ride in an open-cockpit barnstormer; though Dave survived his aeronautical initiation, he chose not to fly again, and he and Jordan never made an air tour of the canyon lands. Perhaps, like Ralph Flanders, Dave would have found it merely "interesting."

The war directly involved many of Rust's clients. Dodge Freeman wrote to Rust early in 1942, saying that he hoped to enter the armed services even though he was over the normal age limit. He signed on as a recruiter for the navy, but soon took a lieutenant's commission and served aboard ships in the European and Pacific theaters. Charles Berolzheimer, although he was the head of California Cedar Products, a major lumber-producing company, enlisted in the Air

Force and flew missions over Germany as a gunner. According to Jordan, who since 1928 had worked for Charles, he had "a fierce hatred for the Nation that tormented his people."[4]

The Rust household, too, was changing. All of Dave and Ruth's children except Helen were now grown; Blanche had left home for California, where she filled in for Jordan's wife Edloe in the office of Charles's company. Nelson went into the army in 1942, serving with the Corps of Engineers in Europe. Quentin, who had been working summers as a surveyor's assistant for the General Land Office, was still living at home during the winters, but by 1944 he received his draft call and decided to enlist in the marines. Dave and Ruth, in turn, opened their house to their relatives' offspring. Five of his half-brother Sidney's grandchildren stayed with the Rusts while they attended Brigham Young University over the years, and there were others. The Rusts could not pay their tuition, but by offering room and board they felt they were materially helping to educate the family. Each of their children had attended BYU, and Dave and Ruth held no value higher.

Beginning in the summer of 1942, Dave found work as a night watchman at the Geneva Steel plant outside of Provo, a new facility built for the war effort. He received a hundred dollars a month for his work and spent the long hours with his favorite books. The pay also helped significantly in the absence of guiding work. Nelson sent money, too, in the form of his poker winnings, which sometimes nearly equaled his father's salary. He wrote home often, occasionally mentioning how much he missed Utah. On April 20, 1944, writing from England, Nelson told his folks, "Can think of no place I would rather be right now than laying back in a Canvas boat, floating lazily down the Colorado."[5] He took part in the D-Day operation, his letters omitting details owing to wartime censorship. Dodge Freeman also participated in this historic event, serving aboard the attack transport U.S.S. *Henrico* during the landings at Omaha Beach.

On August 15, 1944, Dave and Ruth received the telegram that every wartime parent feared. In stark capital letters, it informed them that Private George Nelson Rust had been killed in action in France on August 1.[6] An official letter that followed contained no further details. Soon thereafter, a long letter that Ruth had written to Nelson was returned, bearing the words "deceased" on the envelope. He was buried at the Normandy American Cemetery overlooking Omaha Beach. The Rusts received many letters of sympathy from their friends and relations, but

Dave's own thoughts are not recorded in his diary. His daughter, Blanche, recalled that her parents' sorrow was allayed with pride at their son's sacrifice, and that they were relieved that Nelson did not have a family of his own.

Following the war, Dave's life continued to focus on home and family. No longer would he saddle his horses at Jim Pace's ranch in Torrey to head across the Waterpocket Fold or up onto the Aquarius Plateau. A new generation of explorers was discovering the canyons in rubber rafts, jeeps, and autos. Norm Nevills of Mexican Hat continued to offer float trips on the San Juan and Colorado rivers during the war, but his business picked up considerably beginning in 1945. Nevills advertised through an eight-page typewritten brochure featuring homely line drawings; the guiding business was then in its infancy and professionally printed color booklets were decades away. Among the boatmen he hired were Harry Aleson and Otis "Dock" Marston, both of whom would correspond and visit with the Rusts over the next few decades. Nevills, like Rust, enjoyed taking his clients up Forbidding Canyon to visit Rainbow Bridge; in 1946 he shepherded at least thirty-five paying visitors to the bridge on five separate trips.[7] This was far more traffic than Dave ever handled, and marked the beginning of a major commercial enterprise in the region.

Private groups were also beginning to scout the canyon country using war-surplus rafts and jeeps. These included Sierra Club outings from California, Boy Scout troops from Utah and other states, and an enterprising LDS church group from Salt Lake City's South Cottonwood Ward (SOCOTWA) that made regular float trips down Glen Canyon starting in 1948. The availability of used army jeeps at auctions throughout the West allowed almost anyone to get far back into the canyons. Ward Roylance, a Utah guidebook author and tourism promoter, was one of the first to exploit this mode of transportation. His 1986 memoir *The Enchanted Wilderness* recounts his joy at discovering out-of-the-way places such as the Circle Cliffs, Dead Horse Point, and the Escalante canyons, all the while having to change flat tires and dig his vehicle out of treacherous stream crossings.

The national press also took notice of this seemingly unexplored territory. *National Geographic* ran articles with such titles as "Escalante—Utah's River of Arches," "Utah's Arches of Stone" (on Arches National Monument), "Desert River through Navajo Land" (on floating the San Juan and Colorado rivers), and "Flaming Cliffs of Monument Valley."[8] Visits to the region's parks and monuments burgeoned as well. At Natural Bridges, which recorded only 112 visitors in 1944, more than a thousand people were arriving by 1948. Utah's two national parks, of course, saw much greater numbers: Bryce Canyon recorded more than 125,000 visitors in 1946, while Zion saw 212,000 arrivals. The era of "windshield tourism" had arrived, and everyone in the business, from highway officials to the Park Service, was eager to boost the numbers.

To Dave, auto tours were a poor substitute for exploring with a pack string. Returning from a visit to J. O. Brew's excavations at Awatovi in the Hopi country in 1938, he drove from Flagstaff to Provo in a single day. He told Emery Kolb "how terrible, you can't see a thing at that speed."[9] While he had lobbied in the early part of the century for better roads to Kane County, he could now see how the automobile compressed distances, utterly changing the character of travel. When meeting his guests on his early pack trips, he would often take three or four days to ride north from Kanab to the rail stations at Marysvale, Richfield, or Manti. His affinity for leisurely travel may have accounted for the few auto tours he took after the war.

He remained interested in the history of the canyon country, avidly clipping items from the *Salt Lake Tribune* about the outdoorsmen and explorers he had known. "About all a man has left after 60, is the fond collection of recollections which may be looked over," he wrote. He found it delightfully stimulating when members of his old network of river runners would call on him and Ruth in Provo. Arth Chaffin, the ferryman at Hite, stopped by every year or so, as did his nephew Ned, who had traveled with Dave on two of his Peabody expeditions. Bert Loper was another welcome guest. "Mighty thrilling to see the old 'rats,'" Rust wrote to his friend Harry Aleson, another maverick explorer who stopped by often. In 1945 Aleson made a boatless descent of the lower Grand Canyon with his friend Georgie White, both of them wearing only life jackets.[10] In 1948 he and White floated down the Escalante River in rubber rafts, the first to boat the length of this shallow but entrancing stream.

"Precious visits," Dave wrote of these occasions. He downplayed his own role as a river veteran. When Harry Aleson wrote to arrange a photo session with him, Rust replied, "If you care to risk photographic equipment, surely I must yield to your request for a pioneer picture even though I'm unworthy of such title."[11] In truth, he must have been pleased with the recognition.

In 1952 the Park Service invited Rust to attend a celebration at the South Rim honoring the fiftieth anniversary of the Kolb brothers' work at the Grand

Canyon. He sent his regrets to Emery, but noted: "Am pleased to be numbered among the old timers. Nearly 45 years since we first met. And now I recall many precious episodes we enjoyed together such as horsebacking [*sic*] with little Edith on the Kaibab and years later trailing into Thunder River with her and Emma."[12]

There were also occasional sad dispatches. In 1946 newspapers around the West reported the death by suicide of ace river runner Haldane "Buzz" Holmstrom near the end of a run down Oregon's Rogue River. Holmstrom had distinguished himself in a daring solo voyage through Cataract Canyon and the Grand Canyon in 1937, running nearly all of the Colorado's major rapids. The following year he completed the first descent of all of the rapids of the Green and Colorado. Dave followed Holmstrom's whitewater adventures with interest, comparing his 1937 trip favorably to Charles Lindbergh's solo flight across the Atlantic ten years before. Rust told Emery Kolb that Holmstrom endured "the strain of many days compared to the strain of a few hours."[13] As someone who had never faced the Colorado's worst rapids, Dave held in high esteem anyone who had taken on the challenge. But to him, Holmstrom's death evinced a regrettable lapse in character. Dave shared his observations with Harry Aleson: "Every member of the Sacred Order of River-rats will be shocked and chagrined that one of their star members should falter in the face of any small disappointment. And he so young—it might be entirely honorable for one past 70, providing he chose to jump in the river. Maybe we should have a springboard where the old boys could finish. But to use such a sordid escape as an old gun! Stupid and unworthy."[14] Rust, with his strong moral compass, could not forgive such an action, although his comments to Aleson reveal how he tried to assuage the difficulties of growing old with a little humor.

In September 1946 Rust received a telegram from Dodge Freeman, inviting him to join Dodge and his bride, Ann Rutledge, during their honeymoon at the Grand Canyon. Dave was delighted to be able to see his young trail companion again, who now worked as a mining engineer for Peabody Coal Company. They rendezvoused at Jacob Lake in early October, possibly the finest time of year to be on the Kaibab. The threesome stayed two nights at the Grand Canyon Lodge's cabins on the North Rim (Dave joked with his family that he bunked up with Dodge as in the old days). They took a leisurely drive out to Cape Royal and Point Imperial—a "glorious day," Rust noted, with the aspen leaves turning golden and the air crisp and bracing. Dee Woolley's old outfitting cabin was no longer there, and a good road wound through the forest where Dave had led his pack string thirty-five years before. Dodge and Ann took Dave back to Kanab, where they picked apples at the home of one of Ruth's family. Rust cherished the memory of this trip, the last time he would see Dodge.

Earlier that year Dave's son Richard, who was living in Vernal, Utah, invited Dave and Ruth to come along on a trip to the Midwest, where they could visit some of the important shrines of Mormon history.[15] Many Latter-day Saints try to make a pilgrimage to Nauvoo, Illinois, the scene of pivotal events in the church's development, and Dave was also drawn to his father's and grandfather's history there. Accompanied by two other family relations, they left in late May, driving over the Rockies to visit Dave's daughter Laura in Littleton, Colorado. He was thrilled to see the snowy Continental Divide at Berthoud Pass; this appears to have been his first crossing of the Rockies. Traveling through the Great Plains and following the route of the Mormon emigrants, Dave savored the chance to relive some history, reading to the group from the 1847 journals of William Clayton, Howard Egan, and Harriet Young. After touring Nauvoo and making an excursion southward to Mark Twain's birthplace in Hannibal, Missouri, they returned via Winter Quarters in Kansas, where George S. Rust had courted Eliza Brown. Back home in Provo, with time to reflect on the journey, he wrote that "it seems like we went round the world.... Continue in spirit crossing the Plains & Rivers & Mountains while I plant some corn in the garden." Such trips were rare, however, as Dave and Ruth could not afford to travel much on their own. Even their midwestern journey was taken on the cheap, renting inexpensive tourist cabins (Dave noting the cost of each one) while he further economized by bringing his sleeping bag.

Richard Rust organized another car trip with Dave in 1948 to revisit some of Dave's old southern Utah haunts, bringing along his two oldest sons.[16] They searched unsuccessfully for the remains of the family homesteads in Grass Valley and Caineville, traveling through the Waterpocket Fold via Capitol Wash just as in the pioneer days. Then they took the narrow, winding road over the eastern shoulder of the Aquarius Plateau, bouncing along sandstone ledges and climbing up to the Wildcat Ranger Station in its lovely forest setting. A new station had been built near the one Walter Hanks used when Rust and George Fraser visited in the summer of 1915. Then it was on to Boulder, still relatively secluded amid its Navajo Sandstone domes, where an automobile passing through still evoked comment.

They headed on toward Bryce Canyon, following the breathtaking path over the slickrock nominally called State Route 23, which ventured south from

Boulder into the Escalante River canyon. Only seven years before, Dave had led Dodge Freeman into the wildest parts of those canyons; the country was still mostly the province of cattlemen from Boulder and Escalante. Progress was making inroads, however. An old stock trail leading east to Henrieville had recently been upgraded and opened to auto traffic, providing a more direct alternative to the historic road that followed Main Canyon up to a pass between the Table Cliff and Aquarius plateaus. The state highway map for 1947 still showed the former route as a trail, but it would eventually become the modern Highway 12 that connects Boulder and Escalante to Bryce Canyon and the towns in the Paria River valley. Only seventy-five years before, Almon H. Thompson had led his exploring party over this pass on his way to discovering the Escalante River.

At Bryce Canyon they were back in tourist country—175,000 people visited the park that year. The Rusts stayed in the comfort of the park's tourist cabins, bringing their circuit of the slickrock country to a close. The Rust grandchildren recalled that Dave enjoyed talking with the old-timers he knew in the villages along their route, but he was not one to reminisce in his journal about the changes coming to the canyon country. Only as the rest of the nation began to discover the Escalante region would outsiders begin to value its feeling of wild remoteness.

This was Dave's last visit to the red-rock country. Back in Provo he increasingly led the life of the mind, and his journals continued to record the free range of his thoughts. He kept track of notable dates in history that he felt were worthy of celebration. These included the birthday of Robert Burns, for which he and Ruth "read several Burns verses, a sketch of his life, close by singing 'Coming through the Rye.'" Mozart's birthday came up soon after, then Susan B. Anthony's ("emancipation for freedom of females in America"). Washington's birthday was occasion to read his biography. On December 15, 1956, he celebrated Bill of Rights Day by planting a blue spruce in his front lawn. (Few Americans would have known there was such a day to commemorate.) He noted the birthday of labor leader John L. Lewis and lauded his efforts on behalf of "enslaved coal miners." On March 22, 1955, he marked the passing of the civil rights leader Walter White, "another outstanding human rights benefactor." After seeing a local production of *Old Man River*, he recalled the great theatrical performances of Paul Robeson. His diary indicates he voted Republican in the 1956 election, so his regard for the downtrodden (and for blacklisted actors) took no partisan aspect.

Dave and Ruth celebrated their fiftieth wedding anniversary in May 1953.

All of their eight living children came to Provo to honor their parents and renew acquaintances. Jordan by this time had become manager of the California Cedar Company, where he took a strong interest in research and development. He had acquired another business, the Ry-Lock Company, which manufactured the first horizontal sliding aluminum windows. He made it a practice to send a monthly check to his parents to help them in their retirement, and several of his siblings chipped in at times as well.

Dave's brother Will, who had been living in Manti, Utah, since 1945, died in 1952. Of his brothers and sisters, Dave felt closest to him; he recorded that he often dreamt of their times together. They had prospected the sandbars of the Colorado, farmed the wastes of the Arizona Strip, and enjoyed the cool forests of the Kaibab, sharing hardships and adventures. They had seen the country change from a hardscrabble frontier to one of the nation's premier tourist destinations, and both had taken part in its development.

All of Dave's older siblings had passed away; only his younger brother Roy remained. Dave felt the encroachment of age and growing infirmity. "Cannot write much any more, cannot see or hear or walk or ride horses as we did 20 years ago," he wrote to Emery Kolb in 1953, when he was nearly eighty. "But my memory is keen and enjoyable and I manage to keep in touch with present as well as past events by reading with one reliable eye."[17]

He tried to stay active within the confines of Provo. His grandchildren recalled that he often walked to the library, keeping a brisk pace. In the summer of 1957 Dave noted that he mowed his lawn, "an item of record for an 83-year old duffer handicapped in both hind legs." But his continued interest in the world remained his most notable characteristic. He refused to settle into a predictable point of view; where he might criticize the Democrats in one diary entry, he would record his admiration for President Kennedy in another. In a letter to a friend in 1960, he noted that he might vote "bipartisan" that year.[18] This was a man who had switched tickets in Kane County to run as a Democrat for the state legislature.

In the summer of 1956 the Rusts were pleased to receive a visit from their friend Helen Candland and her husband Henry Stark of Wilmington, Delaware. Helen had taught school in Kanab when Dave was district superintendent. She had gone on to become a writer and essayist with an interest in Jungian psychology and Eastern mysticism. Although she had spent only one year in Kanab, Helen held fond memories of discovering the scenic lands of the region. During her visit with the Rusts she was impressed with Dave's active mind. They talked about the June 30 plane crash in the Grand Canyon in which two airliners collided in midair, killing 128 passengers. Dave, with his long connection to the Canyon, felt especially saddened by this disaster. Helen was surprised at his almost mystical response, in which he told her that he had in some fashion relived the tragedy. In an unpublished essay that she sent to the Rusts, she quoted Dave as saying, "'I have been there. I have seen those people and I have gone into their homes. I have tried to bless those who remain [in the Canyon].'"[19]

Dave told the Starks that he understood time and space to be relative, and that the mind could explore freely beyond its physical confines. "Memory and imagination still served him," she wrote, "and he could call up at will a center for his activity." Her impressions of her old friend and mentor serve as a worthy summary of his life: "The years have not been easy for my friend. He has known family tragedy. He has never made much money. But like Matthew Arnold, he has always sought to touch life at many points. He has loved not only knowledge, but good conduct and beauty as well."

Toward the end of their conversation, Dave offered the Starks some advice, taking note of the many miles back to Wilmington: "'It is a long way home' he counseled us. 'Stop often and look.' He told us, then, of a member of one of his expeditions from whom he had learned much about looking. Once the pack horses got away in a particularly uninviting stretch of terrain, entailing a long wait. This man knelt on the seemingly barren desert and turned over a stone to reveal, going on beneath it, the fascinating life of insects." Rust clearly was describing his friend George C. Fraser—whom he had described years earlier as "a man who has taught me much about seeing." Dave was not simply suggesting that the Starks pull over at scenic turnouts on the way home. "Stop often and look" was his prescription for an interesting life. It was practical advice from someone who had not only stood at the Southwest's most impressive vista points, but who had never ceased to use his mind.

By no means was his home life always filled with lofty themes; several of his grandchildren recalled that he could be quite gruff, and a progressive hearing loss increasingly isolated him from ordinary conversation. He told Emery Kolb in 1960 that he had been a "shutin" for four years. One grandchild observed that Dave felt overlooked in the publicity that attended the new generation of Colorado River runners and canyon explorers.[20] But he would follow the high school sports scores and discuss the games with the youngsters, and he still knew how to get a laugh from them.

His correspondence, written in a shaky but neat hand, connected him to friends around the country. Dodge Freeman wrote occasionally, and George Fraser Jr. and Sarah Fraser also kept in touch. He treasured his friendship with Emery Kolb in a series of warm letters. "Thinking of Ellsworth and Israel [Ellsworth Kolb and Israel Chamberlain], takes me back into Bright Angel where I lived for four years in behalf of E. D. Woolley's hobby. Most nearly all of my old friends are gone. Hope to meet them *over there*" [his emphasis].[21] He included his "gentile" (non-LDS) friends in his hopes for the hereafter.

Donald C. Scott and his wife, Louise, had corresponded with him ever since their climb of Navajo Mountain in 1919, recalling their trips together and keeping up on family news. The Scotts came to visit Dave and Ruth nearly every year following the war as part of their business and pleasure trips out West. They were less sanguine than Dave about the transformation of the canyon country, especially as the pace of change accelerated after World War II. "How unattractive all this geiger-counter buzzing over the areas which were still so noble and unspoiled when we traveled through them," Donald Scott remarked in 1955. Two years later, he told Dave that he "read with some horror of the plans for the Glen Canyon Dam and the roads and towns which will intrude upon that lovely wilderness, to say nothing of the flooding of that beautiful canyon."[22]

Rust, however, generally supported economic activity that might better the lives of local people, such as improved roads to link the communities of his homeland. He never joined some of his clients in protesting the progress that was coming to the canyon country. He had no objection to the Echo Park and Split Mountain dams that were proposed for Dinosaur National Monument in the early 1950s, telling river historian Dock Marston "am not interested in 'Dam' controversy." Nor did he seem to have qualms about the Glen Canyon dam, even though it would flood the stretch of river he had guided on from 1923 to 1939. He felt that the new reservoir would be a suitably scenic replacement for the flooded canyon, and would give many more people the opportunity to see the desert canyons than had ever floated the river. Perhaps Dave envisioned inquisitive tourists boating along the lake's shoreline, investigating side canyons and stopping to admire the newly accessible scenery. This was, in fact, how many people traveled the lake in its first few decades. Rust would likely have taken a less appreciative view of Lake Powell in its current form, which, at some seasons at least, seems to be a party destination for thousands of adrenaline-charged youths who take to its waters in powerboats and jet skis.[23]

Dave, in any event, marveled at the current age's technological progress. In March 1962 he expressed to Barbara Ekker, a friend from Hanksville who shared his love of history, his amazement at the feat of astronaut John Glenn: "The entire account is so fabulous, unbelievable! To orbit the earth 3 times in one day. What can Columbus say? Or Lindberg even?"[24] At the age of eighty-eight, he could still let his mind soar in astonishment and wonder.

In November 1962, a few weeks before her eightieth birthday, Ruth fell in the backyard of their home and suffered a broken hip. This was her second such injury; she had fractured her other hip in 1948. She came through a consequent operation well and spent several weeks in the hospital. Dave noted on December 1 that she was "improving splendid." He was faced with living on his own for a while, which he managed with help from his daughter Blanche, who drove down from Salt Lake City nearly every day. He fully expected Ruth to recover. For many years he had told his children that he was "preparing Ruth to be a widow," since she was eight years younger than he. Ruth continued to improve, and in January Blanche helped her move to a convalescent home. Family members wrote and offered to pay the expense. Dave continued to live on his own. Toward the middle of the month, he became sick from eating a meal he had left out too long; Blanche took him to the hospital, but he remained weak. After a few days he asked to be transferred to the same nursing home as Ruth so they could be together, for he missed her a great deal. But on January 21, Ruth died unexpectedly.

Her passing was a great loss to Dave. They had been close companions for sixty years. He still referred to her as "The Queen of our Family," recognizing her long and stable influence on him and on their children. At the funeral service, Dave turned to Blanche and reminded her that he had hoped to precede Ruth to their reward. With a slight smile, he said, "I can't believe that Mother would go and take a trip without me."[25]

With no family members in town, he had only Blanche's visits to look forward to. Throughout his life Dave expressed in his writing a fear of too much solitude; one of his poems repeated the refrain "Oh! save me from living alone." Ruth, as her children and grandchildren recalled, supplied the Rust home with much of its warmth. It seemed as though Dave was loath to live without her.

On January 27, 1963, still at the nursing home, Dave passed away shortly after going to bed. His last days' thoughts are not recorded, but they must have been filled with hope and anticipation as well as with sadness. His faith had always been that a new life with Ruth awaited him, and that they would be joined, in proper time, by their whole family. His last letters to his canyoneer friends suggest that he also anticipated renewing his acquaintance with the men and women with whom he spent many fine days on the trails of the Plateau Province.

In his evenings along the Colorado River in Glen Canyon, when dinner and camp chores were through and the golden light spilled out over the cliffs, Rust often liked to read to his trip mates from some favorite geological or literary work. One of these was Henry van Dyke's poem, "God of the Open Air." It ended with a fitting wish:

> Let me once more have sight
> Of the deep sky and the far-smiling land,—
> Then gently fall on sleep,
> And breathe my body back to Nature's care,
> My spirit out to thee, God of the open air.

If Dave felt in 1956 that he could journey in essence back to the Grand Canyon on an errand of compassion, then surely at times he directed his thoughts to other canyons and mesas he had known, and to the men and women with whom he had shared the trail. No doubt many of his clients joined him in this remembrance. They had come west for adventure, and had found it in the unending wild country; but they were equally drawn to the company of Dave Rust—a dusty cowboy with his eyes set on the distant view, a native son with a thirst for the greater world.

EPILOGUE | *The Wonder around the Bend*

> I shall never forget the night we came down to the river by
> Bullfrog, I believe, and camped on a point some miles above
> California Bar. The moon turned the muddy Colorado to the
> brightest silver, fringed by the green cottonwoods and other
> growth in the talus, and all protected by the silent uprising cliffs.
>
> DONALD C. SCOTT
> From a 1957 letter to Dave Rust

AT A NAMELESS POINT on the North Rim of the Grand
Canyon near the head of Bright Angel Creek, a small wooden sign points the
way to the Old Bright Angel Trail—a narrow footpath that plunges down a
steep hillslope through thickets of manzanita and cat's-claw acacia. Underneath
a nearby ponderosa pine lies a coil of rusted steel cable, hinting at the origins of
the trail. Another faint track leads back from the rim into the forest, past a venerable aspen tree bearing the date "3 May 1907" carved into its bark. This path
winds for three miles over meadows and through blowdowns to the former site
of the Grand Canyon Transportation Company's little outfitting cabin in Fuller
Canyon. These remains tell of Dave Rust's and Dee Woolley's dream to link the
opposite rims of the Grand Canyon with a tourist trail.

Few hikers venture down the old path, which was officially abandoned in
1928 when the Park Service completed the North Kaibab Trail through Roaring
Springs Canyon. Those who linger here on a summer's day can revel in the solitude, the wind in the tall pines punctuated by a rumble off to the southwest as a
thunderhead builds over the canyon. The deserted atmosphere at this trailhead
contrasts with the activity at Bright Angel Point a few miles away, where buses full
of tourists pull up to the Grand Canyon Lodge and cars fill the parking lot where
the Wylie tent camp once stood. Pickups jockey for spaces in the designated park
campground; overflow sites back toward Jacob Lake accommodate those who
arrive too late. Hikers and mule riders converge on the North Kaibab trailhead,
which originates at a good-sized parking lot of its own; a few lucky backpackers
carry the coveted permit that allows them to camp within the canyon.

Today's park crowds exceed anything that Rust and Woolley could have
hoped for in 1909, when Dave hauled his first paying passengers across the Colorado in his creaking steel tramcar. Nearly three hundred thousand people drove

to the North Rim in 2004,[1] and cabins at Phantom Ranch, which replaced Rust's Camp at the bottom of the canyon, are typically booked two years in advance. But Park Service planners intended this outcome almost from the beginning. Stephen Mather and Horace Albright envisioned tourists speeding over good roads to arrive at key assembly points on the rim, where they could take in the splendor of America's greatest natural wonder. Park administrators ever since have worked hard to fulfill this dream—and to cope with the consequences. Today, a new management plan envisions shuttle buses taking tourists to the facilities at Bright Angel Point and out to Cape Royal, relieving summertime traffic congestion; Zion National Park already has gone this route.[2]

In the remaining wild sections of the park, the hardiest hikers can wander among the rocks in relative solitude. But Rust's weeklong rides along the North Rim would hardly be possible today. Camping permits are strictly rationed, and roads have replaced the cattlemen's trails that once led to Skidoo Point, Point Sublime, and Powell Plateau. Pack strings still take supplies down to Phantom Ranch, and mule rides depart daily from both rims, but other than these permitted uses, the old ways have departed.

Elsewhere in Rust's "Wilderness Park"—the canyon lands of the Colorado Plateau that he so loved—adventure seekers now probe every slot canyon and ascend improbable cliffs. Detailed topographic maps and dozens of trail guides lead the modern, satellite-guided explorer to hidden arches and rock art sites. Roads and jeep tracks reach within a few miles of almost every mesa and canyon. Visitors who chafe at having to walk can choose from a variety of capable vehicles to shrink the distances. Some employ cunningly designed rock-crawling machines to tackle boulder-filled creek beds and steep slickrock, sometimes performing before a cheering audience. The region's breathtaking red-rock spires and thousand-foot dropoffs form a rugged backdrop to advertise sport-utility vehicles—beckoning the well-equipped wanderer to find his personal paradise. (The canyons, though, are rarely as unpopulated as the ads suggest.)

Where Rust and Woolley once wondered how to get the world to come see their country, today's public officials grapple with crowd control. Tourism has broken the bounds that Rust took for granted, when "sagebrushers" in their Model As set up tents in out-of-the-way spots and a cabin at Bryce or Zion represented the peak of luxury. Even the airplanes that Rust predicted would someday fly across the Grand Canyon now are regulated, and the visitor to Point Sublime finds that aircraft noise is audible seventy-six percent of the daylight hours.[3]

Change is the constant accompaniment to Western civilization, as Rust well knew. Even in the 1930s he observed the growing mechanization of travel, and was willing to grant that most tourists would keep themselves tethered to their automobiles. "Every traveler has a right to his own attitude, just as he will reap his own reward," he wrote in his essay "Genuine Travelers." But he clearly preferred the greater quest that waited out in the far distances. Four decades into the twentieth century, when he was conducting the last of his backcountry excursions, it was still possible to saddle a horse and head out into a little-known territory of dry washes and soaring sandstone cliffs, seeking out places nowhere described in print. There was a tremendous sense of discovery that awaited the adventurer. Ken Sleight, one of Rust's postwar successors in Glen Canyon, observed how his customers were "always in wonder of what lay around the next bend."[4] Rust's gift was to share these discoveries with many others who came to this region not quite knowing what they would find.

Glen Canyon, of course, underwent a complete transformation, and the old-timers such as Sleight who remember the river voyage often wonder why it was allowed to happen. The dam was built with little controversy, but the clamor from its opponents has built steadily ever since. At least two citizen organizations are trying to attract support for the notion of unplugging the dam and restoring as many of Glen's wonders as can be resurrected. The lost canyon has become an icon of a vanished Eden. Why did no one anticipate this in the 1920s or 1930s? The answer partly lies in the different attitude Americans had in those years toward the ideal of progress. Great reclamation projects symbolized all that was good about America—a can-do attitude that held that the power of nature should be harnessed to help humanity. Indeed, the Progressive movement, of which Dave counted himself part, stipulated that resources were to be used, not fenced off.

Many of Rust's fellow Utahns seemed to harbor this apparent contradiction—a fond regard for the wild country they grew up in, all the while welcoming the changes that inevitably displaced the old ways. Was it myopia, or simply a calm acceptance of that which must be? While many of the canyon country's native citizens have a deep appreciation for the landscape, they have listened to the stories of their elders and they see the country in a different light than outsiders. Often in their extended family there are those who remember when few or none of the roads were paved, when a doctor was a day's journey away, when fresh fruit and vegetables were a rare enjoyment in winter, or when floods washed out a whole town's water supply. Progress had tangible benefits for the citizens of Kanab, Hanksville, and Escalante.

Roads, dams, and mines were not the only great changes to come over the canyon country, however. A less visible, though equally profound, transformation had been quietly taking place during Rust's lifetime, and it was his hero, John Wesley Powell, who set it in motion. Powell, as scholars have observed, came to the Plateau Province not primarily for adventure, but to increase mankind's understanding of it. He sought to study the region's topography, stratigraphic relationships, geologic processes, irrigation prospects, and native peoples. The crude and incomplete measurements that his untrained men obtained in 1869 and afterward (Wallace Stegner would call the whole show, not unkindly, "Major Powell's Amateur Hour") were but a first step to remove the region from obscurity. The Powell Survey and its successor, the U.S. Geological Survey, produced the first topographic sheets that pinned down features from the Book Cliffs to the Uinkaret Plateau with reasonable (for the day) accuracy. Rust would use the maps for many years; they would not be supplanted, in some cases, until the 1950s.

Maps made the land comprehensible. The geologists, historians, botanists, and archaeologists who followed added a layer of intellectual depth to what was otherwise mere scenery. As ordinary citizens—the weekend explorers of the canyon country—avail themselves of this knowledge, they find reason to cherish and protect the landscape, not just as a backdrop for thrilling adventure, but as a fascinating exposition of the earth's history and of humans' attempts to settle it.

Rust once told an interviewer that he had "come out of the wilderness," referring to his emergence from his family's precarious existence in the frontier settlements of south-central Utah. He meant a figurative emergence, too, as he discovered the world of human knowledge that existed over the horizon. The hills and hollows that once had promised only a stinting existence now offered intriguing insights into the earth's slow evolution, as well as the sense of continuity that comes from knowing its human history.

In his thirty-three-year career as a guide and outfitter, Rust never led a trip outside of the Colorado Plateau. His painted hills and dusty deserts offered enough for a lifetime of contemplation. He began his career building trails and lobbying for roads that would smooth the path to the North Rim for thousands of travelers. He ended his work by taking one young man on a three-week pack trip through the Escalante River canyons, which even then was a refuge from the hurried pace of automobile tourists. Rust's last trips had become elemental—a trusted saddle horse for each rider, a pack mule or two, a simple bedroll, and a basic kitchen. There were spectacular vistas, of course, and exciting discoveries as they rounded a bend in the canyon to behold an elegant natural bridge. But many of his camps held no high glories. Settling in by a lake on the Aquarius, the dark spruce forest edging a starlit sky, the nighttime air spreading campfire smoke low across the water—these quiet moments brought out one's deeper longings.

A man seeking to make a big showing in the Utah canyon country of the early twentieth century had few options: gather together a significant cattle herd, as Al Scorup did in the 1880s, or locate a major mineral discovery, as Charlie Steen did in the 1950s, or rise in the world of politics and business like Dave's mentor, Dee Woolley. Dave Rust dabbled in all of these pursuits, but none became anything more than an avocation. He earned little more from his guiding than from his placer and hard-rock prospects, but that was of small concern. It was the landscape of the Plateau Province that commanded his attention. He was intent on mining a rich vein of knowledge that ran through the country. That single-minded, lifelong pursuit drew him into the company of his many distinguished guests and immeasurably enriched his own life. In this quest, and in these friendships, he found his mother lode.

Rust left little mark on the land. He seems not to have chiseled any inscriptions on canyon walls, and his prospect holes never turned into profitable mines. Few heard the echoes of his horses' hooves in those far-off canyons. His influence was on the minds of those who, as he said of Clarence Dutton, had eyes to see and a heart to understand.

The trails of the mind still beckon. Although the wilderness of today is much more circumscribed and regulated, scenes of great beauty—of awfulness and sublimity, to use an old phrase—still await the traveler who is willing to push a few miles beyond the tourist centers. And anyone with a little curiosity can come to understand, at least in broad terms, the long and fascinating story of the Colorado Plateau's creation. If the scientists' language seems a bit arcane at times, one can always walk out to Cape Final on the North Rim of the Grand Canyon, or climb Mount Ellen in the Henry Mountains, or hike up Barrier Canyon to the Great Gallery, and simply stare in wonder at these amazing pictures. If Rust's scientist-heroes have removed some of the mystery from the landscape, they have also added richness to its story. The Plateau Province that Dave Rust knew has changed, but the opportunity to come to a deep understanding of the land and its people, as he would have wished us to do, has only increased.

Notes

Full citations to both published and unpublished works are given in the Bibliography. Web pages cited were last accessed on May 28, 2007.

ABBREVIATIONS FOR MANUSCRIPT COLLECTIONS

EDW-BYU   Edwin D. Woolley Jr. and Erastus Snow Family Collection, L. Tom Perry Special Collections, Harold B. Lee Library, Brigham Young University, Provo, Utah.

EDW-RC   Edwin Dilworth Woolley [Jr.] Papers, within the David Dexter Rust Collection, Church Archives, The Church of Jesus Christ of Latter-day Saints, Salt Lake City, Utah.

EDW-SUU   Edwin D. Woolley Jr. Collection, Gerald R. Sherratt Library, Southern Utah University, Cedar City, Utah.

KC   Emery Kolb Collection, Cline Library, Northern Arizona University, Flagstaff.

NPS-ENM   National Park Service, Canyonlands National Park, Moab, Utah: "Correspondence, Escalante Proposed Area."

ORM   Otis R. Marston Papers, Huntington Library, San Marino, Calif.

USHS   Utah State Historical Society, Salt Lake City.

RC   David Dexter Rust Collection, Church Archives, The Church of Jesus Christ of Latter-day Saints, Salt Lake City, Utah.

PROLOGUE

1. Merrill, "Dave Rust, Lover of the Grand Canyon," 473.

2. Neither Rust nor Scott kept a contemporaneous journal of this trip, although they each recalled the summit scene on Navajo Mountain in their correspondence and other writings. See, especially, note 3 below.

3. Donald C. Scott to Rust, April 26, 1920 (RC, box 5, fd. 3).

4. The "Plateau Province" was John Wesley Powell's term for what we now call the Colorado Plateau, a 140,000-square-mile region centering roughly on Glen Canyon and the lower San Juan River. A good introductory description is provided by Annabelle Foos in "Geology of the Colorado Plateau," www2.nature.nps.gov/geology/education/foos/plateau.pdf. Geographers have refined the Colorado Plateau's boundaries since Powell's day. In this book I use "canyon lands" to denote the Canyonlands Section of the Colorado Plateau, the central part

of the province that includes the classic exposures of Navajo, Wingate, Entrada, and Cedar Mesa sandstones.

5. Rust proudly recalled his efforts at getting an education in his various journals and unpublished essays, including "Private Journal—Deseret" (January 1, 1901); "Dan Duncan," a set of autobiographical sketches; and "Genuine Travelers," an unpublished essay from the 1930s, when Rust was looking back on his career and the changes that had come to the tourist business.

6. Henry Dodge Freeman, one of Dave's favorite clients, told this to Harold Rust, Dave's grandson, in July 1983 (Harold Rust, interview with author, July 26, 1999).

7. Merrill, "Dave Rust, Lover of the Grand Canyon," 473.

8. Brew, "Donald Scott and His Collection."

9. Fraser, "Memoranda of a Trip," July 30, 1914. George C. Fraser was Rust's companion on six trips from 1914 to 1930 (see Fraser, *Journeys in the Canyon Lands*).

CHAPTER 1

1. Quoted letters: Jane Fraser to Dave Rust, August 2, 1921 (RC, box 3, fd. 1); "Le Colonel" [an unknown correspondent] to Rust, June 20, 1957 (RC, box 2, fd. 6).

2. Rust, "A Deer Hunt." The youthful writing in this undated essay suggests he may have written it while attending high school in Richfield. He places the incident as six years before he wrote the essay, which would put his age at no more than thirteen. Boys started early in the outback in those days.

3. Rust, "Seven Decades of Dave Rust." Quotations in this chapter not otherwise attributed are from this unpublished autobiographical essay.

4. Carvalho, *Incidents of Travel and Adventure in the Far West*, ch. 29.

5. George Smith Rust's early years are sketchily documented; my sources are "Seven Decades of Dave Rust"; a brief account in the Sons of Utah Pioneers' *Conquerers of the West*; and Ethel Jensen's *Beneath the Casing Rock*. Jensen lived with George and Eliza Rust for a time and also interviewed Dave in the 1930s.

6. George S. Rust's mineral find is briefly (and variously) described in Harris, *The Towns of Tintic*, 16–17, and in Dixon, *Peteetneet Town*, 23; it is also mentioned in a retrospective article titled "Utah Thrives on Tintic Mineral Discoveries" (*Millard County Chronicle*, Fillmore, Utah, March 11, 1937). None of these accounts, nor those in the Rust family records (such as in Jensen's *Beneath the Casing Rock*), give the same story. George Rust continued his mineral quest for years and was secretary of several mining companies operating in Nevada in the early 1900s.

7. Jensen, *Beneath the Casing Rock*, 120.

8. Local practice at the time was to call the stretch of the Fremont River below Fruita the "Dirty Devil." This usage persisted into the 1900s; today, it is applied only to the river below Hanksville.

9. Capitol Gorge, or Capitol Wash as local people called it, was used as the main route through the Waterpocket Fold until 1962, when Highway 24 was constructed along the Fre-

mont River. There was a shorter route via Grand Wash, but it involved more crossings of the Fremont River. See Jensen, *Beneath the Casing Rock*, 184.

10. Hunt, *Geology and Geography of the Henry Mountains*, 19.

11. Rust, "Dan Duncan."

12. Monnett, "The Mormon Church and Its Private School System in Utah"; Danielson, "History of Education in Sevier County."

13. Rust, "Dan Duncan." A collection of sketches and aphorisms intended for use in a novel he never completed, "Dan Duncan" contains many seemingly autobiographical references and descriptions of the landscape around Caineville and the Henry Mountains.

14. Dutton, *Geology of the High Plateaus of Utah*, 286–87; Stegner, "Coda: Wilderness Letter," in Stegner, *Where the Bluebird Sings*.

15. Fraser, *Journeys in the Canyon Lands*, 86.

16. Jensen, *Beneath the Casing Rock*, 165–66. Rust corroborated the story of his making a fiddle in "Seven Decades of Dave Rust," though in less detail.

17. Rust, "I Came Out of the Wilderness."

18. Nora Rust Mickelson, interview with author, March 21, 2007.

19. Rust, "I Came Out of the Wilderness"; Jensen, *Beneath the Casing Rock*, 190, 191.

20. Rust, "I Came Out of the Wilderness."

21. Snow, *Rainbow Views*, 288.

22. Hunt, *Geology and Geography of the Henry Mountains*, 19.

23. Stegner, *Where the Bluebird Sings to the Lemonade Springs*, 20–21.

CHAPTER 2

1. Stanton, *Hoskaninni Papers*, 79n5.

2. Baker, *Trail on the Water*, 70.

3. Crampton, *Standing Up Country*, 134.

4. Will Rust inscription: Crampton, *Historical Sites in Glen Canyon*, fig. 22; mining boom in 1896: Crampton, *Outline History of Glen Canyon*, 30–31; Ed Meskin: William Rust, "The Story of My Life."

5. Crampton, *Standing Up Country*, 134.

6. Dave's work in Glen Canyon with his brothers is detailed in William Rust's memoir, "The Story of My Life," and in Dave's testimony in the Colorado River Bed Case (Utah State Attorney General, Records of the Colorado River Case, 1929–1931, 4238–39).

7. Stanton, *Hoskaninni Papers*, 102.

8. Ned Chaffin, interview with author, Torrey, Utah, May 28, 2005.

9. Stanton's railroad and mining ventures are described in Crampton, *Standing Up Country*, 131–34 and 138–41. C. Gregory Crampton, who edited Stanton's *Hoskaninni Papers*, noted that Stanton based his hopes on samples from older gravel bars above river level, which indeed contained coarser gold particles, and which "were in fact the most profitable placer areas in the canyon" (Stanton, *Hoskaninni Papers*, 70n5).

10. Rust to Otis R. Marston, February 4, 1948 (ORM, box 202, fd. 18).

11. Rowing upstream: Colorado River Case, 4240; Will Rust's trip: William Rust, "The Story of My Life."

12. Rust to Marston, May 7, 1950 (ORM, box 202, fd. 19).

13. Rust, "Boating on the Colorado."

14. Quoted in Ethel Jensen, *Beneath the Casing Rock*, 199. No date is given for the poem.

15. Crampton quote: *Standing Up Country*, 135; Rust quote: "Dan Duncan"; Powell crewmember quote: W. D. Johnson Jr., "Powell's Colorado River Exploring Expedition, May 10, 1872" ("Correspondence," *Deseret Evening News* [Salt Lake City], August 14, 1872); Rust's interest in Glen Canyon: Merrill, "Dave Rust, Lover of the Grand Canyon."

16. Teaching certificate, Emery school (RC, box 10, fd. 3).

17. David Rust to Eliza Rust, August 15, 1900, in Jensen, *Beneath the Casing Rock*, 211. Dave's notes suggest that he may also have visited Seattle and worked in logging camps in Washington during this trip.

18. Rust, "Private Journal—Deseret."

19. Brigham Young Academy, *The White and Blue*, vol. 5, nos. 2–12 (1901–2).

20. John Dewey, "My Pedagogic Creed," *The School Journal*, vol. 54, no. 3 (January 16, 1897), 77–80; reprinted in *John Dewey: The Early Works, 1882–1898*.

21. Ibid.

22. Rust's move to Fredonia and meeting Ruth is drawn from Ruth Woolley Rust's unpublished memoirs.

23. Chamberlain, "Sketch of the Life of Edwin Dilworth Woolley, Jr.," 6.

24. "President Visits Utah, Idaho and Montana," *Eureka* (Utah) *Reporter*, June 5, 1903.

25. Missionary certificate, LDS Church, August 13, 1903 (RC, box 10, fd. 3).

26. Ruth Woolley Rust to Mrs. E. D. Woolley, October 19, 1903 (RC, box 11, fd. 9).

27. Davis's most influential popular article, "The Rivers and Valleys of Pennsylvania," appeared in *National Geographic Magazine* for July 1889. His legacy is discussed in Ranney, *Carving Grand Canyon*, 73–76.

CHAPTER 3

1. Granger, *Arizona Place Names*, 71.

2. Powell's *Exploration of the Colorado River* (1875) gives "Kaibab" as the plateau's Indian name, but his preliminary report of April 30, 1874 goes into more detail: "... with a certain tribe in Northern Arizona, kaivw is the word signifying mountain; a-vwi' means reclining or lying down; Kai'-vav-wi, a mountain lying down, is the name for a plateau. A great plateau north of the Grand Cañon of the Colorado is called by them Kai'-vav-wi, and the small tribe of Indians inhabiting it are Kai'-vav-wits" (Powell, *Report of Explorations in 1873*, 26). Thus "Kaibab Plateau" is, in its original meaning, redundant.

3. Dutton, *Tertiary History of the Grand Cañon District*, 140.

4. Dutton's influence on generations of Grand Canyon lovers is celebrated in Stegner, *Beyond the Hundredth Meridian*, 164–74, and Pyne, *How the Canyon Became Grand*, 68–87.

5. Chamberlain, "Sketch of the Life of Edwin Dilworth Woolley, Jr.," 8.

6. Cody trip: Woodbury, *History of Southern Utah*, 190–91; Talmadge trip: Carroll, *History of Kane County*, 168–69; school outing: Chamberlain, "Sketch of the Life of Edwin Dilworth Woolley, Jr.," 17.

7. Michael F. Anderson's *Living at the Edge* gives a thorough account of the early South Rim tourist entrepreneurs.

8. "Articles of Incorporation of the Grand Canyon Transportation Company" (EDW-BYU, box 1, fd. 11).

9. The company's certificate and plat sketch was filed in book 308-9-10 of the Coconino County Recorder's Office. A copy is in the Rust Collection, box 11, fd. 10, and is shown as fig. 5 in Anderson, "Grand Canyon National Park Toll Roads and Trails," in Anderson, *A Gathering of Grand Canyon Historians*. Anderson shows the Guffy-Henry plat as fig. 2 in the same article.

10. Chamberlain, "Sketch of the Life of Edwin Dilworth Woolley, Jr.," 6–7.

11. Matthes, "Breaking a Trail through Bright Angel Canyon."

12. "Hoyt's Point" is shown on a sketch map of the trail that was prepared by a surveyor (RC, box 11, fd. 10). The map shows their trail zigzagging down into Bright Angel Canyon, the upper part of which they called "Marble Canyon."

13. T. C. Hoyt to Rust, June 26, 1903 (RC, box 1, fd. 8).

14. One of the oddities of Grand Canyon nomenclature is that the original Bright Angel Trail ran on the opposite side of the canyon from Bright Angel Creek. Today, the name is used for the trail leading down from the South Rim to Indian Gardens, which was originally developed by Ralph Cameron and Pete Berry as the Bright Angel Toll Road, and its extension on down Pipe Creek to the Colorado River and Phantom Ranch. See Anderson, *Living at the Edge*, 86.

15. Forest Supervisor to Commissioner, General Land Office, November 22, 1904 (EDW-SUU, box 4, fd. 1).

16. George Sutherland to E. D. Woolley, April 28, 1905; Gifford Pinchot to Hon. George Sutherland, May 6, 1905; Overton W. Price to Lorum Pratt, Forest Supervisor, Fredonia, Arizona, May 29, 1905 (EDW-RC, box 11, fd. 6).

17. Newspaper coverage: Reilly, *Lee's Ferry*, 197; Senators' trips: Woodbury, *History of Southern Utah*, 192.

18. Rust to "Mother & folks," April 30, 1905 (RC, box 11, fd. 9).

19. J. S. Amundsen to Rust, April 25, 1906 (RC, box 1, fd. 9).

20. Rust, "Grand Canyon Journal," September 19, 1906. His journal gives no particulars of the other men at work on the tram.

21. Rust, "Grand Canyon Journal." The journal entries are dated from July 4, 1906, to November 20, 1909, becoming more sporadic in 1908 and 1909, with a final paragraph dated December 31, 1910, reviewing that summer's activities. Subsequent excerpts in this chapter not otherwise identified are also from this journal.

22. Bowman & Company, May 19, 1905, to Zions Cooperative Mercantile Institution, Salt Lake City (RC, box 11, fd. 7).

23. Trent Engineering & Machine Co. to E. D. Woolley, Jr., August 22, 1905 (RC, box 11, fd. 7).

24. Rust interview, probably by Ethel Jensen, 1936 (EDW-BYU, box 1, fd. 8). An article in *Popular Mechanics* for October 1917, titled "Cableway at Bottom of World's Greatest Gorge," said that the men divided the cable into "7 pairs of coils which were strapped to 7 pack horses."

25. "Blueprint for Aerial Tramway," Trent Engineering & Company (EDW-SUU, box 4, fd. 1).

26. Dee Woolley's grandson, Julius Dalley, remarked to the author that Rust "had to be brilliant" to have successfully installed the cable tram. At the very least he drew on the same native insight that many miners and river-bank engineers displayed in frontier settings. Julius Dalley, interview with author, October 23, 2005.

CHAPTER 4

1. Rust, "Grand Canyon Journal," December 20, 1906, to January 25, 1907. Subsequent excerpts in this chapter are from this journal.

2. In 2003 the U.S. Board on Geographic Names officially changed Nail Canyon to Naile Canyon to reflect Nagle's Anglicized spelling of his name (Minutes, U.S. Board on Geographic Names, October 1, 2003, http://geonames.usgs.gov). Zane Grey, in his 1908 book *Last of the Plainsmen*, gave a more colorful explanation, describing the canyon's walls as resembling an old-fashioned nail: "long, straight and square sided."

3. Rust to E. D. Woolley, January 21, 1907. Collection of Blanche Rasmussen.

4. The Forest Service apparently did not issue a permit for occupancy of the two-acre site until April 1911, suggesting that such matters were fairly informal at the time. A copy of the company's "Special Use Permit," issued by Supervisor James Pelton, is in the Rust Collection, box 10, fd. 1.

5. Rust to E. D. Woolley, March 9, 1907 (EDW-SUU, box 4, fd. 1).

6. Ruth Woolley Rust, Memoirs, 15.

7. Rust did not record the exact length of the cable used, but the Park Service's "Swinging Bridge" that replaced the tramway in the same location measured five hundred feet between its supports, according to a June 1921 article in *National Geographic Magazine* (Chalmers, "The Grand Canyon Bridge," 647).

8. Rust to Harry Aleson, December 1957 (USHS, Harry LeRoy Aleson papers, box 12, fd. 1).

9. Reilly, *Lee's Ferry*, 205. The hybrids are sometimes called *cattalo*, but Jones spelled it *catalo*.

10. Kolb, *Through the Grand Canyon*, 137.

11. Rust, "Notes Gathered While Working in the Tourist Business."

12. Woolley to E. S. Clark, September 4, 1907, October 14, 1907, and February 5, 1908 (EDW-SUU, box 4, fd. 1). Historian Michael F. Anderson's books *Living at the Edge* and *Polishing the Jewel* recount Ralph Cameron's frequent run-ins with the railroad and federal officials at the Grand Canyon.

13. May, "The United Order Movement," *Utah History Encyclopedia* (http://historytogo. utah.gov/utah_chapters/pioneers_and_cowboys/theunitedordermovement.html).

14. Ruth Woolley Rust, Memoirs, 16–17.

15. "Alvin Heaton Arrested," *Richfield* (Utah) *Reaper*, May 7, 1908; "Orderville Man Found Guilty," *Richfield Reaper*, September 7, 1922 (reprise of case).

16. Ruth Woolley Rust, Memoirs, 16–17.

17. Author interview with Joseph C. Rust, July 10, 1999.

18. United States Civil Service Commission, "Departmental Service—Forest Ranger Examination" (1908). Forest History Society, Durham, NC (www.lib.duke.edu/forest/ Research/usfscoll/people/Ranger_Life/ranger08.html).

19. Rust, "Notes Gathered While Working in the Tourist Business."

20. Ibid.

21. Rust to Grand Canyon Transportation Company, May 5, 1908 (RC, box 5, fd. 4).

22. Rust to Otis R. Marston, April 29, 1954 (ORM, box 202, fd. 20).

23. Rust, "I Came Out of the Wilderness."

24. Muir, "The Grand Cañon of the Colorado." The essay was reprinted in Muir's 1916 book *Our National Parks*.

25. Rust to "Ma & Pa" (Mr. & Mrs. George S. Rust), April 30, 1909. Collection of Blanche Rasmussen.

26. Ruth Woolley Rust, Memoirs, 18.

27. This appears to be the Forest Service's ranger cabin at Harvey Meadow, two miles north of Bright Angel Point. It was occupied by "Uncle Jim" Owens but served as a gathering place for others using the Kaibab. Frank Onstott was a ranching partner with Dee Woolley.

28. Alter, *Through the Heart of the Scenic West*, 216, 220.

29. Anderson, *Living at the Edge*, 135; Alter, "Utah Recovers the Grand Canyon of Arizona."

Chapter 5

1. Woodbury, *History of Southern Utah*, 193. Accounts of the motorists' trip are also given in Carroll, *History of Kane County*, 95–98, and Chamberlain, "Sketch of the Life of Edwin Dilworth Woolley, Jr.," 9–11.

2. Gordon Woolley to Edwin D. Woolley Jr., May 23, 1909 (EDW-BYU, box 1, fd. 2).

3. Edwin D. Woolley Jr. to Gordon Woolley, n.d. (EDW-BYU, box 1, fd. 10).

4. For a map of the Woolley-Rust wagon route, see Anderson, *Living at the Edge*, 131.

5. Rust, "From Salt Lake to the Grand Canyon." Subsequent quotations about the Woolleys' trip are from this article. The first airplanes reached the South Rim in 1919 and may have flown across the Canyon at that time. See "Grand Canyon Aviation History," Grand Canyon Pioneers Society *Bulletin*, vol. 6, no. 10 (October 2002).

6. Pomeroy, *In Search of the Golden West*, 152; James, *In and Around the Grand Canyon* and *The Grand Canyon, How to See It*.

7. Anderson, *Living at the Edge*, 137.

8. Rust, "I Came Out of the Wilderness."

9. May, *Zane Grey: Romancing the West*, 49.

10. Rust, "Grand Canyon Journal," March 29, 1907.

11. Rust to Otis R. Marston, Sept. 24, 1960 (ORM, box 202, fd. 20); second quotation is from Rust, "Genuine Travelers."

12. Zane Grey, letter to Lina Grey, cited in Pauly, *Zane Grey*, 84. Rust never made such a claim in his journals or correspondence; Thunder River was most likely discovered by prospectors in 1872 during a minor gold rush to the Kanab Creek area (Huntoon, "Opening of Deer Creek"). Perhaps Dave was indulging Grey just a little with a good story.

13. Rust, "Genuine Travelers." Stephen May, in *Zane Grey: Romancing the West* (59–60) places Rust on this trip, but this seems unlikely, as Rust's later recollections make no mention of traveling with Grey.

14. Zane Grey to Rust, January 2, 1910 (RC, box 4, fd. 7).

15. In his unpublished essay "Genuine Travelers," Rust observed that Zane Grey indignantly refused to join Rust's and Nathaniel Galloway's 1908 grizzly-trapping adventure, yet "he did not hesitate to shoot defenseless lions which had been put up a tree by a pack of blood-hounds."

16. Zane Grey to Rust, December 4 [1910] (RC, box 4, fd. 7).

17. Navajo trip: Zane Grey to Rust, January 15, 1911 (RC, box 4, fd. 7); Rust to Marston, Sept. 24, 1960 (ORM, box 202, fd. 20).

18. Joseph C. Rust, "From the Dirty Devil to the Bright Angel."

19. "Camp Fire Dinner for Buffalo Jones," *New York Times*, December 5, 1909.

20. Webb, *Call of the Colorado*, 87.

21. Nathaniel Galloway to Rust, December 7, 1907, and February 7, 1908 (Gary Topping papers, USHS, box 9, fd. 4). Rust kept these charming letters and sent them to Dock Marston, who transcribed them.

22. Rust to Marston, February 4, 1948 (ORM, box 202, fd. 18); Galloway to Rust, November 22, 1909 (P. T. Reilly Collection, Cline Library, Northern Arizona University, box 7, fd. 101).

23. Rust to Marston: see note 22. Brown's drowning: Ghiglieri and Myers, *Over the Edge: Death in Grand Canyon*, 139–40.

24. Suran, *With the Wings of an Angel*, chapter 2.

25. Ellsworth L. Kolb to Rust (RC, box 4, fd. 8).

26. Ghiglieri and Myers, *Over the Edge: Death in Grand Canyon*, 186–87.

27. Rust described his trip with Helen White Sargent in "Grand Canyon Journal," December 31, 1910 (RC, box 1, fd. 4).

28. Woodbury, in *History of Southern Utah* (114–5) discussed the native peoples' names believed to have been used for Zion Canyon. He pointed out that local Paiute and Shivwits bands used different names for various aspects of the canyon (e.g., *Pahroos* [swift, turbulent stream], or *Unga-timpe pai-ave* [red rock canyon]), and there was rarely a precise correspondence with Anglo nomenclature. In his *Report on the Exploration of the Colorado River* (1875), Powell places his exploration of the Mukuntuweap as 1870, when he actually made the

journey in 1872 (see Stegner, *Beyond the Hundredth Meridian*, 148). Dutton's descriptions are from the *Tertiary History*, 48, 58; Dellenbaugh's from "A New Valley of Wonders," 2.

29. Hinton, "Getting Along," 314.

CHAPTER 6

1. Alter, *Through the Heart of the Scenic West*, 215.

2. Rust, "Journal, Grand Canyon," November 20, 1909 (RC, box 1, fd. 4, vol. 10).

3. Woodbury, "Biotic Relationships of Zion Canyon, Utah."

4. Ruth Woolley Rust, Memoirs, 20.

5. John A. Widtsoe to Rust, April 17, 1911 (RC, box 1, fd. 9).

6. Rust to Edwin D. Woolley, Jr., March 9, 1907 (EDW–SUU, box 4, fd. 1). The law in question was the Act of June 11, 1906.

7. William Slauson Rust, *The Story of My Life*.

8. Ruth Woolley Rust, Memoirs, 19.

9. Carroll, *History of Kane County*, 222.

10. Alter, *Early Utah Journalism*, 94.

11. Mary Woolley Howard to Arthur Woolley, June 26, 1912 (RC, box 1, fd. 10). Mary Woolley was a plural wife of Kanab resident Thomas Chamberlain; she used the pseudonym "Howard" to avoid calling outside attention to the union. This, and the council's election and actions, are discussed in Turley, "Kanab's All Woman Town Council."

12. "Kanab Women Retire Deserving High Honors," *Kane County News*, January 9, 1914. George Fraser included a copy of this article in his "Memoranda of a Trip, 1914," opposite p. 102.

13. Townsend quotation: "Attempting to Make National Park of Kaibab," *Kane County Independent*, September 5, 1912; revenue problems: Carroll, *History of Kane County*, 222; Borlase and Dobson: Alter, *Early Utah Journalism*, 94.

14. Kane County Commission, Minutes, November 11, 1912; Carroll, *History of Kane County*, 204. The record gives no explanation of why Rust's overwhelming election in 1912 was followed by defeat two years later.

15. Opening of high school: Carroll, *History of Kane County*, 201–2; Helen Candland: Stark, "A Vacation and the Nature of God."

16. Carroll, *History of Kane County*, 233–34.

17. "For a Railroad," *Washington Country News* (St. George, Utah), November 4, 1909; "Rio Grande to Extend Its Road," *Carbon County News* (Price, Utah), June 6, 1910.

18. Clarence Dutton noted the character of this forest in his *Tertiary History* (1882, p. 174): "Wherever we go the grand old trees are above us and the grassy lawn beneath our feet. The ground is unencumbered with undergrowth, and the beautiful vistas of open parks, winding glades, and vanishing avenues of tree trunks, the long nodding grasses, and flowers, invite the fancy to wander forever in Paradise."

19. Edwin D. Woolley Jr. to Reed Smoot [1907?] (EDW–SUU, box 4, fd. 2). A board foot is 12 inches by 12 inches by 1 inch; a mature ponderosa might contain five to ten thousand board feet or more.

20. Timothy C. Hoyt to Woolley, September 26, 1909 (EDW–SUU, box 4, fd. 3).

21. "Are After Timber," *Washington County News*, December 15, 1910.

22. "Utah & Grand Canyon Railroad," www.utahrails.net/utah–rrs/utah–rrs–inc–7. php#8702.

23. T. C. Hoyt to Rust, July 10, 1912 (RC, box 1, fd. 10).

24. The timbering plans were reported in various newspapers in Utah, including the following articles in the *Washington County News*: "Railroad Certain, Says Governor Spry," October 30, 1913; "Railroad Will Be Built to Grand Canyon," January 8, 1914; and "Proposed Railroad into Kaibab Forest," October 8, 1914. Graves's quote originally appeared in a magazine called *Railroad Review*. The Bryan bill was featured in the *Washington County News*, September 24, 1914 ("Will Not Recommend Bryan Kaibab Bill"); May's in the *Parowan Times*, February 16, 1921 ("Utah and Utahns").

25. *Salt Lake Tribune*, November 12, 1911.

26. Compare Dutton, *Tertiary History of the Grand Cañon District*, 54.

27. "Auto Road Will Be Built to the Grand Canyon," *Richfield Reaper*, July 17, 1913.

28. Heath, *In the World: The Diaries of Reed Smoot*, 326.

29. Woodbury, *History of Southern Utah*, 195; "Zion Canyon Is Most Beautiful," *Washington County News*, October 30, 1913 (reprint from *Deseret News*).

30. "Wonderful Scenery: Little Zion Canyon," *Washington County News*, November 27, 1913 (reprint from *Salt Lake Tribune*).

31. Parts of the old road are still visible; a two-mile-long section follows upper Jacob Canyon between forest roads 246 and 461 north of Jacob Lake. Watch for a clump of aspen bearing the names of early twentieth-century travelers.

32. Rishel, *Wheels to Adventure*, 71–74.

33. "The Best Way," *Washington County News*, June 18, 1914; "Held Road Meeting," ibid., August 20, 1914.

34. Woolley to E. S. Clark, July 13, 1909 (EDW–SUU, box 4, fd. 3).

35. "Kane County Comes Through," *Kane County News*, Good Roads Issue, January 15, 1915 (copy at EDW–SUU); "Kane County is O.K.; Working for Highway," Chas B. Parry, *Washington County News*, January 21, 1915.

36. "State Convicts to Complete Highway," *Washington County News*, April 8, 1915.

CHAPTER 7

1. Rust, miscellaneous writings (RC, box 11, fd. 4).

2. The primitive road that the Transportation Company built between the cabin and the head of Rust's trail is still visible, though blowdowns and new growth are obscuring it. It exits the southern end of the meadow in Fuller Canyon, climbs to a low divide, and veers east up a shallow draw.

3. Alter, "To the Grand Canyon of Arizona by Auto: The Route and the Road Described," *Salt Lake Tribune*, August 31, 1913. Alter wrote this article and a companion piece on Zion Canyon as an inducement for auto tourists, even though he and his wife had made the journey in a light horse-drawn buggy.

4. Alter, "Utah Recovers the Grand Canyon of Arizona," 913–15.

5. Alter, "A Pilgrimage to Little Zion, The Mukuntuweap," *Salt Lake Tribune*, January 4, 1914.

6. Ibid.

7. "Agreement between D. D. Rust and Nicholas Roosevelt, signed at Kanab Utah, June 24th, 1913" (RC, box 5, fd. 2).

8. Nicholas Roosevelt to Rust, telegram, July 8, 1913 (RC, box 5, fd. 2).

9. Will Rust, "Visit of Col. Theodore Roosevelt" (EDW-BYU, box 2, fd. 12); Nicholas Roosevelt, *Theodore Roosevelt, The Man As I Knew Him*, 112.

10. "Roosevelt in Electrical Storm," *New York Times*, July 17, 1913, quoted in Grand Canyon Historical Society *Bulletin*, vol. 8, no. 3, March 2004; Suran, *With the Wings of an Angel*, chapter 5.

11. Roosevelt wrote of his adventure on the Kaibab in "A Cougar Hunt on the Rim of the Grand Canyon" (*The Outlook*, October 4, 1913). In it he mentions the snafu with the Grand Canyon Transportation Company, but gives no details. More of Nicholas Roosevelt's observations are found in Babbitt, "Across the Painted Desert."

12. May, *Maverick Heart*, 47–48, 53–54.

13. Technically, the Union Pacific Railroad was co-owner, along with Senator William A. Clark, of the San Pedro, Los Angeles & Salt Lake Railroad, also known as the Salt Lake Route. The Union Pacific acquired Clark's interest in the railroad in 1921. See Hemphill, *Union Pacific: Salt Lake Route*.

14. Ensign's story is given in Richards, "A Pleasure Trip in 1914."

15. "Pathfinders Back from Southern Utah," *Salt Lake Tribune*, September 18, 1914.

16. Quoted in Angus Woodbury papers (Marriott Library, University of Utah, box 6, fd. 7). Woodbury was an early ranger-naturalist at Zion who researched the history of Zion, Bryce, and Grand Canyon national parks for his book, *History of Southern Utah*.

17. J. H. Manderfield to Woolley, June 24, 1913 (EDW-SUU, box 4, fd. 6); Manderfield to Rust, March 5–April 19, 1915 (RC, box 1, fd. 10).

18. Rust to Manderfield, April 26, 1915 (EDW-SUU, box 4, fd. 4).

19. Woolley to Manderfield, June 3, 1915, (EDW-SUU, box 4, fd. 4).

20. Manderfield to Rust, March 5, 1915 (RC, box 1, fd. 10).

21. The text of Rust's prospective brochure from 1915 is found in the Rust Collection (box 11, fd. 4). Moran's trip is described in Hughes, *In the House of Stone and Light*, 38–39.

22. Anderson, *Living at the Edge*, 151.

23. Goss, *Making Concessions in Yellowstone*.

24. "Return from Trip to Southern Utah," *Washington County News*, August 24, 1916. Reprint from *Deseret News*, Salt Lake City.

25. The Wylie camp is described in a tourist brochure, "Zion Canyon, Utah's Scenic Wonderland," released as the July 1917 issue of *The Arrowhead*, a publication of the Union Pacific's Salt Lake Route in July 1917 (copy at USHS). According to Angus Woodbury, Parry made the initial application for a camping facility in 1917. Wylie soon filed a competing

application, and the two men threw in together, with Wylie handling the camp and Parry the transport (Angus Woodbury papers, Marriot Library, University of Utah, box 6, fd. 7).

26. Mills, *Your National Parks*, 239–41.

27. Albright, *Creating the National Park Service*, 245. Horace M. Albright served as acting director from 1917 to 1919 while Stephen T. Mather was incapacitated. He became superintendent of Yellowstone National Park in 1919 and replaced Mather as director in 1929.

28. Woodbury, *History of Southern Utah*, 201.

29. United States Railroad Administration, "Zion National Monument, Utah."

30. Franklin Lane to Stephen Mather, May 13, 1918, in Foss, *Conservation in the United States*, 187.

31. Rishel, *Wheels to Adventure*, 65–69.

32. Murphy, *Seven Wonderlands of the American West*, 226.

CHAPTER 8

1. J. Cecil Alter to George C. Fraser, May 5, 1914 (RC, box 3, fd. 2). Alter presumably was referring to Parunuweap Canyon on the East Fork of the Virgin River as the other "Mukuntuweap." There is only one Toroweap, however.

2. Rust kept no journals of his trips with George Fraser. Edited and abridged versions of three of Fraser's detailed accounts can be found in Fraser, *Journeys in the Canyon Lands*. The originals of these journals, along with a fourth journal covering a 1922 trip to the Crossing of the Fathers, are at the Princeton University Library's Department of Rare Books and Special Collections.

3. Dutton, *Tertiary History of the Grand Cañon District*, 81.

4. Ibid., 96. The lava flows at Toroweap and downstream dammed the Colorado repeatedly, at times building to a depth of as much as two thousand feet and flooding the river canyon as far upstream as Moab (Ranney, *Carving Grand Canyon*, 138–39).

5. Fraser, *Journeys in the Canyon Lands*, 41–58.

6. Dutton, *Tertiary History of the Grand Cañon District*, 207.

7. Rust annotation to George Fraser's 1914 journal, "Memoranda of a Trip," following p. 158.

8. Fraser, *Journeys in the Canyon Lands*, 63. This was not the first time that such signals failed to work; in 1907 Bass missed seeing the fires of the Buffalo Jones–Zane Grey party and would have left them stranded at the river, had he not ridden down anyway to attend to other business at his tram (Pauly, *Zane Grey*, 75).

9. Rust to George C. Fraser, August 6, 1914, in Fraser, "Memoranda of a Trip," following p. 205.

10. Fraser to Rust, August 12, 1914 (RC, box 3, fd. 2).

11. See note 7 above.

12. Fraser to Rust, December 11, 1914 (RC, box 3, fd. 2).

13. Ibid., January 26, 1915.

14. Ibid., June 1, 1915.

15. Fraser to Rust, June 12, 1915 (RC, box 3, fd. 3).

16. Fraser, *Journeys in the Canyon Lands*, 176.

17. Andrus quote: "Initial Trip Over Monumental Highway," *Washington County News*, July 5, 1917; Rust journal: RC, box 1, fd. 5, vol. 2.

18. Fraser to Rust, August 16, 1916 (RC, box 3, fd. 3). Fraser's letter to Manderfield was quoted in the Salt Lake City *Evening Telegram*, August 24, 1914.

19. Fraser, "Diaries, January 1, 1886 to December 18, 1886," entry for March 28, 1886.

20. Fraser to Rust, March 20, 1917 (RC, box 3, fd. 4).

21. Ibid., May 10, 1917.

22. Rust, "Genuine Travelers."

23. Rust did not keep a record of this trip, but Jeffers recalled it in his 1923 book *The Call of the Mountains*.

24. David Jordan Rust, Oral History Transcript.

25. Jeffers, *The Call of the Mountains*, 216.

26. Scrattish, "The Modern Discovery, Popularization, and Early Development of Bryce Canyon, Utah." "Bryce Canyon" denotes both the national park and the canyon of Bryce Creek, which flows eastward past the town of Tropic. It was initially called Bryce's Canyon. The great amphitheater of upper Bryce Canyon affords one of the most spectacular (but by no means the only) views in the park.

27. Dutton, *Geology of the High Plateaus*, 254.

28. National Park Service, "Bryce Canyon Historic Resource Study," www.cr.nps.gov/history/online_books/brca/hrs2.htm.

29. Ibid. See also Presnall, "Early Days in Bryce and Zion"; O. J. Grimes, "Utah's New Wonderland: Bryce's Canyon, One of Nature's Masterpieces in Sculpture and Coloring," *Salt Lake Tribune* (magazine section), August 25, 1918.

30. Woodbury, *History of Southern Utah*, 208.

31. National Park Service, "Bryce Canyon Historic Resource Study."

32. Woodbury, *History of Southern Utah*, 204.

33. Ruth Woolley Rust, Memoirs, 22.

34. "Statement of Charles R. Pugh" (RC, box 10, fd. 1).

35. Rust described his election to the state legislature and his experience serving his single term in a short, undated essay titled "My Best Stroke of Luck."

36. George C. Fraser to Rust, November 15, 1916 (RC, box 3, fd. 2).

37. Grand Canyon Highway measure: "Will Strive for Grand Canyon Road," *Washington County News*, January 11, 2007; Rust's reminiscence of legislative session: Rust, "My Best Stroke of Luck"; election loss: Kane County Commission, Minutes, 1928.

38. Jensen, "The Trip to Grand Canyon," in *Beneath the Casing Rock*, 254–63. Jensen interviewed Rust on several occasions for this family history. Dave's words are probably based on her recollection and do not appear to be from contemporaneous notes.

39. Anderson, *Living at the Edge*, 153.

CHAPTER 9

1. Hopkins, "Log and Story of Monumental Highway Thro' America's Wonderland," *Good Roads Automobilist* (Salt Lake City), January 1918.

2. Rochester, *Little St. Simons Island*, 67.

3. Horace M. Albright to Arnold W. Koehler Jr., April 28, 1919. Albright's letter is included in Berolzheimer and Koehler, "Our Western Trip."

4. Rust to Koehler, May 12, 1919. Berolzheimer and Koehler, "Our Western Trip."

5. Quentin Rust quote: interview with author, Salt Lake City, December 17, 2000. Following quotations are from Rust, "The Worth of a Boy."

6. George C. Fraser to Rust, May 7, 1919 (RC, box 3, fd. 5).

7. Rust, "I Came Out of the Wilderness."

8. Berolzheimer and Koehler, "Our Western Trip" and "A Trip to Utah." Details of their 1919 trip, and all quotations not otherwise attributed, are from the first journal.

9. Anderson, *Living at the Edge*, 137.

10. Ibid., 118.

11. Bernheimer, *Rainbow Bridge*, 6–7.

12. Hassell, *Rainbow Bridge: An Illustrated History*, 16–17. Luckert, in *Navajo Mountain and Rainbow Bridge Religion*, recorded Navajo beliefs regarding these features, such as that rain clouds arose from a sacred spring or pool on the summit of Navajo Mountain. Both the mountain, which is known to the Dineh as "Head of Earth Woman," and the bridge were used for ceremonial offerings.

13. Jett, "The Great 'Race' to 'Discover' Rainbow Natural Bridge in 1909." He points out that prospectors such as Cass Hite and others working in the area from the 1880s onward may well have happened across the bridge without bothering to publicize it. Hank Hassell, in *Rainbow Bridge: An Illustrated History*, discusses the various discovery claims in detail and believes that the Cummings-Douglass party has priority, with Cummings the more dignified of the two in representing his claim.

14. Bernheimer, *Rainbow Bridge*, 8.

15. Ibid., 100.

16. Sproul, *A Bridge between Cultures*, chapter titled "Making it Work: Monument Development, 1910–1955."

17. Sources for the early trips to the White Canyon bridges are: Redd, "History of the Natural Bridges"; Dyar, "The Colossal Bridges of Utah"; and Crampton, *Standing Up Country*, 152–54.

18. Kelly and Martin, "Zeke Johnson's Natural Bridges," 13; Redd, "History of the Natural Bridges."

19. Holmes, "The Great Natural Bridges of Utah."

20. Ibid., 204.

21. Berolzheimer and Koehler, "Our Western Trip," 44.

22. Rust, "I Came Out of the Wilderness."

23. Ibid.

24. David Jordan Rust, Oral History Transcript, 24.

CHAPTER 10

1. Robert W. Righter, in "National Monuments to National Parks: The Use of the Antiquities Act of 1906," explains how Interior Department personnel repeatedly sought to have national monuments declared for lands they felt merited protection but were unlikely to become national parks soon. In many cases the monuments served as way stations on the road to eventual park legislation.

2. Rust, "Notes Gathered While Working in the Tourist Business."

3. Special use permits, Kaibab National Forest, April 3, 1911 (Woolley cabin) and April 10, 1911 (Rust's Camp) (RC, box 10, fd. 1).

4. Herbert Woolley to Edwin D. Woolley Jr., November 1, 1911; reply, November 12, 1911 (EDW–SUU, box 4, fd. 2).

5. Supervisor, Kaibab National Forest to Rust, March 31, 1919 (RC, box 1, fd. 11).

6. Rust to Grand Canyon National Park, Nov. 24, 1919, and December 16, 1919 (RC, box 2, fd 1).

7. Chamberlain, *Sketch of the Life of Edwin Dilworth Woolley, Jr.*, 9.

8. Rust to Ellsworth Kolb, November 18, 1914 (KC, box 14, fd. 1697); Adams, "The Grand Canyon Bridge."

9. Anderson, *Polishing the Jewel*, 14.

10. Shankland, *Steve Mather of the National Parks*, 207–8. Maps of the proposed tramway alignments are shown in Ohlman, "The 1919 Transcanyon Aerial Tramway Survey," in Anderson, *A Gathering of Grand Canyon Historians*. In the 1920s the Fred Harvey Company installed a cable tram to access its Hermits Rest camp, but it did not span the river (Anderson, *Living at the Edge*, 104). Davol was not the only man to have extravagant plans for the canyon. Dee Woolley told Senator Reed Smoot in 1910 that "as soon as it is settled that a [rail] road is coming to the rim, I want to get busy and build a cog road across the canyon. That is one of my latest dreams" (Woolley to Reed Smoot, January 14, 1910, EDW–SUU). He had brought up the idea in various letters as early as 1905.

11. Anderson, *Living at the Edge*, 156.

12. Rust, "Notes Gathered While Working in the Tourist Business." Woolley was an inveterate booster who saw no difficulty in inviting a potential rival to locate at the North Rim.

13. Chamberlain, "Sketch of the Life of Edwin Dilworth Woolley, Jr.," 9; Ned Chaffin, interview with author, May 27, 1999.

14. Judd, *Men Met Along the Trail*, 79–80.

15. Rothman, "Foreword," in Fraser, *Journeys in the Canyon Lands*, x.

16. Fraser's travels among the Indian reservations of Arizona and New Mexico are described in Jett, "The Journals of George C. Fraser '93." To see how Rust's friends Buffalo Jones and Jim Emmett regarded the Navajo, read Zane Grey's description of their lion chases on the Powell Plateau in *Tales of Lonely Trails*. Their Navajo wrangler came in for condescension and outright harassment.

17. Kanab Town Board, Minutes, 1920.

18. Chamberlain, "Sketch of the Life of Edwin D. Woolley Jr.," 6–7; Carroll, *History of Kane County,* 229.

19. Fraser to Rust, June 4, 1920 (RC, box 3, fd. 6).

20. Ibid., July 6, 1920.

21. Jensen, *Beneath the Casing Rock,* 278.

22. Powell, *Exploration of the Colorado River,* 109.

23. Dutton described his ride with W. H. Holmes, in which they traveled beneath the Vermilion Cliffs to this viewpoint, in *Tertiary History,* 54–60.

24. Fraser to Rust, July 25, 1920 (RC, box 3, fd. 6); Jane G. Fraser to Rust, December 9, 1921 (RC, box 3, fd. 7). Ruth's comment is from Ruth Woolley Rust, Memoirs, 22.

25. Fraser to Rust, March 24, 1921 (RC, box 3, fd. 6), and March 21, 1925 (RC, box 3, fd. 7).

26. Ibid., March 21, 1921 (RC, box 3, fd. 6).

27. "Democratic Platform for Sixth Judicial District," *Richfield Reaper,* September 4, 1924.

28. Kanab Town Board, Minutes, 1920.

29. Fraser to Rust, December 1, 1921 (RC, box 3, fd. 7).

30. Kanab Town Board, Minutes, January 3, 1922.

31. Fraser to Rust, October 17, 1921 (RC, box 3, fd. 7).

32. "North Rim of Grand Canyon Particularly Attractive," *Richfield Reaper,* August 24, 1922.

33. The relationship of the National Park to Park Highway to Utah's early parks and monuments is discussed in McKoy, *Cultures at a Crossroads,* 86–88.

34. Hough, "The President's Forest," 58.

35. John Dickinson Sherman, "The President's Forest," *Manti Messenger,* March 10, 1922. Sherman's article appeared in a number of southern Utah newspapers. The Grand Canyon Cattle Company's letter to President Warren Harding, giving their surprising agreement to the proposal, was reprinted in this article.

36. Glen Miller, N. H. Bertham, and Rosco Breeden, "Wants Kaibab Forest Made National Park," Letter to *Salt Lake Tribune,* reprinted in *Washington County News,* October 9, 1913.

37. Anderson, *Polishing the Jewel,* 56. In 1975 Congress expanded the park to include both the Grand Canyon National Monument, west of the existing park, and Marble Canyon National Monument upstream to Lees Ferry.

38. Alter, *Through the Heart of the Scenic West,* 214.

39. Ibid., 217, 220.

Chapter 11

1. Quotation from Berolzheimer and Koehler, "A Trip to Utah," 18. Details of Rust's 1920 trip with Charles Berolzheimer and Arnold Koehler, and all quotations not otherwise attributed, are from this journal.

2. George C. Fraser to Rust, January 24, 1920 (RC, box 3, fd. 6).

3. Charles Berolzheimer to Rust, March 20, 1920 (RC, box 2, fd. 9). "Nonnezosshe" (or Nonnezoshe) was one of the supposed Navajo names for Rainbow Bridge. According to Stephen Jett ("The Great 'Race' to 'Discover' Rainbow Bridge," addendum), the Navajo actually used different names for the span.

4. Thompson, "Diary," June 6, 1872, 81–82.

5. Frank Millikan, the historian of the Joseph Henry Papers Project at the Smithsonian, notes that G. K. Gilbert claimed that Powell named the range in 1869 during his first Colorado voyage; why Almon Thompson, Powell's close associate, would not be using the name in 1872 is unclear (Millikan, "Henry Namesakes," note 6, http://siarchives.si.edu/history/jhp/joseph22.htm).

6. Breed, "First Motor Sortie into Escalante Land."

7. Gregory and Moore, *The Kaiparowits Region*, 5.

8. Roundy, *Advised Them to Call the Place Escalante*, 144.

9. Crampton, *Standing Up Country*, 111–12.

10. Dutton, *High Plateaus*, 284.

11. Charles and Arnold heard this figure from a local sheepherder.

12. F. B. Woolley, "Report of Reconoitering Expedition." Franklin B. Woolley was ten years older than his brother, Edwin D. Woolley Jr. He was killed by Mojave Indians near San Bernardino, California, in 1869.

13. George C. Fraser to Rust, May 23, 1922 (RC, box 3, fd. 7).

14. Fraser, "Notes of journey, June 23rd to August 11th, 1922," entry for July 11, 1922.

15. Ibid., July 15, 1922.

16. Otis R. Marston to Mrs. Leighton H. Coleman (Jane Fraser), December 28, 1954, in Fraser, "Notes of journey, June 23rd to August 11th, 1922." George Fraser described the Crossing of the Fathers in his article "El Vado de los Padres," but he did not indicate that he knew of the steps' exact location at that time.

17. Fraser, "Notes of journey, June 23rd to August 11th, 1922."

18. Fraser to Rust, August 14, 1922 (RC, box 3, fd. 7).

19. Fraser to David Jordan Rust, April 25, 1923 (RC, box 9, fd. 4).

20. David Jordan Rust, Oral History Transcript.

21. Fraser to Rust, January 26, 1925 (RC, box 4, fd. 1).

22. Fraser to Rust, July 7, 1924 (RC, box 4, fd. 1). Fraser evidently did not keep Rust's letters; these would have rounded out our understanding of a fine, unusual friendship.

23. Rust to David Jordan Rust, March 18, 1925 (RC, box 9, fd. 3).

CHAPTER 12

1. J. P. Proctor to Rust, August 1925 (RC, box 2, fd. 1).

2. David Jordan Rust, "Journal, June 26th through July 29th [1923]."

3. Merrill, "Dave Rust, Lover of the Grand Canyon," 471.

4. Dellenbaugh, *A Canyon Voyage*, 140.

5. Both Dave and his son Jordan kept journals of their 1923 excursion, which form the main sources for this narrative. Jordan Rust's, titled "Journal, June 26th through July 29th,"

comes to six typewritten pages; Dave's journal is retrospectively titled "Charles & Arnold— First River Trip for Fun 1921." The 1921 date is in error; their trip clearly took place in 1923. Rust added the title years later and remembered the date wrong. For clarity, I have filled out Rust's many abbreviations in his river journal.

6. Robinson, "The Editor and His Uniquely Glorious Trip." Robinson's comments anticipated by several years the local movement to create a Wayne Wonderland—eventually Capitol Reef—National Park.

7. Stanton, *The Hoskaninni Papers*, 151–52.

8. Judd, "Beyond the Clay Hills."

9. Rust to Secretary, USHS, Jan. 11, 1950. Collection of Blanche Rasmussen.

10. Freeman, Lewis R., "Diary of the U.S.G.S. Grand Canyon Voyage of 1923," cited in Westwood, *Rough-Water Man*, 133n10.

11. River historian Roy Webb, in his book *Call of the Colorado* (p. 126), gives a brief summary of Rust's river guiding activities. Crampton's *Standing Up Country* (p. 165) mentions that "David E. Rust" started running Glen in 1917; he probably got this date from the abstract of Rust's 1929 testimony in the Colorado River Bed case, in which Rust gave the impression that he had been running Glen for twelve years. Rust probably was thinking of his brief row up from Lees Ferry with George Fraser in 1916. I have found no evidence that he boated the length of Glen Canyon between his mining days in 1897–1898 and his trip in 1923. His 1923 journal certainly suggests that he was seeing many of Glen's features, such as Music Temple, for the first time.

12. Rust's brief account of this trip is found in "Oastler Voyage, July 1, '25."

13. Emma Rust's accounts of her 1924 and 1925 trips appear in Joseph C. Rust, "From the Dirty Devil to the Bright Angel," 35.

14. Maude Oastler to Rust, April 17, 1937 (RC, box 2, fd. 4).

15. Rust did not elaborate on his moonlight voyage with Ed Meskin, one of Glen Canyon's colorful but little-known placer miners. Will Rust worked with Meskin occasionally starting in 1896, but did not offer any description of him.

16. Jerry Johnson to Rust, August 1925 (RC, box 2, fd. 1); J. P. Proctor to Rust, August 1925 (RC, box 2, fd. 1).

17. Vaughan Roche, "'Seldom Seen Smith' mourns a lost canyon and dead foes," *High Country News* (Paonia, Colo.), October 18, 1993.

CHAPTER 13

1. Rust to George H. Dern, October 12, 1925. Utah State Archives, Governor Dern correspondence, (series 204, box 217-19-6-6).

2. Charles Kelly stated that Dr. A. L. Inglesby of Salt Lake City made the first auto trip down Crescent Creek in 1933. See Kelly, "Proposed Escalante National Monument," 21.

3. Grimes, Oliver J., "Down the Colorado River by Canoe," *Salt Lake Tribune*, May 9–11, 1926; George H. Dern, "Down the Colorado with the Governor," *Deseret News*, May 8, 15, and 22, 1926.

4. Dern, "Down the Colorado with the Governor."

5. Rust testimony, Colorado River Bed Case, Transcript of Testimony, 4254–55 (Utah State Archives, Salt Lake City).

6. Grimes, "Down the Colorado River by Canoe."

7. George C. Fraser to Charles Kelly, July 1, 1933 (ORM, box 202, fd. 17). Fraser's letter does not indicate whether he and Rust found the steps on their 1922 trip or whether he learned of them later from Rust.

8. Quoted in Kelly, "Sand and Sagebrush."

9. "Explorers Find Exact Spot Where Escalante Crossed Colorado River," *Deseret News*, August 21, 1937.

10. "Aged Manufacturer from Ohio on Colorado River Trip," *Richfield Reaper*, September 29, 1938; Kelly, "At Eighty-Three He Is an Explorer."

11. Rust, "Dodge Freeman 1939"; Rust to Otis R. Marston, August 12, 1949 (ORM, box 202, fd. 18); L. F. H. Lowe to Charles Kelly, May 11, 1939 (USHS, Charles Kelly papers, box 2, fd. 6). See also Bert Loper's acid comment about Frazier's claim in Dimock, *The Very Hard Way*, 337. Kelly and Frazier were not entirely responsible for the hoopla over finding the steps; local newspapers were eager to trumpet the "discovery" as well.

12. Dern, "Down the Colorado with the Governor."

13. Rust to Herbert E. Gregory, January 19, 1926 (RC, box 5, fd. 5). Gregory's study of the Kaiparowits region, which included economic geology, was published in 1931.

14. Rust, "Harry and Ben" [1927]. Quotations from this trip are from this journal.

15. Phillip Rollins to Dan D. Spencer, May 17, 1927 (RC, box 2, fd. 2).

16. Rust to Phillip Rollins, May 26, 1927 (RC, box 2, fd. 2).

17. Rust, "Boating on the Colorado," 510.

18. "Howard A. Kelly 1858–1943," Natural History Society of Maryland (www.marylandnature.org/aboutus/people/phowardkelly.htm).

19. *Deseret News*, September 4, 1929.

20. Dr. Pack described the trip in his unpublished autobiography, "History of Frederick James Pack," 153–56. Rust apparently kept no record of the trip.

21. Webb, *Call of the Colorado*, 122–23. Webb describes Nevills's remarkable river running career in his 2005 book *High, Wide, and Handsome*.

Chapter 14

1. Rust, "Unusual Campout Excursions." Subsequent quotations in this chapter not otherwise identified are from this typescript.

2. Visitation figures to the Grand Canyon are from Anderson, *Polishing the Jewel,* appendix 1; auto use at both rims is from Anderson, *Living at the Edge*, 110, 156.

3. Improvements at Zion and Bryce are from Woodbury, *History of Southern Utah*, 207–8; at Cedar Breaks, from Rothman, "Shaping the Nature of a Controversy."

4. William Slauson Rust, "The Story of My Life."

5. Michael McGerr, in *A Fierce Discontent: The Rise and Fall of the Progressive Movement in America*, states that the average wage of a worker in a manufacturing plant in 1915 was only

$568 (p. 251) and "families of clerks and small shop owners" would typically have an annual income of a thousand dollars or so (p. 43).

6. Merrill, "One of the Fourteen Points," *Deseret News*, May 24, 1924.

7. Rust, "I Came Out of the Wilderness."

8. Donald C. Scott to Rust, March 6, 1928 (RC, box 5, fd. 3).

9. Nora Mickelson, interview with author, March 21, 2007.

10. Robert H. Stewart to Rust, April 13, 1927 (RC, box 2, fd. 2); "The Larz Andersons Take to the 'Covered Wagon' in Zion Park," *Boston Transcript*, January 14, 1928. A "cookee" is a kitchen helper.

11. Pomeroy, *In Search of the Golden West*, 15.

12. Merrill, "One of the Fourteen Points."

13. Woodbury, *History of Southern Utah*, 204.

14. Hinton, "Getting Along."

15. Al Richmond, "Rails At Both Rims," in Anderson, *A Gathering of Grand Canyon Historians*, 16.

16. Presnall, "Utah Exceeds All World in Scenic Wonders."

17. Suran, *With the Wings of an Angel*, ch. 9.

18. Woodbury, *History of Southern Utah*, 208.

19. "J. F. Tolton Praises Democratic Nominee for State Senate," *Richfield Reaper*, November 1, 1928; Kane County Commission minutes, Utah State Archives, series 83799; "Utah Elects Junior Senator, Governor and Secretary from Democratic Ranks," *Richfield Reaper*, November 8, 1928.

20. Blanche Rust Rasmussen, interview with author, Salt Lake City, July 13, 2005. Rust left no written record of their move to Provo. The *Garfield County News* (Panguitch) noted on June 7, 1929, that Rust resigned from the town library board "because he will be in Kanab so little after this."

21. Joseph C. Rust, interview with author, July 10, 1999. See also Joseph Rust's *From the Dirty Devil to the Bright Angel*, 36, 41–42.

22. "River Bed Case May Go to High Court," *Times-Independent* (Moab, Utah), March 29, 1928.

23. Utah State Attorney General, Colorado River Case, 4240.

24. Ibid., 4250.

25. Frederick Dellenbaugh diary, Arizona Historical Society, October 12, 1929. Courtesy of Brad Dimock. See also Dimock, *The Very Hard Way*, 306–7.

26. George C. Fraser to Rust, November 9, 1928 (RC, box 4, fd. 2).

27. Baker, *Trail on the Water*, 22. Bert Loper's life and river-running exploits are also presented in Dimock, *The Very Hard Way*.

28. Sarah Fraser Robbins, interview with author, November 1, 2000.

29. Ibid.

30. Frank M. Barrios, "An Appointment with Death: The Howland-Dunn Tragedy Revisited," in Anderson, *A Gathering of Grand Canyon Historians*, 146.

31. George C. Fraser to Rust (RC, box 4, fd. 3).

CHAPTER 15

1. Judd, *Men Met Along the Trail*, 79–80; *Archaeological Investigations North of the Rio Colorado*, 139.

2. Elliott, *Great Excavations*, 164.

3. William H. Claflin to Rust, May 12, 1927 (RC, box 2, fd. 2).

4. Rust to Claflin, May 16, 1927 (RC, box 2, fd. 2).

5. "Archaeological Discovery in Wayne County," *Richfield Reaper*, September 2, 1926. The shields are now thought to be of comparatively recent origin, perhaps around A.D. 1700.

6. Quotations from Rust's 1927 trip with Claflin and Emerson are from his unpublished journal, "Exploring with Peabody."

7. S. J. Guernsey to Rust, April 16, 1928 (RC, box 2, fd. 3).

8. "Group of Prominent Men Buy Evening Post," *New York Times*, January 14, 1922. Rust's 1928 trip with Donald and Louise Scott is described in his unpublished journal, "Donald Scott and Wife 1928."

9. Donald C. Scott to Rust, May 18, 1926 (RC, box 5, fd. 3).

10. Archaeologist Polly Schaafsma studied the Scotts' rock art photographs and published an analysis in *The Rock Art of Utah: A Study from the Donald Scott Collection*.

11. Frye, *From Barrier to Crossroads*, 29n17.

12. Fowler and Aikens, *1961 Excavations*, 5–6. They note that "apparently [Donald] Scott was unaware of the abundance of sites there."

13. Rust, "Peabody Museum Archaeological Expedition 1930."

14. Rust, "Donald Scott and Wife 1928." This ruin, apparently used as a kiva, was already known to local cowboys. A University of Utah team investigated the ruin in the 1950s and found Kayenta-style pottery and woven sandals in it, indicating use by Puebloan (Anasazi) people (Gunnarson, "1957 Excavations, Glen Canyon Area"). The site is now under the waters of Lake Powell.

15. Donald C. Scott to Rust, Nov. 29, 1955 (RC, box 5, fd. 3).

16. See Morss, *Notes on the Archaeology of the Kaibito and Rainbow Plateaus*.

17. Morss, *The Ancient Culture of the Fremont River in Utah*, 2–3.

18. Fawcett and Latady, "Archaic and Ancestral Pueblo Peoples in the Vicinity of the Coombs Site," 146–47; Lister, "Kaiparowits Plateau and Glen Canyon Prehistory," 81.

19. Morss, *The Ancient Culture of the Fremont River in Utah*, 5. Morss's investigations in the vicinity of Capitol Reef are also described in Houk, *Dwellers of the Rainbow*.

20. Morss, *The Ancient Culture of the Fremont River in Utah*, 14.

21. Spangler and Spangler, *Horned Snakes and Axle Grease*, 3.

22. Morss, *The Ancient Culture of the Fremont River in Utah*, 76.

23. The term "Anasazi" was applied to the ancient Puebloan inhabitants of the canyon country by Alfred V. Kidder in 1936 (Aton and McPherson, *River Flowing from the Sunrise*, 173n1.) J. O. Brew, one of Rust's friends from the 1931 Peabody Museum expedition to northeastern Utah, took exception to the term in his 1946 paper on Alkali Ridge. He noted that the word "is used by the Navajo to refer to the ancient people who occupied the ruins" and

called it an "unfortunate choice." He preferred the term "Pueblo" (Brew, *Archaeology of Alkali Ridge*, ix–x). In recent years the term "ancestral Puebloans" seems to be gaining favor.

24. "A Conversation with Ned Chaffin," interview by Gary Cox and Cynthia Beyer, November 20–22, 1990, 44 (Moab, Utah: National Park Service, Canyonlands National Park [www.nps.gov/cany/historyculture/nedchaffin.htm]).

25. Ibid., 26–27.

26. Rust, "Exploring with Peabody." The name "Great Gallery" may have originated with members of the Biddlecome family, whom Rust knew. They ran cattle out of what is now known as the Robbers Roost (or Ekker) ranch and down Horseshoe Canyon (phone conversation with Cynthia Cox, National Park Service, Canyonlands National Park, March 23, 2007).

27. Tipps, "Barrier Canyon Rock Art Dating." Tipps writes that the spalled paint fragment from the Great Gallery that her group tested using a mass spectrometer method probably belongs to the "first millennium B.C."

28. Rust's brief notes on this expedition are found in Rust, "Peabody Museum Archaeological Expedition 1930." See also "Complete Successful Exploration Trip," *Times-Independent* (Moab, Utah), August 14, 1930.

29. Rust, "Exploring with Peabody," also "Peabody Museum 1931."

30. J. O. Brew to Rust, Jan. 31, 1947 (RC, box 2, fd. 5); Elliott, *Great Excavations*, 165.

31. Brew, "Donald Scott and His Collection," in Schaafsma, *The Rock Art of Utah*, xvi.

32. Donald C. Scott to Rust, April 9, 1931 (RC, box 5, fd. 3).

33. Brew, *Archaeology of Alkali Ridge*.

34. Madsen, *Exploring the Fremont*, 21–23.

CHAPTER 16

1. George C. Fraser to Rust, June 27, 1935 (RC, box 4, fd. 4).

2. Edloe Rust to David Rust [1935] (RC, box 7, fd. 10).

3. J. Cecil Alter to Rust, November 19, 1935 (RC, box 2, fd. 4). Rust's letter to Alter is, unfortunately, unavailable.

4. James T. Dennison to Rust, February 18, 1934 (RC, box 2, fd. 3). Note to modern-day explorers: climbing into ruins damages them and is no longer considered good sport.

5. Rust to James T. Dennison, April 2, 1934 (RC, box 2, fd. 3).

6. Rust, "Dennison Party 1934." Quotations in this chapter not otherwise attributed are from this journal.

7. Dutton, *Geology of the High Plateaus*, 15.

8. Harrison R. Merrill, "One of the Fourteen Points." *Deseret News*, May 24, 1924.

9. Rust, "Genuine Travelers."

10. Hunt, *Geology and Geography of the Henry Mountains Region*, 4.

11. Snow, *Rainbow Views*, 148.

12. Statistics for total annual visits to the National Park System are found at www2.nature.nps.gov/Npstats/select_report.cfm?by=year.

13. Frye, *From Barrier to Crossroads*, 125. A 1925 article in the *Richfield Reaper* ("Wayne Wonderland Booklet Issued," June 25) suggests that Hickman was already using the term "Capitol Reef" to describe the domes and cliffs of the Waterpocket Fold, years before the Park Service formally bestowed the name.

14. Ibid.

15. "Wayne Beauty Lures Tourists," *Salt Lake Tribune*, April 25, 1926.

16. Frye, *From Barrier to Crossroads*, 135–50. For a map of the monument's initial boundaries, see figure 6 in Frye.

17. Kelly, "Valley of the Cathedrals." Fremont reaching Cathedral Valley: Hal Schindler, "A New Focus on Fremont Explorer Validated Travels Through Daguerreotypes," *Salt Lake Tribune*, December 10, 1995; 1950 Park Service party: "Memorandum to Superintendent, Zion and Bryce Canyon from Asst. Superintendent, Chester A. Thomas, July 26, 1950" (National Archives, Denver, Record Group 79, National Park Service, series 8NS-079-94-1434, box 138, fd. O-35—Proposed Monuments).

18. Quoted in Barnes, *Canyon Country Arches and Bridges*, 222.

19. Sproul, *A Bridge between Cultures*, 95–96.

Chapter 17

1. Hall's expeditions are described in Topping, *Glen Canyon and the San Juan Country*, 236–41.

2. Freeman, "Vanadium and Uranium Deposits." Before the nuclear era, uranium was used as a source of radium and pigments; vanadium was in demand as an alloy for aircraft steel.

3. Rust, "Dodge Freeman Excursion 1935." Subsequent quotations in this chapter not otherwise attributed are from this journal.

4. Van Cott, *Utah Place Names*, 9.

5. "A Conversation with Ned Chaffin," interview by Gary Cox and Cynthia Beyer, November 20–22, 1990, 56 (Moab, Utah: National Park Service, Canyonlands National Park [www.nps.gov/cany/historyculture/nedchaffin.htm]).

6. Rust may have been referring to Candlestick Tower, a prominent butte located west of the Island in the Sky plateau east of the Green River; he could also have meant one of several other towers closer by on the west side of the Green and Colorado, such as the Sewing Machine on the south side of a plateau called the South Block. In any event, the views were stupendous.

7. Harry Aleson to B. F. Bingham, March 10, 1947 (Harry LeRoy Aleson Papers, USHS, box 2, fd. 1). See also Scholl, "Arth Chaffin & Cass Hite," *Canyon Country Zephyr* (Moab, Utah), April–May 1996, 17.

8. Henry Dodge Freeman to Ken Sleight, March 6, 1965 (ORM, box 202, fd. 17).

9. A Park Service staffer named Paul Brown visited Horse Mountain in 1943 and found the view just as entrancing: "This should be the tourists introduction to the Escalante Canyon land. Here can be pointed out to them, over the desert wastes and serpentine canyons

what they will later come to know more intimately in their travels into and along the Colorado and Green Rivers' canyons. And those who will not be privileged to enjoy orchestra seats in the pit below can come here to a gallery bench and see the lavish display of fantastic scenery on the distant stage of the Escalante circus" (Brown, "Narrative Report on the Trip to Horse Mountain").

10. Frye, *From Barrier to Crossroads*, 133–44.

11. "National Park Officials Visit Moab by Airplane," *Times-Independent* (Moab, Utah), June 6, 1935; "River Trip Pleases Park Service Men," *Times-Independent*, June 20, 1935.

12. A. E. Demaray to Secretary, Department of the Interior, December 28, 1934 (NPS-ENM). Ickes's approval was given without comment as a note added to the bottom of Demaray's letter.

13. The preliminary boundary for the Escalante National Monument, dated May 1935, is shown on a map entitled "Proposed Escalante National Monument," along with the "recommended" boundary as released the following year (Utah State Archives, State Planning Board, Escalante National Monument files, box 1, fd. 4).

14. West, "The Proposed Escalante National Monument."

15. Transcript of public meeting held in Price, Utah, May 9, 1936 (Utah State Archives, Series 22028, State Planning Board, Proposed Escalante National Monument records, 1936–1940).

16. Rust interview, "I Came Out of the Wilderness." The language suggests that this typescript may have been notes he prepared for the interview.

17. "Lions Declare in Favor of Creating a National Monument," *Times-Independent*, February 17, 1938.

18. "Creation of Escalante Area Nears Agreement," *Times-Independent*, February 22, 1940.

19. Richardson, "Federal Park Policy in Utah."

CHAPTER 18

1. Author interviews with Blanche Rust Rasmussen and Quentin Rust, Salt Lake City, December 17, 2000.

2. This trip is described in Flanders, *Senator from Vermont*, 153–57. Subsequent quotations by Flanders in this chapter that are not otherwise identified are from this book.

3. Quentin Rust interview.

4. Ralph Flanders to Rust, April 26, 1961 (RC, box 2, fd. 14).

5. Rust, "John S. Chafee Party June 25–July."

6. Breed, "First Motor Sortie into Escalante Land." The McKees' photo of the main river canyon near the mouth of Silver Falls Canyon is at the Cline Library, Northern Arizona University (NAU.PH.95.48.946).

7. Local residents celebrated the completion of this year-round road on June 21, 1940, with a barbeque in Boulder and an evening dance in Escalante (Woolsey, *The Escalante Story*, 194). Today's paved highway follows roughly the same route; several older alignments, including the original wagon road, can be seen cut into the cliffs in several places.

8. Rust, "Freeman, Lowe, King, July 1937." Subsequent quotations from this trip that are not otherwise identified are from this journal.

9. Crampton, *Historical Sites in Glen Canyon*, 28.

10. Henry Dodge Freeman to Ken Sleight, March 6, 1965 (ORM, box 202, fd. 17).

11. Rust, "Lowe and Hartshorne 1938."

12. "Party Equips Here for River Trip," *Richfield Reaper*, July 7, 1938.

13. The poem "God of the Open Air" was written by Henry van Dyke (1852–1933).

14. Cutter, "Then and Now."

15. Nevills's journal for July 7, 1938, in Webb, *High, Wide, and Handsome*, 38.

16. L. F. H. Lowe to Charles Kelly, May 11, 1939 (USHS, Charles Kelly papers, box 2, fd. 6).

17. Rust, "Dodge Freeman 1939."

18. Brad Dimock recounts Rust and Freeman meeting Loper in 1939 in *The Very Hard Way*, 344–45.

19. Rust's notes of his 1940 trip with Freeman are found in "Dodge Freeman 1939."

20. Farmer, "Undiscovered to Undiscoverable," 105, 116; Gregory and Moore, *The Kaiparowits Region*, 144.

21. Norman D. Nevills to Harry L. Aleson, November 28, 1939 (USHS, Harry Aleson papers, box 1, fd. 6). Nevills's trip even received publicity in the *New York Times* ("Find New Natural Bridge," August 2, 1940). A full account of Nevills's promotion of the bridge is found in Farmer, "Undiscovered to Undiscoverable."

22. Rust, "Freeman 1941."

23. Henry Dodge Freeman to Ken Sleight, March 6, 1965 (ORM, box 202, fd. 17).

24. Rust journal, May 25, 1941 (RC, box 1, fd. 1).

25. Rust journal, September 20, 1941 (RC, box 1, fd. 1). See also "Hole in Rock Trip Scheduled for September 20," *Garfield County News* (Panguitch, Utah), August 28, 1941.

CHAPTER 19

1. Rust's journal for 1941 is found in the Rust Collection, box 1, fd. 1. Unless noted, quotations in this chapter are from this journal. Rust entered many of his notations for subsequent years on the same date in his 1941 journal, apparently to save paper, but this creates some confusion for those reading his memoirs.

2. Rust, "Dan Duncan."

3. David Jordan Rust to Dave Rust, January 1943 (RC, box 7, fd. 10).

4. Ibid.

5. George Nelson Rust to Dave and Ruth Rust, April 20, 1944 (RC, box 6, fd. 7).

6. Telegram and correspondence from the Adjutant General, U.S. Army, August 15, 1944 (RC, box 9, fd. 7).

7. Rainbow Bridge visitor register, National Park Service, Glen Canyon National Recreation Area, Page, Arizona.

8. Moore, "Escalante—Utah's River of Arches"; Breed, "Utah's Arches of Stone" and "Flaming Cliffs of Monument Valley"; Bailey, "Desert River Through Navajo Land."

9. Rust to Emery Kolb, March 1, 1938 (KC, box 8, fd. 980).

10. Accounts of Rust's river-running friends can be found in Webb, *Call of the Colorado*; Topping, *Glen Canyon and the San Juan Country*; and Dimock, *The Very Hard Way*.

11. Rust to Harry Aleson, June 22, 1947 (USHS, Harry Aleson Papers, box 2, fd. 8).

12. Rust to Emery Kolb, October 21, 1952 (KC, box 11, fd. 1281).

13. Holmstrom's exploits are detailed in Webb, *Call of the Colorado*, 79, and Welch, Conley, and Dimock, *The Doing of the Thing*. Rust's impressions of Holmstrom are from a letter to Emery Kolb, March 1, 1938 (KC, box 8, fd. 980).

14. Rust to Harry Aleson, May 22, 1946 (USHS, Harry Aleson Papers, box 2, fd. 2).

15. Joseph C. Rust, "From the Dirty Devil to the Bright Angel," 38–39.

16. Ibid., 39–40.

17. Rust to Emery Kolb, July 17, 1953 (KC, box 11, fd. 1306).

18. Rust to Barbara Ekker, August 4, 1960. Collection of Barbara Ekker.

19. Stark, "A Vacation and the Nature of God."

20. Author interview with Joseph C. Rust, July 10, 1999.

21. Rust to Emery Kolb, January 15, 1960 (KC, box 11, fd. 1404).

22. Donald C. Scott to Rust, Nov. 29, 1955 and June 27, 1957 (RC, box 5, fd. 3).

23. Rust on Glen Canyon Dam: Rust to Otis R. Marston, April 24, 1955 (RC, box 3, fd. 12); author interviews with Quentin Rust, Salt Lake City, December 17, 2000, and Blanche Rasmussen, Salt Lake City, September 30, 2004. The evolving uses of Lake Powell are detailed in Farmer, *Glen Canyon Dammed*, 173–75.

24. Rust to Barbara Ekker, March 2, 1962. Collection of Barbara Ekker.

25. Dave's final weeks were recalled by Blanche Rasmussen (interview with author, May 6, 2005).

EPILOGUE

1. "Visitation Counts by Gate and Mode of Travel—2004, Grand Canyon National Park," U.S. Department of the Interior, National Park Service, Grand Canyon National Park (www.nps.gov/grca/facts/chart-2000s.pdf).

2. "Grand Canyon Wilderness Management Plan, April 1998," U.S. Department of the Interior, National Park Service, Grand Canyon National Park (www.nps.gov/grca/wilderness/draftwmp.htm).

3. U.S. Department of the Interior, National Park Service, Effects of Aircraft Overflights on the National Park System, table 9.2. September 12, 1994.

4. Vaughn Roche, "'Seldom Seen Smith' Mourns a Lost Canyon and Dead Foes," *High Country News* (Paonia, CO), October 18, 1993.

Bibliography

The principal source for this book was the David Dexter Rust Collection in the Church Archives of the Church of Jesus Christ of Latter-day Saints, located in Salt Lake City, Utah (here abbreviated "RC"). This extensive collection consists of Rust's personal diaries, unpublished writings by Rust and others, correspondence, news clippings, and ephemera. More than a thousand photographs taken by Rust and his clients, uncatalogued and largely unidentified, are also stored in this collection. Much additional material and many photographs came from the collection of Rust's daughter, Blanche Rasmussen.

Manuscripts referred to in the text are listed under the author's name. Abbreviations used for certain manuscript collections are given under Notes, above. Web pages cited were last accessed on May 28, 2007.

Adams, Harriet Chalmers. "The Grand Canyon Bridge." *National Geographic Magazine*, vol. 39, no. 6 (June 1921): 644–50.

Albright, Horace M., and Marian Albright Schenk. *Creating the National Park Service—The Missing Years*. Norman: University of Oklahoma Press, 1999. Web version: "Exploring a New World of Parks—1917" (www.cr.nps.gov/history/online_books/albright2/index.htm).

Alter, J. Cecil. *Early Utah Journalism: A Half-century of Forensic Warfare, Waged by the West's Most Militant Press*. Salt Lake City: Utah State Historical Society, 1938.

_____. "The Temple of the Gods." *Improvement Era*, vol. 22, no. 5 (March 1919): 393–400.

_____. *Through the Heart of the Scenic West*. Salt Lake City: Shepard Book Company, 1927.

_____. "Utah Recovers the Grand Canyon of Arizona." *Improvement Era*, vol. 23, no. 10 (August 1920): 909–17.

Anderson, Michael F. (ed.) *A Gathering of Grand Canyon Historians: Ideas, Arguments, and First-Person Accounts*. Grand Canyon, Ariz.: Grand Canyon Association, 2005.

_____. *Living at the Edge: Explorers, Exploiters and Settlers of the Grand Canyon Region*. Grand Canyon, Ariz.: Grand Canyon Association, 1998.

_____. *Polishing the Jewel: An Administrative History of Grand Canyon National Park*. Grand Canyon, Ariz.: Grand Canyon Association, 2000.

Aton, James M., and Robert S. McPherson. *River Flowing from the Sunrise: An Environmental History of the Lower San Juan*. Logan: Utah State University Press, 2000.

Babbitt, James E., ed. "Across the Painted Desert: Nicholas Roosevelt in Northern Arizona, 1913." *Journal of Arizona History*, vol. 28, no. 3 (Spring 1987).

Baker, Pearl. *Trail on the Water*. Boulder, Colo.: Pruett Publishing Company, 1969.

Bailey, Alfred M. "Desert River through Navajo Land." *National Geographic Magazine*, vol. 92, no. 3 (August 1947): 149–72.

Barnes, F. A. *Canyon Country Arches & Bridges and Other Natural Rock Openings*. Moab, Utah: Canyon Country Publications, 1987.

Bernheimer, Charles L. *Rainbow Bridge: Circling Navajo Mountain and Explorations in the "Bad Lands" of Southern Utah and Northern Arizona*. New York: Doubleday, Page & Co., 1926.

Berolzheimer, Charles P. and Arnold W. Koehler. "Our Western Trip: Crossing the Navajo Indian Reservation on Horseback, Summer 1919." Collection of Charles P. Berolzheimer II.

_____. "A Trip to Utah, August 1920." Collection of Charles P. Berolzheimer II.

Breed, Jack. "First Motor Sortie into Escalante Land." *National Geographic Magazine*, vol. 96, no. 3 (September 1949): 369–404.

_____. "Flaming Cliffs of Monument Valley." *National Geographic Magazine*, vol. 88, no. 4 (October 1945): 452–61.

_____. "Utah's Arches of Stone." *National Geographic Magazine*, vol. 92, no. 2 (August 1947): 173–92.

Brew, John Otis. *Archaeology of Alkali Ridge, Southeastern Utah*. Cambridge, Mass.: Papers of the Peabody Museum of American Archaeology and Ethnology, vol. 21 (1946).

_____. "Donald Scott and His Collection," in Schaafsma, *The Rock Art of Utah*.

Brigham Young Academy, *The White and Blue* (Provo, Utah).

Brown, Paul V. "A Narrative Report on the Trip to Horse Mountain and a Gallery Seat in the Escalante Area." U.S. Department of the Interior, National Park Service, Region Three, Santa Fe (August 14, 1943) (NPS-ENM).

Bryce, James. *Memories of Travel*. New York: The Macmillan Company, 1923.

Carroll, Elsie Chamberlain, ed. *History of Kane County*. Salt Lake City: Kane County Daughters of Utah Pioneers, 1960.

Carvalho, S. N. *Incidents of Travel and Adventure in the Far West; with Col. Fremont's Last Expedition across the Rocky Mountains: Including Three Month's Residence in Utah, and a Perilous Trip across the Great American Desert, to the Pacific*. New York: Derby & Jackson, 1857. Web version: www.jewish-history.com/WildWest/carvalho/.

Chalmers, Harriet. "The Grand Canyon Bridge." *National Geographic Magazine*, vol. 39 (June 1921): 645–50.

Chamberlain, Mary E. W. "A Short Sketch of the Life of Edwin Dilworth Woolley, Jr." Typescript, Utah State Historical Society, MSS A 1999. Reprint, Salt Lake City: Daughters of Utah Pioneers, 1934.

Crampton, C. Gregory. *Historical Sites in Glen Canyon: Mouth of Hansen Creek to San Juan River*. Salt Lake City: University of Utah Department of Anthropology, Anthropological Papers No. 61 (December 1962).

_____. *Outline History of the Glen Canyon Region, 1776–1922*. Salt Lake City: University of Utah Department of Anthropology, Anthropological Papers No. 42 (September 1959).

_____. *Standing Up Country: The Canyon Lands of Utah and Arizona*. Salt Lake City: Peregrine Smith Books, 1983. (Orig. pub. New York: A. A. Knopf, 1964.)

Cummings, Byron. "The Great Natural Bridges of Utah." *National Geographic Magazine*, vol. 21, no. 2 (February 1910): 157–67.

Cutter, Lois Jotter, "Then and Now." *Boatman's Quarterly Review* (Grand Canyon River Guides), Fall 1997. Web version: www.gcrg.org/bqr/10-4/then.html.

Danielson, Melvin D. "History of Education in Sevier County." Master's thesis, University of Utah, 1951.

Dellenbaugh, Frederick S. "A New Valley of Wonders." *Scribner's Magazine*, vol. 35, no. 1 (January 1904): 1–18.

_____. *A Canyon Voyage: The Narrative of the Second Powell Expedition Down the Green-Colorado River from Wyoming.* New York: G. P. Putnam's Sons, 1906. Reprint, Tucson: University of Arizona Press, 1984.

Dewey, John. *John Dewey: The Early Works, 1882–1898: Vol. 5, 1895–1898: Early Essays.* Carbondale, Ill.: Southern Illinois University Press, 1972.

Dimock, Brad. *The Very Hard Way: Bert Loper and the Colorado River.* Flagstaff, Ariz: Fretwater Press, 2007.

Dixon, Madoline C. *Peteetneet Town: A History of Payson, Utah.* Provo, Utah: Press Publishing Company, 1974.

Dutton, Clarence E. *Report on the Geology of the High Plateaus of Utah.* Washington, D.C.: U.S. Department of Interior, Geographical and Geological Survey of the Rocky Mountain Region, 1880.

_____. *Tertiary History of the Grand Cañon District, with Atlas.* Department of the Interior, Monographs of the United States Geological Survey, volume II. Washington D.C.: Government Printing Office, 1882. Reprint, Salt Lake City: Peregrine Smith, Inc., 1977. Reprint, Tucson: University of Arizona Press, 2001.

Dyar, W. W. "The Colossal Bridges of Utah: A Recent Discovery of Natural Wonders." *Century Magazine*, vol. 68, no. 4 (August 1904).

_____. "Colossal Natural Bridges of Utah." *National Geographic Magazine*, vol. 15, no. 9 (September 1904): 367–69.

Elliott, Melinda. *Great Excavations: Tales of Early Southwestern Archaeology, 1888–1939.* Santa Fe: School of American Research Press, 1995.

Farmer, Jared. *Glen Canyon Dammed: Inventing Lake Powell and the Canyon Country.* Tucson: University of Arizona Press, 1999.

_____. "Undiscovered to Undiscoverable: Gregory Natural Bridge," *Utah Historical Quarterly*, vol. 63, no. 2 (Spring 1995): 100–121.

Fawcett, William B., Jr., and William R. Latady. "Changes in the Organization of Technology and Labor Among Archaic and Ancestral Pueblo Peoples in the Vicinity of the Coombs Site, South-Central Utah," in *Proceedings of the Fourth Biennial Conference on Research on Colorado Plateau*, ed. Charles van Riper III and M. A. Stuart. Report Series USGS/FRESC/COPL/1999/16, United States Department of the Interior, U.S. Geological Survey. Web version: http://sbsc.wr.usgs.gov/cprs/news_info/meetings/biennial/proceedings/1997/cultural_resources/FawcettandLatady.pdf.

Flanders, Ralph E. *Senator from Vermont.* Boston: Little, Brown and Company, 1961.

Foss, Phillip O., ed. *Conservation in the United States: A Documentary History.* New York: Chelsea House Publishers, 1971.

Fowler, Don D., and Melvin Aikens. *1961 Excavations, Kaiparowits Plateau, Utah*. Salt Lake City: University of Utah Department of Anthropology, Anthropological Papers No. 66 (June 1963).

Fraser, George C. "Diaries, January 1, 1886 to December 18, 1886, During Journey to Egypt, the Holy Land, Ephesus, Greece, Constantinople, Up the Danube, Vienna, Switzerland, Germany and London." George C. Fraser journals, Princeton University Library.

_____. "El Vado de los Padres." *Natural History*, vol. 23, no. 4 (1923): 344–57.

_____. *Journeys in the Canyon Lands of Utah and Arizona, 1914–1916*. Edited by Frederick H. Swanson. Tucson, Ariz.: University of Arizona Press, 2005.

_____. "Memoranda of a Trip Taken by G. C. Fraser, Sr. and Jr., to Southwestern Utah and Northwestern Arizona, Sunday, June 28, 1914 to Thursday, August 6, 1914." George C. Fraser journals, Princeton University Library.

_____. "Notes of Journey, June 23rd to August 11th, 1922, with Jane Fraser, Jr. to Southwestern Utah; Portland, Oregon; Victoria, B.C.; Seattle, Washington and East via C. M. & St. Paul Railway." George C. Fraser journals, Princeton University Library.

Freeman, H. Dodge. "Vanadium and Uranium Deposits in the Triassic and Jurassic Sandstones of the Plateau Area of Southwestern Colorado and Southeastern Utah." Senior thesis, Princeton University, 1935.

Freeman, Lewis R. *Down the Grand Canyon*. New York: Dodd, Mead and Company, 1930.

Frye, Bradford J. *From Barrier to Crossroads: An Administrative History of Capitol Reef National Park*. Cultural Resources Selections no. 12, Intermountain Region. Denver: U.S. Department of the Interior, National Park Service, 1998.

Ghiglieri, Michael P., and Thomas M. Myers. *Over the Edge: Death in Grand Canyon: Gripping Accounts of All Known Fatal Mishaps in the Most Famous of the World's Seven Natural Wonders*. Flagstaff, Ariz.: Puma Press, 2001.

Gilbert, Grove Karl. *Report on the Geology of the Henry Mountains*. Department of the Interior, U.S. Geographical and Geological Survey of the Rocky Mountain Region. Washington, D.C.: Government Printing Office, 1877.

Goss, Robert. *Making Concessions in Yellowstone: A Who's Who of Explorers, Exploiters, Enthusiasts and Enterprises in Yellowstone National Park*. Privately published, 2001.

Granger, Byrd H. *Will C. Barnes' Arizona Place Names*. Tucson: University of Arizona Press, 1960.

Gregory, Herbert E., and Raymond C. Moore. *The Kaiparowits Region: A Geographic and Geologic Reconnaissance of Parts of Utah and Arizona*. United States Department of the Interior, Geological Survey Professional Paper 164. Washington, D.C.: Government Printing Office, 1931.

Grey, Zane. *The Heritage of the Desert*. New York: Harper & Row, 1910. Reprint, American Reprint Company, n.d.

_____. *The Last of the Plainsmen*. New York: Outing Publishing Company, 1908. Reprint, New York: Grosset & Dunlap, 1911.

_____. *Riders of the Purple Sage, A Novel*. New York: Harper & Brothers, 1912.

_____. *Tales of Lonely Trails*. New York: Harper & Brothers, 1922.

Gunnarson, James H. "1957 Excavations, Glen Canyon Area." Salt Lake City: University of Utah Department of Anthropology, Anthropological Papers No. 43 (September 1959).

Harris, Beth Kay. *The Towns of Tintic*. Denver: Sage Books, 1961.

Hassell, Hank. *Rainbow Bridge: An Illustrated History*. Logan: Utah State University Press, 1999.

Heath, Harvard S., ed. *In the World: The Diaries of Reed Smoot*. Salt Lake City: Signature Books, 1997.

Hemphill, Mark W. *Union Pacific: Salt Lake Route*. Erin, Ontario: Boston Mills Press, 1995.

Hinton, Wayne K. "Getting Along: The Significance of Cooperation in the Development of Zion National Park." *Utah Historical Quarterly*, vol. 68, no. 4 (Fall 2000): 313–31.

Holmes, Edwin F. "The Great Natural Bridges of Utah." *National Geographic Magazine*, vol. 18, no. 3 (March 1907): 199–204.

Hough, Emerson. "The President's Forest." *Saturday Evening Post*, vol. 194 (January 21, 1922): 23, 58–63.

Houk, Rose. *Dwellers of the Rainbow: The Fremont Culture in Capitol Reef Country*. Torrey, Utah: Capitol Reef Natural History Association (rev. ed.), 2005.

Hughes, J. Donald. *In the House of Stone and Light: A Human History of the Grand Canyon*. Grand Canyon, Ariz.: Grand Canyon Natural History Association, 1978.

Hunt, Charles B. *Geology and Geography of the Henry Mountains Region, Utah*. U.S. Department of the Interior, Geological Survey Professional Paper 228. Washington, D.C.: Government Printing Office, 1953.

Huntoon, Peter. "The Opening of Deer Creek and the History of the Thunder River Trail" (abstract). *The Ol' Pioneer*, Grand Canyon Historical Society, vol. 18, no. 1 (Jan/Feb/Mar 2007).

James, George Wharton. *The Grand Canyon, How to See It*. Boston: Little, Brown and Company, 1910.

_____. *In and Around the Grand Canyon: The Grand Canyon of the Colorado River in Arizona*. Boston: Little, Brown, and Company, 1901.

Jeffers, Le Roy. "The Temple of the Gods in Utah." *Scientific American*, vol. 119, no. 14 (October 5, 1918).

_____. *The Call of the Mountains: Rambles among the Mountains and Canyons of the United States and Canada*. New York: Dodd, Mead and Company, 1923.

Jennings, Jesse D. *Glen Canyon: An Archaeological Summary*. Salt Lake City: University of Utah Press, 1998.

Jensen, Ethel R. *Beneath the Casing Rock: The George Smith Rust Family*. Provo, Utah: Stevenson's Genealogical Center, 1981.

Jett, Stephen C. "The Great 'Race' to 'Discover' Rainbow Natural Bridge in 1909," *Kiva*, vol. 58, no. 1 (1992): 3–66. Web version: www.nps.gov/rabr/jett.htm.

_____. "The Journals of George C. Fraser '93: Early Twentieth Century Travels in the South and Southwest." *Princeton University Library Chronicle*, vol. 35 (Spring 1974): 290–308.

Judd, Neil M. *Archaeological Investigations North of the Rio Colorado*. Smithsonian Institution, Bureau of American Ethnology, Bulletin 82. Washington, D.C.: Government Printing Office, 1926.

_____. "Beyond the Clay Hills: An Account of the National Geographic Society's Reconnaissance of a Previously Unexplored Section in Utah." *National Geographic Magazine*, vol. 45, no. 3 (March 1924): 275–302.

_____. *Men Met along the Trail: Adventures in Archaeology*. Norman: University of Oklahoma Press, 1968.

Kanab Town Board. Minutes, 1912–1923. Utah State Archives, Salt Lake City, Series 84960.

Kane County Commission. Minutes. Utah State Archives, Salt Lake City, Series 83799.

Kelly, Charles. "At Eighty-Three He Is an Explorer," *Saturday Evening Post*, vol. 211 (May 6, 1939).

_____. "Proposed Escalante National Monument." *Desert Magazine*, vol. 5, no. 4 (February 1941): 21–22.

_____. "Sand and Sagebrush: Little Journeys to Odd Corners of the Desert." Charles Kelly papers, Marriott Library, University of Utah, 1949.

_____. "Valley of the Cathedrals." *Desert Magazine*, vol. 13, no. 2 (December 1949): 4–7.

_____, and Charlotte Martin. "Zeke Johnson's Natural Bridges." *Desert Magazine*, vol. 11 , no. 1 (November 1947): 12–15.

Kolb, E. L. *Through the Grand Canyon from Wyoming to Mexico*. New York: The Macmillan Company, 1914.

Lister, Florence C. *Kaiparowits Plateau and Glen Canyon Prehistory: An Interpretation Based on Ceramics*. Salt Lake City: University of Utah Department of Anthropology, Anthropological Papers No. 71 (July 1964).

Luckert, Karl W. *Navajo Mountain and Rainbow Bridge Religion*. Flagstaff: Museum of Northern Arizona, 1977.

Madsen, David B. *Exploring the Fremont*. University of Utah Occasional Publication No. 8. Salt Lake City: Utah Museum of Natural History, 1989.

Marr, John E. *The Scientific Study of Scenery*. London: Methuen & Co., 1900.

Matthes, F. E. "Breaking a Trail through Bright Angel Canyon." *Grand Canyon Nature Notes* (November 21, 1927). Grand Canyon, Ariz.: Grand Canyon Historical Society. Web version: www.grandcanyontreks.org/matthes.htm.

May, Dean L. "The United Order Movement," *Utah History Encyclopedia*. http://historytogo.utah.gov/utah_chapters/pioneers_and_cowboys/theunitedordermovement.html.

May, Stephen J. *Maverick Heart: The Further Adventures of Zane Grey*. Athens: Ohio University Press, 2000.

_____. *Zane Grey: Romancing the West*. Athens: Ohio University Press, 1997.

McGerr, Michael. *A Fierce Discontent: The Rise and Fall of the Progressive Movement in America, 1870–1920*. New York: Free Press, 2003.

McKoy, Kathleen L. *Cultures at a Crossroads: An Administrative History of Pipe Spring National Monument*. Cultural Resources Selections No. 15, Intermountain Region. Denver: National Park Service, 2000. Web version: www.nps.gov/pisp/adhi/adhi.htm.

Merrill, Harrison R. "Dave Rust, Lover of the Grand Canyon." *Improvement Era*, vol. 32, no. 6 (April 1929): 471–73.

Mills, Enos A. *Your National Parks*. New York: Houghton Mifflin, 1917. Reprint, 1920.

Monnett, John D., Jr. "The Mormon Church and Its Private School System in Utah: The Emergence of the Academies 1880–1892." PhD dissertation, University of Utah, 1984.

Moore, W. Robert. "Escalante: Utah's River of Arches." *National Geographic Magazine*, vol. 108, no. 3 (September 1955): 399–425.

Morss, Noel. *The Ancient Culture of the Fremont River in Utah: Report on the Explorations under the Claflin-Emerson Fund, 1928–1929*. Cambridge, Mass.: Papers of the Peabody Museum of American Archaeology and Ethnology, Harvard University, vol. 12, no. 3, 1931.

———. *Notes on the Archaeology of the Kaibito and Rainbow Plateaus in Arizona: Report on the Explorations, 1927*. Cambridge, Mass.: The Museum [Peabody Museum of American Archaeology and Ethnology, Harvard University], 1931.

Muir, John. "The Grand Cañon of the Colorado." *Century Illustrated Magazine*, vol. 65 (November 1902): 107–16. Reprinted in Muir, *Our National Parks* (Boston and New York: Houghton Mifflin Co., 1916).

Murphy, Thomas D. *Seven Wonderlands of the American West*. Boston: L. C. Page & Co., 1925.

National Park Service. "Bryce Canyon Historic Resource Study." www.cr.nps.gov/history/online_books/brca/hrs2.htm.

Newell, Maxine, and Terby Barnes. *The Untold History of Utah's Grand Staircase–Escalante National Monument*. Moab, Utah: Canyon Country Publications, 1998.

Pack, Frederick J. "History of Frederick James Pack: An Autobiography from February 2, 1875 to Aug. 26, 1933." Frederick J. Pack Papers, Marriott Library, University of Utah.

Pauly, Thomas H. *Zane Grey: His Life, His Adventures, His Women*. Chicago: University of Illinois Press, 2005.

Pomeroy, Earl. *In Search of the Golden West: The Tourist in Western America*. New York: Alfred A. Knopf, 1957.

Powell, John Wesley. *Report of Explorations in 1873 of the Colorado of the West and Its Tributaries, by Professor J. W. Powell, under the Direction of the Smithsonian Institution*. Washington, D.C.: Government Printing Office, 1874. Reprint, Ann Arbor: University of Michigan Library, 2005. Web version: www.hti.umich.edu/cgi/t/text/text-idx?c=moa;idno=AJA3599.

———. *Report on the Exploration of the Colorado River of the West and Its Tributaries, Explored in 1869, 1870, 1871, and 1872, under the Direction of the Secretary of the Smithsonian Institution*. Washington, D.C.: Government Printing Office, 1875.

———. *Second Annual Report of the United States Geological Survey to the Secretary of the Interior, 1880–81*. Washington, D.C., Government Printing Office, 1882.

Presnall, C. C. "Early Days in Bryce and Zion," *The Utah*, vol. 2, no. 6 (July 1936): 13–15, 55.

———. "Utah Exceeds All World in Scenic Wonders." *The Utah*, vol. 1, no. 1 (October 1935): 24–30, 38.

Pyne, Stephen J. *How the Canyon Became Grand: A Short History*. New York: Viking, 1998.

Ranney, Wayne. *Carving Grand Canyon: Evidence, Theories, and Mystery*. Grand Canyon, Ariz.: Grand Canyon Association, 2005.

Redd, J. Wiley, "History of the Natural Bridges," U.S. Department of the Interior, National Park Service, Canyonlands National Park, Moab, Utah, Natural Bridges National Monument files, series 2631, fd. 48, n.d.

Reilly, P. T. *Lee's Ferry: From Mormon Crossing to National Park*. Logan: Utah State University Press, 1999.

Richards, H. V. "A Pleasure Trip in 1914." *The Utah Magazine*, vol. 2, no. 7 (August 1936): 42–43.

Richardson, Elmo. "Federal Park Policy in Utah: The Escalante National Monument Controversy of 1935–1940." *Utah Historical Quarterly*, vol. 33, no. 2 (Spring 1965): 109–33.

Righter, Robert W. "National Monuments to National Parks: The Use of the Antiquities Act of 1906." *Western Historical Quarterly*, vol. 20, no. 3 (August 1989): 281–301. Web version: www.cr.nps.gov/history/hisnps/npshistory/righter.htm.

Rishel, Virginia. *Wheels to Adventure: Bill Rishel's Western Routes*. Salt Lake City: Howe Brothers, 1983.

Robinson, William J., "The Editor and His Uniquely Glorious Trip," *Critic and Guide*, vol. 25a (October 1923): 367–430. RC, box 13, fd. 5.

Rochester, Junius. *Little St. Simons Island on the Coast of Georgia*. Little St. Simons Press, 1994.

Roosevelt, Nicholas. *Theodore Roosevelt: The Man As I Knew Him*. New York: Dodd, Mead and Company, 1967.

Roosevelt, Theodore. "A Cougar Hunt on the Rim of the Grand Canyon." *The Outlook*, vol. 105 (October 4, 1913): 259–66.

Rothman, Hal. "Shaping the Nature of a Controversy: The Park Service, the Forest Service, and the Cedar Breaks Proposal." *Utah Historical Quarterly*, vol. 55, no. 3 (Summer 1987): 213–35.

Roundy, Jerry C. *Advised Them to Call the Place Escalante*. Springville, Utah: Art City Publishing, 2000.

Roylance, Ward J. *The Enchanted Wilderness: A Red Rock Odyssey*. Torrey, Utah: Four Corners West, 1986.

Rust, David D.

Published works:

_____. "Boating on the Colorado." *Improvement Era*, vol. 4, no. 7 (May 1901): 507–12.

_____. "The Bright Angel." *Improvement Era*, vol. 11, no. 3 (January 1908): 175–77.

_____. "De Motte Park." *Improvement Era*, vol. 14, no. 10 (August 1911): 873–76.

_____. "Fleeing to Zion—For Scenery." *Improvement Era*, vol. 32, no. 8 (June 1929): 662–63.

_____. "Rio Virgen." *Improvement Era*, vol. 36, no. 5 (March 1933): 282–84.

_____. "From Salt Lake to the Grand Canyon." *Improvement Era*, vol. 13, no. 5 (March 1910): 408–12.

_____. "The Worth of a Boy." *Improvement Era*, vol. 14, no. 3 (January 1911): 263–65.

Rust, David D.

Manuscripts:

_____. "Crossing Green River" [1895]. RC, box 10, fd. 12.

_____. "Dan Duncan." RC, box 1, fd. 5.

_____. "A Deer Hunt." RC, box 10, fd. 12.

_____. "Dennison Party 1934." RC, box 1, fd. 3, vols. 4–5.

_____. "Dodge Freeman Excursion 1935." RC, box 1, fd. 3.

_____. "Dodge Freeman 1939" [includes "River Trip" and "1940"]. RC, box 1, fd. 2, vol. 2.

_____. "Donald Scott and Wife 1928." RC, box 1, fd. 4.

_____. "Exploring with Peabody." Collection of Harold Rust.

_____. "Freeman, Lowe, King, July 1937." RC, box 1, fd. 3, vols. 4–5.

_____. "Freeman 1941." RC, box 1, fd. 4.

_____. "Genuine Travelers." RC, box 10, fd. 12.

_____. "Grand Canyon Journal 1906-7-8-9". RC, box 1, fd. 4, vol. 12.

_____. "Harry and Ben" [1927]. RC, box 1, fd. 4, vol. 7.

_____. "I Came Out of the Wilderness" and "Interview." Transcripts of interviews, KSL Radio, Salt Lake City [1937?]. RC, box 10, fd. 12.

_____. "If I Were Rich." RC, box 11, fd. 2.

_____. "John S. Chafee Party, June 25–July" [1937]. RC, box 1, fd. 3, vols. 4–5.

_____. "Lowe and Hartshorne 1938." RC, box 1, fd. 3, vol. 5.

_____. "My Best Stroke of Luck." RC, box 10, fd. 12.

_____. "Notes Gathered While Working in the Tourist Business." Interview by Mary E. W. Chamberlain (EDW-BYU, box 1, fd. 11).

_____. "Oastler Voyage, July 1, '25." RC, box 1, fd. 2, vol. 2.

_____. "Peabody 1929." RC, box 1, fd. 4.

_____. "Peabody Museum Archaeological Expedition 1930." RC, box 1, fd. 3, vols. 4–5.

_____. "Peabody Museum 1931." RC, box 1, fd. 4.

_____. "Preserve the Ruins." RC, box 11, fd. 2.

_____. "Private Journal—Jan 1. 1901 to Mar 12, 1901, Deseret." RC, box 1, fd. 4, vol. 12.

_____. "Seven Decades of Dave Rust." Collection of Blanche Rasmussen.

_____. "Stretching the Dollar" [1914]. RC, box 11, fd. 2.

_____. "Unusual Campout Excursions." RC, box 11, fd. 2.

Rust, David Jordan. David Jordan Rust Oral History Transcript, Charles Redd Center for Western Studies, Brigham Young University. Interview by Thomas G. Alexander, January 23, 1976.

_____. "Journal, June 26th through July 29th [1923]." Collection of Blanche Rasmussen.

Rust, Joseph C. "From the Dirty Devil to the Bright Angel: The History of David D. and Ruth W. Rust." Collection of Joseph C. Rust.

Rust, Ruth Woolley. Memoirs [1942]. Collection of Blanche Rasmussen.

Rust, William Slauson. "The Story of My Life." Church Archives, The Church of Jesus Christ of Latter-day Saints, Salt Lake City, Utah.

_____. "Visit of Col. Theodore Roosevelt," EDW-HBLL, box 2, fd. 12.

Schaafsma, Polly. *The Rock Art of Utah: A Study from the Donald Scott Collection*. Salt Lake City: University of Utah Press (reprint, 1999). Orig. pub.: Cambridge, Mass: Peabody Museum of Archaeology and Ethnology, Harvard University, *Papers of the Peabody Museum of Archaeology and Ethnology*, vol. 65, 1971.

Scrattish, Nick. "The Modern Discovery, Popularization, and Early Development of Bryce Canyon, Utah," *Utah Historical Quarterly*, vol. 49, no. 4 (Fall 1981): 348–62.

Sellars, Richard West. *Preserving Nature in the National Parks: A History*. New Haven: Yale University Press, 1997.

Shankland, Robert. *Steve Mather of the National Parks*. New York: A. A. Knopf, 1951.

Snow, Anne. *Rainbow Views: A History of Wayne County*. Springville, Utah: Art City Publishing Company, 1953.

Sons of Utah Pioneers. *Conquerors of the West: Stalwart Mormon Pioneers*, vol. 4. Salt Lake City: National Society of the Sons of Utah Pioneers, 1999.

Spangler, Jerry D., and Donna K. Spangler. *Horned Snakes and Axle Grease: A Roadside Guide to the Archaeology, History and Rock Art of Nine Mile Canyon*. Salt Lake City: Uinta Publishing Co., 2003.

Sproul, David Kent. *A Bridge Between Cultures: An Administrative History of Rainbow Bridge National Monument*. Cultural Resource Selections no. 18, Intermountain Region. Denver: National Park Service, 2001. Web version: www.nps.gov/rabr/adhi/adhit.htm.

Stanton, Robert B. *The Hoskaninni Papers: Mining in Glen Canyon, 1897–1902*. Edited by C. Gregory Crampton. Salt Lake City: University of Utah Department of Anthropology, Anthropological Papers No. 54 (November 1961).

Stark, Helen Candland. "A Vacation and the Nature of God." RC, box 11, fd. 1.

Stegner, Wallace. *Beyond the Hundredth Meridian: John Wesley Powell and the Second Opening of the West*. Lincoln: University of Nebraska Press. Reprint, 1982. (Orig. pub. Boston: Houghton Mifflin, 1954.)

_____. "Coda: Wilderness Letter." In *The Desert Reader: Descriptions of America's Arid Regions*. Edited by Peter Wild. Salt Lake City: University of Utah Press, 1991.

_____. *Where the Bluebird Sings to the Lemonade Spring: Living and Writing in the West*. New York: Random House, 1992.

Stone, Julius F. *Canyon Country: The Romance of a Drop of Water and a Grain of Sand*. New York: G. P. Putnam's Sons, 1932.

Suran, William C. *With the Wings of an Angel: A Biography of Ellsworth and Emery Kolb, Photographers of Grand Canyon*. Grand Canyon, Ariz.: Grand Canyon Historical Society, 1991. Web version: www.grandcanyonhistory.org/kolb.html.

Swanson, Frederick H. "Dave Rust in Glen Canyon: A 1923 River Diary." *The Confluence* (Colorado Plateau River Guides Assoc.), no. 22 (February 2001): 10–14.

Thompson, Almon H. "Diary of Almon Harris Thompson." *Utah Historical Quarterly*, vol. 7, nos. 1–3 (Jan.–April 1939).

Tipps, Betsy L. "Barrier Canyon Rock Art Dating," in National Park Service online publication, *Archaeology of Horseshoe Canyon* (www.nps.gov/cany/planyourvisit/upload/HorseshoeBook.pdf).

Toll, Roger. "Removals from List of Proposed National Parks and Monuments." Roger Toll Collection, Denver Public Library.

_____. "Reports on Proposed Parks and Monuments." Roger Toll Collection, Denver Public Library.

Topping, Gary. *Glen Canyon and the San Juan Country*. Moscow: University of Idaho Press, 1997.

_____. Papers, 1824–1998. USHS, Salt Lake City.

Turley, Kylie Nelson. "Kanab's All Woman Town Council, 1912–1914: Politics, Power Struggles, and Polygamy." *Utah Historical Quarterly*, vol. 73, no. 4 (Fall 2005): 308–28.

United States Department of the Interior, National Park Service. Report to Congress on Effects of Aircraft Overflights on the National Park System, September 12, 1994. Web version: www.nonoise.org/library/npreport/intro.htm.

United States Railroad Administration. "Zion National Monument, Utah." Chicago: Rathbun-Grant-Heller Co., 1919.

Utah State Attorney General. Records, Colorado River Case, 1929–1931, 4234–4263. Utah State Archives, Salt Lake City.

Utah State Planning Board. Records. Utah State Archives, Salt Lake City.

Van Cott, John W. *Utah Place Names: A Comprehensive Guide to the Origins of Geographic Names: A Compilation*. Salt Lake City: University of Utah Press, 1990.

Webb, Roy. *Call of the Colorado*. Moscow: University of Idaho Press, 1994.

_____, ed. *High, Wide, and Handsome: The River Journals of Norman D. Nevills*. Logan: Utah State University Press, 2005.

Welch, Vince, Cort Conley, and Brad Dimock. *The Doing of the Thing: The Brief, Brilliant Whitewater Career of Buzz Holmstrom*. Flagstaff, Ariz.: Fretwater Press, 1998.

West, Ray B. "The Proposed Escalante National Monument: Preliminary Report to Governor Henry H. Blood." Utah State Planning Board, May 1936. Marriott Library, University of Utah.

Westwood, Richard E. *Rough-water Man: Elwyn Blake's Colorado River Expeditions*. Reno: University of Nevada Press, 1992.

Wheeler, George M. *Report upon United States Geographical Surveys West of the One Hundredth Meridian*. Washington, D.C.: Government Printing Office, 1875.

Woodbury, Angus M. "Biotic Relationships of Zion Canyon, Utah with Special Reference to Succession," *Ecological Monographs*, vol. 3, no. 2 (April 1933): 147–245.

_____. *A History of Southern Utah and Its National Parks*. Rev. ed. Salt Lake City: Utah State Historical Society, 1950.

Woolley, F. B. "Report of Reconoitering Expedition, Mouth of Green River, 1866." Utah State Historical Society, Salt Lake City.

Woolsey, Nethella Griffin. *The Escalante Story*. Springville, Utah: Art City Publishing Co, 1964.

Index

Abajo Mountains, 228, 241, 249, 255

Affleck, David, 62, 63, 90

Agassiz, George A., 69, 70, 77, 208

airplanes, 271, 293, 305n5

Albright, Horace, 128–29, 148, 212, 249, 293, 310n27; at Grand Canyon, 212; in Zion Canyon, 107

Aleson, Harry, 73, 254, 282, 283, 284

Alter, J. Cecil, 81, 100, 110–11, 216–17, 239; quotations of, 30, 60, 144; "Temple of the Gods," 122; *Through the Heart of the Scenic West*, 144, 157; trips with Rust, 94–98, 157–58; "Utah Recovers the Grand Canyon of Arizona," 30

Anasazi. *See* Puebloans, Ancestral

Anderson, Larz and Isabel, 209–10

Andrus, Dolph, 117–18, 127–28

Andrus, James, 166–67

Angel Trail, 252

Antiquities Act of 1906, 144, 226, 235

Aquarius Plateau: xvi, xviii, 1, 195, 206, 207, 215, 222; Bowns Point on, xviii, 166–67, 197, 212, 241; Chokecherry Point on, 197; Donkey Point on, 240; early exploration of, 161, 166–67; lakes on, 165, 241; Rust's visits to, 164–67, 171, 179, 196–97, 226–27, 229, 238, 240–42, 265–67, 273, 285; sheep grazing on, 166, 265

archaeology: "Aztec" ruins, 220; in Colorado Plateau, 221, 235–36; of Fremont culture, 230, 233, 235–36; on Kaiparowits Plateau, 227; "Moki" houses, 220; private collecting, 222, 226, 229; pot hunting, 235. *See also* Claflin-Emerson expeditions; Puebloans, Ancestral

Archaic culture, 232

Arch Canyon, 249

arches, 134, 160–61, 227, 274, 275

Arches National Monument, 262–63, 282

Arizona Strip, 30–32, 101, 145; development of, 85, 87; dry farming in, 78–80; roads across, 90, 92, 103, 106, 123; Rust's travels in, 74, 87–88, 97, 194

Atchison, Topeka & Santa Fe Railway, 32, 37, 50, 83, 84, 88, 145, 146, 148

Atoko Point, 105, 120, 152

Augusta Natural Bridge, 139, 140

Aurand, Harry A., 258

automobiles: Cadillac, 101; difficulties with, 62–63, 87–88, 97–98, 101–2, 120, 210–11; at Grand Canyon, xx, 61–64, 90, 102, 109, 203, 228, 251; Locomobile, 62; in Monument Valley, 127–28; Pierce Arrow, 101; Rust's views on, 63–64, 204, 210, 261, 283, 294; in southern Utah, xx, 63, 90, 107–9, 133, 176, 190, 204, 211, 246, 267, 278; Thomas Flyer, 62

Awapa Plateau, 7, 170

Awatovi ruins, 234, 283

Aztec (Forbidding) Canyon, 184, 229, 269, 282

Bailey, T. C., 121

Baker, Frank, 252, 253

Baker, Pearl, 17, 217, 252

Barney, Lewis, 6

Barrier Canyon. *See* Horseshoe Canyon

Barrier Canyon style, 232

Bartol, Henry G. "Harry," Jr., 194–99 *passim,* 229

Bar Z Ranch, 99

"Basket Makers," 220, 222

Bass Camp, 114–15

Bass trail, 32–33, 115

Bass, William W., 32–33, 66, 73, 111, 114–15, 310n8

bears, 52, 65, 67, 81, 306n15

Bears Ears, 141, 254

Beck, Eldon, 273

Beckwith, Frank, 248

Behunin, Mosiah, 7

Benedict, R. E., 84

Bernheimer, Charles, 134–38, 249

Berolzheimer, Charles P., 128; head of California Cedar Co., 280; trips with Rust, 128–39, 140–42, 159–60, 163–71, 177–85; visits with Rust family, 186, 247; in World War II, 280–81

Berolzheimer, Philip, 128, 264

Biddlecome ranch, 233, 252

Big Park. See De Motte Park

Big Springs, 40, 44, 63, 90

Bird, Charles Sumner, 68–69, 77

Birdseye, Claude H., 185

Black Trail, 268, 276

Blake City (Green River), UT, 12, 279

Blue Dugway, 178

"Boating on the Colorado" (Rust), 17, 24, 69, 176, 199

boats, 73, 257; in Glen Canyon, 18, 21; of Grand Canyon Transportation Company, 40, 48; Rust's, 177–78, 182, 190–91, 199, 202, 215

Book of Mormon, 116

Borlase, Jack, 82

Boulder mail trail, 162, 227, 273

Boulder Mound (Coombs) site, 223, 228, 229

Boulder Mountain. See Aquarius Plateau

Boulder, UT, 162, 165, 196, 223–29 passim, 267, 285–86, 322n7

Bowl Creek, 179

Bowman, Harold, 124

Bowman & Co., 39

Bowns, Will, 166, 276

Bowns Canyon, 276

Bowns Point. See under Aquarius Plateau

Box, The, 34, 39, 57

Brahma Temple, 97, 126

Brant, Charles, 55

Brew, John Otis, xx, 234, 235, 239, 283, 319n23

Bridge Canyon, 136, 184

Bridge Creek, 135, 136

Brigham Young Academy, xvii, 13–14, 17, 23, 24, 25, 27

Brigham Young University, 13, 173, 213, 237, 244, 273, 281

"Bright Angel" (Rust), 58–59

Bright Angel Canyon, 33, 35, 38, 57, 58, 78, 289, 292

Bright Angel Creek, xviii, 30, 33–45 passim, 53, 57–59, 79, 97

Bright Angel Creek trail (Rust's). See Rust Trail

Bright Angel Point, 90, 96–97, 207; autos to, 61–63, 89, 102; Rust at, 96–97, 125; tourism at, 103, 109, 125–26, 148, 203, 211–12, 292–93

Bright Angel Spring, 111

Bright Angel trail (Ralph Cameron's), 32–33, 35, 42, 50, 53, 97, 303n14

Broaddus, J. E., 247–48

Bromide Basin, 23, 179, 180

Brown, Catherine Slauson, 5

Brown, Frank M., 71, 72, 73

Bryce Canyon, 120–22, 160, 311n26

Bryce Canyon National Park, 122, 151–52, 160, 196, 199, 213; lodge and cabins at, 122, 160, 204; as national monument, 122, 160; tourism at, 160, 199, 203–4, 211, 246, 283, 286; as Utah National Park, 122

Bryce, Ebenezer, 120

Bryce, James, 44, 56

Buckskin Mountain. See Kaibab Plateau

buffalo, 133

Buffalo Jones. See Jones, Charles J.

Bull Creek, 179

Bullfrog Creek, 224, 292

Bullfrog rapid, 190

Bull Pups Club (Kanab), 83
Burroughs, John, 56, 279
Burrville, UT, 6, 8, 9

Cable Mountain, 89, 97
Caine, John T., 7
Caineville, UT: description of, 8, 285;
    Rust's childhood in, 7–10; Rusts' move
    to, 7; floods affecting, 15; typhoid fever
    in, 14–15
Calf Creek, 162, 267, 268
California Cedar Products, 281, 287
Call of the Mountains (Jeffers), 120
Cameron, Ralph, 32, 33, 40, 50, 91, 303n14,
    304n12. *See also* Bright Angel trail
Cammerer, Arno, 262
Camp Fire Club of America, 69
Candland, Helen. See Stark, Helen Cand-
    land
Canyon Country (Stone), 280
canyon lands. *See* Colorado Plateau Pro-
    vince
Canyonlands National Park, 251, 258, 262
Canyon Voyage (Dellenbaugh), 69, 183, 270
Cape Final, xxiv, 207, 296; Rust at, 113, 120
Cape Royal, 93–94, 203, 293; Rust at, 113,
    120, 284
Capitol Gorge. *See* Capitol Wash
Capitol Reef, 247–48, 321n13
Capitol Reef National Monument, 247–49
Capitol Reef National Park, 168, 226, 321
Capitol Wash, 7, 9, 178, 200, 265, 285,
    300n9
Cárdenas, Garcia López de, 193
Caroline Natural Bridge, 139, 140
Carpenter, William, 183, 190, 217
Cassia Stake Academy, 29
Cassidy, Butch, 124, 251, 252
catalo, 49, 65, 73, 84, 94, 133, 304n9
Cataract Canyon, 175, 181, 201, 215, 216,
    253, 271, 284
Cathedral Valley, 248–49

Cedar Breaks National Monument, 203,
    210, 211
Cedar City, UT, 92, 101–5 *passim*, 123, 195,
    210, 211
Cedar Mesa Sandstone, 139, 255, 300n4
Chafee, John H., 266
Chafee, John S., 266
Chaffin, Arthur L. "Arth," 214, 253–54, 283
Chaffin, Faun, 231, 253
Chaffin, Lou, 19, 214
Chaffin, Ned, xxiii, 19, 149, 231
Chamberlain, Israel, 45, 55, 56, 78, 289
Chamberlain, Mary Woolley, 148, 307n11
Chamberlain, Thomas C., 33, 52, 307n11
Chenoweth, William, 273
Chimney Rock, 168
Chinle Formation, 169, 189, 196, 277
Circle Cliffs, 119, 163–64, 221, 266, 282
Claflin-Emerson expeditions, 221–24, 228–35
Claflin, William H., 221–24 *passim*, 227, 235
Clark, E. S., 33, 50, 91
cliff dwellings. *See* Puebloans, Ancestral,
    dwellings of
Clover, Elzada, 270–71
Coconino County, AZ, 30, 33, 35, 36, 91, 133,
    303n9
Coconino Plateau, 167
Cody, William F. "Buffalo Bill," 31, 208
Collet (Twentyfive Mile) Gulch, 172
Colorado Plateau Province: defined, 299n4;
    early descriptions of, 167, 243; mapping
    of, 161; Rust's interest in, 22, 29, 109, 202,
    205, 295
Colorado River: boating on, 17, 21, 24,
    69–73, 150, 177, 182–85, 187–88, 189–93,
    216–17, 257, 270–71, 274, 284; bridge
    over, 133, 176; cable crossings of, 32, 35,
    111; confluence with Green River, 167,
    255, 271; dams on, 189, 193–94; ferries
    at, 133, 156, 163, 254; floods in, 53, 57,
    68; fords of, 162, 163, 172, 191–93; gold
    in, 16–18, 20–22, 190, 214; guiding on,

201–2, 274, 282, 316n11; hazards of, 73, 187, 190–91, 199–201, 271; lava flows at, 112, 310n4; oil drilling along, 256; River Bed Case, 214–15; surveys of, 185; swimming in, 185, 217

Companion Alcove, 97

convict labor, 88, 91–92, 103, 124

Coombs site, 223, 228, 229

cougars. *See* mountain lions

cowboys, 30–31, 96, 157–58, 252–53, 274–76; Rust as, 12–13, 174, 280; as symbol, 100, 245

Coyote Gulch, 163, 274, 275

Coyote Hole, 162

Coyote Natural Bridge, 257

Crampton, C. Gregory, 19, 22, 182, 301n9, 316n11

Crescent Creek, 19, 175, 178, 181, 186, 189–90, 225, 254

Critic and Guide (Robinson), 179

Crossing of the Fathers, 119, 172, 183; discovery of steps at, 192–93; history of, 185; Rust's visits to, 184–85, 187, 190, 217, 269–70, 272

Culmer, H. L. A., 140

Cummings, Byron, 117, 134, 135, 139, 143, 221, 312n13

Cummings, Jesse, 99

Curtis, Milo, 251

dances, 8, 9, 11, 20, 24, 26, 179, 180

Dandy Crossing, 22, 176, 182, 192, 253–54; ferry at, 176, 254; named, 181

Davis Gulch, 228, 267, 268

Davis, William Morris, 28, 29, 302n27

Davol, George, 147–48, 313n10

Death Hollow, 162, 171, 266–67, 273

Dellenbaugh, Frederick, 69, 74, 107, 177, 195, 215–16; "A New Valley of Wonders," 74

Dellenbaugh, Mount, 218

Demaray, Arthur, 258

De Motte Park, 61, 95–96, 125, 146, 157, 204

"De Motte Park" (Rust), 95–96

Dennison, Henry S., 233, 239–42 *passim*, 264

Dennison, James, 233, 234, 239–42 *passim*

Dennison Manufacturing Company, 240

Denver & Rio Grande Railway, 83, 86, 87, 151, 178, 211, 225

Depression, Great, 231, 237, 240, 246, 248, 250, 257

Depression of 1921, 153–54

Dern, George, 189–91, 193, 247

Deseret Stake Academy, 24–25

Deva Temple, 97, 125–26

Devil's Garden, 227

Dewey, John, 25, 28; "My Pedagogic Creed," 25

diphtheria, 15

Dirty Devil River: description of, 7; Escalante River mistaken for, 161; floods in, 15; called Fremont River, 7, 300n8; mouth of, 181, 200; naming of, 58; Rust's childhood on, xvii, 7–8; Rust's trip to, 252–53, 266

Dobson, Will, 82

Dodds, Pardon, 161

Dodge, Frank, 185

Dominguez-Escalante expedition, 171–72, 185, 191–93

Doolittle, H. J., 110

Douglass, William B., 135, 312n13

Doyle, Al, 68

Down the Colorado (Freeman), 185

drought, 246, 252, 273

dry farming, 78–79, 122

Dudley, Frank A., 86

Dunham, Scott, 52, 59, 73, 78, 85, 98–99

Dutton, Clarence, xix, 10, 17, 116, 174, 242–43, 296, 302n4; on Aquarius Plateau, 164; on De Motte Park, 96; on Grand Canyon, 31, 97, 125; on Kaibab Plateau, 307n18; on Pink Cliffs, 120–21; on Toroweap, 112–14, 245; on Vermilion

Cliffs, 87; on Zion Canyon, 74, 152; *Geology of the High Plateaus of Utah*, 10, 120, 242; *Tertiary History of the Grand Cañon District*, 31, 74, 96, 111, 114, 174

Dutton Point, 120, 158, 207

Dyar, W. W., 140

Eagle City, UT, 23

East Kaibab monocline, 132

Echo Cliffs, 132–33

Eddy, Clyde, 216

Edwin Natural Bridge, 139, 140, 254

Elk Ridge, 169, 255

Ellen, Mount, xviii, 23, 195, 206, 207, 296; Rust's visits to, 116, 179, 197, 225, 251

Ellsworth, Mount, 195, 206, 241; Rust's visit to, 181

El Tovar hotel, 32, 55, 84, 126, 145

El Vado de los Padres. See Crossing of the Fathers

El Vado de los Padres (Fraser), 315n16

Emerson, Raymond, 221, 222, 224

Emery, UT, 22

Emmett, James, 33, 36, 49, 52, 66, 313n16

Emmett Creek. *See* Roaring Springs Creek

Enchanted Wilderness (Roylance), 282

Enlarged Homestead Act of 1909, 78

Ensign, Frank, 101

Entrada Sandstone, 162, 196, 248, 299n4

Escalante, UT, 161–67 *passim*, 172, 222–29 *passim*, 267, 286

Escalante canyons, xviii, xxxi, 195, 278, 282, 286, 321n9; Rust's explorations of, xviii, 119, 159, 162–64, 196, 222–23, 225, 228, 266–68, 273–78, 296

Escalante National Monument proposal, 258–62, 321n9, 322n13

Escalante River, xviii, 21, 267, 278, 283; discovery of, 161; inundation of, 273; roads to, 162–63, 225, 267, 286, 322n7

Exploration of the Colorado River (Powell), 74, 152, 183

False Creek, 161

Fewkes, Jesse Walter, 142, 221

Fiftymile (Soda) Gulch, 273, 274

Fiftymile Mountain, xvi, 119, 150, 171, 174, 191, 272; Rust's visits to, 161–63, 227–28, 272, 274–76

"First Motor Sortie into Escalante Country" (Breed), 267

Fish Creek Cove, 230

Fish Lake, 2, 7, 170, 247

Fishlake Plateau, xvii, 2, 116, 240

Flagstaff, AZ, 26, 45, 48, 65, 66, 283

Flanders, Nancy, 264

Flanders, Ralph, 1, 264–66, 280; *Senator from Vermont*, 264

flash floods, 7, 178, 266–67

"Fleeing to Zion—For Scenery" (Rust), 243–44, 245

Floral Ranch, 226

Forbes, Waldo Emerson, 233, 234

Forbidding (Aztec) Canyon, 184, 229, 269, 282

Forest Homestead Act of 1906, 79

Fort, Gerritt, 106

"Fourteen Points," 206, 251

Fraser, Ann, 150, 151

Fraser, George Corning, 1, 110, 133, 138, 149, 159, 186, 192, 196, 248, 257, 264, 288, 315n16; childhood travels, 118; death of, 238–39; correspondence with Rust, 115–19, 123, 130, 139, 150, 153, 155, 216, 238; friendship with Rust, 153–55, 173–74, 237, 239; trips with Rust, 110–21, 135, 151–53, 171–73, 177, 185, 205, 216; *El Vado de los Padres*, 315n16

Fraser, George Corning, Jr., 111, 117, 289

Fraser, Jane (wife of George C.), 1, 117, 151, 153, 216

Fraser, Jane (daughter of George C. and Jane), 151, 171, 185

Fraser, Myra, 117

Fraser, Sarah, xxiv, 217–18, 289

Frazier, Russell, 192–93, 272, 317n11

Fred Harvey Company, 147, 205, 313n10

Fredonia, AZ, 25–30 *passim*, 36, 37, 44, 63, 90, 109, 155

Freeman, Charles Y., 250

Freeman, Henry Dodge, 1, 193, 250–57, 260–64, 268, 271–81, 284–85, 289

Freeman, Lewis, 185

Fremont, John C., 3, 248

Fremont culture, 229, 232–33, 235–36; disappearance of, 236; naming of, 230

Fremont River, 7, 14, 168, 178, 197, 230, 300n8. *See also* Dirty Devil River

Fruita, UT, 168, 197, 217, 225, 232

Fuller Canyon, 33, 90, 93, 96, 112, 125, 308n2

Galloway, Nathaniel, 52, 79, 280; in Glen Canyon, 20–21; in Henry Mountains, 23, 179; river-running method, 21; river trips, 69–71, 192

Geneva Steel plant, 281

Geology and Geography of the Henry Mountains (Hunt), 15, 272

Geology of the Henry Mountains (Gilbert), 227

Geology of the High Plateaus of Utah (Dutton), 10, 120, 242

Gilbert, Grove Karl, 17, 120, 134, 182, 226, 245, 315n5; *Geology of the Henry Mountains*, 227

Glen Canyon: description of, 1, 175–76; gold discovered in, 17–18; history of, 17–19, 175–76, 191–93, 272; rapids in, 21, 24, 69, 182, 184, 187, 190, 199; Rust mining in, xviii, 15–16, 19–22; Rust's boating trips in, 1, 116, 177–91, 197–201, 212, 216–19, 238, 268–71, 316n11; Rust's horseback trips to, 19, 171–72, 225

Glen Canyon Dam, 185, 193–94, 294; Rust's views on, 194, 289

Glen Canyon National Recreation Area, 163

Goblet of Venus, 186

"God of the Open Air" (Van Dyke), 270, 291

gold mining. *See* mines and mining

Good Hope Bar, 21, 182, 190

Good Hope Mining Company, 21

Goodridge (Mexican Hat), UT, 138

Good Roads Automobilist, 127, 129

Goosenecks (of San Juan River), 249

Grand Canyon: airplane crash in, 288; airplanes at, 305n5; early automobiles to, 61–64, 90; descriptions of, 44, 61, 97, 112, 125; North Rim of, 31–34, 83–84, 89, 96–97, 102, 104–15 *passim*, 120, 125–26, 146, 156–57, 203–4, 211–12, 292–93; road proposed across, 260; roads to, 88–92, 94–95, 101–4, 109, 123–24; South Rim, 32, 37, 50, 60, 65, 114–15, 145, 156, 203; tourism at, 31–33, 57, 60, 84, 102–10, 126, 145, 156, 203, 292–93

Grand Canyon Auto Road, 88–90, 95

Grand Canyon Cattle Company, 132, 157, 314n35

Grand Canyon Forest Reserve, 79

Grand Canyon Game Preserve, 32, 65, 115, 145–46

Grand Canyon Highway, 90–92, 101–2, 109, 123–24

Grand Canyon Lodge, 212, 292

Grand Canyon National Monument, 84, 144–45; designation of, 32, 314n37

Grand Canyon National Park: designation of, 107, 144–46; expansion of, 107, 157; railroad to, 146; tourism at, 84, 93, 212, 292–93. *See also* Grand Canyon, tourism at

Grand Canyon Supergroup, 113

Grand Canyon Toll Road, 33

Grand Canyon Transportation Company: clients of, 85, 98–99; employees of, 45, 52, 59, 85, 94; facilities of, 145; finances of, 33, 52, 77–78; incorporation of, 33; outfitting cabin of (*see* Woolley cabin);

relations with Forest Service, 146; road
application by, 35–36; Rust hired by,
36–37. *See also* Rust Trail
Grand Staircase, 191
Granite Ranch, 178
Grant, Heber J., 212
Grass Valley, 2, 6–7, 167, 285
Graves, Henry S., 84, 85, 86, 308n24
Great Gallery, 232, 297, 320n26–27
Greenland. *See* Walhalla Plateau
Green River, 12, 150, 201, 234, 256, 258,
270–71; confluence with Colorado, 166,
255
Green River, UT, 12, 178, 201, 261
Gregory Natural Bridge, 273–75
Gregory, Herbert, 134, 162, 173–74, 207,
273; Rust and, 194, 251
Grey, Zane, 65–68, 100, 245, 304n2,
306n12–15, 313n16; Rust's experiences
with, 66–68
Grey, Zane, works by: *Heritage of the Desert*,
67, 132; *Last of the Plainsmen*, 66; *Riders
of the Purple Sage*, 68; *Tales of Lonely
Trails*, 313n16
Griffin, Ken, 227–28
Griffiths, Rees B., 52, 59, 85, 106
Grimes, Oliver J., 121, 189–92
Grinnell, George Bird, 138, 149, 156
Guernsey, S. J., 224
Guffy, Porter, 33
Gunsight Pass, 192

Hall, Ansel F., 250
Hall, Charles, 19, 163, 223; wagon road of,
19, 163, 268
Halls Crossing, 18, 21, 176, 269, 272, 277
Hanks, Ephraim, 226
Hanks ranch, 167–68, 241
Hanksville, UT, 13, 15, 178–80, 246, 251–52
Hansen, Archie, 272
Harris Wash, 159, 161, 163, 223; road
through, 163

Hartnet, 10–11, 271, 279
Hartshorne, Harold, 268
Harvey Meadow, 33, 305n27
Hatch, Bus, 201
Hays, H. H., 9, 106
Heaton, Alvin, 51
Hells Backbone road, 267
Henry, Wash, 33
Henry Mountains, xvi, 7, 134, 266, 272;
naming of, 161, 315n5; Rust in, xviii,
13–14, 23, 180–81, 225, 238, 265
Heritage of the Desert (Grey), 67, 132
Hickman, Joseph, 247
Hickman Natural Bridge, 168, 217, 226
High Plateaus Province, 116
Highway 12, 162, 286
Highway 24, 178, 300n9
Hite, Ben, 21
Hite, Cass, 17, 21, 139, 176, 181, 217, 312n13
Hite, UT, 18–19, 21, 178, 180–82, 186, 225,
253–54
Hite Crossing. *See* Dandy Crossing
Hite ferry, 176, 254
Hole-in-the-Rock: automobiles at, 278;
Mormon emigrant party at, 19; Rust's
visits to, 183, 187–88, 191, 218–19, 269;
trail to, 19, 162
Hollwith, George C., 212
Holmes, Edwin F., 140, 141
Holmes, Mount, 241
Holmes, W. H., 113–14, 121, 314n23
Holmstrom, Haldane "Buzz," 284
homesteading. *See* Enlarged Homestead
Act; Forest Homestead Act
Honda (Broken Bow) Arch, 275
Hoover Dam, 194
Hopi Indians, 140, 220
Hopkins, W. H., 127
Horsecollar Ruin, 139
Horse Mountain, 255, 321n9
horses, 12, 21, 34, 39, 42, 99, 111, 119,
265–66, 304n24; compared to auto-

mobiles, 87–88, 108, 127, 206, 211; horse trading, 168; Rust's, 11, 14, 53–54, 69, 77–78, 117, 138, 240, 251, 274

Horseshoe Canyon: called Barrier Canyon, 231; prehistory in, 231–33; Rust at, 231–33, 252–53, 257

Horseshoe Shelter site, 233

Horsethief Trail, 256

Hoskaninni Mining Company, 20, 23, 140, 301n9

Hotel Highway, 132, 210

Hough, Emerson, 156

House Rock Desert, 49, 259

Howard, Mary. *See* Chamberlain, Mary Woolley

Howell, Joseph, 36

Hoyt, Timothy C., 33, 34, 36, 85–86, 146

Hoyt's Point, 34, 303n12

Humphrey, J. W., 120

Humphries, Tom, 181

Hunt, Charles B., 15, 272; *Geology and Geography of the Henry Mountains*, 15, 272

hunting: of bears, 52, 67, 81; on Kaibab Plateau, 31–33, 41–42; of mountain lions, 49, 52–53, 65–66, 68–69, 99, 212, 222; Rust's views on, 67, 115, 119–20

Hurricane, UT, 75, 90, 92, 97

Hurricane Gulch, 274

Ickes, Harold, 258–59, 322n12

Improvement Era, 24, 176

Indian Gardens, 35, 45, 50, 54

influenza, 137, 155

Inglesby, A. L., 199–200, 316n2

Inscription House, 134

inscriptions, historic, 18, 193, 218, 268, 272, 296

Intelligencer tour company, 199–200

Jacob Hamblin Arch, 275

Jacob Lake, 46, 63, 90, 125, 292

James, George Wharton, 64, 245

Jeffers, Le Roy, 119–22, 127, 311n23; "Temple of the Gods in Utah," 121

Jensen, Aldus "Blondie," 106

Jensen, Ethel, 4, 6, 11, 15, 23, 151, 300n5; trip to North Rim, 124–26

Jett, Stephen C., 135, 312n13, 313n16, 315n3

Johnson, Ezekiel "Zeke": as guide, 129, 137, 141, 186, 187, 208; at Natural Bridges N. M., 139, 235, 247, 254

Johnson, Frank, 133, 185

Johnson, Jerry, 133, 185, 188

Johnson, W. Louis, 212

Johnson Canyon, 63, 90, 94, 248

Jones, Charles J. "Buffalo," 49, 65–69 *passim*, 73, 133, 304n9, 313n16

Jordan, David Starr, 27

Jotter, Lois, 270, 271

Judd, Neil, 149, 183, 221

Judd, Thomas, 74

Kachina Natural Bridge. *See* Caroline Natural Bridge

Kaibab Plateau: deer herds, 33, 115; description of, 30–31, 95–96; as game preserve, 32; livestock grazing on, 156–57; named, 30–31, 302n2; as national monument, 32; "President's Forest" proposed for, 156–57; railroad proposed for, 85–86; Rust's travels on, 45–46, 58, 61, 65, 73, 94–95, 115, 120, 124–25, 152, 158, 284–85; timbering proposed for, 84–86; tourist lodge on, 204. *See also* Grand Canyon (North Rim); hunting

Kaibab squirrel, 125

Kaibito, AZ, xvi, 133

Kaibito Desert copper mine, 155

Kaibito Plateau, 132, 134, 138

Kaibito Spring. *See* Kaibito, AZ

Kaiparowits Plateau, 19, 150, 162, 166, 171, 191, 207; archaeology of, 227, 319n12; Rust's visits to, 172

Kaiparowits Region (Gregory), 162, 172

Kalamazoo Canvas Boat Company, 177

Kanab, UT, 26, 78, 132, 153; first autos to, 63; Commercial Club of, 83, 91; Hotel Highway in, 210; newspapers in, 80–82; roads to and from, 32, 44, 63, 83, 85, 87–88, 90–91, 94, 105, 123–24; Rusts' home in, 44, 80, 94, 106, 112, 122, 147, 213–14; schools in, 82–83, 287; town council of, 81, 150, 154, 307n12; water system, 150

Kanab Canyon, 111

Kanarra Valley, 75

Kane County, UT, 26, 51, 79, 92, 243, 283; school system in, 82; elections in, 123, 213, 307n14

Kane County Independent, 82

Kane County News, 80, 82

Kane Creek, 172, 192

Kelly, Charles, 192–93, 248, 271–72

Kelly, Howard A., 200, 201

Kidder, A. V., 231, 319n23

Kidder, Alfred, Jr., 231

King, Wesley E., 87–88

King ranch, 179, 197, 225

kivas. *See under* Puebloans, Ancestral

Klondike Bar, 19

Knight, Jesse, 52

Knowles, Emery, 140

Koehler, Arnold, Jr., 128; trips with Rust, 128–39, 140–42, 159–60, 163–71, 177–85

Kolb, Blanche, 43, 58

Kolb, Edith, 58

Kolb, Ellsworth, 42–43, 45, 49, 54, 147, 257, 283, 289; river running, 71–73; trips with Rust, 58

Kolb, Emery, 43, 58, 257, 283–84, 287–89; river running, 70–73, 185, 212; trips with Rust, 70–71, 212, 284

Kolb studio, 43, 57

laccoliths, 134

Laguna Creek, 128

Lake Canyon, 193, 198, 221, 272

Lake Powell, 176, 254, 289–90

Lamp Stand, 164

LaRue, E. C., 185

La Sal Mountains, 256

Last Chance Creek, 20, 171, 188

Last of the Plainsmen (Grey), 66

Latter-day Saints, Church of Jesus Christ of, 15, 25–27, 30, 51, 122–23, 212; emigration of, 3–5, 243–44; school system of, 9, 29; Zane Grey's depiction of, 67–68

La Verkin, UT, 74

Lee, John D., 185

Lees Ferry, 33, 68, 69, 133, 185, 188, 272

LeFevre Ridge, 90

Lions Club of Moab, 262

Little De Motte Park, 95, 157

"Little Giant" engine, 54–55

Little Rockies, xvi, 181, 206. *See also* Mounts Ellsworth and Holmes

Little Zion. *See* Zion Canyon

Loa, UT, 14, 15, 18, 240, 247, 48

Long, Horace J., 140

Long Valley, 50, 75, 87, 90, 94

"Lookout Ridge." *See* Navajo Mountain

Loper, Bert, 17–18, 73, 215, 283, 317n11; at River Bed Case hearing, 214; river running, 272; trip with Rust, 216–17

Lowe, L. F. H., 268, 269, 270, 271

Lund, UT, 83, 86, 103, 105, 110, 210

Lyman, Francis, 165

Mace, Charley, 157–58

MacFarland, J. M., 259

Mancos, CO, 13

Manderfield, J. H., 101–7, 110–11

Manti, UT, 15, 27, 151

maps, 127, 146, 250; of Colorado River, 183, 192; highway, 206, 286; by Powell Survey, 113, 161, 295; of Rust trail, xviii, 303n12

Marble Canyon, 67, 71, 73, 132, 185, 270

Marble Canyon Lodge, 272

Marble Canyon National Monument, 32, 314n37

Markagunt Plateau, 1, 67, 203; Rust's visits to, 52, 69, 75–76, 116, 210

Marston, Otis R. "Dock," 73, 282

Marysvale, UT, 83, 86, 87, 211

Mather, Stephen T., 108, 148, 156, 157, 186, 212, 249

Matthes, Francois E., 34

McDougal, Les, 231

McKee, Edwin, 267, 322

McKee, Elizabeth Wylie, 126

Memories of Travel (Bryce), 44, 56

Merrill, Harrison R., xix, 176–77, 206, 210, 244

Mesa Verde National Park, 128, 156, 205, 229, 244; Rust at, 141–42, 221; tourism at, 142

Meskin, Ed, 18, 20, 188, 316n15

Metate Arch, 227

Mexican Hat, UT, 138, 206

Middle Desert, 10, 248

Miller, Louis, 269

Miller, Ralph, 272

mines and mining: on Colorado River, 17–21, 181, 190, 269; at Grand Canyon, 35, 63, 144, 146; in Henry Mountains, 23; Klondike discovery, 18; for oil, 163, 256; at Tintic, 5, 8 52; for uranium, 250–51, 263, 321n2. *See also under* Rust, David Dexter

Minnie Maud Canyon, 230, 233–34

Moab, UT, 201, 256, 262

Moki steps, 275

Monett, Ed, 217

Monument Canyon, 175

"Monumental Valley." *See* Monument Valley

Monument Valley, xvi, 128, 241, 249; first auto to, 127–28; Rust's visits to, 117–18, 138

Moody canyons, 276–77

Moore, Raymond C., 171, 172

Moqui Canyon, 183

Moran, Thomas, 93, 104, 121

Mormon Battalion, 4

Mormons, Mormon Church. *See* Latter-day Saints, Church of Jesus Christ of

Moroni Slopes, 240–41

Morss, Noel, 228–30, 233, 235; *Ancient Culture of the Fremont River in Utah*, 230, 235

Mound Canyon, 175, 183

mountain lions, 33, 65–67, 98, 106, 222, 306n15

Mount Carmel, UT, 63, 76, 87

Muav Canyon, 33, 66, 114–15

Muav Saddle, 73, 114–15

Muir, John, 56, 64

Mukuntuweap. *See* Zion Canyon

Mukuntuweap National Monument. *See* Zion National Park

mules, xvii, 10, 51–52, 196, 211, 234, 277, 278, 293

Muley Twist Canyon, 63, 163, 223, 268

Mulford, Clarence, 230

Music Temple, 183–84, 269

"My Pedagogic Creed" (Dewey), 25

Naile Canyon, 63, 90, 304n2

Nasja Begay, 117, 135, 137. *See also* Old Nasja

National Geographic Magazine, xix, 140, 141, 147, 183, 267, 282

national parks. *See* individual names of

National Park Service: policies, 108, 147–48, 226, 259–60, 293; promotion of tourism, 108, 128, 156, 203, 211, 248, 260, 283, 293; Rust's relationship with, xx, 146–49. *See also* Escalante National Monument; individual national parks and monuments.

National Park to Park Highway, 156

National Park Transportation and Camping Company, 107. *See also* Utah Parks Company

natural bridges, 121–22, 139–40, 168, 171, 217, 241, 246–47, 257, 273–75

Natural Bridges National Monument, 139–41, 186, 254, 259, 283; tourism at, 140–41

Nauvoo, IL, 4, 285

Navajo Indian Reservation, 117–18, 127–29, 137, 142, 219; tourism on, 138

Navajo Indians, 133–37 *passim*, 142, 150, 313n16, 315n3, 319n23. *See also under* Navajo Mountain

Navajo Mountain: descriptions of, 136, 141; geology of, 134; Navajo spirituality on, 135, 312n12; Rust's visits to, xv, xvii, 133–37; views from, xv–xvi, 173–74, 206

Navajo National Monument, 134

Navajo National Park (proposed), 249

Navajo Sandstone, 135, 196, 267

Needles, 255

Nevills, Norman, 188, 201, 250, 269–71 *passim*, 274, 275, 278, 282

Newberry, J. S., 243

"New Valley of Wonders" (Dellenbaugh), 74

New York Evening Post, 224

Nine Mile Canyon, 230, 248

Noble, Howard, 42

North Kaibab Trail, 292

North Rim. *See under* Grand Canyon

North Trail, 253

North Wash, 19, 178, 189, 254, 271. *See also* Crescent Creek

Oastler, Frank R., 186, 187, 249, 262

Oastler, Maude, 187

Ohio Oil Company, 163

Old Bright Angel Trail. *See* Rust Trail

Old Nasja, 137

Onstott, Frank, 59, 61, 305n27

Orange Cliffs, 231, 251, 253, 255, 263

Orderville, UT, 50–51, 76, 77

Orderville Gulch, 152

Otter Creek, 2, 167

Owachomo Natural Bridge. *See* Edwin Natural Bridge

Owens, James T. "Uncle Jim," 60, 63, 65–66, 99, 133, 305n27

Owens, William T., Jr., 213

Oyler, Michael Valentine "Tine," 225

Oyler ranch, 217, 225

Pace, Jim, 214, 240, 242

Pack, Frederick J., 199–201

Padre Creek, 172, 185, 192

Pagahrit, Lake, 198

Pahreah, UT, 20, 185, 194, 279

Paiute Indians, xv, 84, 135, 137–38, 150; names given by, 30, 74, 152, 302n2, 306n28. *See also* Nasja Begay; Old Nasja

Panguitch, UT, 82, 86, 120, 123, 213

Panguitch Lake, 52, 75

Paria River, 20, 69, 120, 161, 191, 194–95, 222

Parry, Chauncey, 107, 189–91, 269

Parry, Gronway, 107

Parsons, Herbert, 85

Parunuweap Canyon, 74, 131, 152, 310n1

"Pathfinder" expeditions, 90, 102

Paunsaugunt Plateau, 120–22, 151–52, 195–96, 206, 222, 273

Payson, UT, 3, 5

Peabody Museum of American Archaeology and Ethnology, 221, 224–28, 230–35

Peale, Mount, 256

Pearl of Great Price (Smith), 116

Pectol, Ephraim P., 222, 226, 229, 247–48

Pelton, James, 90, 95

Peterson, J. Q., 259

petroglyphs. *See under* Puebloans, Ancestral, rock art of

Phantom Creek, 45, 221

Phantom Ranch, 45, 147, 149, 293, 303n14

pictographs. *See* Puebloans, Ancestral, rock art of

Pinchot, Gifford, 84–85

Pine Alcove Creek, 224

Pine Valley Mountains, 76, 116, 206, 207, 251

Pink Cliffs, 75, 120–21

Pioneer Day (Utah), 172, 183

Pipe Creek, 35, 53, 303n14

Pipe Spring, AZ, 26, 74, 103; Rust's property at, 80, 122, 214; Will and Sarah Rust at, 80

Pipe Spring National Monument, 74

Plateau Province. *See* Colorado Plateau

Point Imperial, 94, 152, 284

Point Sublime, 58, 94, 114, 228

polygamy, 9, 30, 307n11

ponderosa pine, 61, 84–85, 164, 307n19

Powell, John Wesley, xix, 116, 152, 182, 295; names given by, 58, 74, 95, 113, 152, 161, 167, 175, 184, 224, 299n4, 302n2; surveys of, 30–31, 160, 161, 218; expeditions of, 17, 69, 220; *Exploration of the Colorado River*, 74, 152, 183

Powell Plateau, 66, 73, 94, 114, 152, 158

Powell Point, 160–61, 171, 196, 242, 266

Presnall, C. C., 211

primitive areas, 261–62

Proctor, J. P., 175, 187–88, 221

Progressive Era, 108, 130, 294, 317n5

progressivism. See Progressive Era

Provo, UT, 14, 25, 28; Rust's retirement to, 213–14

Puebloans, Ancestral, 137, 220–30, 232–36, 319n23; disappearance of, 229, 232; dwellings or ruins of, 41, 134, 138, 139, 142, 149, 163, 183, 198, 220–24, 226–30, 232–36, 249, 255, 277, 319n14, 320n4; Kayenta Anasazi, 229, 319n14; kivas of, 142, 228, 319n14; naming of, 319n23;

rock art of, 197, 217, 220, 225–27, 230–32, 241, 248, 320n27

Pugh, Charles, 123

railroads: as homesteading promoters, 78; to Kaibab Plateau, 83–86; to South Rim, 32, 37, 145; as tourism promoters, 102–4, 106–8, 121–22, 145, 203, 211. *See also* individual names of

Rainbow Bridge, xvi, 138, 274, 282, 312n11, 315n3; discovery of, xvi, 117, 135, 312n13; Rust's visits to, 135–36, 184, 188, 198, 212, 269

Rainbow Bridge–Monument Valley Expedition, 250

Rainbow Lodge, 138, 212

Rainbow Plateau, 134, 159

Rainbow Trail, 135, 136

Rauch, Thomas, 122

Raymond & Whitcomb company, 209

Redbud Pass, 137

Redd, Charles, 259–60

Red House ruin, 134

Red Wall. *See* Vermilion Cliffs

Richardson, Elmo R., 262

Richardson brothers, 138

Richardson's trading post, 133

Richfield, UT, 88, 123, 247, 283; *Richfield Reaper*, 268–69; Rust attending school in, 9, 13

Richmond, William, 69

Riders of the Purple Sage (Grey), 68

Rincon, 223

Rio Virgen. See Virgin River

Rishel, Bill, 90, 108

Ritchie, Elizabeth, 187–88

River Bed Case, 214–15

roads: to Bryce Canyon, 121; to Cedar Breaks, 203; condition of, 32, 62–63, 75, 87–89, 97–98, 101–3; construction of, 89–92, 123–24; to Escalante canyons, 162, 172, 267–68, 285–86, 322n7; to

Glen Canyon, 178, 206; to Grand Canyon, 32, 63, 89–90, 93, 126, 156, 203, 284, 308n31, 308n2; to Hanksville, 178, 197; to Natural Bridges National Monument, 254, 259; on Navajo Reservation, 127–28, 137, 138; pioneer, 7, 10, 19, 163, 183, 225, 272; Rust's interest in improving, 88, 124, 156; to Zion Canyon, 109, 203. *See also* Grand Canyon Auto Road; Grand Canyon Highway

Roaring Springs Creek, 38

Robbers Roost Canyon (Ariz.), 61, 63, 125

Robbers Roost Canyon (Utah), 231, 252, 256–57, 320n26

Roberts, Henry, 230–33 *passim*, 235

Robinson, William, 179–80

rock art. *See under* Puebloans, Ancestral

Rock Art of Utah (Schaafsma), 235

Rockville, UT, 74

Rollins, Phillip, 195

Roosevelt Camp, 147. *See also* Rust's Camp

Roosevelt, Franklin Delano, 224, 258, 262

Roosevelt, Nicholas, 98–99

Roosevelt, Quentin, 100

Roosevelt, Theodore, xx, 27, 32, 68, 98, 100, 139, 309n11

Roosevelt, Theodore, Jr., 100

Rothman, Hal, 149

Ruby, Glen M., 189–91 *passim*, 196

Ruesch, Walter, 107, 141

Ruess, Everett, 267

Ruetz, Joseph, 269

Ruin Park, 232, 255

ruins. *See under* Puebloans, Ancestral

Russell, Charles, 217

Rust, Blanche (Mrs. Elden Rasmussen, daughter), xxiii, 213, 281, 282, 290

Rust, David Dexter "Dave": automobiles, views on, 63–64, 204, 210, 261, 283, 294; birth of, 3; at Brigham Young Academy, 13–14, 17, 23, 24–25, 27; in California, 23, 27–29, 214; childhood of, 6–11; children, *see* individual names; cost of trips, 67–68, 103, 198, 201, 205, 222, 224; death of, 290–91; education of, xvii, 6, 9, 13–14, 23–25, 27–29; as farmer, 78–79; fiddles and fiddling, 11, 23; "Fourteen Points," 206–7, 251; Glen Canyon Dam, views on, 289; as guide, xviii, xx, 118, 158, 208, 234, 242; Forest Service and, 51–52, 145–46; Fraser family, friendship with, 153, 289; in Grand Canyon, 37–71; with Zane Grey, 65–68; as homesteader, 78–80, 122, 214; horsemanship of, 12, 51–52, 234; Kolb brothers, friendship with, 42–43, 45, 54, 58–59, 71–73; Emery Kolb, trips with, 58, 70–71, 212; LDS Church mission, 27; as legislator, xvii, 123–24; and literature, xx, 24, 208, 244–46, 279–80; marriage, 27; as mayor of Kanab, 154–55; menus and provisions on trips, 169, 209, 253, 255, 276; as miner, xviii, 15–16, 18–23, 155–56, 180, 214; as Dave Naab, 67; National Park Service and, xx, 109, 145–47; as newspaper publisher, 80–82; physical appearance of, xx; political activities and views, 123–24, 154–55, 213, 286, 287; poverty and, 7–9, 77, 237; prehistory, views on, 235; religious beliefs of, 58–59, 280; retirement years, 279–90; in River Bed Case, 214–15; as river runner, 21, 70–71, 182–91, 197–98, 201–2, 215–17, 316n11; river safety and, 69, 71–73, 199, 201, 215; scenery, interest in, xv, xix, 116, 151, 176, 206–7, 244–46; as school principal, 14, 24–25, 29, 36, 50–51, 82, 129; as school superintendent, 82–83; as schoolteacher, xvii–xviii, 13, 22–23, 213; and sheepherding, xvii, 2, 9–11; siblings, *see* individual names of; at Stanford University, 27–29; tourism ventures, 37–73 *passim*, 102–6; tourism, views on, xix, 93, 105–6, 109–10, 113–14, 126, 148, 158, 204,

243–46, 261–62, 264, 289, 294; wedding anniversary, 286–87; wilderness, views on, 157, 211

Rust, David Dexter, articles by: "Boating on the Colorado," 17, 24, 69, 176, 199; "The Bright Angel," 58–59; "De Motte Park," 95–96; "Fleeing to Zion—For Scenery," 243–45; "From Salt Lake to the Grand Canyon," 61, 64; "Worth of a Boy," 127, 130

Rust, David Jordan (son), 28, 51, 173, 238, 280, 287; trips with Dave, 120, 130–31, 142, 159–60, 163, 166–67, 170–71, 175, 177–82, 184–88, 218, 247

Rust, Eliza Brown (mother), 3–6 *passim,* 8–9, 11, 13–15 *passim,* 22–23, 27, 36, 151, 285; trip with Dave, 124–26

Rust, Emma (daughter), 29, 51, 284; trips with Dave, 186, 199

Rust, George Brown (brother), 5, 7, 8, 9, 161

Rust, George Nelson (son), 237, 268; death of, 281–82; trip with Dave, 234

Rust, George Smith (father), 3–11, 15, 124–26, 151, 170, 178

Rust, Helen (daughter), 237, 281

Rust, Joseph C. (grandson), xxiii, 51, 68

Rust, Julia (sister), 3, 8, 151

Rust, Laura (sister), 8, 22, 151

Rust, Laura (daughter), 80, 285

Rust, Milton (son), 57; trips with Dave, 195, 222, 225, 227–28, 240–41

Rust, Orion (brother), 7, 8, 13, 18, 19, 151, 176

Rust, Quentin (son), 100, 130, 153, 281; trips with Dave, 242, 265

Rust, Richard (son), 39, 51, 285

Rust, Roy (brother), 8, 9, 14, 23, 151, 287

Rust, Ruth Woolley (wife), xvi, 36, 44, 57, 80, 143, 285; courtship and marriage, 26–27; death of, 290–91; and Fraser family, 153, 173; in Fredonia, 30; at Grand Canyon, 58, 212–13; in Idaho, 29;

in Orderville, 51; in Palo Alto, 27–28; in Provo, 213–14, 237, 281; wedding anniversary, 286–87

Rust's Camp, 45, 50, 52, 76, 79, 106, 146–47; as Roosevelt Camp, 147

Rust, Sabra Beckstead (father's second wife), 5, 9

Rust, Sarah (sister-in-law), 79–80, 98, 132, 151, 210

Rust, Sidney (half brother), 14, 281

Rust, William Slauson (brother), 4, 98–99, 124–25, 151, 210; death of, 287; as homesteader, 79–80; Hotel Highway of, 132, 210; Kaibab tourist lodge of, 204; as miner, 18–21, 23

Rust, William Walker (grandfather), 4

Rust Trail, xviii, xx, 29–30, 77–78, 83, 93–94; abandonment of, 292; construction of, 32–39, 42, 45–46, 50, 52–53; Theodore Roosevelt on, 99; route of, 33–35; use of, 55–57, 59–60, 103–4, 106

Rust tram, 35; abandonment of, 147; construction of, 39–41, 44–50; description of, 39–40; engine for, 54–55; first passengers on, 49–50; remnants of, 37; use of, 57, 59–60, 99

Ryan, AZ, 63

Salt Lake Commercial Club, 87, 101, 140, 156–57

Salt Lake Route. *See under* Union Pacific Railway

"Salt Lake to the Grand Canyon" (Rust), 61, 64

Sanderson, Robert, 229

sand waves, 177, 190–91, 199, 215, 270

Sandy Creek ranch, 251

San Juan County, 184, 250

San Juan River, xvi, 137, 138, 191, 249, 258; gold discoveries on, 18; navigability of, 214; river running on, 201, 214, 270, 278, 282

San Pedro, Los Angeles & Salt Lake Railroad (Salt Lake Route). *See under* Union Pacific Railway

San Rafael desert, 12, 231

San Rafael Swell, 240

Santa Fe, NM, 4, 84, 187

Santa Fe Railway. *See* Atchison, Topeka & Santa Fe Railway

Sargent, Helen White, 73

sawmills, 40, 75, 85, 89

Schock, William, 225

Schroeder, Gilliat, 194

Scientific Study of Scenery (Marr), 246

Scorup, James A., 140

Scorup, John A. "Al," 296

Scott, Donald C., xv, xvi, xviii, 149, 208, 237, 289, 292, 319n12; on Claflin-Emerson expeditions, 224–29 *passim*, 233, 234, 235, 241

Scott, Donald C., Jr., 232, 233

Scott, Louise, 208, 225–28 *passim*, 289

Seegmiller, William W., 80, 124

Senator from Vermont (Flanders), 264

Sentinel Rock, 270

Sevier River, 12, 152, 210

Sevier Stake Academy, 9

sheep, 1, 2, 53, 81, 169, 259; on Aquarius Plateau, 166, 265; on Kaibab Plateau, 145–46, 156. *See also under* Rust, David Dexter

sheepherders, xix, 166, 265

Sheffield road, 268

Shinumo Creek, 32, 73, 114, 115

Shivwits Plateau, 76, 119, 218

Short Creek, AZ, 79, 88, 103

Shunesburg, UT, 152; Old Shunesburg Trail, 131

signal fires, 114, 115, 310n8

Silver Falls Canyon, 163, 223, 225, 322n6

Sipapu Natural Bridge. *See* Augusta Natural Bridge

Skidoo Point. *See* Point Imperial

Sleight, Ken, 188, 294

Smith, Joseph, 4, 116

Smith Fork, 225, 272

Smithsonian Butte, 97, 152

Smoot, Reed, 36, 78, 88, 107, 131, 157, 174

Snow, Coleman, 171

Snow, Erastus, 4, 25, 30

Soap Creek, 133

Soap Creek rapid, 71–72

Sockdolager rapid, 70–71

South Desert, 10, 248

Southern California Edison Co., 185

South Rim. *See under* Grand Canyon

Spencer's trading post, 138

Spring Creek, 3

Springdale, UT, 75, 78, 98, 107, 111, 131, 138

Spry, William, 89, 90, 106, 148

Stanford University. *See under* Rust, David Dexter

Stanton, Robert Brewster, 20, 23, 70, 73, 254

Stark, Helen Candland, 82–83, 287

Steamboat, 97

Stegner, Wallace, 10, 16, 295

Stevens Arch, 274

Stevens, Mary, 51

Stewart, Robert H., 209

Stone, Julius, 70, 192, 280

Straight Cliffs, 162, 227

Strong, Fred, 256, 257

Sturges, Benjamin, 194–98 *passim*

Sturges, Libby, 238

Sumner, Jack, 23

Sun Beam claim, 5

Sutherland, George, 36, 53

Swamp Point, 114, 115

Swapp, Joseph, 123

Sylvan Gate, 95

Syrett, Ruby, 122, 160, 196

Table Cliff Plateau, 121, 174, 195, 206, 207; Rust's trips to, 160, 196, 242, 266

Taft, William Howard, 74, 144

"Take a Rest," 38

Tales of Lonely Trails (Grey) 313n16

Talmadge, James E., 32

Tapeats Sandstone, 113

Tavaputs Plateau, 234

Taylor, Loren, 260

Teasdale, UT, 171

Temple (Pleasant) Creek, 167, 229

"Temple of the Gods" (Alter), 122

"Temple of the Gods in Utah" (Jeffers), 121

Tertiary History of the Grand Cañon District (Dutton), 31, 74, 96, 111, 114, 174

Thomas, A. L., 36

Thompson, Almon H., 161, 195, 215, 286, 315n5

Thompson's Point, 58

Thousand Lake Mountain, 10, 116, 168–69, 207, 240, 241, 271

Through the Heart of the Scenic West (Alter), 144, 157

Thunder River, 66, 284, 306n12

Ticaboo Canyon, 181, 182, 217

Ticaboo rapid, 182

Tillotson, Miner R., 249, 257–59

Tintic, UT, 5, 8, 52. *See also* Rust, George Smith

Tipoff, 53

Toll, Roger, 248, 249, 258

Tolton, J. F., 213

Tonto Platform, 50, 53, 54, 97

Toquerville, UT, 75, 98, 101, 103, 111, 238; Commercial Club of, 91

Toroweap, 104, 189, 207, 310n4; mine at, 155, 214; Rust at, 112, 206, 210–11, 218, 244–45, 251

Torrey, UT, 247

tourism: xxi, 100, 101, 108, 203, 260–62, 283, 293; railroads' interest in, 145, 211; "sage-brushers," 211, 293. *See also under* individual national parks; Rust, David Dexter

Towers of the Virgin, 152

Townsend, Charles H., 80, 82

Trachyte Canyon, 181, 182, 225

Trachyte Creek, 178

Trachyte rapid, 182

Trail on the Water (Baker), 17, 217

tramways, 147–48, 269, 313n10. *See also* Bass trail; Rust tram

Transept, 97

Trent Engineering & Machinery Co., 39, 44

Tsegi Canyon, 138, 221

typhoid fever, 14

Uinkaret Plateau, 111, 112, 160, 245, 295

Uinta mountains, 233–34

Uncle Jim Owens. *See* Owens, James T.

Unconformity, Great, 113

Under the Ledge, 231, 233, 253

uniformitarianism, 29

Union Pacific Railway, 86, 106–7, 110, 148, 195, 211, 212, 309n13; Salt Lake Route of, 83, 85, 89, 145, 210, 309n13. *See also* Manderfield, J. H.; Utah Parks Company

United Order, 51

Untold History of Utah's Grand Staircase–Escalante National Monument (Newell and Barnes), 258

uranium, 250–51, 263, 321n2

U.S. Forest Service, 32, 50, 79, 107–8, 261–62, 305n27; at Bryce Canyon, 120–22, 160; at Cedar Breaks, 203; and Grand Canyon Transportation Company, 35–36, 45, 93, 145–46, 304n4; and "President's Forest," 157; road construction by, 63, 89–90, 95, 103; Rust applies to work with, 51–52; Kaibab timber sale proposed by, 84–86

U.S. Geological Survey, 34, 120, 162, 174, 183, 184, 185, 192, 295

Utah–Grand Canyon Highway, 90–92, 101, 102, 109, 123

Utah & Grand Canyon Railroad Company, 86

Utah National Park. *See under* Bryce Canyon National Park

Utah Parks Company, 122, 148, 198, 203, 204, 211. *See also* National Park Transportation and Camping Company

"Utah Recovers the Grand Canyon of Arizona" (Alter), 30

Utah State Planning Board, 257, 259

Utah State Road Commission, 88

Ute Ford, 191–92. *See also* Crossing of the Fathers

Ute Indians, 3, 6

Vaca, Cabeza de, 193

Van Dyke, John C., 245

Vermilion Arid Farming Association, 79

Vermilion Cliffs, 30, 67, 87, 112, 132, 259

Victorian era, 129–30, 239

Virgin River, xviii, 74, 89, 97, 106–7; East Fork, 74, 131, 152, 310n1; North Fork, 69, 75, 107, 111

Virginian, The (Wister), 65

Vishnu Temple, 93, 242

V. T. Park. *See* De Motte Park

Walhalla Plateau, 36, 49, 93, 126

Wallace, Grant, 49, 77

War God Spring, xvi, 135, 137

Wasatch Plateau, 12, 22

Wash Henry trail, 53

Wasp House ruin, 198

Waterhole Flat, 231, 233, 253

Waterpocket Fold: described, xvi, 7; roads through, 19, 163, 178, 223; Rust's trips to, 268, 273, 276–77; scenic value of, 168, 169, 179–80, 246. *See also* Black Trail; Capitol Reef National Monument

"water-ponies," 195, 202

Wayne Wonderland, 168, 247–48, 257

Weber, Albert, 251–52

West, Ray, 259

Western Temple, 97

Wetherill, John, 76, 128, 129, 137, 183, 208, 249; Rainbow Bridge and, xvi, 117, 135, 138

Wetherill, Louisa, 135, 143

Wheeler Point, 152

White Canyon, 119, 139–41, 181, 186, 249, 254

White Cliffs, 87

Widtsoe, John A., 79

Widtsoe, UT, 172, 178, 197

Wildcat Ranger Station, 265, 285

wilderness, 10, 108, 145, 156, 175, 296; appreciation of, 64, 100, 165, 260–62; Rust's views on, 61, 64, 203, 211, 250, 261–62, 280

Wildhorse Bar, 19, 20

Willow Gulch, 274, 275

Wilson, Bates, 262–63

Wilson, Junius, 274

Wilson, Woodrow, 107, 123, 154, 206, 213

Wingate Sandstone, 164, 169, 196, 198, 253, 255, 267, 276, 300n4

Wister, Owen, 65

Woodruff, Len, 232, 256

Woolley, Edwin D., Jr., 26, 27, 29, 44, 49, 87, 98, 150; Buffalo Jones and, 49; as cowboy, 31; death of, 150–51; Grand Canyon National Park and, 146–49; with Zane Grey, 66, 67; Hotel Highway and, 132; Kaibab railroad and, 85–86, 313n10; Kaibab timber sale and, 84–85; and *Kane County News*, 80; at North Rim, 31–34, 37–38, 102; political activities, 81; road construction and, 88, 90, 91, 103; as tourism promoter, 36, 61–64, 82, 292–93. *See also* Grand Canyon Transportation Company

Woolley, Edwin D., Jr., children of: Mary Elizabeth (*see* Chamberlain, Mary Woolley); Rae, 28; Royal, 26; Ruth (*see* Rust, Ruth Woolley)

Woolley, E. G. "Gordon," Jr., 61–63

Woolley, Emma Bentley, 26
Woolley, Florence, 26
Woolley, Franklin B., 166–67, 315n12
Woolley cabin, 33, 93–94, 103, 125–26,
    145–46, 148, 292
Woolley trail. *See* Rust trail
Woolley's Station, 33
World War I, 119, 127, 203
World War II, 279, 280–82, 289
"Worth of a Boy" (Rust), 127, 130
Wylie Way camps, 109, 125–26, 131, 142,
    148, 292, 309n25
Wylie Way company, 89, 104, 106, 145, 148
Wylie, William Wallace, 109, 126

Yellow House ruin, 134
Yellowstone National Park, 88, 123, 259;
    autos to, 108; Wylie Way company at,
    89, 102, 104, 106
Yosemite Valley, 74, 98

Young, Brigham, 3, 22, 51
Young, John W., 31
Your National Parks, (Mills), 107
youth culture, 129

Zion Canyon, 74–78, 88–89, 98, 106–7, 111,
    116; Crawford ranch in, 117; early names
    for, 74, 306n28; east rim of, 75, 207;
    sawmill in, 75; tourism at, 89, 106–8
Zion Lodge, 106
Zion National Monument, 131
Zion National Park: designation of, 107,
    131, 142, 145; Kolob Canyons addition
    to, 248; as Mukuntuweap National
    Monument, 107, 144; roads to, 120, 203,
    211; tourism at, 108, 131, 199–200, 203,
    211, 246, 283, 293; Union Pacific's inte-
    rest in, 107, 109, 145
Zoroaster Temple, 97, 126